ACROSS ANTHROPOLOGY
TROUBLING COLONIAL LEGACIES, MUSEUMS, AND THE CURATORIAL

Across Anthropology

Troubling Colonial Legacies,
Museums, and the Curatorial

Edited by
Margareta von Oswald and Jonas Tinius

LEUVEN UNIVERSITY PRESS

The publication of this work was supported by the Centre for Anthropological Research and the Alexander von Humboldt Foundation, the Open Access Publication Fund of Humboldt-Universität zu Berlin, and the KU Leuven Fund for Fair Open Access.

Published in 2020 by Leuven University Press / Presses Universitaires de Louvain / Universitaire Pers Leuven. Minderbroedersstraat 4, B-3000 Leuven (Belgium).

Selection and editorial matter © Margareta von Oswald and Jonas Tinius, 2020
Individual chapters © The respective authors, 2020

This book is published under a Creative Commons CC BY 4.0 Licence.

Further details about Creative Commons licences are available at http://creativecommons.org/licenses/

Attribution should include the following information: Margareta von Oswald and Jonas Tinius, eds, *Across Anthropology: Troubling Colonial Legacies, Museums, and the Curatorial*. Leuven, Leuven University Press. (CC BY 4.0)

ISBN 978 94 6270 218 9 (Paperback)
ISBN 978 94 6166 317 7 (ePDF)
ISBN 978 94 6166 318 4 (ePUB)
https://doi.org/10.11116/9789461663177
D/2020/1869/19
NUR: 761

Lay-out: Crius Group
Cover design: Daniel Benneworth-Gray

Table of contents

List of images   9

Acknowledgements   15

Introduction: Across Anthropology   17
Margareta von Oswald and Jonas Tinius

Museums and the Savage Sublime   45
Arjun Appadurai

Transforming the Ethnographic: Anthropological Articulations in Museum and Heritage Research   49
Sharon Macdonald

"Museums are Investments in Critical Discomfort"   65
A conversation with Wayne Modest

Frontiers of the (Non)Humanly (Un)Imaginable: Anthropological Estrangement and the Making of Persona at the Musée du Quai Branly   77
Emmanuel Grimaud

"On Decolonising Anthropological Museums: Curators Need to Take 'Indigenous' Forms of Knowledge More Seriously"   97
A conversation with Anne-Christine Taylor

Troubling Colonial Epistemologies in Berlin's Ethnologisches Museum: Provenance Research and the Humboldt Forum   107
Margareta von Oswald

"Against the Mono-Disciplinarity of Ethnographic Museums"   131
A conversation with Clémentine Deliss

Resisting Extraction Politics: Afro-Belgian Claims, Women's Activism, and the Royal Museum for Central Africa   143
Sarah Demart

"Finding Means to Cannibalise the Anthropological Museum"   175
A conversation with Toma Muteba Luntumbue

Animating Collapse: Reframing Colonial Film Archives   187
Alexander Schellow and Anna Seiderer

"Translating the Silence"   211
A conversation with le peuple qui manque

Art-Anthropology Interventions in the Italian Post-Colony: The Scattered Colonial Body Project   223
Arnd Schneider

"Dissonant Agents and Productive Refusals"   243
A conversation with Natasha Ginwala

Porous Membranes: Hospitality, Alterity, and Anthropology in a Berlin District Gallery   255
Jonas Tinius

"What happens in that space in-between and beyond this relation"   279
A conversation with Bonaventure Soh Bejeng Ndikung

Material Kin: "Communities of Implication" in Post-Colonial, Post-Holocaust Polish Ethnographic Collections   289
Erica Lehrer

"Suggestions for a Post-Museum"   325
A conversation with Nanette Snoep

Representation of Culture(s): Articulations of the De/Post-Colonial at the Haus der Kulturen der Welt in Berlin   337
Annette Bhagwati

"How Do We Come Together in a World that Isolates Us?"   363
A conversation with Nora Sternfeld

The Trans-Anthropological, Anachronism, and the Contemporary   375
Roger Sansi

List of contributors   383

Visual constellations across the fields   393

Some lists to inspire the reader   421

List of images

Fig. 1.1	*Ganesh Yourself Robot*. Film by Emmanuel Grimaud, © Emmanuel Grimaud	76
Fig. 1.2	Uncanny Valley Graph. Cited in: Mori (2012 [1970]: 99)	79
Fig. 2.1	Boris Gliesmann working in the archive. Photograph by Marion Benoit, © Ethnologisches Museum der Staatlichen Museen zu Berlin – Preußischer Kulturbesitz	106
Fig. 2.2	Buli chair, collected by Werner von Grawert, III C 14966, © Ethnologisches Museum der Staatlichen Museen zu Berlin – Preußischer Kulturbesitz	108
Fig. 2.3	A scan of the inventory book on the page including III C 14966, © Ethnologisches Museum der Staatlichen Museen zu Berlin – Preußischer Kulturbesitz	110
Fig. 2.4	Screenshot of the database entry for III C 14966, © Ethnologisches Museum der Staatlichen Museen zu Berlin – Preußischer Kulturbesitz	110
Fig. 2.5	The entrance door to the archive. Photograph by Marion Benoit, © Ethnologisches Museum der Staatlichen Museen zu Berlin – Preußischer Kulturbesitz	117
Fig. 2.6	The museum library. Photograph by Marion Benoit, © Ethnologisches Museum der Staatlichen Museen zu Berlin – Preußischer Kulturbesitz	117
Fig. 3.1	View into the Weltkulturen Labor, Frankfurt, with furniture designed by Mathis Esterhazy and various fish traps from the Weltkulturen Museum's collection. Photograph by Wolfgang Günzel, 2011	130
Fig. 3.2	Weltkulturen Museum Storage Building, Frankfurt am Main. Photograph by Armin Linke, 2013	135

Fig. 3.3	Thinktank on photography at Weltkulturen Labor with (from left to right) Kokou Azamede, Otobong Nkanga, Martin Guttmann, Armin Linke, Jan-Philipp Possmann, Weltkulturen Museum, Frankfurt am Main. Photograph by Wolfgang Günzel, 2013	135
Fig. 3.4	Clémentine Deliss and Metronome books, exhibition *Think with your feet* at Command N Gallery, Tokyo. Photograph by Masato Nakamura, 2006	137
Fig. 4.1	#NotmyAfricaMuseum sketch. Image Imane Skaljac, © Café Congo	142
Fig. 4.2	View of parliamentary debate with Mireille Tsheusi-Robert, Julie de Groote, and Anne Wetsi Mpoma, ©ASBL Nouveau Système Artistique	156
Fig. 4.3	Mireille Tsheusi-Robert during the parliamentary debate, © ASBL Nouveau Système Artistique	156
Fig. 4.4	Protest inside the museum. Photograph by Lyse Ishimwe, © Lyse Ishimwe	162
Fig. 4.5	Protest outside the museum. Photograph by Lyse Ishimwe, © Lyse Ishimwe	162
Fig. 5.1	4th Lubumbashi Biennal, 2014, © Georges Senga	174
Fig. 5.2	ExitCongoMuseum, Johan Muyle, *L'impossibilité de régner*, 2001, © J.M.Van Dyck	176
Fig. 5.3	ExitCongoMuseum, Philip Aguirre y Otegui, l'Homme de Tarifa, 2001, © Koen de Waal	176
Fig. 5.4	Ligablo (personal document), © Toma Muteba Luntumbue.	179
Fig. 6.1	Still 1/021 [021 from: series of animations, work in progress / since 2015 / 3+3" - loop / 16:9 / BW / silent. Each sequence: approx. 36 drawings, 29,7x42cm, ink on paper	186
Fig. 6.2-5	Stills 007/021/044/061 [from: series of animations, work in progress / since 2015 / 3+3" - loop / 16:9 / BW / silent. Each sequence: approx. 36 drawings, 29,7x42cm, ink on paper	200
Fig. 7.1	'Beyond the Magiciens Effect', symposium performance curated by Aliocha Imhoff & Kantuta Quirós, scenography by Adel Cersaque, © Helena Hattmansdorfer, le peuple qui manque; 2015	210
Fig. 7.2	First Declaration of the Stateless Museum, film directed by Aliocha Imhoff & Kantuta Quirós, La Réunion: La plaine des Sables, 2017	212

Fig. 7.3	First Declaration of the Stateless Museum, film directed by Aliocha Imhoff & Kantuta Quirós, La Réunion: La plaine des Sables, 2017	212
Fig. 8.1	Bronze bust of Rodolfo Graziani during removal from IsIAO premises, Via Aldrovandi, Rome, March 2017. Photograph by Arnd Schneider	222
Fig. 8.2	Corridor of the Museo Prestorico Etnografio "Lugi Pigorini" (part of Museo delle Civiltà), Rome, with model of Sabratha amphitheatre, and painting from colonial period. Photograph by Wolfgang Thaler	225
Fig. 8.3	Leone Contini mounting exhibition *Bel Suol d'Amore – The Scattered Colonial Body*, Museum "Lugi Pigorini", Rome, June 2017. Photograph by Wolfang Thaler	226
Fig. 8.4	Map of colonial Libya (detail), Italy, 1930s, collection of former IsIAO, Rome. Photograph by Arnd Schneider	226
Fig. 8.5	*Bel Suol d'Amore*: The Scattered Colonial Body, Preliminary exhibition design, section view, Museo Prestorico Etnografio "Lugi Pigorini" (part of Museo delle Civiltà), Rome, June 2017. Photograph by Cinzia Delnevo	228
Fig. 9.1	Karrabing Film Collective, installation view at Contour Biennale 8 for *Polyphonic Worlds: Justice as Medium*, Mechelen 2017. Courtesy of the artists and Contour Biennale 8. Image Credit: Kristof Vrancken	242
Fig. 9.2	Installation view, 'Double Lives' 8th Berlin Biennale for Contemporary Art, at Museen Dahlem, 2014, © Angela Anderson	246
Fig. 9.3	Installation view, 'Arrival, Incision: Indian Modernism as Peripatetic Itinerary', part of Hello World. Revising a Collection, Hamburger Bahnhof – Museum für Gegenwart, Berlin 2018, © Mathias Völzke	246
Fig. 9.4	Installation view, 'The Museum of Rhythm' at Muzeum Sztuki, Łódź 2017. Image Credit: Piotr Tomczyk	248
Fig. 10.1	A passerby peeking into the gallery during the exhibition *Circling Around Oneness* (2016) by Mwangi Hutter, Galerie Wedding, © Fernando Gutiérrez Juárez	254
Fig. 10.2	View of the gallery membranes from Müllerstraße during the exhibition *Circling Around Oneness* (2016) by Mwangi Hutter, Galerie Wedding, © Fernando Gutiérrez Juárez	256

Fig. 10.3	One part of the video projection, with visitors sitting on the radiators in front of the gallery membrane facing Müllerstraße, during the exhibition *Circling Around Oneness* (2016) by Mwangi Hutter, Galerie Wedding, © Fernando Gutiérrez Juárez	257
Fig. 10.4	Exhibition view of Viron Erol Vert's dreamatory, *The Name of Shades of Paranoia, Called Different Forms of Silence* (2017) in Galerie Wedding, © Johannes Berger	264
Fig. 10.5	Visitors during the opening of Viron Erol Vert's dreamatory, *The Name of Shades of Paranoia, Called Different Forms of Silence* (2017) in Galerie Wedding, © Johannes Berger	265
Fig. 10.6	Emeka Ogboh's 'Beast of No Nation' beer bottle, on the railings of the subway station of the district. *BEAST OF NO NATION* (2018), © Emeka Ogboh	268
Fig. 10.7	A view of the gallery during Simon Fujiwara's exhibition Joanne (2018), Galerie Wedding, © Galerie Wedding.	269
Fig. 11.1	'Monday' by iQhiya, installation view of *That, Around Which the Universe Revolves: On Rhythmanalysis of Memory, Times, Bodies in Space* at SAVVY Contemporary (2017), © Raisa Galofre	278
Fig. 11.2	*Canine Wisdom For the Barking Dog – The Dog Done Gone Deaf* at the Dak'Art Biennale 2018; Ibrahim Mahama *No Time for Curation* (1966-2014-2018), © SAVVY Contemporary	280
Fig. 11.3	*Canine Wisdom For the Barking Dog – The Dog Done Gone Deaf* at the Dak'Art Biennale 2018; Ibrahim Mahama *No Time for Curation* (1966-2014-2018), © SAVVY Contemporary	281
Fig. 11.4	*We Have Delivered Ourselves from the Tonal – Of, with, towards, on Julius Eastman* at SAVVY Contemporary, March 2018; The Otolith Group *The Third Part is the Third Measure*, © Raisa Galofre	282
Fig. 11.5	*We Have Delivered Ourselves from the Tonal – Of, with, towards, on Julius Eastman* at SAVVY Contemporary, March 2018; Eastman Archive, © Raisa Galofre	283
Fig. 12.1	One of two panels (the righthand) from Zygmunt Skrętowicz's The Gassing, from his Auschwitz series (1963). Warsaw State Ethnographic Museum. Photograph by Wojciech Wilczyk	288

Fig. 12.2	Terkotkas on display at the Kraków Ethnographic Museum (Brzezowa near Myślenice, 1929), gift from the girl's junior high school. Object inventory no. 3764. © Erica Lehrer.	297
Fig. 12.3-7	Left to right: Figural beehive (Zabierzów, late nineteenth century; archival photo); masks worn by "Jew" character in Christmastime carolling groups, (Silesia, 1956); Emaus Jewish figurine (early twentieth century). Photographs by Jason Francisco	299
Fig. 12.8	One of two panels (the lefthand) from Zygmunt Skrętowicz's *The Gassing*, from his Auschwitz series (1963). Warsaw State Ethnographic Museum. Photograph by Wojciech Wilczyk.	301
Fig. 13.1	*Prolog #1-10 Stories of People, Things, and Places*, Museum für Völkerkunde, Dresden, 2017, © Vera Marusic	324
Fig. 13.2	Open Space *Die Baustelle*, Rautenstrauch Joest Museum, Cologne, 2019, © Vera Marusic	326
Fig. 13.3	*Maîtres du Désordre (Masters of Chaos)*, Musée du Quai Branly, Paris, 2012, © Nanette Snoep	330
Fig. 13.4	*Megalopolis – Voices from Kinshasa*, Grassi Museum für Völkerkunde, Leipzig, 2018, © Mo Zaboli	330
Fig. 14.1	Anthropozän-Projekt/ Anthropocene Project, 2013, Eine Eröffnung/An Opening, Metabolic, Kitchen, raumlabor Berlin, Haus der Kulturen der Welt. Photograph by Joachim Loch	336
Fig. 14.2	Sample pages from the programme brochures (*Pixihefte*), which appeared twice a month. Photographs by the author	341
Fig. 14.3	Nalini Malani, Titel: Hamletmachine, 2000. Video installation with four lcd projectors, four dvd players, amplifiers, speakers, salt, mylar, mirror. Installed as projections on three walls and salt-bed (variable). Closed room 1100 x 800 x 400 cm (variable). Video loop 20 minutes, © Nalini Malani, Mumbai	350
Fig. 14.4	Anthropozän-Projekt/ Anthropocene Project, 2013, Eine Eröffnung/An Opening, Haus der Kulturen der Welt, Jan Zalasiewicz. Photograph by Sebastian Bolesch	357

Fig. 14.5	Wohnungsfrage, 2015, Haus der Kulturen der Welt, Berlin, urban model, housing model, Kooperatives Labor Studierender (Kolabs) und das Architekturbüro Atelier Bow-Wow, Tokio/ and the Tokyo architecture office Atelier Bow-Wow. Photograph by Jens Liebchen, © HKW	357
Fig. 15.1	'Fires need audiences' (tote bag), 2015. Photograph by Sarah Peguine, © Ariel Schlesinger	362
Fig. 15.2	Nora Sternfeld, Isa Rosenberger, and the Retired Firemen of Bergen, THE MUSEUM OF BURNING QUESTIONS. The Partisan Café (at Bergen's historic fire station) with Jenny Moore, Freja Bäckman, Kabir Carter, Tora Endestad Bjørkheim, Johnny Herbert, and Arne Skaug Olsen. Educational and Performative Cafe designed by Isa Rosenberger, in collaboration with Heidi Pretterhofer, Bergen Assembly, 2016. Photograph by Thor	368

Acknowledgements

This research was funded by the Alexander von Humboldt Foundation as part of the research award for Sharon Macdonald's Alexander von Humboldt Professorship, and was carried out at the Centre for Anthropological Research on Museums and Heritage (CARMAH) at the Department for European Ethnology, Humboldt-Universität zu Berlin.

We are grateful to Sharon Macdonald for her guidance throughout our fellowships, her critical and always attentive eye, and her generous thinking through and editing of our contributions. We thank all of our colleagues at CARMAH for their extremely helpful feedback and critical engagement with the arguments and fieldwork developed in this book. Without the carefully curated context of CARMAH, we would not have arrived at these converging observations. We further acknowledge the subvention from Sharon Macdonald's Alexander von Humboldt award towards making this publication open-access. Likewise, we would like to acknowledge the additional support of the Humboldt-Universität zu Berlin and KU Leuven open-access funds in making possible this publication.

At Leuven University Press, we would like to thank Mirjam Truwant and her colleagues for their support in the drafting of the manuscript, for welcoming us in Leuven and elsewhere, and for guiding us through the production process.

We are grateful to participants at the panel "Anthropological Representation: Contemporary Art and/in the Ethnographic Museum" at the 4th Major Conference *Art, Materiality, and Representation* of the Royal Anthropological Institute, British Museum, in London (1-3 June 2018), which served as an initial point of departure for conversations around our book's argument. We greatly benefited from conversations with colleagues – including Saskia Köbschall, Lotte Arndt, Silvy Chakkalakal, Ignacio Farias and others – which bolstered the development of this book. In another iteration of this project in our co-sponsored panel at the Annual Meeting of the American Anthropological Association in Vancouver, B.C. (20-24 November 2019), panellists, colleagues, and friends, including Anthony

Shelton, Nicola Levell, Christopher Green, Arnd Schneider, Sowparnika Balaswaminathan, and Denise Ryner – engaged with us and provided vibrant feedback. We also thank Thomas Fillitz and an anonymous reviewer for feedback on the introduction and the entire manuscript, as well as Friedrich von Bose and James Clifford for their thoughts on this book. We wish to express our gratitude as well to Marion Benoît, Phillip Röcker, and Sol for generously hosting us during a writing retreat in Bordeaux, in their ateliers at *Maison Merveille*, which provided us with just the right environment to write, delete, and rewrite.

The back and forth with the authors assembled for this book, as well as with interlocutors in the broader fields from which *Across Anthropology* emerged, has continued to trouble us in all the best ways, and we are very grateful to them.

Introduction: Across Anthropology

Margareta von Oswald and Jonas Tinius

While it might seem as though only one thing is certain about anthropology – namely, that it is in "a permanent identity crisis" (Geertz 2000: 89) – this volume takes a different look at what anthropology is and how it is rendered meaningful. After decades of intense and productive critique of anthropological practices and knowledge production from 'within', we address the ways in which anthropology has been reformulated, rethought, and even repractised 'elsewhere' and 'otherwise'. What is anthropology? Where and how is it negotiated? What new understandings of anthropology emerge from beyond the classical fields, practices, institutions, and modi of anthropological knowledge production?

As editors, we come to these questions through our fieldwork on museums, colonial legacies, contemporary art, and curatorial practice as they are articulated in Europe, specifically Berlin. We have witnessed and been struck by the extent to which both anthropology as a discipline (including its history and institutions, such as museums and archives), its methods (among them fieldwork and participant observation), and themes associated with it (such as alterity, race and racism, ontology and personhood, materiality and agency, statehood and citizenship) have become central areas of inquiry in fields and practices beyond the discipline and its institutions. Put differently, anthropology, far from being self-contained, is the subject in other fields of cultural production. Most notably, contemporary artistic research, theorising, education, and practice have turned towards anthropology, its methods, histories, turns and promises. The emergence of the curatorial has been integral in this movement, insofar as it transposes and translates across artistic, activist, and exhibition practices.

Where curatorial practices focus on the legacies of the European colonial project, these inquiries further multiply the possible meanings of anthropology. In this book, we seek to capture and theorise these fields, practices, and meanings as 'trans-anthropological'. This introduction outlines the emergence of the contestations, contexts, and the unfolding of our fieldwork, all of which ground our argument. Facing forward and expanding through its contributors' thick accounts, *Across Anthropology* wishes to trouble and stimulate debate on the futures, frictions, and colonial legacies of museums, art, and the curatorial in a post-colonial Europe.

Emergence: The legitimacy of anthropology

In recent years and especially across European countries, the renaming, reform, and even reconstruction of anthropological museums is embedded within and reinforced by a fierce debate about the legitimacy of anthropology. This debate encompasses the practice of fieldwork, the writing about, display, and visual representation of culture and society (ethnography), and the broader theoretical construction of accounts of human existence (anthropology). We use "anthropology", then, as a term encompassing the multiplicity of traditions, especially those of Anglo-American social and cultural anthropology, as well as the many European iterations of *Ethnologie* and *Volkskunde*. The range and transformations of these traditions are themselves testament to the chronic reshuffling of the very meaning of what anthropology is.

Anthropological museums and collections materialise and embody traditions and styles of anthropological knowledge. We write of "anthropological" museums, therefore, as an umbrella term for museums and collections that emerged in relation to and which facilitated certain kinds of anthropological knowledge production. We use it also in distinction to forms of display and collections drawing on anthropology that may be found in other types of museums and exhibition-contexts. These museums and collections have turned into sites for the contestation and renewal of anthropology, from within as well as from without. Several contributions to this book explore the extent to which the processes of critique, renaming, and reform in museums are related to the different national histories of anthropology's colonial entanglement, asking, for instance: To what extent are anthropological museums caught up in their genesis and disciplinarity? Tasked to reflect on their past, they often reproduce the epistemological frameworks they are seeking to transcend. Among the questions we pose, it seems urgent to us to ask: What are ways to overcome such dilemmas of reflexivity? Which role, if any, can contemporary anthropological knowledge production and research play in these museum infrastructures themselves? What would it mean to conceive of an anthropological museum without anthropologists, or without collections? Or are these processes of transformation a possibly fruitful pathway for the renewal of anthropological relevance?

Proposing terms such as the "post-ethnological" and "post-ethnographic museum", Clémentine Deliss (2012) and Benoît de L'Estoile (2015), among others, have sought to reckon with the consequences of these frictions for contemporary curatorial and anthropological practice. For Deliss, "one can no longer be content to use earlier examples of material culture for the purpose of depicting ethnos, tribe, or an existing range of grand anthropological themes" (2012: 63). In other words, she wants us to move beyond the "logos of ethnos" (2013: 2).

Ruth B. Phillips tackles an aspect of this critique when she characterises exhibition histories in anthropological museums as defined by "the persistent and modernist paradigms of art and artefact" (2007: 98). The differences between exhibitions presenting collections as 'art' or 'culture' are consequential, insofar as they tend to imply particular self-understandings of anthropological museums. They affect how and what is put on display; either they represent, reconstruct, or explain 'culture' through 'context' – and thus mobilise a "translation of difference" (Lidchi 1997: 171) – or they value objects as 'art'. This occurs not seldom against the backdrop of implicit Western aesthetic assumptions and market criteria for defining art, both of which serve to 'elevate' anthropological collections into particular canons. As Haidy Geismar argues,

> [t]he legacies of modernism still continue to inflect the emergent practices of contemporary artists in ethnographic collections, who use art as a vehicle for overriding other categories and values surrounding the objects on display (2015: 184).

Exhibitions in the history of the love-hate relationship between art and anthropology, and their critical reception, pay witness to this deeply engrained, unresolvable, and strangely resilient modernist conflict across the entire twentieth century. Among the nodes in this genealogy, we count landmark exhibitions (as discussed, for instance, in the series Exhibition Histories by Afterall Books), as well as avant-garde movements (such as Surrealism) and their relation to anthropology and colonialism, manifested for example in the editorial project *Documents* (1929-1931). Central for us are also long-term institutional practices and reflexivity, like those of Musée d'Ethnographie de Neuchâtel, documenta, and Berlin's HKW. They include particular cases and debates, like the international reception of the ways anthropological collections were restructured in France, which led to opening in

2006 of the Musée du Quai Branly-Jacques Chirac (see Clifford 2007; Price 2007; Shelton 2009). Across all these, the tracing of independent curatorial practice in the field of contemporary art and its trans-national institutional inscriptions form a central part of this book's backbone. The recurrent concern for disciplinary and epistemological sovereignty in the fields of art and culture points us instead to the generative promiscuity of a *trans-*position.

Contemporary art has long been a central field in which such trans-positions across art and anthropology have been posited and contested. As Marcus and Myers put it, "(b)y virtue of cross-cultural training (...), most anthropologists encounter the category of 'art', internal to our own culture, with a suspicion and a sense of its strangeness", while they themselves tend to "simplify the complex internal dynamics of conflict within art worlds over the issue of autonomy (...) and modern art's own internal 'assault on tradition'" (1995: 6). In the same volume, Hal Foster notes that "advanced art on the left" since the 1990s has adopted a "quasi-anthropological model", struggling to grasp alterity and the "social and cultural other" (1995: 302). Okwui Enwezor reframed the relation between the artistic, the curatorial, and the ethnographic through the lens of appropriation, distance, and proximity (2012); a relation historically grounded in the unfolding of cultural anthropology's ties to modern art and aesthetics (Chakkalakal 2019; Harney and Phillips 2019). Roger Sansi (2015) traced the canonisation of 'the ethnographic turn' in relational art around the turn of the last century, focusing on the emergence and prevalence of notions of gift and exchange since the Situationists and Duchamp's role in modern art in the mid-twentieth century (see also Rutten et al. 2013; Sansi and Strathern 2016). Sansi's idea of a post-relational anthropology brings into conversation the long-standing modern – and then more contemporary – transgressions and rebuilding of both the autonomy of art and anthropology (Canclini 2014). In his account of the intense proximity between and even assimilation of artistic and anthropological practices, he speculates whether "anthropology, like art, will disappear as a discipline, along with its experts, and (...) would become just one of the things that everyone can do in their daily life – as, in fact, it has always been" (Sansi 2015: 163).

The observations of this book are amplified by a particular historical moment with paradoxical consequences for the public role of anthropology. While Europe is facing renewed nationalist populisms that partly respond to perceived threats from migration and globalisation, ever more institutions – cultural and political – are calling for the diversification of its staff, publics, and programmes (Mignolo 2009; Ahmed 2012; Partridge and Chin 2019). At the same time, we witness the return of neo-nativist arguments about threatened indigenous cultures in the Euro-American West among predominantly white nationalist movements (Beliso-De Jesús and Pierre 2019; Mazzarella 2019). In Europe, this has prompted public debate about the role of identity and culture, along with its physical borders and political limits, as well as nationalist centring and cosmopolitan decentring (Römhild 2017; Adam et al. 2019; Bock and Macdonald 2019). It would thus appear as if anthropological understandings of the complexity and representation of human difference and diversity, articulated in both extremes of globalisation and nationalisation, diversity and racism, could be more relevant than ever. Curiously, however, European anthropological institutes and museums do not act as the principal sites for offering publicly consequential and broadly received ways of addressing the above issues, prompting us to ask where and how they are negotiated.

One reason for this paradoxical moment is that anthropology has for some time occupied an ambivalent position: at once associated with colonial complicity and the problematic invention of human difference, as well as with post-colonial reckonings and the critical nuancing of how human difference is constituted and mobilised. As Sherry Ortner put it, "[i]t is hard to overstate the degree to which the colonial framework has reshaped the way anthropology relates to the world today" (2016: 51). How, then, does colonialism reappear in the present, as subject of critical and historical discourse and as material culture? To what extent does an engagement with the legacies of the European colonial project become a pathway to challenge institutions, discourses, and hierarchies of anthropological museums, anthropological practice, and the field of contemporary art today? To what degree does this challenge, as articulated most prominently in re-readings and new generations of post-colonial theory, offer ways to rethink and reshape anthropological museums and practice? Anthropology's different iterations and ties to notions like *Volk*, *Heimat*, *race*, and *ethnos* are underlining its difficulties to situate itself publicly, testified to by the renamings of museums, professional associations, and departments linked to anthropology across Europe (see, e.g., Pagani 2013; Macdonald 2016; Vermeulen 2018). As such, the *critique* and *negotiation* of anthropology are politically consequential, even more so when its patterns or logics are challenged.

Argument: The trans-anthropological

The problematisation of anthropology beyond itself describes contexts and modes of research that turn anthropology into a subject of inquiry, yet also includes those that mobilise anthropological modes of inquiry themselves. Our wording 'across anthropology' signals this type of movement. Working through different ways of tackling the above questions in our own research, we came to use the term "trans-anthropological". Trans-anthropological, for us, means the frictions and dynamics that arise when people are grappling with the where, what, and how of anthropology. It also encompasses the ways in which anthropological knowledge is produced, analysed, and presented – its styles of authorship, universality, and authority – as well as the *problematisation* of what falls within the legitimate remit of its subjects and objects of analysis. It speaks, thus, to the contestation and rethinking of the institutions – predominantly museums, collections, archives, and university institutes or departments – associated with anthropology. In some ways, the grappling with what constitutes anthropology, and the calling into question of its core methods, theories, and epistemologies, is itself most firmly embedded within the academic tradition of the discipline itself. It is then no longer counterintuitive to see crisis and critique of anthropology as signs of vitality, perhaps even of unexpected and fundamental innovation.

With this book, we chart a relational – rather than temporal – transformation, in which the 'trans' in trans-anthropological describes an uneasy encounter with critique against anthropological institutions, practices, and knowledge. 'Trans' means through, across, and beyond, but fundamentally it avoids an either-or dichotomy. Trans-gender and trans-cultural, for instance, do not deny the existence or association with particular identities but express a discomfort to processes of stabilisation and fixation. In the same vein, we want to highlight the meaning of the hyphen ("-") between "trans" and "anthropological" as it underlines the uncertain *relation* between these two terms; an uncertainty that the debates in this book unravel, analyse, and themselves provoke.

Echoing the signification of "post" in "post-colonial" as the ongoing reverberations of the graspable legacies of the colonial today, we underline how contestations of anthropology's past continue to shape anthropology in the present (see Hall 1995; Trouillot 2003). Anthropology's own "difficult heritage" thus renders a "positive, self-affirming contemporary identity" in a way "contested and awkward" (Macdonald 2009: 1). Just as 'post-colonial' neither ignores the evident changes and divergent temporalities of different colonial projects nor declares the end of colonialism per se – and thus exceeds a temporal meaning – we seek to capture the persistent ambivalence and unsettling of anthropology in a move not just against itself but also towards a 'beyond', as Homi Bhabha put it (1994: 1–2). The rejection of modernism in post-modernism, likewise, is not possible without a continual reckoning with modernism and its own genealogies – in nuanced difference yet not altogether unrelated to the complex temporal reflections in analyses of post-socialism (see Derrida 1994 [1993]; Yurchak 2006; Ssorin-Chaikov 2017).

What makes these frictions and dynamics trans-anthropological is that, while they fundamentally concern anthropology, they do not necessarily take place within anthropology, that is, within the professional confines of conferences, journals, departments, and museums associated with the discipline. Implicit in this observation is the question whether anthropology can only take place within anthropology, or if this is not a form of disciplinary narcissism (Gordon 2007). For this reason, we chose the *adjectival* form trans-anthropological, offering a term that works as a tool in relation to fields, practices, moments, or modes of thinking that problematise anthropology. This is, crucially, also an ethnographic observation. In conversations with the interlocutors of this book, they often came to and engaged with anthropology in a transversal way, that is, variously rejecting and embracing yet altogether invoking it.

Using the term "trans-anthropological", we do not wish to return to but, rather, to build on the many twists and turns of the crisis of representation in anthropology, crystallised around the *Writing Culture* turn (Clifford and Marcus 1986; Marcus and Fischer 1986; Behar and Gordon 1995; Clifford 1999), along with its repercussions on museums (Karp and Lavine 1991; Macdonald 1997, 1998) and continuations of this unresolved albeit generative debate within anthropology as it unfolds around more recent calls for its decanonisation, decolonisation, and diversification (Allen and Jobson 2016; McGranahan and Rizvi 2016; Sanchez 2018).[1]

The kind of anthropology we propose between the lines would take these trans-anthropological reflections seriously as *part* of the movement of anthropology. Our argument is not about redrawing the boundaries of where anthropology begins and ends, or what counts as anthropological research, but to observe and think through the possibilities of multiplying and diversifying the *modi* and *loci* of anthropological practice. This has consequences, not least for the ways in which we engage with expertise and knowledge production of and with our interlocutors in fieldwork (see also Blanes et al. 2016; Chua and Mathur 2018; Schneider 2015).

At present, however, it remains indeed unclear in which direction, for instance, the critique levelled against anthropological museums from the field of contemporary art and from activist initiatives calling for their decolonisation will drive these institutions and the discipline of anthropology. The uncertainty we look at and consider here is thus not to be understood as a confusion or a chaos but, rather, as an 'emergence' of different, as yet unknown, possibilities and "phenomena that can only be partially explained or comprehended by previous modes of analysis or existing practices" (Rabinow 2007: 4). This is why we open this inquiry from a range of contemporary standpoints, seeking dialogue with artists, curators, and scholars precisely to update these modes of analysis. We are interested in scoping and analysing beyond and across anthropology in order to rethink what these modes could be – not simply challenging but also adding to, enriching, and providing grounding for a different trajectory ahead.

Fieldwork: Berlin convergences

As our point of departure we take fieldwork conducted at a time of significant transformations in Berlin's museum landscape as well as in contemporary art and curatorial practice. In our research, we have witnessed the emergence and consolidation of what we call trans-anthropological *fields*, marked by a multiplication of diverse interdisciplinary voices (activist, artistic, curatorial, scholarly), locations (museums, biennales, project spaces, galleries), and means (exhibitions, curatorial concepts, artistic projects, demonstrations) by which the where, what, and how of anthropology is disputed and negotiated. These observations draw on ethnographic research in Berlin and on Germany yet additionally offer a broader conceptual toolkit. Influenced by the overlapping of concerns of our interlocutors and the research exchanges that led to this book, we tried to make sense of these various developments that took place in Berlin – and indeed their reverberations in Europe.

One recurrent focal point in our research is the contested Humboldt Forum in the reconstructed Prussian-era City Palace on Berlin's Museum Island. Exhibiting parts of the vast collections of the Ethnological Museum and the Museum of Asian Art, among others, and erected on the former site of the GDR's Palace of the Republic, the project has since its official parliamentary confirmation in 2002 become a national matter of public concern (Binder 2009). It has been a "catalyst for critique" (Bose 2017b: 127) for simmering conflicts and frictions regarding nationalism and religious identity, migration and cosmopolitanism, racism and discrimination, urban politics, as well as Germany's public reckoning with its difficult imperial, socialist, and fascist pasts (see Mandel 2008; Bach 2017; Thiemeyer 2019). Germany's colonial project took centre stage in this context through the hesitant unravelling of its entanglements with Berlin's museum collections (Zimmerman 2001; Penny 2002; Penny and Bunzl 2003; Perraudin and Zimmerer 2011; Eckert and Wirz 2013).

Particularly since the start of the City Palace's architectural reconstruction in June 2013, this process focalised previously active and variously repressed, marginalised, and ignored positions concerning the memory of German colonialism. Central to understanding the genealogy of this process is the formation of *No Humboldt 21!*, a coalition which assembled a broad range of activist, artistic, academic, and civic initiatives. It was formally announced through the publication of what they called the *Moratorium für das Humboldt-Forum im Berliner Schloss (Stop the planned construction of the Humboldt Forum in the Berlin Palace)*. The organisations it brought together – among others, *Berlin postkolonial, Initiative Schwarze Menschen in Deutschland, AfricAvenir, AFROTAK TV CyberNomads, Artefakte // anti-humboldt*, and the *Tanzania-Network* – had, in some cases for more than a decade, been making requests for the recognition and reparation of German colonial injustice (Bauche 2010). These included calls for the repatriation of human remains, the restitution of museum collections acquired during colonial contexts, the renaming of city streets commemorating colonial officials, and, in a broader sense, a debate about race and Germany as a post-colonial nation (see Sow 2008, Ha 2014; Jethro 2018; Aydemir and Yaghoobifarah 2019).

The Humboldt Forum became a cipher for Berlin and Germany's investment in rehabilitating a nostalgic Prussian past, its reconstruction alone being predicted at a total sum of 644.2 million euros in November 2019, according to the German government (Schönball 2019; Bundesregierung 2019). The Forum continues to attract media commentaries, scholarly analyses, as well as public rumours, tabloid attention, and even ridicule. As the often overturned plans about the constituent institutions and teams were gradually announced to the public between 2015 and 2020, the project garnered more consistent and critical attention in regard of its content and conceptual direction – or, rather, its lack thereof. For example, the 2015 nomination of the former head of the British Museum, Neil McGregor, as founding co-director of the Humboldt Forum, was first enthusiastically welcomed. Now, though, it has disappeared from any running commentary, and other events have since set the tone for a fast-paced, and predominantly national, debate on the Humboldt Forum and Germany's colonial heritage. Much-cited and discussed as a turning point in this genealogy of events, art historian Bénédicte Savoy's quitting of the Forum's advisory board in the summer of 2017 and her public denunciation of the project's ignorance regarding the colonial provenance of its collections (Häntzschel 2017) further facilitated the shift in focus towards the colonial ties and provenance of Berlin museum and heritage institutions and collections.

Noticeably, these shifts did not bring any *new* questions to the table. Rather, they changed the means, locations, and publics by which Germany's colonial past was addressed and received. No longer primarily problematised in vain by marginalised initiatives, they were now transferred onto the front-pages and *feuilletons* of major national newspapers. A new context emerged in which negotiations of German colonialism – and therefore also and in particular collections and institutions associated with anthropology – became subjects of renewed and broader concern.

Conducting research on curatorial practices, museums, and contemporary art in this context between 2013 and the time of writing through 2020, inevitably meant observing convergences between these fields. Coinciding with the start of construction for the Humboldt Forum and the organised formation of resistance to it by *No Humboldt 21!*, Margareta began fieldwork in the Ethnologisches Museum Berlin, working closely with staff in its Africa Department. Amid the museum's preparation for the move of its exhibitions into the Humboldt Forum, she looked at how museum staff were grappling with the museum's own colonial entanglements and the relevance of anthropology in this debate more broadly. During this time, she also took part in and accompanied the realisation of the Humboldt Lab Dahlem (2012-2015), a project initiated and funded by the German Federal Cultural Foundation, designed to 'experiment' with anthropological exhibition-making, integrating artistic, and other collaborative practices beyond the museum. This process raised questions about self-reflexive anthropological framing and, among other things, the "trouble with the ethnological" (Macdonald 2015). Margareta's inquiry served to foreground the question of how the engagement with the collections and their entangled histories has co-produced the critique from *within* the institution – and where it has possibly failed to do so (Boast 2011, Deliss and Keck 2016; Macdonald, Lidchi, and Oswald 2017). Where have unexpected coalitions between the museums and critique appeared? How is post-colonial critique appropriated as an institution's "strategic reflexivity" (Bose 2017a)? The anticipated opening of the Humboldt Forum, along with the closure of the Ethnologisches Museum Berlin in its current location in 2016, prompted more than mere conversation. Rather, it incited further artistic and curatorial interrogations of anthropology and anthropological museums.

Until this point in 2013, these dynamics and frictions around Berlin's museum and heritage landscape were both entangled with, yet even more curiously detached from, the city's internationally recognised field of contemporary art. The affordances of the emerging context we sketched above meant that these fields coalesced around more closely interrelated, or more *relatable*, areas of problematisation. It was not that new problems as such emerged, but that the conditions for speaking about and the nodes at which they intersected became more recognisable. Therefore, when the coalition *No Humboldt 21!* organised a major conference and book launch on *Prussian Colonial Heritage* (No Humboldt 21! 2018) and, later on, hosted the first German discussion of Bénédicte Savoy and Felwine Sarr's restitution report (2018), these events already took place against the backdrop of a set of shared reference points.

This was the focus and entry point for Jonas' fieldwork. He accompanied several curators and the spaces they directed, looking at how they crafted their own forms of thinking and practising a troubling of these colonial legacies, constructions of alterity, and different forms of knowledge production beyond the academy. Most of his time was spent with Bonaventure Soh Bejeng Ndikung, Antonia Alampi, and Elena Agudio at SAVVY Contemporary; Alya Sebti at the ifa-gallery (Institut für Auslandsbeziehungen); and Solvej Ovesen at the district gallery of Berlin-Wedding. These curators enacted what we seek to describe with transversal agency, staging their proposals, critique, and imaginations in curatorial concepts. This agency found expression in pamphlets on the Humboldt Forum (Ndikung 2018) and in exhibitions and conferences, such as *Wir sind alle Berliner. 1884 – 2014* (SAVVY and ICI, 2015). It was similarly made manifest in the long-term trans-disciplinary projects *Untie to tie: On Colonial Legacies and Contemporary Societies* (2017-2020, ifa gallery, see Tinius 2020c), in colonial archives, and in critiques of hegemonic cultural production (Tinius 2020a).

These curatorial practices were recursive, enacting models for thinking about the European colonial project and anthropology that had been pioneered by curatorial precursors since the 1990s. Primarily, however, this more recent wave of curatorial work since the 2010s that we investigated in our fieldwork thickened the terrain of inquiry and contributed to catapulting these conversations onto a national and international stage. They brought artworks and projects on restitution, contested collections and museums, and colonial legacies – not to mention, notably, their relationships with anthropology – into major exhibitions, including documenta14 (2017), the Berlin Biennale (2018), and Dak'Art Biennale (2018). These also added to the curators' international reputation as agitators, critics, and commentators.

It is easy to overstate the importance of curatorial work at a time when its celebration as a political remedy has almost turned in on itself. We find it important nonetheless to begin at least to contribute to connecting the dots of small-scale organisations and independent curators in the fields we try to conjure from Berlin, even if the lines between 'independent' and 'state-funded' are fuzzy. Organisations styled as 'small', 'independent', or 'project-based' are for the most reliant on public funding. They are thus hardly removed from public evaluation and accountability, juries, and financing – and certainly not 'independent' from the politics and patronage of city and state administrations. Their entanglement with exhibitions and discursive programmes that translate British, US, and French theoretical and artistic positions on Empire and the colonial condition is visible in the archives particularly of the documenta, the Haus der Kulturen der Welt, or the daadgalerie's official artist-in-residency programme, which are direct organs of the German government's cultural policy and politics. These should be considered as intellectual and curatorial precursors of celebrated articulations of Germany's reckonings with its colonial past, such as *German Colonialism. Fragments Past and Present* (2016-2017), a landmark exhibition in the *German Historical Museum*, widely received and visited.

Our studies in and of Berlin were enhanced by comparative perspectives. We conducted research in the context of the multi-sited project *Making Differences: Transforming Museums and Heritage in the Twenty-First Century*, funded as part of Sharon Macdonald's Alexander von Humboldt Professorship at the Centre for Anthropological Research on Museums and Heritage (CARMAH) of the Humboldt-Universität zu Berlin.[2] While the larger project comprised fourteen scholars working across Berlin's heritage, art, and museum institutions, we focused, together with Larissa Förster, on the thematic area *Transforming the Ethnographic*. Therein, we developed questions on collections, curating, and colonialism, including the very understanding of 'ethnographic', 'ethnological', 'anthropological', and related terminologies and distinctions. The conversations across our fieldsites sparked intense discussions, for instance, on the convergences of provenance and the role of policy work and the media (see CARMAH 2017; Förster 2018; Förster, et al. 2018; Förster and Bose 2018); on contemporary art, diversity, and experimental forms of curatorial collaborations (Tinius 2018a, 2018b, 2020b); and on the contested moves of collections and the construction of 'Africa' in the Humboldt Forum (Oswald and Rodatus 2017; Oswald 2018).

The convergences that we analysed in our research, and which this book takes as its point of departure, capture how a loosely related albeit pioneering set of institutions, initiatives, and actors across the fields of contemporary art, curating, activism, and museums had begun creating a recognisable and translatable set of means and reference points for grappling with anthropology in its imbroglio with German colonial legacies. Gradually and cumulatively, these became near impossible to ignore for policy makers and directors of major cultural institutions at a federal and indeed European level. The current transformations of anthropological museums, contemporary art, and post-colonial critique and activism have arguably become the most productive and vibrant trans-anthropological fields – and the ones most closely associated with our fieldwork. They articulate each other and inter-relate, while having distinct genealogies and historicities. The next section highlights these convergent discursive terrains and institutional constellations, offering a route through the constituent chapters and conversations. They are meant as initiations to a way of seeing relations rather than conclusive statements and, in the process, hope to open future inquiries and problems.

Expanding: The contributions

Across these fields and discursive terrains, curators have acted as particularly noticeable translators, initiators, researchers, theorists, activists, and transversal agents, whose work has generated and catalysed the core conundrum of this book. Thinking against, with, and across anthropology, our conversations during fieldwork and otherwise inspired the argument to think trans-anthropologically. Hence, we accorded them positions across, in-between, around, and 'nearby' the other contributions by university-based scholars, many of whom are working themselves as curators, thus complicating these distinctions and recursive moves of the expanded curatorial field even further (see Sansi 2020; Tinius and Macdonald 2020).

In what follows, we have devised a varied and varying set of interviews and position pieces with individuals and collectives in these various roles. These contributions show how we consider curatorial practice to be transversally agentive across the three main sections of this book: museums, contemporary art, and colonialism. We consider these to be fields that both challenge anthropology and mobilise it in an especially generative way. Notably, however, we conducted interviews with curators whose positionality has come to be known under the unsatisfactory umbrella label of 'independent'. Their emergent significance, particularly since the beginning of the 1990s, owes much to the multiplication of biennials around the world, substantiated by the proliferation of reflexive discourses on curating itself and promoted not least by the accompanying professionalising and institutionalising of such 'independent' curatorial expertise. Even so, this interstitial role comes with a price: the pressure for conceptual innovation; work conditions that are project-based and, thus, temporally limited and bureaucratically saturated; competition among peers and exposure to the ambivalent economy of self-promotion. In all, such circumstances create, for some, a predicament of insecurity and precarity.

The format of the interview *by*, *with*, and *among* curators has become part and parcel of this distribution of the curatorial. Published conversations established themselves, alongside the curatorial concept, as perhaps the most prominent form of curatorial theorising. In this volume, we sought to pry open the format and generation of theory by engaging in an explicit conversation about understandings of curatorial labour, anthropology, museums, and colonial legacies. Since many contributions address curatorial work as the subject of inquiry, albeit often in collaborative manner, the conversations we conducted together over the course of the two years 2018/19 operate refractorily, pick up echoes, and set impulses throughout the entire book.

Below we discuss the ways in which these conversations take us into anthropological institutions and also beyond them, offering a series of practice-based reflections on core anthropological themes as they are addressed in curatorial practice and in the field of contemporary art. The curatorial positions articulate in a multitude of ways post-colonial critiques (*of* anthropology) and contemporary exhibition making (*across* and *with* anthropology) on the trans-disciplinary ecologies of knowledge production, indigeneity, objecthood and agency, restitution and ownership, ethnography and fieldwork, and the legacies of the colonial project in Europe. The contributions in this volume complement the interviews with in-depth analyses of particular case studies of institutional transformations, curatorial collaborations, exhibitions, activist mobilisations, and archival inquiries in and across different national contexts and their entanglement in the global colonial oecumene.

It is quite the undertaking to summarise twenty-one contributions. In this section, we trace the actions and reactions across anthropology of the chapters and conversations. In their own ways, they expand the argument of this book, each responding to our grappling with the core questions we posed to ourselves: What is anthropology? Where and how is it negotiated? What new understandings of anthropology emerge from beyond the classical fields, practices, institutions, and *modi* of anthropological knowledge production?

In 'Museums and the Savage Sublime', anthropologist **Arjun Appadurai** crystallises a fundamental charge against anthropological museums, namely that they "became sites of deep misunderstanding of both the European self and the colonised, objectified other." For him, the fundamental contradiction facing museums is whether they "can be a space for the sacred, the scientific, the educational, and the spectacular, all at the same time." Anthropologist **Sharon Macdonald** contextualises these conundrums across transformations of (anthropological) museums and across heritage practices in Berlin and Europe today. Focusing on her research project, from which this volume emerged, she puts forward an ethnographic analysis of the role of 'difference-making'. Her assembly work speaks across and with institutions that enact themselves as key sites for the articulation and formation of Europe's past and future. In conversation with us, **Wayne Modest** nuances Arjun Appadurai's challenge to the museum. As head of the Research Center of Material Culture in Leiden (NL), he invites us to think with and through the anthropological as a category in the museum. A self-proclaimed "firm believer" in the discipline, he nevertheless claims that anthropology "cannot come without the histories that it is haunted by" and form an integral part of its structure, especially within the museum. Modest sees in art practices and activism from indigenous communities the driving force for the generative critique against the museum. He imagines the trans-anthropological to mean "the distribution of a certain kind of criticality where the museum and anthropology are now articulated in a broader network of critique."

Anthropologist **Emmanuel Grimaud** takes us right into a much-discussed example of what he terms an explicitly "anthropological exhibition", namely *Persona* (2016) at the Musée du Quai Branly-Jacques Chirac. Questioning the reasoning and relations between the supposed binaries subjects and objects, human and non-human forms of existence, his analysis opens up the process of conceiving and curating the exhibition, showing how curatorial, artistic, and anthropological collaborations can act beyond exoticisation and yet within a major public institution. In our conversation with **Anne-Christine Taylor**, former director of the Quai Branly's research department and co-curator of *Persona* (with Emmanuel Grimaud), she offers a synoptic view on the involvement of indigenous curatorial positions and restitution claims within state museums and an ever-evolving anthropological landscape. She relates the routes and roots of many European collections with communities of implication in Latin America and the Pacific. Speaking from and for established national research and heritage contexts in Paris, she takes apart the different elements of what curating means as a translating and transversal practice, "mediating between different communities of interest". Anthropologist **Margareta von Oswald** conducted fieldwork in Berlin's Ethnologisches Museum in a phase that saw the preparation of its collections for their move into the Humboldt Forum against the backdrop of calls for the decolonisation of museum infrastructures. In her contribution, she draws on in-depth analysis of documentation and data practices through an ethnography of provenance research on colonial-era objects. Her research highlights the complex negotiations of anthropology's colonial legacies and epistemologies as they are materialised within museum categories, ordering mechanisms, and ways of knowing collections. In our conversation with curator and cultural historian **Clémentine Deliss**, she takes issue with anthropological museum epistemologies and infrastructures, reflecting on her experimental approaches to making and theorising exhibitions. In doing so, she puts forward a position "against the mono-disciplinarity of ethnographic museums". As the former director of the Weltkulturen Museum in Frankfurt, she pioneered a critical engagement that sought to go beyond received disciplinary framings of anthropology, while her central premise of remediation liaised her museum work closely with self-reflexive anthropological theorising. Arguing for a reconceptualisation of the museum-university, she urges rethinking the relationship between the university, the museum, and the art school – three "central civic institutions" – through "the question of decolonial methodologies".

Drawing on fieldwork among women activists, sociologist **Sarah Demart** addresses what she frames as extraction politics in the context of the renovation of the Royal Museum for Central Africa (RMCA) in Tervuren and Belgian post-colonial reckonings. In chronicling the activist calls for and the unfolding of restitution and ownership claims in Belgium, she problematises the appropriation of Afro-descendant identity politics in the context of contemporary museum and heritage processes. In our conversation with curator, art historian, and educator **Toma Muteba Luntumbe**, he addresses his own curatorial prodding into colonial institutional entanglements in Belgium through the practices and developments in contemporary art. His exhibition *ExitCongoMuseum!* (2001, with Boris Wastiau) at the RMCA offers a pioneering example of the "ideological decoding of its collection". He affirms his insider critique and long-standing engagement with the museum, though he refuses to consider it as "post-colonial" since its re-opening in 2018, or to speak of Belgian "decolonisation". He argues nonetheless for anthropology as "necessary to analyse the most urgent phenomena of our contemporaneity". Thickening the perspectives from within curatorial and ethnographic work across a number of Belgian and French exhibition contexts, including the RMCA, philosopher **Anna Seiderer** and artist **Alexander Schellow** suggest a particular toolkit of methods for reframing colonial film archives. They discuss how moving between institutional contexts reshuffles ways of looking at colonial images, while analysing cognitive responses and visual perceptions to these through estrangement. In doing so, they problematise their "incapacity" and "desire to dissociate the images from their colonial framework".

The Paris-based curatorial collective *le peuple qui manque* draws on literature, philosophy, anthropology, and film to propose an "ontological expansion of art". They put forward curating as interstitial and transversal "between epistemological regimes", whose politics is first and foremost one of translation. Considering anthropology as the "structuring base for thinking about the space of art", the collective wishes to shift towards thinking of the history of this discipline as "a poetic, formal, and political history of the configurations of enunciations". Echoing Grimaud's reflection on the making of an exhibition, anthropologist **Arnd Schneider** ponders the ambivalences and serendipities of art-anthropology interventions in a former colonial museum in Rome. He analyses the difficulties of working through the legacies of ethnographic collections amassed during Italy's colonial enterprise in Libya. Engaging in oral history, as well as in artistic performances as part of an exhibition he co-curated, his contribution highlights in particular the violent colonial traces inscribed in plaster casts of the collection, in addition to the ambiguities of revisiting the "colonial amnesia" in Italy today.

The conversation with curator and writer **Natasha Ginwala** unravels the idea of the curator as a simple translator and reacts *against* our prompts in the interview. For her, curatorial practice should offer forms of "productive refusal" and be a "dissonant agent". This occurs at the kinds of intersection between curating and anthropology, where we find a "non-conformative kinship of academia and artistic thinking" that allows for "a mutation of forms". She traces her positionality among a generation of curators, who "have not waited for institutions to reset their agenda towards a 'non-western' compass, or to craft a more inclusive dialogue". Anthropologist **Jonas Tinius** conducted fieldwork among curators of this generation who are crafting such kinds of reorientations in exhibition practice. Looking at what he terms "district curating", he describes two longer-term curatorial exhibition and research programmes implemented in Berlin's district-gallery of Wedding, called *Unsustainable Privileges* and *Post-Otherness Wedding*. These programmes constituted public efforts to transform the gallery, but they created tensions and ambivalences about what it means to curate a contemporary art gallery in and of a district stereotyped as working-class. Each exhibition took the gallery's physical location in the district as a starting point, and investigated the "porous membranes" of the gallery thresholds, walls, and windows, initiating a difficult and oftentimes incomplete process of description, projection, and reflection on accessibility, locality, and gentrification. SAVVY Contemporary founder and artistic director **Bonaventure Soh Bejeng Ndikung**, who also co-curated the Galerie Wedding programmes, begins our conversation with a counter-question that further complicates our argument of the trans-anthropological. Asking "How do we avoid making the artistic, and in this case the curatorial, just another tool of anthropological research?", he criticises the "audacity" and "disciplinary sovereignty" of the anthropologist to claim the authority of dealing with issues such as indigeneity, humanness, or alterity.

As curators, Ndikung claims, "we are constantly engaged – not in a negation but, rather, in a form of contradiction – with the eyes of anthropologists", though crucially involved in a practice of "situating them as *one* among other forms of trajectories".

Anthropologist and curator **Erica Lehrer** discusses her research in post-colonial, post-Holocaust Polish ethnographic collections, most notably "awkward objects" that push the frameworks of contemporary museums of national culture. Proposing the terminology of "communities of implication", her chapter expands discussions of reimagining the museum today by refusing localised and temporal othering in discussions about restitution, repair, and redress. Describing herself as an "applied reflexive anthropologist", curator and director of Cologne's Rautenstrauch-Joest-Museum **Nanette Snoep** underlines the institutional and political constraints at play when implementing participatory curatorial work in European anthropological museums. Echoing conversations and practices throughout this book, she pushes artistic, anthropological, and what she calls trans-disciplinary curating to engender transformations towards and "suggestions for a post-museum". In a personal and retrospective account, **Annette Bhagwati**, anthropologist and director of the Museum Rietberg in Zurich, examines the notion of cultural representation and traces its impact and genealogy throughout the history of Berlin's Haus der Kulturen der Welt (HKW) from the 1990s until today. Her chapter weaves together various kinds of archival traces, memories, and reflections that put centre stage the transformations of curatorial approaches in an exhibition context without collections: from geographically-bound and "representative" to "research-, process-, and topic-oriented". As such, she highlights how the institution repeatedly questioned its own models of representing cultures, confronting itself with challenges from contemporary artistic practice and incorporating cultural critique in anthropological theorising of the time.

Educator, curator, and documenta-professor **Nora Sternfeld** sees the role of the curatorial subject position in the rendering "liveable" of conflicts. Underscoring her collective curatorial work with *freethought* for the *Bergen Assembly* (2016), she unfolds the neoliberal and institutional forces which trouble curatorial work. Departing from observations about the traditions of criticality in anthropology, Sternfeld raises the question of where and how agitation becomes complicit with the maintenance of existing power relations. And how, if at all, we can "align to use it to agitate?" Anthropologist **Roger Sansi** takes the film *Statues also die* (1953) by Alain Resnais and Chris Marker as his point of departure, in order to discuss the colonial legacies of (European) anthropology museum and their collections. In particular, he understands these institutions as caught up in a temporal dilemma: being at the same time sites for the negotiation of contemporary identity politics and the recognition of colonial pasts, while remaining caught up in a paradoxical anachronism. "What, then, constitutes the contemporary at a time of anachronism?", he asks, prodding at the fraught relation between contemporary art, modernism, and post-modernism to think of a possible anthropology of the contemporary.

Note

1. We also do not intend to associate the concerns articulated in this book to those revolving around post*human* debates on robotics and artificial intelligence (Braidotti 2013; Atanasoski and Vora 2019). In this sense, our propositions are related to but distinct from experimental methodologies and analytics, such as the "alter-anthropological" (Hage 2012: 286), where "critical anthropological thought can generate new problematics (...)", and the "para-sitical" offered for debate by Deeb and Marcus (2011) to reflect on the creation of ethnographic situations.
2. The research that led to this piece was also funded by the Alexander von Humboldt Foundation as part of the research award for Sharon Macdonald's Alexander von Humboldt Professorship. We are grateful to CARMAH and all colleagues who contributed to making our joint research stimulating and productive. Additionally and in particular, we wish to thank Sharon Macdonald, Thomas Fillitz, and anonymous reviewers for helpful comments on our introduction.

References

Adam, Jens, Regina Römhild, Manuela Bojadzijev, Michi Knecht, Pawel Lewicki, Nurhak Polat, and Rika Spiekermann. Eds. 2019. *Europa dezentrieren. Globale Verflechtungen neu denken*. Frankfurt/New York: Campus.

Ahmed, Sara. 2012. *On Being Included. Racism and Diversity in Institutional Life*. Durham, N.C.: Duke University Press.

Allen, Jafari Sinclaire, and Ryan Cecil Jobson. 2016. 'The Decolonizing Generation: (Race and) Theory in Anthropology since the Eighties'. *Current Anthropology* 57(2): 129–148.

Atanasoski, Neda, and Kalindi Vora. 2019. *Surrogate Humanity. Race, Robots, and the Politics of Technological Futures*. Durham, N.C.: Duke University Press.

Aydemir, Fatma, and Hengameh Yaghoobifarah. Eds. 2019. *Eure Heimat ist unser Albtraum*. Berlin: Ullstein.

Bach, Jonathan. 2017. *What Remains? Everyday Encounters with the Socialist Past in Germany*. New York: Columbia University Press.

Bauche, Manuela. 2010. 'Postkolonialer Aktivismus und die Erinnerung an den deutschen Kolonialismus'. *Phase 2. Zeitschrift gegen die Realität*. 37. http://phase-zwei.org/hefte/artikel/postkolonialer-aktivismus-und-die-erinnerung-an-den-deutschen-kolonialismus-134/ (last accessed 17 January 2020).

Behar, Ruth, and Deborah A. Gordon. Eds. 1995. *Women Writing Culture*. Berkeley/Los Angeles/London: University of California Press.

Beliso-De Jesús, Aisha M., and Jenima Pierre. 2019. 'Introduction Special Section: Anthropology of White Supremacy'. *American Anthropologist*. Online Early View: https://doi.org/10.1111/aman.13351 (last accessed 9 January 2020).

Bhabha, Homi. 1994. 'Introduction: Locations of Culture', in: *The Location of Culture*. London: Routledge, pp. 1–27.

Binder, Beate. 2009. *Streitfall Stadtmitte. Der Berliner Schlossplatz*. Cologne: Böhlau.

Blanes, Ruy, Maïté Maskens, Alex Flynn, and Jonas Tinius. 2016. 'Micro-utopias: anthropological perspectives on art, creativity, and relationality'. *Cadernos de Arte e Antropologia/Journal of Art and Anthropology*. 5(1): 5–20.

Boast, Robin. 2011. 'Neocolonial Collaboration: Museum as Contact Zone Revisited'. *Museum Anthropology* 34(1): 56–70.

Bock, Jan-Jonathan, and Sharon Macdonald. 2019. 'Introduction: Making, Experiencing and Managing Difference in a Changing Germany', in: *Refugees Welcome? Differences and Diversity in a Changing Germany*. Oxford/New York: Berghahn Books, pp. 1–38.

Bose, Friedrich von. 2017a. 'Strategische Reflexivität. Das Berliner Humboldt Forum und die postkoloniale Kritik'. *Historische Anthropologie* 25(3): 409–417.

——— 2017b. 'Plädoyer für die Unabgeschlossenheit. Einige Überlegungen zum Humboldt Forum im Berliner Schloss'. *Schweizerisches Archiv für Volkskunde. Halbjahresschrift im Auftrag der Schweizerischen Gesellschaft für Volkskunde* 113(2): 125–130.

Braidotti, Rosi. 2013. *The Posthuman*. Cambridge: Polity Press.

Bundesregierung. 2019. 'Eröffnungstermin, Kostensteigerung, kulturelle Nutzung und Veranstaltungskonzept des Humboldt Forums in Berlin'. Drucksache 11774 (19 July 2019), https://kleineanfragen.de/bundestag/19/11774-eroeffnungstermin-kostensteigerung-kulturelle-nutzung-und-veranstaltungskonzept-des-humboldt-forums-in-berlin (last accessed 09 January 2020).

Canclini, Néstor García. 2014. *Art beyond Itself: Anthropology for a Society without a Storyline*. Durham, NC: Duke University Press.

CARMAH. 2017. *Media Review on Museums*. www.carmah.berlin/media-review-on-museums/ (last accessed 15 June 2019).

Chakkalakal, Silvy. 2019. 'Ethnographic Art Worlds: The Creative Figuration of Art and Anthropology'. *Amerikastudien/American Studies* 63(4): 489–515.

Chua, Liana, and Nayanika Mathur. 2018. *Who are 'We'? Reimagining Alterity and Affinity in Anthropology*. New York/Oxford: Berghahn.

Clifford, James. 1999. 'After Writing Culture' (book review essay). *American Anthropologist* 101(3): 643–65.

———. 2007. 'Quai Branly in Process'. *October* 1 (120): 3–23.

Clifford, James, and George E. Marcus. Eds. 1986. *Writing Culture. The Poetics and Politics of Ethnography*. Berkeley/Los Angeles/London: University of California Press.

Deeb, Hadi Nicholas, and George E. Marcus. 2011. 'In the Green Room: An Experiment in the Ethnographic Method at the WTO'. *PoLAR: Political and Legal Anthropology Review* 34(1): 51–76.

De L'Estoile, Benoît. 2015. 'Can French Anthropology Outlive Its Museums? Notes on a Changing Landscape', in: *Anthropology at the Crossroads. Views from France*, edited by Sophie Chevalier, pp. 81–94.

Deliss, Clémentine. 2012. 'Performing the Curatorial in a Post-Ethnographic Museum', in: *Performing the Curatorial: Within and beyond Art*, edited by Maria Lind. Berlin: Sternberg Press, pp. 61–75.

———. 2013. 'Trading perceptions in a post-ethnographic museum', Thought piece on *Theatrum Mundi*, published 17 June 2013, http://theatrum-mundi.org/library/trading-perceptions-in-a-post-ethnographic-museum/?pdf=178 (last accessed 07 January 2020).

Deliss, Clémentine, and Frédéric Keck. 2016. 'Occupy Collections!* Clémentine Deliss in Conversation with Frédéric Keck on Access, Circulation, and Interdisciplinary Experimentation, or the Urgency of Remediating Ethnographic Collections (before It Is Really Too Late)'. *South Magazine* No. 7. Issue documenta14 #2. http://www.documenta14.de/en/south/456_occupy_collections_clementine_deliss_in_conversation_with_frederic_keck_on_access_circulation_and_interdisciplinary_experimentation_or_the_urgency_of_remediating_ethnographic_collections_before_it_is_really_too_late (last accessed 15 June 2016).

Derrida, Jacques. 1994 [1993]. *Spectres of Marx: The State of the Debt, the Work of Mourning, and the New International*. New York/London: Routledge.

Eckert, Andreas, and Albert Wirz. 2013. 'Wir nicht, die anderen auch: Deutschland und der Kolonialismus', in: *Jenseits des Euzentrismus. Postkoloniale Perspektiven in den Geschichts- und Kulturwissenschaften*, edited by Regina Römhild, Shalini Randeria, and Sebastian Conrad. Frankfurt/Main: Campus, pp. 506–525.

Enwezor, Okwui. 2012. 'Intense Proximité: de la disparition des distances', in: *Intense Proximité. Une Anthologie du Proche et Du Lointain. La Triennale 2012.* Paris, edited by Enwezor, Okwui, Mélanie Bouteloup, Abdellah Karroum, Émilie Renard, and Claire Staebler. Paris: Éditions Artlys, pp. 18–36.

Fillitz, Thomas, and Paul van der Grijp. Eds. 2018. *An Anthropology of Contemporary Art: Practices, Markets, and Collectors*. London: Bloomsbury.

Foster, Hal. 1995. 'The artist as ethnographer?' in: *The Traffic in Culture. Reconfiguring Art and Anthropology*, edited by George E Marcus and Fred R. Myers. Berkeley et al.: University of California Press, pp. 302–309.

Förster, Larissa. 2018. 'Provenance', in: *Otherwise. Rethinking Museums and Heritage*, edited by Christine Gerbich, Larissa Förster, Katarzyna Puzon, Margareta von Oswald, Sharon Macdonald, and Jonas Tinius. Berlin: Centre for Anthropological Research on Museums and Heritage, pp. 16–26. Open-access version: http://www.carmah.berlin/wp-content/uploads/2018/07/CARMAH-2018-Otherwise-Rethinking-Museums-and-Heritage.pdf (last accessed 7 January 2020).

Förster, Larissa, and Friedrich von Bose. 2018. 'Concerning Curatorial Practice in Ethnological Museums: An Epistemology of Postcolonial Debates', in: *Curatopia: Museums and the Future of Curatorship*, edited by Conal McCarthy and Philipp Schorch. Manchester: Manchester University Press, pp. 95–122.

Förster, Larissa, Iris Edenheiser, Sarah Fründt, and Heike Hartmann. Eds. 2018. *Provenienzforschung zu ethnografischen Sammlungen der Kolonialzeit. Positionen in der aktuellen Debatte*. Berlin: Humboldt-Universität zu Berlin. Open-access publication accessible via: https://edoc.hu-berlin.de/handle/18452/19768 (last accessed 17 January 2020).

Geertz, Clifford. 2000. 'The State of the Art', in: *Available Light. Anthropological Reflections on Philosophical Topics*. Princeton: Princeton University Press, pp. 89–142.

Geismar, Haidy. 2015. 'The Art of Anthropology. Questioning Contemporary Art in Ethnographic Display', in: *The International Handbooks of Museum Studies: Museum Theory*, volume edited by Kylie Message and Andrea Witcomb. Handbook series edited by Sharon Macdonald and Helen Rees Leahy. Hoboken, New Jersey: John Wiley & Sons, pp. 183–210.

Gordon, Lewis R. 2007. *Disciplinary Decadence: Living Thought in Trying Times*. London: Routledge.

Ha, Noa. 2014. 'Perspektiven urbaner Dekolonisierung: Die europäische Stadt als "Contact Zone"'. *sub\urban. zeitschrift für kritische stadtforschung* 2(1): 27–48.

Hall, Stuart. 1995. 'When was the "Post-Colonial"? Thinking at the Limit', in: *Post-Colonial Question: Common Skies, Divided Horizons*, edited by Ian Chambers and Curti Lidia. London: Routledge, pp. 242–260.

Häntzschel, Jörg. 2017. '"Das Humboldt-Forum ist wie Tschernobyl". Bénédicte Savoy über das Humboldt-Forum', *sueddeutsche.de*. 20 July 2017. http://www.

sueddeutsche.de/kultur/benedicte-savoy-ueber-das-humboldt-forum-das-humboldt-forum-ist-wie-tschernobyl-1.3596423?reduced=true (last accessed 15 June 2019).

Harney, Elizabeth, and Ruth B. Phillips. Eds. 2019. *Mapping Modernisms. Art, Indigeneity, Colonialism*. Durham, N.C.: Duke University Press.

Jethro, Duane. 2018. 'Decolonizing Streets'. *Africa is a Country*. 10 April 2018. www.africaisacountry.com/2018/10/decolonizing-streets/ (last accessed 15 June 2019).

Lidchi, Henrietta. 1997. 'The Poetics and Politics of Exhibiting Other Cultures', in: *Representation. Cultural Representation and Signifying Practices*, edited by Stuart Hall. Milton Keynes, pp. 151–222.

Karp, Ivan and Steven D. Lavine. Eds. 1991. *Exhibiting Cultures: The Poetics and Politics of Museum Display*. Washington, DC: Smithsonian Institution Press.

Macdonald, Sharon. 1997. 'The Museum as Mirror: Ethnographic Reflections', in: *After Writing Culture. Epistemology and Praxis in Contemporary Anthropology*, edited by Allison James, Jenny Hockey, and Andrew Dawson. London/New York: Routledge.

———. 1998. *The Politics of Display: Museums, Science, Culture*. London/New York: Routledge.

———. 2009. *Difficult Heritage. Negotiating the Nazi Past in Nuremberg and Beyond*. London/New York: Routledge.

———. 2015. 'The Trouble with the Ethnological', in: *The Laboratory Concept. Museum Experiments in the Humboldt Lab Dahlem*, edited by Martin Heller, Agnes Wegner, and Andrea Scholz. Berlin: Nicolai, pp. 211–226.

———. 2016. 'New Constellations of Difference in Europe's 21st-Century Museumscape'. *Museum Anthropology* 39(1): 4–19.

Macdonald, Sharon, Henrietta Lidchi, and Margareta von Oswald. 2017. 'Engaging Anthropological Legacies toward Cosmo-Optimistic Futures?' *Museum Worlds: Advances in Research* 5 (Special Issue: Engaging Anthropological Legacies): 95–107.

Mandel, Ruth. 2008. *Cosmopolitan Anxieties. Turkish Challenges to Citizenship and Belonging in Germany*. Durham, NC: Duke University Press.

Marcus, George E., and Fred R. Myers. 1995. 'The Traffic in Art and Culture: An Introduction', in: *The Traffic in Culture. Refiguring Art and Anthropology*. Berkeley: University of California Press, pp. 1–51.

Mazzarella, William. 2019. 'The Anthropology of Populism: Beyond the Liberal Settlement'. *Annual Review of Anthropology*. 48(1): 45–60.

McGranahan, Carole, and Uzma Z. Rizvi. 2016. 'Decolonizing Anthropology'. *Savage Minds*. Part of the series *Decolonizing Anthropology*, edited by Carole McGranahan and Uzma Z. Rizvi, https://savageminds.org/2016/04/19/decolonizing-anthropology/ (last accessed 03 January 2020).

Mignolo, Walter D. 2009. 'Epistemic Disobedience, Independent Thought and De-Colonial Freedom'. *Theory, Culture & Society*. 26(7-8): 1-23.

Ndikung, Bonaventure Soh Bejeng. 2018. *Those Who Are Dead Are Not Ever Gone. On the Maintenance of Supremacy, the Ethnological Museum and the Intricacies of the Humboldt Forum*. Pamphlet 1. Berlin/Milano: Archive Books.

No Humboldt 21!. 2018. *Dekoloniale Einwände gegen das Humboldt-Forum*. Berlin: AfricAvenir.

Oswald, Margareta von, and Verena Rodatus. 2017. 'Decolonizing Research, Cosmo-optimistic Collaboration? Making Object Biographies'. *Museum Worlds* 5(1): 211-223.

Oswald, Margareta von. 2018. 'Post-Ethnological', in: *Otherwise. Rethinking Museums and Heritage*, edited by Jonas Tinius, Christine Gerbich, Larissa Förster, Katarzyna Puzon, Margareta von Oswald, Sharon Macdonald. Berlin: Centre for Anthropological Research on Museums and Heritage, pp. 55-67.

Ortner, Sherry. 2016. 'Dark Anthropology and Its Others. Theory Since the Eighties'. *HAU: Journal of Ethnographic Theory* 6(1): 47-73.

Pagani, Camilla. 2013. 'Ethnographic Museums: Towards a New Paradigm', in: *European Museums in the 21st Century: Setting the Framework*, edited by Luca Basso Peressut, Francesca Lanz, and Gennaro Postiglione. Milan: MeLa Books, pp. 151-170.

Partridge, Damani J., and Matthew Chin. 2019. 'Interrogating the Histories and Futures of "Diversity": Transnational Perspectives'. *Public Culture* 31(2): 197-214.

Penny, H. Glenn. 2002. *Objects of Culture. Ethnology and Ethnographic Museums in Imperial Germany*. Chapel Hill, NC: University of North Carolina Press.

Penny, H. Glenn and Matti Bunzl. Eds. 2003. *Worldly Provincialism: German Anthropology in the Age of Empire*. Ann Arbor: University of Michigan Press.

Perraudin, Michael, and Jürgen Zimmerer. Eds. 2011. *German Colonialism and National Identity*. New York/London: Routledge.

Phillips, Ruth B. 2007. 'Exhibiting Africa after Modernism: Globalization, Pluralism, and the Persistent Paradigms of Art and Artifact', in: *Museums After Modernism: Strategies of Engagement*, edited by Griselda Pollock and Joyce Zemans. Malden, MA: Blackwell Publishing, pp. 80-103.

Price, Sally. 2007. *Paris Primitive: Jacques Chirac's Museum on the Quai Branly*. Chicago: University of Chicago Press.

Rabinow, Paul. 2007. *Marking Time. On the Anthropology of the Contemporary*. Princeton: Princeton University Press.

Rogofff, Irit. 2013. 'The Expanding Field', in: *The Curatorial: A Philosophy of Curating*, edited by Jean-Paul Martinon. London: Bloomsbury, pp. 41-48.

Römhild, Regina 2017. 'Beyond the Bounds of the Ethnic: For Postmigrant Cultural and Social Research'. *Journal of Aesthetics & Culture* 9(2): 69-75.

Rutten, Kris, An van. Dienderen, and Ronald Soetaert. Eds. 2013. 'Revisiting the Ethnographic Turn in Contemporary Art'. *Critical Arts: South-North Cultural and Media Studies* 27(5): 459–473.

Sansi, Roger. 2015. *Art, Anthropology and the Gift*. London: Bloomsbury.

———. 2020. 'Introduction', in: *The Anthropologist as Curator*, edited by Roger Sansi. London: Bloomsbury, pp. 1–16.

Sansi, Roger, and Marilyn Strathern. 2016. 'Art and Anthropology After Relations'. *HAU: Journal of Ethnographic Theory* 6(2): 425–439.

Schneider, Arnd and Chris Wright. Eds. 2006. *Contemporary Art and Anthropology*. London: Bloomsbury.

Schneider, Arnd. 2015. 'Towards a New Hermeneutics of Art and Anthropology Collaborations'. *EthnoScripts* 17(1): 23–30.

Schönball, Ralf. 2019. 'Bund bewilligt 160 Millionen Euro mehr fürs Museum der Moderne'. *Tagesspiegel online*, 14 November 2019, https://www.tagesspiegel.de/berlin/doppelt-so-teuer-wie-geplant-bund-bewilligt-160-millionen-euro-mehr-fuers-museum-der-moderne/25229586.html (last accessed 07 January 2020).

Shelton, Anthony Alan. 2009. 'The Public Sphere as Wilderness: Le Musée du Quai Branly'. *Museum Anthropology* 32(1): 1–16.

Siegenthaler, Fiona. 2013. 'Towards an ethnographic turn in contemporary art scholarship'. *Critical Arts: South-North Cultural and Media Studies* 27(5): 737–752.

Sow, Noah. 2008. *Deutschland Schwarz Weiß: Der alltägliche Rassismus*. Norderstedt: Books on Demand.

Ssorin-Chaikov, Nikolai. 2017. *Two Lenins. A Brief Anthropology of Time*. Chicago: University of Chicago Press.

Thiemeyer, Thomas. 2019. 'Cosmopolitanizing Colonial Memories in Germany'. *Critical Inquiry* 45(4): 967–990.

Trouillot, Michel-Rolph. 2003. 'Anthropology and the Savage Slot: The Poetics and Politics of Otherness', in: *Global Transformations. Anthropology and the Modern World*. New York: Palgrave, pp. 7–28.

Tinius, Jonas. 2018a. 'Awkward Art and Difficult Heritage: Nazi Art Collectors and Postcolonial Archives', in: *An Anthropology of Contemporary Art: Practices, Markets, and Collectors*, edited by Thomas Fillitz and Paul van der Grijp. London: Bloomsbury, pp. 130–145.

———. 2018b. 'Alterity', in: *Otherwise. Rethinking Museums and Heritage*, edited by Christine Gerbich, Larissa Förster, Katarzyna Puzon, Margareta von Oswald, Sharon Macdonald, and Jonas Tinius. Berlin: Centre for Anthropological Research on Museums and Heritage, pp. 40–54. Open-access version: http://www.carmah.berlin/wp-content/uploads/2018/07/CARMAH-2018-Otherwise-Rethinking-Museums-and-Heritage.pdf (last accessed 7 January 2020).

———. 2020a. 'Troubling Diversity and Iterations of Difference: Reflections on Curatorial Tensions and a Mapping Survey', in: *Beyond Afropolitan & Other Labels: On the Complexities of Dis-Othering as a Process*, edited by Kathleen Louw. Brussels: BOZAR, pp. 53–58.

———. 2020b. 'The Anthropologist as Sparring Partner: German Colonial Legacies, Fieldwork, and the Expanded Curatorial Field'. *Berliner Blätter. Ethnologische und Ethnografische Beiträge* 82. Open-access publication.

Tinius, Jonas. Ed. 2020c. 'Traces, Legacies, and Futures: A Conversation on Art and Temporality' (with Nora-Al-Badri, Khadija von Zinnenburg Carroll, Silvy Chakkalakal, Alya Sebti, and Jonas Tinius). *Third Text* Forum. 01/2020. Open-access version: http://www.thirdtext.org/tinius-et-al-conversation (last accessed 14 January 2020).

Tinius, Jonas, and Sharon Macdonald. 2020. 'The Recursivity of the Curatorial', in: *The Anthropologist as Curator*, edited by Roger Sansi. London: Bloomsbury, pp. 35–58.

Vermeulen, Hans F. 2018. 'History of Anthropology and a Name Change at the German Ethnological Society Meeting in Berlin: Conference Report'. *History of Anthropology Newsletter*. 22 February 2018. http://histanthro.org/news/history-of-anthropology-and-a-name-change-at-the-german-ethnological-society-meeting-in-berlin-conference-report/ (last accessed 5 March 2018).

Yurchak, Alexei. 2006. *Everything Was Forever, Until It Was No More: The Last Soviet Generation*. Princeton: Princeton University Press.

Museums and the Savage Sublime

Arjun Appadurai

I am honoured to provide a preface to this timely, stimulating, and courageous volume, animated by thinkers and practitioners who value museums as a form but are worried about many of their existing deformations. Rather than speak for them (which I am not qualified to do in any case), I offer a provocation which grows out of reading this volume.

We generally agree that the ethnological museum as an institution emerges from ideas of collection, display, learning, and taste with deep roots in Europe's troubled encounters with those societies that were under Imperial rule or came under some sort of Western sovereignty. Though the history of most Western ethnological museums has indisputably come out of prior histories of conquest, commerce, and political exploitation, the museum has struggled from its beginnings to be a forum for the broadening of knowledge and for the transformation of curiosities into popular experiences of the Savage Sublime. It joins the university, the scientific laboratory, the archive, the church and the prison in a complex of institutions devoted to the collected and researchable Sublime. The governing ideology of this evolution is of the best values of the Renaissance and the Enlightenment: knowledge, learning, curiosity, discovery. In short, it is understanding across languages, cultures, and social experiences.

But a funny thing happened to Western museums on the way to the twentieth century. They became sites of deep misunderstanding of both the European self and the colonised, objectified other. These misunderstandings are multiple, and they tell us something of the archaeology of our current ambivalence about museums. One such misunderstanding is about the difference and the similarity between the museum of fine art and the ethnological museum. Since fine art in the modern world is a product of the canonical discipline of art history (in alliance with archaeology in some cases), the distaste for ethnological museums among fine art curators and patrons reveals in fact both a distaste for the objects of the Savage Sublime and a distaste for anthropology, whether ethnographic or ethnological. This distaste has gradually become mutual, and the Savage Sublime is hostage to this misunderstanding. This is a misunderstanding which has not yet been resolved, as we can see in the strange spectacle of the Humboldt Forum, where several classical fine art museums encircle the newly arrived ethnological specimens from the periphery of Berlin. Much earlier, the controversial exhibition on *"Primitivism" in 20th Century Art: Affinity of the Tribal and the Modern* (1984/1985) at the MoMA in 1984 both revealed and exploited this profound mutual misunderstanding.

Another such misunderstanding was about the very categories into which the objects of the Savage Sublime could be divided: functional, ritual, art, craft, shamanic, decorative, and more categories were invented to help group, store, archive and (‚occasionally) display these objects. Here the tectonic struggle is between ethnological museums and natural history museums, since they do not agree on how and where to draw the line between human and non-human others, a struggle first captured by Donna Haraway in her pioneering work on the American Museum of Natural History in New York. The dioramas in major natural history museums express the heart of this confusion in their effort to capture the living environments, in which various objects of material culture may have had a social life, but their effect is to create strange spaces which look more like cartoons or caricatures of non-modernity. The misunderstanding of the Savage Sublime is thus a three-way misunderstanding between the disciplines of ethnology, natural history, and art history, each of which is in fact a product of the Age of Empire and has a different stake in the proper understanding of the objects of the Other.

The other misunderstanding that has plagued modern museums is the notion that they are also sites of research and teaching, similar to universities and colleges. Hence the busloads of school children that arrive at many Western museums (from the British Museum to the Rijksmuseum) today, to be taught how to enjoy exotic objects and cultures or to develop the ideas of taste that the museum patrons, curators, and docents think fit for young minds. This pedagogical ambition has its roots in figures such as Alexander von Humboldt (and his many replicas) who combined travel, science, research, and collecting as seamlessly linked activities in their lives. But is the museum really meant to be a classroom? Can it entertain and educate at the same time? Is the taste of the elite collectors, patrons, and curators who support the museum really what the middle and working classes need? Is this an illusion of cultural elites confused by the modern idea that their taste has to be the arbiter of all taste, and that their learning needs to be the canonical source of a broad democratic ideology? Does the museum really have the capacities to foster critical thinking and new knowledge in the manner of the best modern universities?

And then we have the sense of the museum as a sacred place, a place of icons, silence, transcendental experiences, a church for those whom a Christian god has failed or become unavailable. Notwithstanding the recent efforts of modern museums to become more interactive, user-friendly, sociable, and welcoming, the truth is that noise, loud commentary, playful explorations of museum spaces, jokes about signage, vulgarities about iconic objects, are strictly discouraged. In this regard, museums continue to think of themselves as churches, in which a powerful clergy provides sacraments and glimpses of the divine to ordinary humans, who for a brief period of time, are lifted into the space of the Savage Sublime or the more elevated Kantian Sublime. They are transported out of the grime and stress of everyday life into the hushed sanctity of the great cathedrals, churches, and shrines of this world. It is also true that the great cathedrals and churches have become museums in their own right, but that is another story. So here lies another foundational misunderstanding about the museum, which propels its strategies, energies, and failures.

I said earlier that there were other categorical errors in the history of the modern museum. It is also sometimes viewed as an archive or repository of Otherness, or as a scientific laboratory for restoration, repair, and recovery of special materials, tools, styles, and forms. These confusions are also tied up with the tension between natural history and art history, and between museums and universities.

Thus, the fundamental contradictions, confusions and conundrums surrounding modern museums are products of a foundational misunderstanding which is about whether the museum is a university, a church, a laboratory, or a place of entertainment. The many debates surrounding museums in Europe and the United States today, including the recent one about the repatriation of objects taken from the sites of Euro-American empire, have roots in our failure to probe whether the museum can be a space for the sacred, the scientific, the educational, and the spectacular, all at the same time. Until we develop a simpler, leaner, more distinctive idea of what the museum ought to be, our dilemmas as scholars, curators, artists, and activists will not be resolved. The doors to engaging these misunderstandings and moving past them in the coming years have been brilliantly opened by the contributors to this collection.

Transforming the Ethnographic: Anthropological Articulations in Museum and Heritage Research

Sharon Macdonald

What transformations are underway within contemporary museums and heritage? Where are the points of – generative – disruption? And which ideas or ways of doing things – including in anthropologies and other areas of theorising and practice – can help release and realise the potential of museums and heritage to contribute to more positive futures?

These are some of the central questions that inform the research project *Making Differences – Transforming Museums and Heritage in the Twenty-First Century*, within which the current volume was conceived.[1] The project was designed to be broad in scope, purposely not restricted to only one type of museum or just to established organisations. Instead, my intention was that it would encourage exploration of how ideas and realisations of difference were being mobilised in various locations, in margins as well as in centres, and in the less remarked crevices of practice as well as in the public or academic spotlight. The idea was that this would highlight the resulting or imaginable constellations of difference above and beyond those of specific sites,[2] and that it would identify the actual and possible traffic of concepts, objects, people, and practices *across* locations. In this way, it would not only transgress conventional boundaries of research focus but would also go beyond anthropological documentation and analysis to propose new potential crossings and possibilities.

At the same time, however, museums with collections that are or have been called ethnographic or ethnological are given special emphasis in the project. This is in recognition of their significant historical and contemporary roles in articulating for wider publics particular, often problematic, notions of difference. Condensation points for certain struggles, especially that of decolonisation, they are the impetus for one of the project's thematic areas, *Transforming the Ethnographic*, within which the editors of this current volume, Margareta von Oswald and Jonas Tinius, work.[3] The aim of this area, as the project brief puts it, is to "begin from the challenges facing ethnographic and ethnological museums today", especially their "difficult and contested heritage, with a particular focus on the enduring, problematic, and multiple legacies of colonialism", and to pursue the question of "What curatorial strategies are being and could be developed to address" these challenges?[4] This volume, with its selection of insightful essays and interviews with a wide range of actors who have been variously reflecting on and devising such curatorial strategies, shows an abundance of creative practice, and deep and critical thought, underway. Moreover, as it also shows, this is not restricted to the academy or established museums but is part of a dynamic distributed field whose frictions and connectivities are not only generating debate but are also transforming the nature of the field itself.

Below, I take up Margareta and Jonas' invitation to provide some comments on the project that formed the broader research context for this volume. In doing so, I first discuss some of the ideas that motivated the *Transforming the Ethnographic* area, noting how *Across Anthropology* addresses these. I then mention some of the other relevant research – and its context – that is also underway at the Centre for Anthropological Research on Museums and Heritage (CARMAH) at the Humboldt-Universität zu Berlin, where we are based. First, however, I offer a brief comment on the motivations behind the term "anthropological" that features in the name of our research centre.

Anthropological articulations

The A provided by "Anthropological" in the name of our research centre was partly acronymically inspired – it helped to produce an acronym that I hoped would be sayable and memorable. But it also stemmed from my conviction that social and cultural anthropology had much to offer museum and heritage research that, as yet, had not been substantially drawn out and developed beyond individual studies.[5] A centre for 'anthropological' research would thus be an opportunity to do that and to see what else that might enable.

In planning this, I saw anthropology itself as plural – consisting not only of Anglo-American traditions but also as comprising many other European and Global South approaches, some of which put their emphasis more on 'anthropology at home' than at a distance, and that variously overlap and engage with sociology, history, or literary studies, among others.[6] At the same time, however, I saw the following interrelated features of many of these anthropologies as especially promising for museum and heritage research. First, there is the commitment in most of them to highlighting the relativity of practice, by which I mean their showing how things might be otherwise (Macdonald 2018). While in some traditions this has been achieved through a focus on what – at first sight at least – appears to be radically other, in others it operates more through estranging the apparently familiar (see Taylor, this volume), perhaps through analogies and contrasts – a mode of operating that we might even characterise as *acrossing*. Second, and connected to the former, is the breadth of these anthropologies in terms of their collective geographical and topic range. What I saw this as capable of doing in relation to museums and heritage was enabling a form of acrossing that could unsettle assumptions within the field, as well as expanding it by opening it up to new input. Here, anthropological commitment, enabled by ethnographic methodologies, to engaging with what goes on at the usually hidden under-bellies of practice – among those whose voices are less often heard in public debate or by other disciplines – seemed to me to be especially needed. At the same time, the emphasis in some anthropologies – including the German *Anthropologie* – on probing into commonalities (a term I choose to use here rather than 'universal', which risks being either banal or overblown) was one that I hoped the anthropological label might prompt.[7]

In addition, the very fact that many of these anthropologies have for decades now been in overt struggle with their own problematic heritages – especially but not only colonial – and modes of operation has led to high degrees of reflexivity within them. Of course, this is not ubiquitous or complete but it nevertheless indelibly shapes most contemporary anthropologies. It does so not only by giving attention to those histories and writing about them but also through a quest for alternative modes of engaging with those who might once have been only the objects of research study, and, partly as a consequence of this quest, it does so through considerable experimentation with the design of anthropological knowledge production. This has resulted in a flourishing of collaborative and action-oriented research, as well as in new formats, especially, and increasingly, those that themselves cross over with and into artistic practice – as is a key part of the focus of this volume and a key potential for transforming the ethnographic.

Troubling the ethnographic

In addition to indexing museums and collections that might be called 'ethnographic', the selection of the term "ethnographic" in the research area title *Transforming the Ethnographic* was also intended to prompt reflection on what might constitute 'the ethnographic' more broadly. This was not in order to come up with a definition but, rather, was to consider whether there were senses of 'the ethnographic' that might bring new angles into the debates about ethnographic (and maybe other) museums and their potentials. Here, the fact that anthropology and other social sciences have long deployed the term "ethnography" methodologically – to indicate particular modes of engagement and knowledge-making – and as applicable to any activities, rather than as a restricted socio-geographical designation, seemed to me to be especially worth exploring (see also Luntumbue, this volume). I should here give recognition to the fact that for museums across Europe (the scope of this volume) and even more so elsewhere, the geographical scope of 'ethnographic' or its near synonyms is not necessarily 'overseas', 'beyond this continent' or even 'beyond this nation', even though it is frequently used in this way in academic debate. Even though 'ethnographic' may encompass 'local' collections (often designated as folk culture or *Volkskunde*, to use the German term) – as Erica Lehrer describes in her chapter in this volume (see also the conversation below with Wayne Modest) – it nevertheless still carries a strong connotation of referring to 'cultures' (which in itself is problematic as Anne-Christine Taylor points out in her contribution) that are non-contemporary in Paul Rabinow's sense (see Clementine Deliss, this volume). That is, they are regarded as somehow not of the here and now – as 'elsewhere' and 'left behind', two categories that elide together and become further self-reinforced in a process of 'deadening' (as Natasha Gimwala puts it, this volume).

Yet this understanding of the scope of the ethnographic has very little traction in contemporary social and cultural anthropology. This is partly because over decades now it has been subject to reflexive critique. It is also on account of the insights that can be gained from giving ethnographic attention to practices of many kinds. Ethnographic research has long been looking at locations such as scientific labs and the stock exchange, at space agencies or the film world; it researches robots or living with and dying from HIV/AIDS, video gamers and burn-out.[8] Here, what 'ethnographic' means is in-depth, first-hand engagement with what goes on in practice, conveying the perspectives of those involved, perhaps critiquing established positions in the process, but also potentially highlighting dimensions that participants don't usually notice or give weight to. That might mean certain patterns or recurrences of action, or particular connections and relationships among participants, or the tracing of implications, including to beyond the immediate context or concerns, or to, say, the agency of the non-human (see Grimaud, *le peuple qui manque*, and Schneider, among others, this volume). While not always to the forefront, a powerful technique for bringing what is readily taken-for-granted to awareness is what Emmanuel Grimaud and Anne-Christine Taylor here call "estrangement". This should not be confused with exoticisation – an unreflective reveling in otherness that serves to produce it – that has been so rightly criticised (Ndikung, this volume). It is, rather, a reflexive technique primarily for throwing one's own presumptions into relief, and, as such, one that is deployed for raising questions rather than confirming expectations. Exhibitions such as *Persona* (which blurred the human/non-human distinction), at the Musée du Quai Branly-Jacques Chirac, discussed here by its curators Grimaud and also Taylor, are good examples of this kind of approach, and thus of the potential for opening up what is meant by 'the ethnographic' in the museum context. So too are others mentioned in this volume, such as *The Popular Culture of Illegality* at the Museum Volkenkunde in Leiden, which was co-conceived by Wayne Modest.

Such topics are important not only to show what ethnography can do and not even just because they make for fascinating exhibitions (though this should never be underestimated!). They also matter because they push against the grain of the ethnographic museum's tendency to non-contemporaneity, and by so doing they repurpose it as a different kind of 'ethnographic'. Whether this should even be called ethnographic remains open to question. Personally I don't think the term "ethnographic museum" is especially helpful, and in the public arena it is probably counter-productive, but for now it is still worth thinking through and against. At present and as this volume shows in many contributions, this pushing against is especially underway in relation to the ethnographic museum's coloniality. This is vital – as it is and has been for anthropology as a discipline – due to the formative role of colonialism in forming these institutions, and to the implications that continue to play out. Bringing these to light and addressing their continuing afterlives is necessary to avoid perpetuating violence. As *Across Anthropology* amply shows, interrogation of the ethnographic museum's coloniality and developing strategies to highlight this and, in a further decolonising move, potentially leading to alternative but nevertheless thoroughly reflexive modes of engagement (as Nanette Snoep argues in this volume), are being undertaken by activists and artists, as well as curators and academics. Moreover, this is often being done – as is a key point of this volume – in collaborations between, or across, these various players (see especially Demart, Seiderer and Schellow, Schneider, Snoep, Sternfeld), in new constellations of collaborative working, sometimes, indeed, with individuals occupying more than one subject position. As noted above and as Natasha Ginwala points out of contemporary anthropology, there is today an exciting expansion of forms – a going beyond the usual formats – that this takes, including artistic. Such expansion and experimentation is also underway in relation to the modes of engaging with the questions that have had some of their condensation points in the ethnographic museum – questions of transforming the ethnographic. As *Across Anthropology* shows so well, this engagement is also realised in a flourishing contemporary art practice, capable of sensitising and estranging, of creatively critiquing. Moreover, as we see in this volume, in the examples of the independent Berlin galleries discussed by Jonas Tinius or the HKW, also Berlin, discussed by Annette Bhagwati, this kind of transformation of the ethnographic takes place in many spaces other than in the ethnographic museum itself.

Making differences

The editorial work of assembling this volume is itself an important form of research – thus central to *Transforming the Ethnographic* – in its careful curation of voices from the wider field. It is one of a number of editorial collections undertaken or underway from the *Making Differences* project – with its broader focus on questions of how difference is being variously made and unmade in contemporary museum and heritage transformations.[9] These collections give significant insight into the wider, translocal, and transdisciplinary field.

At the core of *Making Differences*, however, is a multi-researcher ethnography of ongoing museum and heritage developments in Berlin. The idea here was to mobilise the capacity of ethnographic research to attend carefully to practice – to what happens and to what is said – behind the scenes as well as in public, and to bring this together with anthropological expertise in the analysis of how differences (cultural, social, biological ...) are made and the effects that they have. The focus of this is Berlin. This focus was partly pragmatic, but it was also in recognition of significant museum and heritage developments underway, including as capital of the re-unified nation, engaged in grappling with multiple problematic pasts, as well as with changing demographics. Here, the planned reconstructed City Palace that would contain, among other things, displays of objects from the ethnological collections – in what came to be called the Humboldt Forum – was a major impetus for this focus, especially for the *Transforming the Ethnographic* research theme (see also Oswald and Tinius, this volume). I had been following this from a distance for over a decade, having since the early 2000s been invited to participate in various events connected with it, and having been privileged to learn much from Friedrich von Bose, whose PhD on aspects of the process I had jointly supervised (Bose 2016). Significant as the Humboldt Forum is, however, it was not the only subject of the *Making Differences* project, partly for the above-mentioned reasons of seeking to consider a more diverse palette of heritage-making and in order to investigate connections, parallels, and divergences across and between sites and practices (Macdonald, Gerbich, and Oswald 2018).

As a result, the *Making Differences* project comprises some direct study of aspects of the making of the Humboldt Forum, as well as much that is more indirect – and all conducted in a lively research centre that is located just around the corner from the palace building site (as it still is at the time of writing). Margareta von Oswald's ethnographic research, as can be seen in this volume, is focused on the ethnological collections, partly picking up the making process where the study of Friedrich von Bose left off, though with some differences of emphasis. I too have conducted fieldwork on the making of the Humboldt Forum, doing so primarily with the team making the permanent exhibition, provisionally called *Berlin and the World*. This allowed me to see curators themselves actively and critically reflecting on other parts of the Humboldt Forum, including possible shortcomings of the ethnological displays, especially what they thought might be inadequate attention given to coloniality, and devising progressive alternative strategies. At the heart of this were a raft of participative approaches, including with various communities within Berlin. In their search for critical and insightful modes of display the curators also worked with artists, such as the graffiti artists How and Nosm who will create a work called *Weltdenken* (world thinking) that will include, among other things, reference to colonial exploitation.[10]

In addition to the relatively long-term fieldwork by Margareta and myself on the making of parts of the Humboldt Forum, other members of our team have looked at specific aspects of it. Duane Jethro has investigated the debates about the cross on the palace as part of his more wide-ranging research on post-colonial debates and activism in Berlin; and Debbie Onuoha has deployed her skills as a visual anthropologist to analyse the exhibition of African and European artefacts, *Beyond Compare* (Bode Museum 2017-2019) that is a precursor to display in the Humboldt Forum. In addition, Larissa Förster's *Transforming the Ethnographic* research tackles questions of provenance and restitution, for which the Humboldt Forum has been such a focus in German debate (Förster 2018; Förster and von Bose 2018; Förster, Edenheiser, Frundt, and Hartmann 2018; and see also, Jethro 2019). As Jonas Tinius explains of his own research in this volume, the Humboldt Forum development was something about which not only he, as part of the wider research team, was thinking and experiencing but was one that his museum and gallery interlocutors, including Bonaventure Soh Bejeng Ndikung, who is interviewed in this volume, were at least partly responding to in their curatorial work (see also Tinius and Macdonald 2020).

Most recently, in developments unplanned at the start of our research, some of Larissa Förster's ideas have helped prompt a project that will see objects from Berlin's Ethnological Museum travel to Namibia, where artists will work with them to produce new objects for a Namibian National Museum of Fashion that is currently in the making, as well as for the Humboldt Forum.[11] In addition, *Making Differences* artist-researcher Tal Adler has begun collaborating with Friedrich von Bose, who is now curator at the Humboldt Labor – the Humboldt-Universität zu Berlin's exhibition space within the Humboldt Forum – to create an exhibition experiment – that is, a form of exhibiting that develops a new approach that is itself reflexive about its mode of exhibiting and that may also be research generating (Macdonald and Basu 2006). The exhibition experiment will focus on a contentious object from the university collections, namely a skull that has been used in the development of racial science. In doing so, it will also draw on ideas developed by Tal Adler and others as part of the *TRACES* Project – whose aim was to explore the potential for addressing contentious heritage with the arts – that was partly based at CARMAH, and which also included the work discussed by both Erica Lehrer and Arnd Schneider in this volume.[12] This project sought especially to go beyond the usual models of artists being deployed short-term by cultural institutions to create temporary installations and instead for them to work more closely and collaboratively as part of what Adler terms "creative co-production" (Adler 2020).

Beyond these direct engagements with the Humboldt Forum, the ethnographic work of our project team has also taken us to many other museum and heritage locations within Berlin. This includes the Museum of European Cultures (sometimes talked about as having been 'left behind' by the Humboldt Forum, as it will remain in Dahlem rather than moving to it), the Berlin Museum of Natural History, the Museum of Islamic Art, and the Holocaust Memorial, to name just those that have been the focus of the most intense research.[13] In almost all of these locations – again to an extent unanticipated at the outset of the project – there has been engagement with art in some form. This has included research by Christine Gerbich in the Museum of Islamic Art, which explores among other thing the Eurocentric limitations set by the category of 'Islamic Art' (and see contributions to Puzon, Macdonald, and Shatanawi 2020). It also includes fieldwork undertaken by Katarzyna Puzon with *Kunstasyl (Art Asylum)* – a group of mainly refugees producing various forms of artistic engagements, including an exhibition at the Museum of European Cultures (Puzon 2019; see also Macdonald 2019). Also in the the Museum of European Cultures, Magdalena Buchczyk's research probes, *inter alia*, notions of folk art (cf. Lehrer, this volume) and craft, which she has explored in other contexts too (e.g. Buchczyk 2015). Our partner, the Berlin Museum of Natural History has itself developed a strong artistic programme, to which *Making Differences* researcher Tahani Nadim has contributed, including in a collaboration with the visual artist Åsa Sonjasdotter, as well as reflecting more broadly on the potentials of artistic engagements in such museum contexts (Nadim 2018). Chiara Garbellotto's collaborative research on the Berlin Museum of Natural History's citizen science projects has also involved the input of artists, as well as that of visual anthropologist Debbie Onuoha, who is also developing further creative visual work on the museum's Bobby the Gorilla. Beyond these sustained engagements, our project work has also involved us in complementary analysis of exhibitions and debates, beyond as well as in Berlin, as can be seen in the *Reflections* section of our website.[14]

In many ways, then, the project within which *Across Anthropology* was born has itself, as it has developed since it began in 2015, become even more trans-anthropological – and especially more entangled with artistic practice of various sorts – than was initially planned. It takes place within a very lively research culture of events and guests that brings together not only academics but also curators, activists, and artists from across Berlin as well as beyond.

What is underway is not only debate across and between different actors but also the forging of new coalitions of action, which themselves act as sites for further research, critique, and creative works in this dynamic – multiply trans – field. This volume itself is surely, then, not only an illuminating curation of current debates but also a vital stimulus to further critical and enlivening transformation.

Acknowledgments

I thank the *Making Differences* team and other CARMAH members – and especially Margareta von Oswald and Jonas Tinius as editors of this volume – for so much great work and talk that has shaped my thinking here, though

I am responsible for any errors or shortcomings. My professorship and thus my research time, as well as that of many members of *Making Differences*, has been funded by the Alexander von Humboldt Foundation. In addition, I am grateful to the Berlin Museum of Natural History, the Humboldt-Universität zu Berlin, and the Prussian Cultural Heritage Foundation for funding further members of the team.

Notes

1. The project was funded by the Alexander von Humboldt Foundation from 2015-2020 as part of my Alexander von Humboldt Professorship. Further funding was also received from the Humboldt-Universität zu Berlin, the Berlin Museum of Natural History, and the Prussian Cultural Heritage Foundation. For further information see: http://www.carmah.berlin/making-differences-in-berlin/ (last accessed 4 January 2020) and also Macdonald 2018.
2. See also Macdonald 2016.
3. They did so from January 2016 and June 2016 respectively, and were joined later that year by Larissa Förster. Other researchers within the project, starting subsequently, whose work was conceived at least partly within this research area, were Tal Adler, Duane Jethro, and Debbie Onuoha, as well as Magdalena Buchzyk (funded by an Alexander von Humboldt Fellowship, as was Duane Jethro, the Georg Forster Alexander von Humboldt Post-Doctoral Fellow between 2017 and 2019, before he became a post-doctoral fellow in the *Making Differences* project until September 2020).
4. http://www.carmah.berlin/making-differences-in-berlin/ (last accessed 7 January 2020).
5. In *Memorylands* (2013) I sought to make this argument, as well as to make a start on showing that potential by gathering together existing research in relation to memory practices and heritage in Europe. The argument was also central to the application to the Alexander von Humboldt Foundation that led to the establishing of CARMAH and the *Making Differences*, including its thematic area, *Transforming the Ethnographic*.
6. My personal experience has also been multi- and inter-disciplinary, from my undergraduate degree in Human Sciences, comprised of a mix of social and natural sciences, a DPhil in Social Anthropology in the UK, and since then posts in Sociology as well as in Social Anthropology and in Cultural Anthropology, and now working within an Institute of European Ethnology, as well as engagements with anthropologists worldwide, including, especially, in China.

7. I saw this as also potentially affording engagement with questions of the 'post human' or 'more-than-human' (e.g. Braidotti 2013). Although it can reasonably be argued that the "anthropos" emphasis is too narrow for this (as *le people qui manque* argue in their contribution to this volume), it is evident from the emerging work that anthropology has much to contribute (e.g. Kohn 2013; Smart and Smart 2017; Tsing 2015).
8. See, for example, Traweek 1988, Hertz 1998, Zabusky 1995, Ortner 2013; Robertson 2018; Guo 2016, Irving 2017; Bareither 2017; Löfgren and Ehn 2010.
9. Edited collections wholly or partly from the project that curate a wide range of inputs include Lidchi, Macdonald, and von Oswald 2017; Förster, Edenheiser, Fründt, and Hartmann 2018; Edenheiser and Förster 2019; Macdonald and Bock 2019; Bareither and Tomkowiak 2019; Puzon, Macdonald, and Shatanawi 2020. As regards only inputs from members of the research team, see CARMAH 2018 and an online volume called *Doing Diversity in Museums and Heritage – A Berlin Ethnography* that will appear on http://www.carmah.berlin in 2020.
10. See https://www.stadtmuseum.de/aktuelles/375-quadratmeter-wandbild (last accessed 4 January 2020)
11. See https://blog.smb.museum/collaborative-research-with-namibian-colleagues-at-the-ethnologisches-museum/ (last accessed 4 January 2019).
12. The full project title is: *TRACES: Transmitting Contentious Cultural Heritages with the Arts – from Intervention to Co-Production*. It was funded from 2016-2019 by the European Union Horizon 2020 scheme under grant agreement number 693857. Views expressed here are not those of the EU. For more information about the project see http://www.tracesproject.eu (last accessed 4.1.2020), Schneider 2019, and Hamm and Schoenberger 2020.
13. See http://www.carmah.berlin for more information about research at CARMAH.
14. http://www.carmah.berlin/reflections/ (last accessed 03 January 2020).

References

Adler, Tal. 2020. 'The creative co-production: an experimental model for artistic engagements with contentious cultural heritage', in: *Contentious Heritage and the Arts. A Critical Companion*, edited by Marion Hamm and Klaus Schoenberger. Klagenfurt: Wieser Verlag.

Bareither, Christoph. 2017. *Gewalt im Computerspiel. Facetten eines Vergnügens.* Bielefeld: transcript.

Bareither, Christoph, and Ingrid Tomokowiak. Eds. 2019. *Mediated Pasts – Popular Pleasures. Kulturen populärer Unterhaltung und Vergnügen*. Würzburg: Königshausen & Neumann.

Bock, Jan, and Sharon Macdonald. Eds. 2019. *Refugees Welcome? Difference and Diversity in a Changing Germany*. Oxford: Berghahn.

Bose, Friedrich von. 2016. *Das Humboldt Forum. Eine Ethnographie seiner Planung*. Berlin: Kadmos.

Braidotti, Rosi. 2013. *The Posthuman*. Cambridge: Polity.

Buchczyk, Magdalena. 2015. 'Heterogeneous craft communities. Reflections on folk pottery in Romania'. *Journal of Museum Ethnography* 28: 28–49.

Edenheiser, Iris, and Larissa Förster. Eds. 2019. *Museumsethnologie. Eine Einführung*. Berlin: Reimer.

Förster, Larissa. 2018 'Provenance', in: *Otherwise. Rethinking Museums and Heritage*, edited by Christine Gerbich, Larissa Förster, Katarzyna Puzon, Margareta von Oswald, Sharon Macdonald, and Jonas Tinius. Berlin: Centre for Anthropological Research on Museums and Heritage, pp. 16–26. Open-access version: http://www.carmah.berlin/wp-content/uploads/2018/07/CARMAH-2018-Otherwise-Rethinking-Museums-and-Heritage.pdf (last accessed 7 January 2020).

Förster, Larissa, and Friedrich von Bose. 2018. 'Concerning Curatorial Practice in Ethnological Museums: An Epistemology of Postcolonial Debates', *in: Curatopia: Museums and the Future of Curatorship*, edited by Conal McCarthy and Philipp Schorch. Manchester: Manchester University Press, pp. 95–122.

Förster, Larissa, Iris Edenheiser, Sarah Fründt, and Heike Hartmann. Eds. 2018. *Provenienzforschung zu ethnographischen Sammlungen der Kolonialzeit. Positionen in der aktuellen Debatte*. Berlin: Humboldt-Universität zu Berlin. Available online: https://edoc.hu-berlin.de/handle/18452/19769 (last accessed 7 January 2020).

Hamm, Marion, and Klaus Schoenberger. Eds. 2020. *Contentious Heritage and the Arts. A Critical Companion*. Klagenfurt: Wieser Verlag.

Hertz, Ellen. 1998. *The Trading Crowd. An Ethnography of the Shanghai Stock Market*. Cambridge: Cambridge University Press.

Irving, Andrew. 2017. *The Art and Life of Death. Radical Aesthetics and Ethnographic Practice*. Chicago: HAU Books.

Jethro, Duane. 2019. 'The commemoration service on the occasion of the third repatriation of human remains from former German South-West Africa on the 29th of August 2018 at the Französische Friedrichstadtkirche, Berlin', *Material Religion* 15(4): 522–526.

Kohn, Eduardo. 2017. *How Forests Think. Towards an Anthropology Beyond the Human*. Berkeley: University of California Press.

Lidchi, Henrietta, Sharon Macdonald, and Margareta von Oswald. Eds. 2017. *Engaging Anthropological Legacies*, special section of *Museum Worlds: Advances in Research* 5.

Löfgren, Orvar, and Billy Ehn. 2010. *The Secret World of Doing Nothing*. Berkeley: University of California Press.

Macdonald, Sharon. 2013. *Memorylands. Heritage and Identity in Europe Today*. London: Routledge.

———. 2015. 'The Trouble with the Ethnological', in: Martin Heller, Agnes Wegner, and Andrea Scholz. Eds. *The Laboratory Concept. Museum Experiments in the Humboldt Lab Dahlem*. Berlin: Nicolai, pp.211–226.

———. 2016. 'New constellations of difference in Europe's 21st-Century Museumscape', *Museum Anthropology* 39(1): 4–19.

———. 2018. 'Introduction', in: *Otherwise. Rethinking Museums and Heritage*, edited by Christine Gerbich, Larissa Förster, Katarzyna Puzon, Margareta von Oswald, Sharon Macdonald, and Jonas Tinius. Berlin: Centre for Anthropological Research on Museums and Heritage, pp. 3–15. Available online: http://www.carmah.berlin/wp-content/uploads/2018/07/CARMAH-2018-Otherwise-Rethinking-Museums-and-Heritage.pdf (last accessed 7 January 2020).

———. 2019. 'Conclusion: refugee futures and the politics of difference', in: Jan Bock and Sharon Macdonald. Eds. *Refugees Welcome? Difference and Diversity in a Changing Germany*. Oxford: Berghahn, pp. 311–331.

Macdonald, Sharon, and Paul Basu. Eds. 2006. *Exhibition Experiments*. Oxford: Blackwell.

Macdonald, Sharon, Christine Gerbich, and Margareta von Oswald. 2018. 'No museum is an island: ethnography beyond ethnographic containerism', *Museum and Society* 16(2): 138–156.

Nadim, Tahani. 2018. 'Haunting seedy connections', in: *Routledge Handbook of Interdisciplinary Research Methods*, edited by Celia Lury, Rachel Fensham, Alexandra Heller-Nicholas, Sybille Lammes, Angela Last, Mike Michael, and Emma Uprichard. Abingdon/New York: Routledge, pp. 239–247.

Ortner, Sherry. 2013. *Not Hollywood. Independent Film at the Twilight of the American Dream*. Durham, NC: Duke University Press.

Puzon, Katarzyna. 2019. 'Participatory matters. Access, migration and heritage in Berlin museums', in: *Securing Urban Heritage: Agents, Access, and Securitization*, edited by Heike Oevermann and Eszter Gantner. London: Routledge, pp. 31–46.

Puzon, Katarzyna, Sharon Macdonald, and Mirjam Shatanawi. Eds. 2020. *Islam and Heritage in Europe*. London: Routledge.

Robertson, Jennifer. 2018. *Robo Sapiens Japanicus. Robots, Gender, Family, and the Japanese Nation*. Berkeley: California University Press.

Schneider, Arnd. Ed. 2019. *Art, Anthropology, and Contested Cultural Heritage. Ethnographies of TRACES.* London: Bloomsbury.

Smart, Alan, and Josephine Smart. 2017. *Posthumanism. Anthropological Insights.* Toronto: University of Toronto Press.

Tinius, Jonas, and Sharon Macdonald. 2020. 'The recursivity of the curatorial', in: *The Anthropologist as Curator,* edited by Roger Sansi. London: Bloomsbury, pp. 35–58.

Tsing, Anna Lowenhaupt. 2015. *The Mushroom at the End of the World. On the Possibility of Life in Capitalist Ruins.* Princeton: Princeton University Press.

Traweek, Sharon. 1988. *Beamtimes and Lifetimes. The World of High-Energy Physics.* Cambridge MA: Harvard University Press.

Zabusky, Stacia. 1995. *Launching Europe. An Ethnography of European Cooperation in Space Science.* Princeton: Princeton University Press.

"Museums are Investments in Critical Discomfort"

A conversation with Wayne Modest

When did you first come in contact with anthropology and in what way?
Growing up in Jamaica in the context that I did, anthropology was not a field that I knew about. It is not that it didn't exist, but it was just not a field that I was exposed to. I grew up in a traditional understanding of what one was going to do in life, so I would have become a doctor, or a lawyer, or a teacher, perhaps even an accountant. I eventually ended up studying chemistry. It was not through the university that I came to know anthropology, but through the museum – the museum that we called then the *Museum of History and Ethnography*. It was through that institutional context that I first encountered questions of the anthropological in a disciplinary sense.

My wife, who is an anthropologist, has this really lovely statement: "Jamaica is one of the few places where you travel as an anthropologist and you go through immigration and they ask you, 'What do you do?' and you say, 'I'm an anthropologist.' and they say, 'Oh! Like ... '", and they will call a name. His name is Barry Chevannes. He was one of the leading Caribbean anthropologists and worked on questions of Rastafari, amongst others. In Jamaica itself, Barry Chevannes was one of my mentors, if one could have said that. During my time at work, my contact with anthropology came through the museum and material culture, so through things themselves.

Jamaica is a particular case, because while there is a tradition of anthropologists coming from outside, trying to study Jamaica, there are actually also Jamaican anthropologists [both working in Jamaica and in the diaspora, mostly in the North Atlantic] who have been critically engaged with an anthropology of the country, with a different kind of positionality. How do you do anthropology in a society that was colonised? In a society where the anthropological work was a necessary part of thinking through what the Jamaica of the present is, constituted out of the colonial? So the early work that I was reading from anthropology would be on Rastafari, but also on questions of music, dance, performance – performative traditions that emerged from enslaved populations. So these are my earliest engagements with anthropology, including not just the Black Radical tradition, but performance traditions of the Caribbean.

And so when you conceive of anthropology today, and especially in your practice, are you thinking first and foremost about its legacy, or about its present day practice in academia and museums? Or how would you relate to it today?

I'm always a little bit in-between. Recently, there was a discussion in the Netherlands about a young man who did his PhD in sociology. He was accused of unethical aspects to his work, or some people would say that he abused academic ethics. During a discussion, I remember hearing a colleague of mine saying: 'Oh, if he had studied anthropology in *our* department, that would never have happened.' I was a little bit disturbed by the moral high ground taken about the discipline and how it is taught now. I felt that even after the very long and extensive years of rethinking anthropology, one could still suggest that the colonial still hovers over it or *in* it. The colonial haunts it, in a certain sense. Anthropology in the present, in my sense, cannot come without the histories that it is haunted by. These histories are part of the structure of how I think of the discipline itself, especially within the museum.

That said, I am a *believer* in anthropology, as a discipline. When it is at its most innovative, and when it is, as I would call it, at its most philosophical, anthropological investment is what Tim Ingold would call "a certain kind of positioned wisdom". It is something that I think is important for us to imagine in the present: anthropology as a kind of destabilization of this very sense we have that we are the centre of the world and that everything is about us. My engagement with anthropology now is with some anthropologists who are doing some amazing work. I like their work and I think their work is necessary, but *always* with its hauntings. And once one works in the museum, one realises that the two cannot be unhinged from each other. Not yet, anyway. Until that horizon in the future comes when colonial entailments no longer hold us, defining the calculus within which we live, then we still have work to do in this discipline, but also outside of the discipline (see Hartman 2008).

Shifting specifically to your experiences in the Netherlands and the UK, what kinds of resistances and responses have you encountered in museum institutions, in particular with regards to this negotiation of anthropology's colonial legacies in the present?

First of all, I came to the UK to work at the Horniman Museum. This was a very important experience for me, primarily because I still think that even in its earnestness, the UK has one of the most sophisticated museum structures and practices. Actually, there is a *real* belief in the museum as an institution, but not just an elite institution. I actually enjoyed that it was a place where I could hear children run outside of my office just making all sorts of noise. There was an investment in learning and I believe in that. That was in 2008.

And now, a little over ten years after, what surprises me, to be honest with you, is the overwhelming shift in museological practices in relationship to colonialism. There are many people in the discipline, including Nick Thomas and others, who have been working really hard at thinking through colonialism and its afterlives. But I still remember a moment in that early time, when I would speak to colleagues around the question of the ethnographic museum and its relationship to the colonial, and they would be irritated at me for always bringing up this colonial thing. "Why do you need to talk about that all the time?" The response was, "It was not *only* colonial, right?" I cautiously suggested recently that we've gone the entire other direction. Now we are competing as to who is going to be the person who uses the word "colonial" the most in a sentence. And who can be the best "decoloniser". So the field has shifted significantly in that sense.

If you ask me about institutional resistance, initially it was about making the colonial an issue in a real political sense on which there was necessary work to be done. I struggled and struggle with people who want to think the colonial as just a moment in time that has passed. This created a false distance between the reckoning with colonial afterlives and the work of the museum as a cultural institution, even though the afterlives and legacies of colonialism in the present continued to structure relations or hierarchies which govern our lives today. The work, it was felt, was not ours to be done: We were just there to do exhibitions, and it could be a nice exhibition on Indian music, but it didn't have to tie to anything about the precarity of people of Indian descent in contemporary Britain, for example, or how descendants of formerly colonised people can be told in contemporary Britain to "go back to your own country". So, there was an idea of the museum as a *kind* of cultural space, abstracted from the politics of daily life, as a space that did culture. This was a part of the resistance that I encountered. But I too am complicit, as I too struggle with how to address the political in museums.

One of the things that has also changed is the very nature of our discussion of the decolonial. I am especially interested in how things have changed surrounding questions of multiculturalism, specifically in relation to growing narratives of the failure of the multicultural or plural polity in Europe. I am interested in how such narratives of failure continue to affect the lives of descendants of formerly colonised peoples. The rise of this narrative frightens me, to be honest, because it goes hand in hand with rising exclusionary and xenophobic politics and with a scepticism about the (institutional) commitment to equality and justice, and real change.

The difficulties we now have to attend to are really how colonialism continues to work in the present, its racialising logics that continue to structure humanity as differentially deserving of care, of even life itself. As museums we do not really want to get into those issues even though they are fundamental. Those issues are what continues to animate most of the ethnographic museums that we run today and dictate our work, even if they remain unsaid. People who don't want to talk about structural inequality, racism, discrimination, Whiteness will find this is the work of the future museum, in fact, the work of the museum of today, in all its complexity. And there are still many academics, as well, who think that we should have the right to 'pure' academic work untainted by these issues; an understanding that always surprises me, this thing called 'pure academic work' different from what happens in the real world.

Do you agree that anthropological critique, or the negotiation of what anthropology is, now takes place increasingly outside this pure discipline, and its museums? If so, where and how does this take place?
It is hard to respond to this easily, for many reasons. A commitment to anthropological critique may not necessarily come only from anthropology. I come from cultural studies, and I think of myself as disciplinarily promiscuous. The kind of criticality that is necessary to come to grips with objects within museums and with what is happening in society more generally may require different kinds of critical modes, perhaps different forms of anthropological work. That's the first thing to say.

The second thing to say: To be honest with you, I'm not so sure that there was much real, sophisticated anthropological critique coming out of ethnographic museums for a long time now. There have been a few people who have been doing some really interesting stuff, don't get me wrong. But as a discipline, *inside* the museum, there was a time when we struggled with the work that we needed to be doing. This could arguably be because there has been such an abstract separation between anthropology as a critical field of thought, of practice, and anthropology in the museum. In the museum there has been a real focus on documenting collections and exhibitions work, which while important lacked any kind of criticality. One of my interests in what we do – and of course many others have been asking this – is to ask the question: "How do we bring anthropology as a critical discipline, as a space for critique, back into the museum, and stop seeing these two as separate spheres?" But I wouldn't say we have been successful in answering this yet.

I feel that the generative work that has been done in some parts of anthropology has taken too long to find its way in the museum.

But anthropology is also a broad discipline. While there is still exciting work that comes out of the discipline itself, other work continues to be problematic or not so exciting. At the same time, there is a certain kind of critical practice that has been happening in recent years, outside of the museum – which goes back to your question – and in particular in activism, that the museum could benefit from as well. Many of the activists I have been involved with hate anthropology, as a discipline. They think it is useless.

Also, art practices from indigenous communities and indigenous activism – it is from these kinds of spaces that the most important critique has been voiced that got museums to now start moving. Many of us working in museums can now claim that they are decolonising the institution. But the urgency for decolonisation didn't come from us! It came from activists out there, indigenous communities out there.

If you're attendant to that, if you're the listening anthropologist, as we should be, then what you could imagine your 'trans-anthropological' to mean is actually the distribution of a certain kind of criticality where the museum and anthropology are now articulated in a broader network of critique. It then becomes an assemblage and, as such, a generative space; it would be an exciting space. To be honest, the museum of today is an uncomfortable space. You're constantly on the tip of your toes, not knowing "Am I doing this right thing? Did I mobilise the right this or that?" But this discomfort is a generative space for us to imagine another kind of museum practice in the future. For me, this would be one particularly generative conjuncture – in the Stuart Hall sense: that moment when politics comes together with a certain kind of action in order to reimagine another kind of future. I think we're in that right now.

The question is how do we hold on to that and push it to something that is productive, rather than symbolic, as is also the risk? Now every museum doing the decolonial in many ways works with the same groups of activists, divesting the responsibility for decolonisation to them (activists or artists). Usually, they don't really go back and ask, 'What does it mean for *my* museum to start engaging with the question of the decolonial?' They just simply think that inviting this person in or that one – this activist in, the same one another museum invited in – will solve the problem. That is one of the things that we should be cautious about, if we are to take this moment seriously. It requires deeper work to think through how your specific museum, in your country, articulates with specific forms of colonial afterlives – even if some of the issues we deal with are larger scale structures and discourses.

What kind of role does curating take in this context? Especially with a view to reaching different publics and translating across these fields and conjunctures that you mention.
First of all, I should say that we are speaking at a moment when I, like many of my colleagues, struggle to define the urgent role our museum should be taking in the present, and how we stay in this mode without being symbolic. I believe this urgency is very important, especially for now. But there are two things I urgently believe in in thinking about this: I love objects and I believe in their powers, but I believe in the museum's articulation with a public.

I still believe that there are these things called 'the public humanities' and 'public anthropology' that take place in the museum. As a space to really think through the present, what is happening, how to think of it as historical, in its historical contingencies, and how to map out other possibilities for the future. I do believe that other, more equitable futures can be imagined and fashioned, and that museums have a role in this. The role of the curator in that, for me, is still to serve a real public good. That's why I like the research centre that we have here in our museum. But that real public good is not the reduction of our research to numbers and impact. You need to have impact, of course, but what I mean is that research we do can serve to confront a Europe that is now *so* concerned with the failure of the plural polities in which we live; to show that a commitment to plurality is neither strange nor impossible. We need to put it out there in the museum context: What failure is it that people talk about when we say multiculturalism is a 'failure'? Or if we accept this failure narrative, who is it that is 'responsible' for such failure? Can we, as many now do, project such 'failures' on those racialised groups that are now here? We have to show that such narratives of failure make no sense. Moreover, we need to show that they lack a sense of history in how they are being articulated.

The museum is that space where a certain kind of complexity can be added to reductive thinking. We just did a *tiny* exhibition here, but as an example: The exhibition was tied to a research project called 'The Popular Culture of Illegality'. And one of the simple things we wanted to ask people is: Why do you sit at your TV and watch *The Wire*, or all of those crime series so much? Why is it that you have that emotional engagement with the so-called criminal? And what is the role of popular media in actually stirring your emotions to loving these so-called criminals? How is it possible that we have a board game on this criminal, Pablo Escobar? We simply wanted the public to ask the question about what is the limits of this thing we call 'criminality'? How do we define who is regarded as criminal? Who is a criminal anyway? How does the law work to define what is a crime or who is criminal?

The intention was about how popular culture works through the affective, but it was also about asking the public to think through conceptions of the law to think through the normative, of the normalised.

This is also a question that we need to ask ourselves, for example, about the museum's ownership of objects collected during the colonial period. Because saying it was the law at the time does not account for colonialism's impact on our legal system, or the working of power in how we define what is legal and what isn't. Exhibitions like this, and the curation of exhibitions like this, are to also help our audiences, help ourselves, think critically about these ideas. We also asked the question recently: Why is it that every time Europe now speaks about migration and its crisis, so little, if anything, is said about colonialism? As if migration just comes from nowhere. The role of the curator, the role of these public anthropological spaces, for me, is not translation in its simple sense, but it is also about developing sites for a kind of critical research practice that is embedded or put out in a public domain. To help our visitors – and I do not mean this in a patronizing way – to think about the world we live and share with others, to imagine better ways of living together. That is how I see the curator.

At the same time, I'm deeply committed to inclusive thinking, to collaboration, and collaborative creating. Then the curator is also, for me, somebody who is committed to that kind of collaborative work. In a funny way, you could say that the role of the curator – and I refer to Ingold here again – is to share, but also to develop, wisdom with diverse audiences about this thing we call life, how we live it or could live it. And by that I also mean to just take a back seat sometimes and give space to others. And I don't mean give voice to others in a pejorative patronising way, but rather to suggest that there is expertise on my side, but we can create something together, bringing our wisdom together, yours and mine. That has much more impact.

Could one describe the exhibition on crime as an 'anthropological' exhibition? Or put differently: What in your view makes an anthropological framing in an exhibition? Are there specific display techniques, modes of exhibiting, framings, that you would describe as specifically anthropological?

Funnily enough, I've been thinking through this word 'Volkenkunde', which we used for our museum. It is considered a negative term, nowadays. But I've been thinking about it primarily from our location to suggest that 'Volkenkunde' in my museum is fundamentally interdisciplinary. It can be nothing but that. We have a very large curatorial department of about twenty people. Anthropologists, art historians, historians, people with degrees in cultural studies or material cultural studies, all in one space. Yet the nomenclature that we used to describe ourselves as a museum is 'anthropological'. So, anthropology then, one could say, if we were to take it from my perspective, is fundamentally interdisciplinary. That's the first thing I would say.

Secondly, and I say this with much caution, with trepidation: I continue to believe in anthropology and its museum as a hopeful mode or practice. To go back to Dipesh Chakrabarty's idea of provincializing Europe (2000), for me right now, one of the real reasons why and how we should run these museums is to ensure – in Europe anyway – that we realise we're such a small part of the world, and our wisdom is so tiny in comparison to the wisdom of others. And that wisdom is something – and I go back to Tim Ingold here – one gains through experience. If one were to think of the anthropological project as Ingold probably would sketch it, around this particular experience of lived worlds, which is so diverse in the world, then my investment in the anthropology *I'm* talking about is exactly for our visitors to come and realise that their notion of gender, of sexuality, of giving – of all of these things – is just *one small part* of the possibility of this human and non-human world that we live in. I don't know how you want to define that in terms of methodology, but how I define it in terms of a museum methodology is a commitment to this kind of tension between a universal and a particular – but ensuring that one has at the centre of it other ways of being and knowing in the world.

We've created an engine of the museum around happiness and comfort, as if it is a nice thing, so people should come out feeling good and happy. And it is not that people should come out of the museum feeling traumatised, but I see it as an investment in a critical discomfort. In a particular, a kind of critical discomfort about the taken-for-granted-ness we have of ourselves. Much of the narrative of the constitution of Europeanness is that taken-for-granted-ness: "This is who we are. This is what we are. This is what we should be." It is such a strange thing that I think more museums need to be participating in this critical discomfort, this shaking up, this *demand* that we see and understand otherwise, and in relation. There is a world out there and we share it.

But to answer your question, perhaps some would say that the exhibition on crime, and it is called *Most Wanted*, may be anthropological because the project from which it emerged, the research project was largely an anthropological project.

Until fairly recently, art history focused predominantly on the history of European art, while 'non-European art', was mostly regarded and professionally constituted as the domain of anthropological research. In what sense are you engaging with that specific boundary?

When I started out, I was having a lot of discussions about the relation between art and anthropology museums. And I have basically banished that thought from my modes of thinking. I find it a useless battle. So when an artist says to me, "I do not want to be in an anthropological museum," I'm like, "OK, it's alright." My interest isn't *that*. Because my interest is not in the art structure as we've come to know it, the biennales or museum structure, which you know.

My investment is rather to ask – and this is my promiscuity – what mode of creative production, or of making or of materiality, of lived worlds do I want to explore in this exhibition or research project? What is it that is urgent to study, to explore with our publics? And that then defines what modes of objectness will be part of my inquiry. Kader Attia's exhibition on repair at the Hayward Gallery (London, 2019) could have been as much in an art museum or in an ethnographic museum, because the very nature of the reparative that he's invested in is something that we are also involved in and thinking through. I'm just saying that a part of the project that I'm interested in now is to mobilise, to think through, modalities of care and preservation, to think through how we repair historical injustice. Taking perhaps a queer or feminist studies approach to care, I am interested in how we might care for the human and non-human world we live in – to live in it together and well (Tronto 1993). That's in part what Kader Attia is asking in the exhibition I saw. So the distinctions of art and anthropology, I believe, are necessary for how salaries are paid, how disciplines are constituted, how students are trained, but in terms of the mode of critical engagement that I want to have in the relationship to our publics, it is not so interesting for me.

And there's a second side to it, which I find perhaps even more important. I am not so sure, personally, about what we've come to do now in trying to render the ethnographic museum as obsolete and the art museum as being a space for criticality. I'm not so sure what utility that serves any more or anyone, except the art museum. Primarily because that kind of institutional conversation has no real radicality for me to try and really address some of the issues we face. To follow this logic would require that we demolish one colonial structure, while keeping another. It is trying to clean up one kind of museum and then say, "I'm now in it. I'm a part of it and it is now OK." I'm interested in another kind of radical restructuring. I would like to suggest that what we should have learned from the decolonial conversation is that *all* of our institutions need shaking up. *All* of them structure inequality and exclusion. *All* of them are a part of an ongoing kind of colonial violence and therefore the distinctions are there which will help us articulate our project differently. My promiscuity, my non-borderedness in this sense, is more about the modalities of cultural production or creativity that we need to mobilise to tell the story. At the end of the day that is for me important.

I would like to challenge you with one thing in conclusion. One of the struggles that I have now is how to adopt modes of critique while still feeling that I'm creative. We've been talking here about the work of the brilliant academic Fred Moten, who wrote *In the Break* (2003) and *The Undercommons* (with Stefano Harney, 2013). He just completed a trilogy of critical thinking, which I am trying to read now. Thinking with Moten, I have been wondering how museums can adopt a particular kind of critical positionality but *also* think about how to create, how to imagine, how to do and to make anew? I don't know if it is because I'm old and tired, but I'm at the stage now where I ask myself whether our institutional critique is enough. And that's where my struggles have taken me. Is critique enough? Because the burden should be a burden to be critical so that we can work it through. But it probably is also a burden to imagine ... to create. And that I don't know how to do that yet. If you ask what the curator's role is, that's probably what they *should* be doing.

References

Hartman, Saidiya. 2008. *Lose Your Mother: A Journey Along the Atlantic Slave Route.* New York: Farrar Straus & Giroux.

Tronto, Joan. 1993. *Moral boundaries: a political argument for an ethic of care.* New York: Routledge.

Frontiers of the (Non)Humanly (Un)Imaginable: Anthropological Estrangement and the Making of *Persona* at the Musée du Quai Branly

Emmanuel Grimaud

Introduction

The *Persona* project was the third anthropological exhibition organised by the Musée du Quai Branly-Jacques Chirac (MQB hereinafter), following *What is a body?* (2006) and *The Making of Images* (2010).[1,2] The MQB has a large collection of what is referred to in France as "*arts premiers*", a term used to avoid the notion 'primitive'. Crucially divided into regions, these collections derive mostly from outside of Europe. Most of the exhibitions taking place in MQB focus on a particular region or single out a specific type of art. *Persona* (first called *Strangely Human*) had a different purpose, looking at the moving frontiers of personhood, exploring the past and future of the relationships between the human and the non-human, and trying to visualise unexplored possibilities for future alliances.

Persona had a comparative purpose, putting together artefacts belonging to the MQB collections, albeit in deliberate disregard of the geographic origins of objects, including also robotics and contemporary robotic art, as well as a wide range of other artefacts belonging to the history of technology – ghost hunting devices from the nineteenth century, for instance. Going beyond cultural comparison, building up clashes and confrontations of worlds and devices, the exhibition also had a political dimension and, we hoped, a relevance in our troubled times, as it was to ponder on a wider scale the implications of the *non-human turn* in anthropology.[3] Dealing with what is human and what is not human through a wide range of alien encounters, travelling between the animate and the inanimate, the organic and the inorganic, the infra-human and the more than human as well, *Persona* engaged the visitor in an experience of estrangement, an extended "uncanny valley".[4]

Beyond the "uncanny valley"

Before developing more precisely what is meant by the "uncanny valley", as coined by the Japanese roboticist Masahiro Mori, I will briefly explain how we encountered what I consider one of the most intriguing theories ever proposed in the field of human/non-human interaction. After doing fieldwork on religious automata in India and how idols on ritual platforms had been made into interactive animatronics, I was invited to work in Japan with the artist Zaven Paré in the laboratory of roboticist Hiroshi Ishiguro in Osaka. Paré and I wrote a book on Japanese robotics called *The Day Robots Will Eat Apples* (2011), based on a series of experiments around the *Geminoid*, a tele-operated robot designed by Hiroshi Ishiguro as a copy of himself.[5] Making a simulacrum of a human being is a strange idea, but Ishiguro was working hard to give the appearance of a human to his robot. At heart, Ishiguro's research questioned what it means to be human, to have a human appearance, and especially what constitutes human presence. He studied in particular how "eye movements" between two interacting humans would synchronise with each other or follow predictable loops. Thanks to Ishiguro, Paré and I could develop our own set of anthropological experiments. I call these experiments "anthropological", because we not only wanted to investigate questions such as the limits of animism – a classical topic in anthropology – but we also had to use protocols and tricks inspired by theatre, puppetry, and science fiction, which were altogether different from the usual robotic experiments, in order to reveal hidden possibilities or affordances of the *Geminoid* that nobody had yet considered. This robot was the best way to investigate what the Japanese roboticist Masahiro Mori called the "uncanny valley".

Mori's paper on the uncanny explored an intriguing idea illustrated by a simple graph (Mori 1970). He realised that the more you give a human form to an object and especially a robot, the more you create empathy. Yet at a certain point, when the object appears too similar to human appearance, a reversal of empathy takes place, giving rise instead to disgust or fear – in short, an

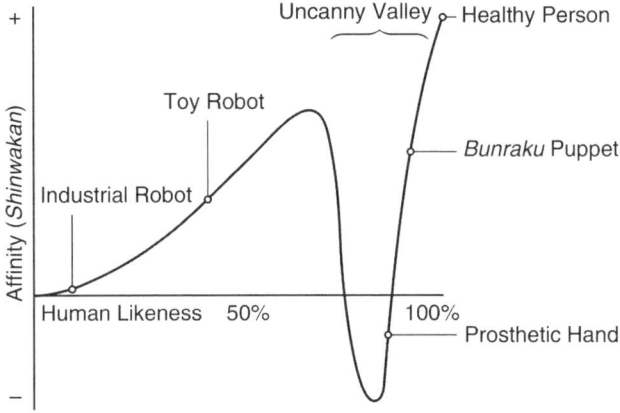

Fig. 1.2 Uncanny Valley Graph. Cited in: Mori (2012 [1970]: 99)

"uncanny" feeling difficult to overcome. To illustrate this "uncanny valley", Mori used the example of a hand prosthesis. Shaking hands with someone with a hand prosthesis without knowing that it is indeed not a 'real' hand might create surprise or fear, because the prosthetic hand is cold and not like a human hand. Inspired by Jentsch's theory developed in *Zur Psychologie des Unheimlichen* (1906), widely discussed by Freud, the "uncanny valley" became a hot topic in humanoid robotics for many years. In this Japanese version of the *unheimlich*, there was a way to go beyond the uncanny. According to Mori, *bunraku* puppet theatre and religious Buddhist art were examples of successful means that had managed to go beyond the 'uncanny' without any complex programming or artificial intelligence. Mori was here addressing a troubled zone for roboticists, inviting them to reflect upon a central question: Do we need to make robots that look like us? Since, if we do, we will always face the risk of falling into the 'uncanny' valley. At the time, Mori already invited roboticists to look at other forms of artificial creatures in a wider perspective. Because the question of knowing whether we want to live with robots marked by human or other appearance is not only a question of design, aesthetics, or 'empathy'; it is a cultural, social, and political issue. Mori's paper was published in French in the MQB-associated journal *Gradhiva* along with a conversation Zaven Paré, Chihiro Minato, and I conducted with him at his home in Tokyo (2012). In the introduction to the issue written with Denis Vidal, we proposed taking the "uncanny valley" further and investigating, with the tools of anthropology, the troubled zones of artificial creature design. Following publication, the museum invited us to propose an exhibition to explore the potentialities of confronting its collections with robotics.

The uncanny valley presented to us a living enigma, a problem still considered an unresolved conundrum worthy of attention by roboticists today. As Mori himself told us: "I just pointed out a problem, but I have no solution." Working in Ishiguro's lab, we realised that he, for instance, had a rather literal interpretation of it. He wanted to go beyond the moment of what we decided to call "ontological confusion", in which one is faced with the uncertainty over whether one is confronted with a machine or a human being. He was convinced that the only way to have an interesting relationship with his robot was to increase his 'humanity'. Here, doubt or uncertainty regarding the ontological status of the robotic entity he was dealing with acted as a kind of provocation in the interaction with a humanoid. Nonetheless, there remained always a moment in which the machine took over and the mechanical behaviours and loops of the humanoid were rendered visible. During several bizarre moments, some of the most 'empathetic' among us were tempted to treat the robot perhaps more like a human being with special needs, caring for it, while the more cynical among us quit the experiment and rejected it as useless mimicry.[6] This posed the question for us, whether we might better assume machines to be machines, rather than trying to fool ourselves with machines in 'human disguise'? This problem opens up an old debate waged since Alan Turing's famous *Imitation Game* (1950).[7] The idea that machines should make themselves more acceptable by looking like animals or humans, then, posed itself as a bizarre 'civilisational' choice that we wanted, carefully, to question.

Anthropological estrangement

Deeply anchored in this mutant world and full of open questions, *Persona* was riskier than most of the exhibitions that had taken place in the MQB museum, seeking to move beyond stereotypes and crass juxtapositions, yet integrating both more 'classic' artefacts from the collection and cutting-edge robotic research. I am still surprised that it was accepted with such enthusiasm by the museum, and I am deeply grateful they took the risk. When the project was almost ready on paper, Hélène Fulgence, the person in charge of exhibitions, welcomed me. Curating this show was a privilege to me, since very few anthropologists had curated exhibitions in the museum. "Anthropologists don't always make good curators", she said, "but people are very fond of anthropological exhibitions, they want more *knowledge*." She went on to clarify a few points:

The idea behind what we call 'anthropological exhibitions' is more question-oriented than artefact-oriented. The aim is to propose global conceptual frameworks, wider perspectives, and not only beautiful objects. We are still trying to find the right formula between the informative and the spectacular.

Early on in our conversation, I realised the kind of challenge *Persona* would pose. From what I understood, it had to be question- or content-oriented but not confusing, informative but not too much to read, pedagogical but not academic, and last but not least, it had to be spectacular but informative. "Anthropological exhibitions give people a conceptual framework much more than exhibitions that are simply artefact-oriented or whose purpose is to introduce an unknown kind of 'curiosities' to the public", she added, "but an exhibition requires a strong storyline. It's storytelling with artefacts after all."

There is great uncertainty about what anthropology is today, given that after the non-human turn of the early twenty-first century, its subjects cover almost anything (non)humanly (un)imaginable. Therefore, it is equally unclear what makes a good 'anthropological exhibition', since it could also be about *estranging* almost everything. There is no single formula for estrangement. But the MQB was ready to experiment, searching for another equilibrium of content, story, and sensory experience. If nothing at our early stage of conceptualisation was really stabilised, our project was at least carefully evaluated in its potential to offer a new kind of fusion between "content" (also referred to as "knowledge" or "information") and "display" (denoting "artefacts" or "objects") inside a "scenario" (or "story"). The previous MQB exhibitions I mentioned had made radically opposite choices of navigation into cultural heterogeneity: the exhibition *What is a body?* (2006) by curators Stephane Breton, Eduardo Viveiros de Castro, and Anne-Christine Taylor presented a chaotic encounter with different cultural worlds, while the careful structuralist grammar of *The Making of Images* curated by Philippe Descola, facilitated a shift from one art to another.[8] With *Persona*, we had no choice but to proceed differently, going deeper into the dark matter of the "uncanny valley", an unfathomable zone with no possibility to escape.

Envisioning the frontiers of personhood

If Mori's theory of the uncanny valley became our magnifying glass to address the issues of personhood, I will now outline how it inspired us to use a scenographic method guiding almost every choice of artefact in *Persona*. In fact, each gallery or display could be seen as a small "uncanny valley" made of various artefacts belonging to eclectic sources in a kind of kaleidoscopic structure. The valley theory invited us to juxtapose, aggregate, and compare objects from diverse sources according to two parameters of Mori's theory, resemblance and familiarity. With our scenographer Constance Guisset, we made these into a principle that became almost a distinctive feature of *Persona*: each series of objects, module, or unit should convey not only a set of possibilities but also a clash, provoking a kind of turmoil in the visitors' minds. This helped us to avoid several risks in terms of scenography.

To summarise its movement, *Persona* was a speculative scenography, leading from one enigma to another, starting with a clash of experiments and finishing with a clash of choices. The main problem that anthropological exhibitions have to face is how to display meaningful heterogeneities, build comparative frameworks, and propose transcultural tools of analysis. Common traps of anthropological exhibitions are well-identified and not very different from those haunting anthropological thought more generally: the great divide in 'cultural areas', the colonial and postcolonial models, including those of the West and the non-West, and evolutionary scaling from the primitive to the modern. These models are still very operational in ethnographic museums today. Attempts to build up alternative modes of organising artefacts are made but often fall into other traps, such as aesthetic formalism, new age mysticism, or para-cultural chaos.[9] If we could have in *Persona* a Hindu god next to a Japanese robot, or a Cameroonian divination mice box next to a Belgian ghost hunter's kit from the nineteenth century, it was not because we disregarded any criteria of comparison, or because we adhered to any specific formal aesthetic criteria, such as surrealism's primitivism, or because there was something called 'robotics' or something called 'divination' that would enable us to put these objects together. It was rather because the people who made these kinds of interfaces tried to solve similar problems and found out very different solutions and responses. In articulating these objects in the same space, we told another story, creating a clash of possibilities in a gallery of virtually infinite choices. Such a clash then underlines the singularity of the speculative solutions invented in history and articulated in the form of objects and devices and helps us to grasp them as 'choices' among others.

The MQB was probably the best playground; it was such an uncanny valley in itself that it was difficult to choose the right objects to display since we could have chosen them all. Additionally, the extensive ethnographic literature on 'personhood' helped us in choosing the most suitable artefacts.

Lévy-Bruhl's seminal text *The "Soul" of the Primitive* (1927), for instance, provides plenty of examples that disturb our preconceived notion of personhood, insofar as it considers how objects, stones, mountains, and plants can be seen as 'persons' in various cultures, yet also how 'personhood' cannot be restricted to 'humans' alone. Personhood, instead, is attached to elements of the surroundings, living or non-living, with whom humans form multi-persons, bi-persons, and so on. Considering some of the artefacts and collections at the MQB from this point of view, we realised to what extent Eduardo Viveiros De Castro was right to say that "the concept of person is anterior and logically superior to the concept of the human" (Viveiros de Castro 2014: 58). Among the entities represented in artefacts, there are actually fewer human and more non-human ones. This process helped us to identify that 'personhood', and not humanity, was the main problem behind the uncanny valley. The problem that we then faced became how we could shift from Mori's humanoid robot to a mask from an entirely different region of the world, or from a Tlinglit figure representing a sea spirit to a Gond tree inhabited by a ghost. It was not possible without changing completely the parameters of Mori's graph. The collections of the MQB became the main resource to go beyond the uncanny valley, but they did not remain the only one.

Deep into a troubled zone

Persona was not only engaged with artefacts from the MQB collections, but also with curiosities from science and technology museums (Henry Lavery's psychograph, Angelo Mosso's 'human circulation balance', for instance), treating them as experimental devices digging into uncanny valleys that nobody had thought of. The brain itself became a troubled area with the psychograph. What the soul consists of remains an unknown zone, too, but becomes yet more palpable with Mosso's balance. We also included in our research, and eventually in the exhibition, contemporary art, especially robotic art that would confront us with variations of the uncanny valley problem. The common feature between the works of art we chose was not only their reflexive edge, their ability to question our relationship to machines. They were pointing out something invisible, pointing out the strangeness of it. *The Good, the Bad and the Ugly* (2005) and *The Questionable Gods of Biomechanics* (2007) by the Dutch artist Christian Zwanikken are exemplary pieces of the kind of effect we were looking for.

They inspired us at the very beginning of the project, because they presented us with hybrid-systems that mix mechanics with living and non-living elements, thus prompting one to spend hours wondering: "Who is there?" One can be scared, fascinated, or amused, but Zwanikken's artworks invite one to enter a special kind of uncanny valley – and yet his animal creatures present a choice completely different to the *Geminoid* created by Ishiguro. To put them in the same room created a 'clash of possibilities' representing choices radically different to the same problem. In the same space, a 'polytheist' machine would allow the visitor to choose his own Hindu god through a manual device designed by us in collaboration with an automata maker from Mumbai. The visitor had the choice to create their own avatar from nine models of upper parts (e.g. the head of a monkey, peacock, or human, etc.), a type of body (multiple arms, etc.), various types of animal lower parts (squid, snake, etc.). There was also a mechanical Buddha with multiple arms, a very hypnotic piece made by the Korean artist Wan Zi Won, which illustrated the possibility for roboticists to go beyond the uncanny valley by incorporating a spiritual dimension into their machines. These were only some of the different options proposed by artists, and put in our exhibition, which responded to Mori's uncanny valley problem.

By chance, whereas robotics produces artefacts that are difficult to categorise, variously designed with a human or an animal face, with animacy and agency, neither purely object nor person, robotic *art* plays with this ambiguity even more. Doubt, or uncertainty about "who is there", as we asked in our exhibition, is part of the interaction in Christian Zwanikken's zoo creatures, Zaven Paré's tele-operated presences, and Yann Minh's sexual interfaces that we included in our exhibition. These robot artistic displays presented us with a great variety of choices that helped us distance ourselves from the flow of commodities produced for a capitalist market, such as commercial robots, increasingly invasive 'spybots', robotic companions endowed with autonomy, or other technical artefacts. These blurred frontiers constitute the proto-robotics world we all inhabit; a world with an uncertain direction and no author. In short, there were many unsolved questions to which *Persona* responded, including questions about animal or robot rights, whether we should support the extension of 'personhood' to machines, or instead protest in the name of an old humanist contract. Still, after working with the MQB museum collections, we realised that these kinds of debates at the frontiers of the human and the non-human are less new than we think. In fact, many other types of contracts have been experimented with, and a wide variety of 'pacts' or alliances with *other than human* entities have been made in societies around the world. That could help us to rethink a Western, proto-robotic world – and maybe even offer alternatives to the choices we have to make.

Persona had a mission: to reset our modes of thinking the relationship between the 'human' and the 'non-human' in all its forms, whether indiscernible, more than human, anthropomorphic or not. Already at preliminary stages of the project, the uncanny effect guided us into critical zones we did not anticipate. In one exhibition space, we had to shift across vastly different historical epochs and through various scientific domains ranging from robotics to astrology, yet also from debates on animal intelligence to the cognition of plants, from biology to the history of spiritualism. And we had to do so step by step. Our research made it clear to us just how very uncertain the frontiers between human, object, animal, and machine have been throughout time, and it forced us to identify more clearly how at various epochs some of these realms had been divided, separated, fused with different kinds of social and political implications. The more we looked at the problem historically, the more we realised that the most *restrictive* notion of personhood was developed in Western societies of the post-Enlightenment era. This limitation was a pillar of an ecologically devastating conception as part of which humans regarded other, living and non-living entities as subordinated, deprived of a 'mind' or 'interiority'. These ontological and political questions, which have become significant issues today due to ecological crises, different kinds of knowledge about the human and non-human world, as well as shifts of attitude, were the first matters of concern for *Persona*. The clash of possibilities that we outlined was thus not only a scenographic method, but also an attempt to challenge our consciousness of the choices which are offered by science and technologies, and on many of which we depend. It is not enough to point out, for instance, that biologists take plant cognition very seriously today, frequently discovering new forms of sensitivity that we had never thought of; or to direct our gaze towards ethologists who discover new abilities in the animal kingdom, such as mental images among cats or forms of culture in baboon societies. We need to go further in our understanding not only of the invisible alliances that make a living milieu possible, but also of the subconscious life of a wide range of entities, including the ones humans produce or cultivate without knowing. It is in this field of unexplored relationships that anthropology helps to clarify the field of possibilities ahead.

From animism to post-anthropomorphism: The structure of the exhibition

This first part of the exhibition, entitled "Is there anybody out there?" set the tone. It showed how people beyond the narrow confines of psychology and the experimental sciences had experimented with perception, hallucination, anthropomorphism, and the extrapolation of non-human presences. We had to start there because the uncanny valley does not make sense if it is not situated in the larger context of "limit experiments" in perception. The most well-known of these, such as the Turing test or the experiments of Heider and Simmel (explained below), are reductionist versions of experiences that have been taken further in artistic, religious, and popular forms.

Indeed, many objects, rituals, and beliefs are the results of experiments designed in forgotten contexts to play with perception, rarely revealing their experimental nature at first glance. The first part of the exhibit thus multiplied experiments in perception, starting with unexpected situations, such as walking in the forest or interpreting noises, encountering 'presences' initially hard to identify. The place accorded to *experiments* in the exhibition was key. All the experiments in experimental psychology that we showed, and even the lesser obvious forms of experiment, like shamanic experiences or encounters with ghosts, implied an *interaction* or an *encounter* with a 'presence'. Mori's idea of the uncanny valley itself is a form of alien encounter characterised by a maximal discomfort with a humanoid robot. We decided to play with the possibility of encountering such 'presences', using alien encounters and ghost experiences as a model. The visitor was invited to go through a series of small theatres ("dioramas"), displaying various situations in which one faced the limits or frontiers of one's perception (in the world of microorganisms, looking at the cosmos, facing another animal, or sitting under a tree, etc). One example of the kind of resonances we tried to create was the "sensory deprivation experiment", which opened the exhibition. It is a well-known way to study the mechanism of hallucination in the dark, or in isolation, but we tried to connect it to a popular classical motif in Christian art, namely that of St Anthony in the desert. The example concerns the hallucinatory presences around St Anthony, which provoke a question that has generated a lot of research in psychology since the end of the nineteenth century, namely: Are hallucinations in one's head or 'out there' in the world?

We connected the well-known experiments conducted in 1944 by the psychologists Fritz Heider and Marianne Simmel on causal attribution with abstract Melanesian 'spirits' and geometrical supernatural entities. The visitor was confronted with having to balance between Heider and Simmel's animated sequence (a very short animated film in which two triangles and a circle moved inside and outside a square) and the possibility of making a 'counter-experience' with objects from the museum collections. Heider and Simmel's audience was asked to interpret the behaviour of their geometric figures, asking, for instance, whether they were following, repelling, or chasing one another. The experiment showed that one is easily tempted, without being compelled, to attribute behaviours to objects or to say, for instance, that the triangle is particularly 'aggressive', 'excited', or 'insistent'; that it does everything to enter the square; or that one of the triangles follows the other at a time, while the small circle may appear 'fragile' or even 'hesitant'.[10] Heider and Simmel's experiment is a good example for a wider discussion of anthropomorphism in experimental psychology, which argues that attributing human features to things that are not apparently human-like is a widespread human cognitive tendency, a kind of 'defence mechanism', or reflex to make sense of the unknown. By contrast, the Melanesian abstract spirits were telling another story, opposite to the idea that *animism* is something happening in the mind, a brain module, or tendency to project living features onto things around us.[11] Animism, in this (psychological) sense, would imply a 'non-living' world; and thus not only a false but also misleading assumption.

Whereas the first part of our exhibition multiplied these kinds of speculative assemblages without giving a final answer, the second part – "Who is there?" – explored the techniques to detect and identify entities, to materialise them, or to guess what they are made of. In this part, we thus displayed divination tools, materials for ghost hunting and spirit research, machines to communicate with the dead, instruments drawn from aura research, and other curious tools from the margins of the history of science and technology. We offered a wide range of 'resources' to allow the visitors to immerse themselves into the field of perceptual experiments, for which we drew on a broad range of approaches: those from astrobiology that worked on imagining aliens; from biology that inquired into the behavioural agency of micro-organisms; or from paranormal activity, ghost hunting, and spirit research. All these activities debate the features and properties of non-human 'entities' and deal with shared questions also at the core of the uncanny valley, namely: How do we make sense of unknown bodies or entities, and how do we categorise and classify such unknown beings?

Only in the third part of the exhibition, "Beyond the uncanny valley" did visitors encounter Mori's theory explicitly. In this section they passed through a garage of detached parts, prosthetics, and *ex votos*, before entering a gallery reproducing Mori's uncanny valley in the form of various objects. There, the visitor would face objects that could be disturbing, or indeed create a kind of uncanny feeling regarding the issue of 'personhood'. We confronted the visitors with entities – hybrids – that were not intuitively classifiable as either objects, persons, animals, humans, or something else, sometimes perhaps even defying classification altogether. Visitors thus had to decide on their own which 'items' to choose in order to figure out their own uncanny valley experience, before proceeding toward the last part of the exhibition.

This fourth and last section, called "Extended personhood or what do we want to be surrounded with?" was constituted by a kind of show house made up of several rooms, including a kitchen, a bedroom, a living room, and a garage composed of quasi-humans. In this section, Japanese wind spirits were displayed next to a sex machine by Yann Minh, roots used in Vodun rituals to attach people, or a robot of the god Ganesha, to name but a few examples of the clashes we wanted to create. The show house proposed new possibilities, many of which were not addressed up until this point in the exhibition, questioning them with regard to their implications for practical living. The section thus asked, for example: What kind of non-humans are we ready to adopt?

Post-anthropomorphism

Persona was definitely using the provocative and not unproblematic means of juxtaposition and what I called 'clash of possibilities' and perhaps unexpected (by standard scientific classifications) objects as a method, but it also tried to provoke a clash in the mind of the visitor. In fact, our familiarity with *both*, science fiction and canonised anthropological literature, might have given *Persona* another distinctive feature. We were inspired in particular by the science fiction writer Philip K. Dick, notably by *The Android and the Human* (1972). In this speculative work, Dick showed remarkable intuition about human/non-human relations, pointing out that the more our environment equipped itself with machines and artificial animacy, the more it would be poised to abound with a multifarious muddle of entities liable to arouse doubt as to their nature. In his view, the challenge was to figure out how to avoid reducing this complex problem to the psychological question of the "the ascription of intentionality". Beginning with the idea that the "primitive mind" has a tendency "to animate its environment", he stresses the very specific role played by modern psychology, which, he writes, requested us for years to withdraw these anthropomorphic projections from what is actually inanimate reality, to *introject* – that is, to bring back into our own heads – the living quality which we, in ignorance, cast out onto the inert things surrounding us (Dick 1972, cited in: Sutin 1995: 183). Introjection, for Dick, therefore describes "the authentic mark of civilization" that distinguishes us from primitive beings that see their natural environment as "pulsing with a purpose, a life". The supposedly mature and scientific individual is therefore condemned to eliminating these "childish projections" for the sake of the principle that "the world is dead, and that life resides solely within himself". "But", Dick continues, "one wonders: has he not also, in this process, reified—that is, made into a thing—other people? Stones and rocks and trees may now be inanimate for him, but what about his friends? Has he not now made them into stones, too?" (Dick 1972: 183) Dick does not only condemn the psychologising of the problem of attribution in the form of introjection and its implications. He also argues that "within the last decade, we have seen a trend not anticipated by our earnest psychologists – or by anyone else – which dwarfs that issue: our environment, and I mean our man-made world of machines [...] is in fact beginning more and more to possess what the earnest psychologists fear the primitive sees in his environment: animation" (Dick 1972, cited in Sutin 1995: 183).

It is worth noting that at the time Dick wrote those lines, a number of currents in psychiatry explored the idea that introjection and analogising non-human diversity constitutes a psychological problem in itself. Harold Searles (1960), for example, noticed that among schizophrenic patients with an advanced level of the disorder, many began to see themselves as machines, or thought they were under the influence of uncontrollable mechanisms. They also saw themselves as animals or plants. But the anxiety was never as intense as when they had the feeling they were composed of circuits and bolts, or under the influence of a machine outside themselves that dispossessed them of their feelings or took over their vital functions. Searles proposed the term "relatedness", to designate persons' feelings of intimate kinship with surrounding non-human elements (atomic structures, molecules, metabolisms, patterns), which involve the maintenance of a "reasonable" relationship, cognisant of the fact that the search for fusion would appear to patients as the disappearance of one's individuality. We know how much Dick enjoyed frightening his readers, using his novels to confront them with wayward forms of relatedness and a proliferation of fusions and personality confusions between humans and machines that would appear as "unreasonable" in the sense espoused by Searles. In doing so, Dick enables us to formulate a hypothesis about a central issue regarding non-human entities like machines: If an individual is conscious of their own introjections and convinced that "the world is dead, and that life resides solely in himself", what kinds of unprecedented forms of relatedness in Searles' sense are available to him?

We made a digression via Dick's description of a technological animist modernity to stress the kind of short circuit we sought to create in the mind of visitors in our exhibition. Considering that anthropomorphism is a widespread, useful, and flexible tool for human beings in their interaction with their environment, the question for us was not only to break with the patronising and discredited idea about animist thought in children and certain groups of people (see Lévy-Bruhl 1927); we also meant to show the 'possibilities' afforded by developing harmonious relationships with our environment, as well as by psychotic scenarios such as Searles' study of schizophrenia. It is not uncommon to give names to objects. Even in our team, we address our computers or speak to our dogs and cats. In Japan, when people leave their house, it is common to salute it. The house is a living entity in itself to which you must show respect. Studies of religious contexts provide us with ample further examples in which objects, conceived as incarnations of invisible entities, come to materialise very subtle 'states' of being. Popular Hinduism is a good example. Most of the idols in India are not alive until they are charged by a priest through an 'opening of the eyes' ritual. And it is very commonplace to see stones or trees considered as 'intermittent persons', hosting goddesses or other spirits, potentially at any time. Gods have a wide range of possible ways to manifest, between the inorganic and the living. For Indian villagers, there is nothing uncanny about it. The uncanny lies somewhere else. When somebody comes with a tele-operated robot of Ganesha, thus enabling anyone to incarnate the deity and to have a conversation, a cruel game starts to evaluate the divinity of the impersonator (Grimaud 2016, see also figure 1.1).

Concluding discussion: MQB as a museum of forgotten possibilities

Persona became a laboratory, not so much because it was intended to be one, or because the first part of the exhibition was inviting visitors to make experiments. Rather, it turned into one because people came and sat for hours in front of objects and devices, experiencing and experimenting with diverse kinds of 'encounters' with non-human entities. And yet, as the Indian physicist Jagadhish Chandra Bose wrote, "The true laboratory is the mind". The uncanny valley hypothesis became our device for provoking visitor estrangement and engagement with the themes of the exhibition. From that point of view, *Persona* had not only an archaeological role to play, digging out past possibilities, but also an exploratory and *prospective* one, trying to figure out a possible alternative for our exploration of the non-human. In this respect, the MQB became for me a museum of forgotten possibilities.

What makes objects 'anthropological' for me, then, are the agentive possibilities they incarnate. Frequently, an object dealing with the non-human realm I explored in this chapter – be it a mask or a divination tool – will evoke a reaction. The experience of such a confrontation, in my understanding of the term, thus creates an anthropological experience regarding the idea of personhood. The collections of the MQB contain a great number of objects with the agency of displacing preconceived Western notions of personhood. Among them are objects treated as 'persons', where the term doesn't refer to a human being, or even a 'human-like' entity. While the desire to reproduce a human being in humanoid robotics appears like a bizarre technological obsession, it can thus be regarded among a range of similar aspirations. The museum also contains objects *made* as persons, such as masks with human or animal features like eyes, mouths, and heads, which are kept deliberately in a state of abstraction or dissemblance to humans, so as to enhance their difference or supernatural characteristics. It was obvious for us that the collections of the museum offered a field from which to extend and revise the troubled zone that lay behind Mori's idea of the "uncanny valley".

We repopulated the 'valley' to such an extent that the theory itself transformed in dialogue with the museum collections and eventually gave rise to an unexpected new form of human/non-human interactions. It became an intriguing thought experiment for us to ask what would happen if we included not only other cases and 'entities' in the uncanny valley scenario but also other parameters in the graph. Beyond familiarity and likeness, there are many other 'testable' criteria of relevance to understand our relation to objects. Among them are, for example: the principles of respondence (the possibility to react or answer); the possibility to 'control' (to be able to influence or control the entity at a distance); animacy (e.g., being static but considered as a person – in the case of a Buddha statue, for example, stillness is interpreted as a state of active meditation); or the possibility to connect (activate or deactivate). Our research on these parameters did not stop with the end of the exhibition, and we subsequently formalised our graph of the *uncanny valley reloaded*, albeit too late to include it in the catalogue.

Through *Persona*, new puzzles emerged as people tried to make sense of the artefacts in our exhibition. We chose many of our objects (minerals, statues, robots), because they showed what might be considered *unexpected* forms of personhood, or because they played with preconceived Western notions of anthropomorphism. Many visitors to the show, however, appreciated the objects because they appeared to them as 'uncanny'. This in itself was surprising for many of the people who had worked on this exhibition, because they had gotten used to manipulating these objects and to facing their 'aura'. One journalist even described *Persona* as "the terrifying exhibition of the MQB", as if visitors had to prepare themselves to enter a kind of horror museum. While the uncanny valley began for us as an apparently minor problem of interaction adjustment for engineers in robotics, it became a more widespread issue once transplanted inside the MQB infrastructure, and turned into a broader question of cosmopolitics.

Another art critic made an interesting observation by stating that all media in the exhibition, irrespective of whether it concerned a painting, a sculpture, a photograph, or a mineral – were equally treated as "possible incarnations". Previously it did not occur to us that what we had adhered to, implicitly, was a fairly simple principle – that if the possibility of animacy was imagined, it materialised in some way and thus existed. In the mind of a visitor, it does indeed not make a difference whether what conjures up this imagination is a photo of a semi-squid/semi-human creature, a robotic rendering, or a painting of it. While it might have been so for an historian of art concerned with the formal means and media of the presentation, what strikes the mind of the visitor – anthropologically speaking – is the possibility of experiencing a transfer, a transformation, and of imagining a world in which the existence of such a being would be possible. In that sense, the different types of media in our exhibition became equivalent, to us, to different 'states of materialisation' of this possibility. It thus became meaningful to juxtapose a robot of a giant squid, such as the one created by Takahashi Shiro, with the photographic work of Danny van Ryswyk depicting human-like beings with aquatic animal heads sitting in a Victorian living-room – that is, to make comparable the virtual imaginary world of Van Ryswyk's photomontage with the mechano-pneumatic stage of Shiro's robotic zoo. Certain possibilities of 'human' and 'non-human' relations might be a dream for some, or a nightmare for others, but with *Persona* we tried to show that curatorial imagination can help envision fields of possibilities that would remain otherwise opaque or unimaginable.

Notes

1. The image on page 76 is Figure 1.1 Ganesh Yourself Robot. Film by Emmanuel Grimaud, © Emmanuel Grimaud.
2. It was curated by a team of anthropologists, Anne-Christine Taylor, Denis Vidal, Thierry Dufrene, and myself.
3. We cannot quote here in extenso the literature that has been produced in the non-human turn, starting with the works of Latour, Descola, Viveiros de Castro

and now widespread in the Anglo-Saxon world. For an earlier account of the first generation of non-human ethnographies, see Houdart and Thiery (2011); and for a conceptual framework dealing with the frontiers of the human, see Vidal (2016). Grusin has recently tried to define the non-human turn of the end of twentieth century and early twenty-first beyond anthropology and the human sciences where it started. He sees it as a more general movement of reaction against social constructivism in the arts and humanities (2015).

4. On the notion of estrangement, see Shklovsky (1917). For tools to estrange our present and rethink the relationship between anthropology and science fiction, see Déléage and Grimaud (2019).
5. After the *Geminoid* experiment, Paré and I made a tele-operated robot of the Hindu god Ganesha to allow anyone to incarnate God and have a conversation. This experiment gave rise to a film called *Ganesh Yourself* (2016).
6. For a detailed account of these experiments, see Grimaud and Paré (2012).
7. Turing proposes to consider the question of the 'intelligence' of machines as less relevant than the question to know in which conditions a machine can fool us and make us believe that she has thinking abilities. See Turing (1950: 433–460).
8. See the catalogue (Descola 2010); and Descola's contribution in Alloa (2015).
9. The Museum of Edinburgh, for instance, deliberately plays with weird arrangements (a Buddha next to a World War I airplane or a series of Chinese vessels). An overdose of these juxtapositions does not always provoke an increase in interest or attention. By contrast, the MQB follows a very strict classical plan divided by regions where the provenance is almost sacred.
10. Many people invent scenarios, saying that "Mrs. Triangle seeks to protect her little one from Mr. Triangle who ends up destroying the house (the rectangle)", or that "Papa Triangle is in competition with Mama Triangle", and so on. One of the main interesting aspects of the experiment is to point out a dynamic process of seeking intentions, causes, and motivations in order to make sense of what we perceive, especially when we are facing objects far removed from human appearance. Heider and Simmel distinguished between cases where the figures are taken in simultaneous movements with instantaneous contact and other cases where we are dealing with simultaneous movements with prolonged contact. In the same way, they differentiated the cases of successive movements with brief contact and the cases of successive movements with prolonged contact, all of which lead to distinct interpretations.
11. *Animism* at the HKW, curated by Anselm Franke, was dealing with these issues in 2012, using contemporary art as a way to investigate in a self-reflexive manner this anthropological question: What are the implications of the living/non-living divide and how variable it has been historically.

References

Breton, Stéphane, Anne-Christine Taylor-Descola, Michael Houseman, and Eduardo Viveiros De Castro. Eds. 2006. *Qu'est-ce qu'un corps?* Paris: Musée du Quai Branly-Jacques Chirac.

Descola, Philippe. Ed. 2010. *La fabrique des images*. Paris: Musée du Quai Branly-Jacques Chirac.

Alloa, Emmanuel. Ed. 2015. *Penser l'image. Anthropologies du visuel*. Paris: Les presses du réel.

Déléage, Pierre, and Emmanuel Grimaud. Eds. 2019. *Estrangemental. Gradhiva* 29. Paris: Musée du Quai Branly-Jacques Chirac.

Dick, Philip K. 1972. 'The android and the human', in: *The shifting realities of Philip K.Dick. Selected literary and philosophical writings*, edited by Lawrence Sutin, 1995. New York: Vintage Books, pp. 183–210.

Grimaud, Emmanuel. 2016. *Ganesh Yourself*. film. Arte/La Lucarne: France. (67')

Grimaud, Emmanuel, and Zaven Paré. 2012. *Le jour où les robots mangeront des pommes*. Paris: Petra.

Grimaud, Emmanuel, Anne-Christine Taylor, Denis Vidal, and Thierry Dufrêne. 2016. 'Qui est là? Présences-limites et effets de personne', in: *Persona, étrangement humain*, edited by E.Grimaud, A-C. Taylor, D. Vidal, and T. Dufrêne. Paris: Actes Sud / Musée du Quai Branly-Jacques Chirac, pp. 11–17.

Grusin, Richard 2015. 'Introduction', in: *The Nonhuman Turn*, edited by Richard Grusin. Minneapolis, MN: University of Minnesota Press, pp. vii–xxx.

Heider, Fritz, and Marianne Simmel. 1944. 'An Experimental Study of Apparent Behavior'. *American Journal of Psychology*. 57(2): 243–259.

Houdart, Sophie, and Olivier Thiéry. Eds. 2011. *Humains, non humains. Repeupler les sciences sociales*. Paris: La Découverte.

Jentsch, Ernst. 1906. 'Zur Psychologie des Unheimlichen.' *Psychiatrisch-neurologische Wochenschrift* 8(22): 195–198; 203–205.

Lévy-Bruhl, Lucien. 1927. *L'âme primitive*. Paris: PUF.

Mori, Masahiro. 1970. 'The uncanny valley.' *Energy* 7(4): 33–35. Republished in: *IEEE Robotics & Automation magazine*. June 2012, pp. 98–100.

———. 2012. 'Le Bouddha dans le robot', in: *Robots étrangement humains*, edited by Emmanuel Grimaud and Denis Vidal. *Gradhiva* 15: 162–181.

Searles, Harold. 1960. *The Nonhuman Environment in Normal Development and in Schizophrenia*. New York: International Universities Press.

Shklovsky, Viktor. 1917. 'Art as Device', in: *Russian Formalist Criticism: Four Essays*, edited by Lee T.Lemon. 1965. Lincoln: University of Nebraska Press, pp. 3–24.

Turing, Alan. 1950. 'Computing Machinery and Intelligence.' *Mind* 49: 433–460.

Vidal, Denis. 2016. *Frontières de l'humain.* Paris: Alma éditions.
Viveiros de Castro, Eduardo. 2014. *Cannibal Metaphysics.* Minneapolis: Univocal Publishing.

"On Decolonising Anthropological Museums: Curators Need to Take 'Indigenous' Forms of Knowledge More Seriously"

A conversation with Anne-Christine Taylor

How would you describe your position in the Musée du Quai Branly-Jacques Chirac (MQB)? Do you see yourself as a curator in the sense of being a transversal, a translating agent? What is your definition of curatorship?

My position at the MQB was certainly that of a transversal and translating agent mediating between different communities of interest. But in France, curators are *conservateurs*, a body of civil servants quite distinct from that of academics and scientific researchers, usually trained in a specific school (*l'Ecole nationale du patrimoine*), and their primary mission is the stewardship of museum collections; they are caretakers rather than translating agents. Part of my brief when I was recruited by the museum in 2005 to head the department of research was precisely to get the *conservateurs* and the academic community, in particular the anthropological one, to work together. As you know from the history of the MQB, a rift had built up during the years of the museum's planning between the academic world and the museum's authorities. This divergence played out in a pile-up of conflicts over the general framing of the collections, who would have the final say about the narrative attached to them, whether they should be presented as ethnographic documents or as art works, and so forth. So there was a lot of diplomatic work to be done to get the parties concerned to reach a level of agreement over the museum's missions, policies, and museographical options. You also have to take into account the fact that half of the MQB's budget is paid by the French Ministry of Research and Higher Education, so the museum obviously had to pay a little more than lip service to the research community.

In an article you published in 2008 about the MQB, you stated that the institution is not an ethnological museum.[1] Can you comment on this claim?
At an early stage, the museum's planners decided, rightly in my view, that it was no longer possible to exhibit cultures in the former panoramic style as self-contained, timeless, substantive entities. In that sense, the MQB was not and did not aim to be an 'ethnological museum'. Its stated goal was to convey to the public an idea of cultural difference – as opposed to the 'representation' of any given culture – through the display of visually striking pieces meant to cue a kind of aesthetic shock. This explains the museum's strategy regarding the information offered to the public. The objects are presented with the bare minimum of information, so as not to interfere with the visitor's immediate experience of them, but he or she also has access to an expanding circle of documentation: first the a variety of audio programs, then the many short multimedia stations dotting the expanse of the permanent collection, then the resources of the reading room, and eventually of the large research library, not to mention the many scientific events (international conferences, work-shops, lectures and seminars, film projections, dramatic performances, etc.) that are held at the museum. Another principle guiding the MQB's museography is to avoid a single and one-sided view on the collections by combining or juxtaposing possibly contradictory discourses – for example, by playing the temporary exhibitions against the style of display of the permanent collection. I think these are defendable strategies for a museum.

But my statement also had a more critical edge. There was a time when I, and a lot of people in the anthropological community, believed that the museum was opening a new and interesting path, on the crest road between being a truly anthropological museum and being a 'primitive art' museum, in short that it had the potential of becoming an anthropological museum of the arts. But I think the MQB never really achieved this, or only partially, because it remains trapped in an ethnocentric view of 'Art' as a universal category, a 'natural' impulse that operates trans-culturally. I did try to promote the idea that the museum should at least select a few pieces or small sections of the permanent collections and do a full job of translating the conceptualisations underlying a given type of production: Why does this object have this form? How is it thought to act on those who perceive it, more generally on the world? In short, how does it work? But the truth is that the department of research, and more broadly the academic community, have virtually no say in the MQB's museography – except in a dedicated section of the space reserved for temporary exhibitions, revealingly labelled in-house as that of '*les expos anthropologiques*'....

Where do you position anthropology in anthropological museums today, and in the MQB in particular? What has been the legacy of this relation between anthropology as a discipline and the museum of anthropology?
As is generally recognised, up until the middle of the twentieth century there was an organic link between ethnographic museums and the discipline of anthropology; in fact, such museums were anthropology writ large, its primary visual regime as well as the site for spelling out its underlying premises – whether evolutionist or later culturalist – for the instruction of the public. But for various reasons I can't deal with here, this link broke down as anthropology shifted to new paradigms increasingly at variance with museums' way of ordering and displaying 'culture'. Consequently, ethnographic museums found themselves in a dire situation, having lost both their public and their scientific *raison d'être*. They were obliged to reinvent themselves, hence the episode of self-critique and renovation that all big ethnographic museums engaged in over the past decades. One of the striking outcomes of this process has been that anthropology as a discipline has largely deserted museums. More accurately, museums have assimilated parts of popularised anthropological ideology, but they actually draw less and less on current anthropological knowledge. This is partly due to the 'aesthetic turn' of museums that have followed in the footsteps of the MQB by displaying ethnographic material as Art. Art has in fact replaced 'Science' as the new language of universalism. But, as I said, the conceptualisation of art underlying these museums' museography remains deeply problematic, as well as disconnected from the kind of knowledge being currently produced by the growing field of the anthropology and history of the arts. That said, even in '*musées de société*' that claim to shun the aestheticisation and presumed exoticisation of other cultures, a real connection to anthropology is also missing, because these museums shy away from the idea of cultural difference and downplay the complexities of cultural translation. And both kinds of museum confront other big problems: the 'arty' museums are facing a huge surge of repatriation claims, not least because the massive inflation in value of anything qualified as Art fuels the process of 'patrimonialisation', which in turn fosters quarrels over property claims, along the lines of: "By what right is *our* art in *your* museum?" *Musées*

de société, for their part, don't know what to do with the collections they have inherited and many of them have in fact given up displaying them.

How has the transformation of anthropological discourse affected the ways in which anthropological exhibitions were set up and articulated? Would there be certain kinds of displays or even exhibition styles that you would still depict as 'anthropological'?
The problem is that a lot of museums, when they think they're doing 'anthropological exhibitions', tend to think in terms of *a culture*. I don't think that this kind of exhibition gets anthropology back into museums – precisely because if there is *one* useful thing that anthropology has done, it is the critical work it has produced on the notion of culture and its essentialisation. But this critical approach to the notion of culture hasn't been sufficiently heard by the general public. Further, this reification of culture is something very difficult to fight against, because you may find yourself fighting against people that you're trying to defend at the same time, and for whom an essentialised idea of culture is the only defence they have against oppression and disempowerment. It isn't easy to deal with that.

To cut to the chase, I see little real anthropology in most supposedly anthropological exhibitions. The main reason for this is that museum curators do not really take indigenous forms of knowledge seriously. Even when 'native' curators are invited to exhibit in museums, the discourse they are implicitly or explicitly encouraged to develop about 'their culture' is heavily marked by a Western way of thinking about culture as objectified patrimony. Instead of colluding with this kind of toothless ethnicism, museums should be less condescending and more exigent with their indigenous interlocutors: not let them put forth statements such as 'this object is sacred to us', but instead push them to formulate what is at stake in this claim, how whatever they translate as 'sacred' reconfigures and challenges what we mean by the sacred. In short, anthropological exhibitions should be about equivocations, about veiled misunderstandings, not about presumed convergence of experience. The crux of the matter is that an 'anthropological exhibition' should be equally interesting and surprising for non-native and native people, for 'insiders' just as much as for 'outsiders'. In fact, indigenous museum partners should be encouraged to invent counter-museum displays. What would an Amazonian group's exhibition of 'Western' culture look like? To be honest, I think museums are such quintessentially Western institutions, so imbued with our own cultural premises – about temporality and history, about what makes up the world and how its elements are combined – that I doubt they can ever become fully decolonised or fully symmetrical. But they still have a wide margin for improvement in dealing with the issue of cultural translation, and thereby fostering greater understanding and tolerance for difference – which is after all the primary mission of museums showing ethnographic collections

What about your own exhibitions? I'm thinking particularly of Persona (see Grimaud, this volume). Would you call this an anthropological exhibition?
The idea for this exhibition emerged from the informal conversations a group of us – anthropologists but also an art historian – were having about various issues related to anthropomorphism. Eventually, we decided that this theme would be interesting to deal with through the medium of an exhibition. We didn't set out to produce an anthropological exhibition in the sense of trying to transpose in visual terms an anthropological argument or theory – although there was, hopefully, a lot of anthropology embedded in this exhibition. Our objective was to convey an approximation to the very common experience of suddenly perceiving a presence in a non-human being – a cloud, an abstract image, a stone, a plant ... – and to explore the variety of ways this experience is dealt with. The show was thus organised into sections. The first, "Who's there?", examined the perceptual and cognitive mechanisms involved in sensing a presence in the absence of any tangible being. The second section dealt with the procedures used to identify the presence, to determine its nature. Then we examined the ways the presence is made to be felt, how its agency is made manifest by its uncanniness, by the fear, awe, or jubilation it cues in the spectator. Another section raised the question of how we cohabit with these presences, what kind of polity we form or could form with them. The final section dealt with the question of shape-shifting: What would we become if our bodies became more, or less, or other than they are now?

When we began organizing the exhibition, we set ourselves a few simple guidelines. First, to deliberately mix 'ethnographic' pieces from the museum's collections with 'Western' objects, past, present, and futuristic, in order to destabilise assumptions about the 'Great Divide' between 'the West and the Rest', between modernity and 'tradition', between Art and ethnography; to show that our ways of dealing with robots, with the frontier between humans and animals, can be usefully compared with the ways other collectives conceptualise and relate to the non-human presences that people their worlds. Another principle was to limit as far as possible the discursive accompaniment to the exhibition: The objects, and their juxtaposition, were meant to speak for themselves. When we used text, it was mostly in the form of enigmatic and/or poetic citations, which we treated as simply another kind of object. We also relied a lot on contemporary artists' creations of uncanny presence, because they produce an interesting analogue to the way many 'ethnographic' artefacts work in their own context.

The public's reactions to this exhibition were very divided, either highly indignant or quite enthusiastic. This in itself might be an indication that *Persona*, for all its shortcomings, was in fact a truly anthropological exhibition ...

How and where do you encounter anthropology today – beyond the MQB?

The good news is that the discipline of anthropology is beginning to find ways of coming back into museums, in ways that are not purely discursive and couched in the language of scientific authority. There is now an interesting convergence between anthropology and contemporary art, building on artists' keen interest in the ethnographic method and the ethnographic gaze. Contemporary artists are wizards at inventing optical devices and immersive installations that can be used to convey and indeed simulate sensorial experiences or techniques of co-referencing that are commonly produced in 'traditional' ritual contexts, for example. Further, many contemporary artists are involved in the business of imagining and giving visual form to non-factual entities, substances, and relations – in other words of challenging our sense of reality and of the here-and-now. This is another field where anthropologists and artists can meet and exchange techniques of description, since anthropologists are used to dealing with all sorts of non-humans and different ways of cohabiting with them.

In Berlin and other European cities, many museums are confronted with calls for their decolonisation. How do you situate these processes in relation to your experience of the recent history of anthropology and its museums?

The discourse on the 'decolonising of anthropology' has been around for a long time. And it's still regularly being promoted as a necessary goal. What exactly it means is another matter. Most of what goes under the name of 'decolonising' is simply adopting a typically Western denunciatory view of anthropology as an irredeemably colonialist practice because it 'exoticises' the Other. Of course, a critical take on colonialist and neo-colonialist oppression is necessary; but it is not enough: Westernised readers and museum visitors are only too happy to adopt late capitalism's self-critical discourse – so long as nothing really changes. What is needed is to upset people's sense that the world is as it is and cannot be anything other, because this is the only way of reactivating the political imagination. That is the payoff of what is often condemned as 'exoticisation', and which I would prefer to call 'estrangement' or 'defamiliarisation'.

Museums have of course assimilated post-colonial critique, and they are often good at dealing with asymmetries of power; but they are very bad at dealing with asymmetries of epistemology; they assume that sharing a predicament – being confronted with AIDS, facing the ravages of climate change, being dispossessed by extractive multinationals or agro business – means that people experience and conceptualise this predicament in the same way – in other words in our way. So there is no way out ... So long as 'ethnographic' museums do not deal with cultural difference in a more symmetrical manner, they will remain 'colonialist' institutions.

I have some hope that the present upsurge in repatriation claims is going to move things on that front. The move towards repatriation is probably inevitable, and in many cases it is entirely justified, because a lot of countries from the Global South have been completely dispossessed of their cultural patrimony. Many of them claim that they need these objects to help reconnect their population – particularly their youth – to some sense of history and tradition, and I am convinced by this argument. But the trend toward repatriation can go two ways. Either it will feed and intensify the current move toward cultural closure – to each his own patrimony and his own discourse on it, the only legitimate one. This would spell the end of universalist museums, as well as do little to redress the scandalous unbalance between the North and the South in terms of culturally significant patrimony. Alternatively, it could push museums into recognizing that they are now in the business of diplomacy through objects, leading them to open all their collections – not just those pieces looted in colonial times – to permanent negotiation about their ownership as well as about the narrative that should be attached to them. Ultimately, what is needed is a radical reconceptualisation of the notion of cultural property or ownership, such that museum collections would be recognised as belonging to the sphere of Commons, the shared property of humanity, and museums (and countries) as stewards rather than owners. But we're still a long way from that ...

Considering the different kinds of institutions and practices you have worked with, what kind of practices did these institutions enable or prevent?
One of the great originalities of the MQB is its combination of museum, research, and university. But it must be said that what had the most effect, in the long-term, on the French – even perhaps the European – anthropological community, was setting up the system of the annual grants and residencies for

young scholars. Proof of that is that about 75 percent of the scholars funded by the museum were recruited by academic institutions within three years of their leaving the museum. This policy has brought a lot of oxygen to the chronically underfunded scholarly community, besides contributing to make the anthropology of the arts a very active front of current research in the social sciences and humanities. Beyond that, the MQB's programming of a rich variety of conferences, seminars, workshops, artistic events, and so forth does certainly contribute to public interest in non-European societies and in the disciplines involved in their study. But it is a permanent battle in this museum as in others to convince museum authorities and curators that these studies are needed to complement their often narrow focus on the documentation of their collections. So, in general terms, ethnographic museums play a useful civic role in informing the public about issues which are beyond their ordinary sphere of experience and knowledge. But as I have said, they still have a way to go to foster a truly reflexive take by the public on its spontaneous anthropology – on its deep-seated premises regarding the problem of cultural difference.

Until recently, European art history and European art museums focused predominantly on the history of European art, while non-European art was mostly collected by – and professionally also associated with – anthropology and its institutions. How do you regard these disciplinary claims now?
They are shifting, clearly, though perhaps more on the side of anthropology than on the side of art history. A lot of art historians are beginning to take an interest in non-European art, but in a 'classical' art historical way, by focusing on questions of stylistic variation, biographies of objects, the history of their collecting, the status of 'artists', and so on. Anthropologists for their part are beginning to work on European art in very innovative ways. In short, the hybridisation between the two disciplines is ongoing, and hopefully growing, even in France, where the art historical establishment tends to be wary of anthropological approaches and resists poaching by other disciplines. A symptom of that is the rather tense relation between the MQB and the Louvre, which still considers the MQB's extension there in the *Pavillon des Sessions* as outside its purview, as an intrusion rather than an addition...

Note

1. Taylor, Anne-Christine. 2008. 'Au Musée du Quai Branly: la place de l'ethnologie'. *Ethnologie française* 2008/4(38): 679–684.

Troubling Colonial Epistemologies in Berlin's Ethnologisches Museum: Provenance Research and the Humboldt Forum

Margareta von Oswald

Engaging with the troubles and troubling of anthropological museums with regard to their colonial legacies, this contribution grapples with how provenance research unfolds in practice.[1/2] Provenance research troubles, on the one hand, the museum's commonly recognised status as legitimate owner of collections. Provenance research is troubling, on the other hand, because it shows how difficult attempts to tackle colonial and anthropological epistemologies are. There is, simply put, no easy way out of particular modes of naming, ordering, and categorising collections. Furthermore, such work risks reproducing asymmetries of access, knowledge, and thus, of the interpretative sovereignty between former colonisers and colonised.

This ambivalent status of provenance research offers me ways to work through anthropological categories, orders and inventories, both past *and* present, in Berlin's Ethnologisches Museum. The contribution underlines the difficulties of being caught up in the seeming impossibility of not reproducing colonial epistemologies from within the institution. All the while, I try to emphasise the persistent professional efforts of grappling with such epistemologies and the museum staff's attempt of "staying with the trouble" (Haraway 2010). How, I ask, are past ways of conceiving, imagining, and classifying cultures reflected in current ways of working with the collections? Where and how do museum staff – and in this chapter, the data base manager and museologist Boris Gliesmann – identify the frictions between these past and present conceptualisations and understandings, and how do they deal with them?

In the German context, provenance has become a keyword in addressing the nation's colonial histories. This is closely related to German politics of remembrance more generally speaking and, in particular, to the policies and research regarding Nazi-looted art. These politics have raised awareness of how, for instance, contested museum acquisitions and collections are to be understood and dealt with. This awareness – not least due to long-lasting activist calls for uncovering collection histories (see introduction, this volume) – has been expanded to collections acquired in colonial contexts (see Bodenstein and Howald 2018: 543; Förster, Edenheiser, and Fründt 2018: 13–18; Förster 2019: 80). When provenance research reveals that processes within a chain of ownership raise ethical or moral doubts, this can be politically consequential, especially when used as a prerequisite for claims for restitution (Splettstößer 2019: 124–28). Put differently, the political role and mandate of provenance research has gained in significance, even beyond conventional understandings of provenance as retracing and situating chains of ownership.

In the context of and, as some claim, in reaction to the debates following France's restitution report in 2018 (Sarr and Savoy 2018), German politics has committed to provenance research regarding "collections from colonial contexts", manifested in the publication of guidelines, policies, and funding schemes (German Museums Association 2018; Koalitionsvertrag 2018;

Fig. 2.2 Buli chair, collected by Werner von Grawert, III C 14966, © Ethnologisches Museum der Staatlichen Museen zu Berlin – Preußischer Kulturbesitz

BPA 2019; German Lost Art Foundation 2019). This political commitment to provenance research has not only been celebrated but also interpreted as serving as a means for externalising questions of colonial guilt. It is seen by some as relegating these difficult queries into the realm of academia, as well as delaying or preventing political consequential actions, such as restitution or financial reparation (Häntzschel 2018; Zimmerer 2019).

This contribution methodologically addresses how provenance research unfolds in the museum by scrutinising the knowledge infrastructures that embed the object. More specifically, it does so by adopting the narrative of the object biography of one particular object, the so-called "Buli stool",[4] which I researched during my fieldwork (2013-2015) at the Africa Department of the Ethnologisches Museum.[5] Produced by groups identified as 'Luba' or 'Luba-ised', the wooden caryatid stool III C 14966 entered the museum in 1902 as a gift by the colonial officer Werner von Grawert in the then Congo Free State. Later, it was attributed the authorship of the 'Buli-Workshop'. Paola Ivanov, the department's co-curator, highlighted the object's significance in the current exhibition's catalogue, as she stated that

> for the Luba and their related peoples, the stools were regarded as the most important objectivization of the power of kings and chiefs (...) embody[ing] the ancestors and the royalty represented by them (Junge, Ivanov, and Ethnologisches Museum 2005: 91).[6]

Doing an *ethnography* of provenance research made me understand over time that I needed to go beyond tracing the histories of colonial entanglement only, as they manifest and materialise in the objects' biographies. I observed the difficulties of provenance research as it continues to operate in and is limited by established knowledge categories and infrastructures – categories and infrastructures that are themselves the result of and rely on colonial knowledge production.

I analyse first how the museum's practices of ordering and classifying inadvertently sustain colonial differences and stereotypes. I describe these practices as *discriminating* in their effect of recognising and marking something as different and distinct. I then work through the production of knowledge about the objects. Caught up in this production are differences that I describe as *unequal distribution*: an imbalance of access, sources, and resources is maintained between the Global North and the Global South. Finally, I analyse the process of valuing the object as art by attributing an author – "Buli" – to a particular group of objects. This process reveals how the construction of this particular difference – inscribing the stool in a system in which 'art' opposes 'culture' – articulates as *appropriation* that benefits Western institutions.

The following sections thus explore how the provenance research articulates in an analysis of the Buli stool's *present* status and genealogy as museum object, its trajectories *before*, and *after*, it entered the museum.

Struggling with the grids: Taxonomy and the continuity of colonial discrimination

Provenance research as a means to identify an object's trajectory includes not only an analysis of the past but also of the present. The present life of an object is shaped and predominated by its status as *museum* object, a status that situates the object in particular museum orders and regulations. When the object described here arrived in the museum in 1902 – once attributed a name and a number – it irrevocably mutated from what it used to be into a museum object. The stool was first registered in the museum's inventory (*Erwerbsbuch*), within the bundle of objects with which it arrived, and then given regional allocations, entering the 'main catalogue' (*Hauptkatalog*). The resulting list resembles a listing of birth dates. As part of the list, the object is converted into a constitutive part of the museum and becomes part of a whole – the collection – with the number 14966. What figures as roughly organised entries in the inventory list, primarily in order to give a number to a

 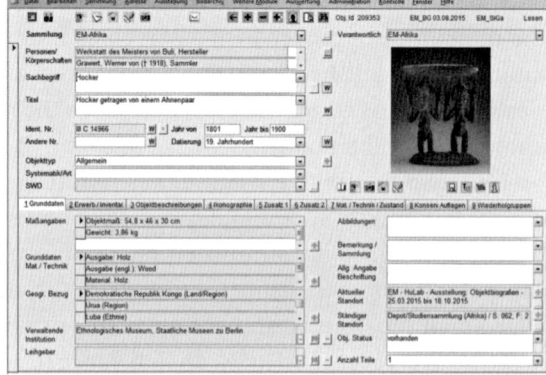

Fig. 2.3 A scan of the inventory book on the page including III C 14966, © Ethnologisches Museum der Staatlichen Museen zu Berlin – Preußischer Kulturbesitz

Fig. 2.4 Screenshot of the database entry for III C 14966, © Ethnologisches Museum der Staatlichen Museen zu Berlin – Preußischer Kulturbesitz

thing, is mirrored, further classified, and solidified in the museum's database, *MuseumPlus*.

The museum's database reflects these museum orders. Past and present practices of naming and categorising are condensed in each particular database entry, which figures and is read by museum staff as a compressed characterisation of the object. The entry, ideally, is supposed to indicate the accumulated knowledge about a particular object. Provenance research thus always starts with looking at the database, provided that an entry of the particular object exists.

The categories 'Collection' and 'Africa'

The first category in the database defines the object's affiliation to a "collection", in this case "EM-Afrika". The database *MuseumPlus* is used in all museums governed by the Stiftung Preußischer Kulturbesitz (SPK – Foundation Prussian Cultural Heritage). An indication of a particular museum – the Ethnologisches Museum – and a particular collection within the museum – "Africa" – is necessary to locate the object. This particular indication thus situates the object within an even more important grouping of collections, namely, Berlin's Staatliche Museen zu Berlin (SMB – State Museum Collections). Objects were attributed to particular collections, which define the objects' primary identity. The primary identity is accompanied by specific value regimes, which establish hierarchical differences between collections. These hierarchies are the result of difference-making through distinction: The ethnological as "the Other to art museums" is neither an art museum, a historical museum, or a decorative arts museum (Bangma 2013: 63).

This hierarchical separation between collections are stabilised through the past and ongoing politics of place on Museum Island in Berlin's centre, confirming these processes of difference-making. On Museum Island, museums associated with 'Ancient and Modern Civilizations' – Islamic, Egyptian, Greek, Roman, as well as nineteenth-century European painting – are situated in opposition to the Humboldt Forum. The Forum, in turn, has been repeatedly presented as a "place for world cultures" integrating the "non-European" collections, both of the Ethnologisches Museum and the Museum für Asiatische Kunst (Parzinger 2011: 6). As Sharon Macdonald (2016) has argued, this particular "constellation of difference" contributes to an understanding of the 'European' which is defined in terms of historic belonging, rather than in geographical terms. It implies the construction of these collections as 'European' heritage, which, conversely, serves as a constitutive part of 'European' history. This history is constructed in contrast to the 'non-European', a history which is excluded from the narrative (see also Bose 2013; 2016). The dichotomy is accentuated by the exclusion of the Museum für Europäische Kulturen in the Forum.

These constellations of difference and their implicit hierarchies are also sustained within the exhibition spaces of the Ethnologisches Museum in the Humboldt Forum through their regional division. Each continent is assigned a separated part in the Forum, which suggests a possible reading of these different continents as self-contained and homogeneous, bringing to mind critiques of colonial imaginations of 'Africa' as an isolated continent deprived from history. Subject to both opposition and celebration, the collection's particular inscription among the institutions of Museum Island relates and mirrors the anthropological modes of classification within its internal technical infrastructure. IIIC 14966, then, both in the database and via its future exhibition location in the Humboldt Forum, will continue to be primarily defined by being 'ethnological' and 'African', implying an opposing difference to being both 'European', or part of European history, as well as 'art'.

In addition to those divisions, the Humboldt Forum's strong architectural frames posed difficulties for productive criticality among those working within the museum. One interlocutor aptly summarised this unresolved question amidst preparations to move the exhibitions:

> When you enter the reconstructed Royal Palace, situated opposite of the museums of 'the Great Civilisations', pass its foyer with an overwhelming display styled like a chamber of curiosity, learn about the glories of Western science and explorers, move up several floors until you find the exhibitions of the Ethnologisches Museum – what room to manoeuvre does one have to challenge all of these framings?

The category 'Geographical Reference'

Similar to what I describe with regard to the category "collection", the category of "geographical reference" (*geografischer Bezug*) facilitated the continued use of anthropological concepts shaped by colonial modes of thinking. Intended to provide precise territorial indications, this part of the database's grid and its sub-categories "Country" (*Land*), "Region", and "Ethnic Group" (*Ethnie*) compounded temporal, geographical, and cultural entities. The database de-historicised contemporary and historic contexts, and finally omitted the most dominant political context of the time of the object's acquisition, namely, the colonial governance of the "Congo Free State". The "country" is indicated as "Demokratische Republik Kongo" (DRC), indicating a particular national constellation, only in place since 1997. The "region" "Urua" referred to a historic entity, on the west side of Lake Tanganyika, which is now located in the DRC's region of Katanga. Leaving "Urua" and "DRC" both without particular dates or denominations trapped them in what has been famously phrased by Johannes Fabian (2014) as an "ethnographic present", denying historicity both to the those who had produced the objects in question, as well as contemporaneity to those currently living in the DRC.

Equally part of the "geographical reference", "Luba" was referenced in the category "Ethnie", which can be translated as "ethnic group". The attribution of names to societies in the context of European colonialism has been subject to critique: They were ideologically accompanied by theories of social evolutionism and historic progress, and sometimes complicit with colonial governance. Similar to the notion of "tribe", which "is now commonly considered an ethnographic, rather than an analytical term" (Sneath 2016), attributions of "ethnicity" continue to be contested (see also Arndt and Hornscheid 2004; Arndt 2011). The origins of the attribution "Luba" predate colonial governance, but were fixed within the colonial context. Mary Nooter Roberts (1998: 60) describes Luba people as a "a wash of myriad clan and lineage groupings that were more or less consolidated as a kingdom from approximately the seventeenth to late nineteenth century". It was, however, not until the colonial period in the late nineteenth century that peoples referred to themselves homogenously as 'Luba', when Arab traders and European explorers and travellers started to name them that way. As Pierre Petit notes, "'Luba' is a most ambiguous category that may refer to five thousand or five million people, depending upon its particular, situationally defined application" (Petit cited in M. N. Roberts and Roberts 1996: 20). Despite the vague definitions and colonial consolidation, the term continues to be used, within and outside the museum context, including by people who identify as Luba today. This renders its use, or the search for alternatives, ever more complex.

Troubling categories

Museum staff, and curators in particular, were aware of the problems and historical genealogy of the museum's database and its discriminatory character. Attempts to circumvent and challenge the categories and their limitations exist and continue to be invented in the museum. These include adding categories to the object description, or erasing and replacing names considered derogatory. One method for challenging historical epistemologies was the introduction of the sub-category "historical depiction" (*historische Bezeichnung*) as part of the category "geographical reference". When I worked at the museum, the category was notably used to indicate historical descriptions of locations and places, such as, in this case, "Congo Free State". The sub-category helped to nuance and render more complex the object's digital presence and to avoid confounding temporalities. The adding of sections in the database allowed for more space to record research results. In my time at the museum, by contrast, the only option to report particular research trajectories was the "Notes" field in the database. Later, in 2016, a category devoted to "provenance" was added to the database.[7]

In 2018, Boris Gliesmann explained during a discussion of the first draft of this chapter that the category of "historical depiction" was also more frequently used to engage in a "transfer of categories" (*Kategorieüberführung*), in which depictions considered "derogatory" (*abwertend*) and "offensive" (*anstößig*) were replaced by depictions considered more neutral.[8] His favourite depiction was "magic" (*Zauber*):

> "Magic", "charm", "holy substance" (*Zauber, Magie, heilige Substanz*) – these are the categories we are now pushing into the subfield of "historical depiction". One method we pursue is to transform all of the "magic things" (*Zaubersachen*) into "medicine things" (*Medizinsachen*).

This was, for example, the case for a research and exhibition project in Tanzania, which featured one important object formerly depicted as "magic bag" (*Zaubersack*) that the curators renamed as a "bag with objects used in the practice of medicine " (*Beutel mit medizinischen Objekten*) (Reyels, Ivanov, and Weber-Sinn 2018: 84, 202).

> If you type anything with magic, or anything with witchcraft into the search machine, there are several hundred things which appear. "Fetish device" (*Fetischgerät*); "miraculous impact" (*wundertätige Wirkung*); "amulet against malicious witchcraft" (*Amulett gegen bösartige Hexerei*); "hunt charm" (*Jagdzauber*); something that has "the power to make rain" (*die Kraft, Regen zu machen*).

Boris Gliesmann explained that it was not only difficult to replace these names with others considered more appropriate. The numerous depictions related to "magic" were also difficult to identify if your aim was to change these depictions, systematically, among thousands of objects in the data base.

I hear the curators say: "Oh, this is a colonial use of language to depict this object, it was only used to depreciate (*abwerten*) those from who it was collected!" I know the debates and, of course, we are working on it. But pragmatically, it is difficult to tackle them, it needs a lot of time, thought, research, and expertise. And also, we cannot record the discussions in the database!

Similar problems arose with the category of *Ethnie*, which Boris Gliesmann depicted as the next "construction site" (*Baustelle*) he and the curators were dealing with in particular in relation to the Africa Department.

There are so many ethnic groups in Africa, more than 300 in the Congo collections alone I believe! "Hottentots" (*Hottentotten*) are just one example, but there are so many more. We cannot continue to use some of these depictions, as they are malicious (*bösartig*). We have different categories which we use, such as "external designation" (*Fremdbezeichnung*) or "ethnic subgroup" (*Ethnie Untergruppe*), but all of them carry their own problems.

Categories as historically situated artefacts

The database's different categories analysed can be understood as "historically situated artefacts", as defined by Bowker and Star (1999: 278). "Historically situated", in this case, concerns the categories' particular genesis in and through colonial systems of governance and anthropological knowledge orders, reproducing particular categories of difference which underlie them. As "artefacts", the museum's processes of categorising IIIC 14966 materialised in a particular politics of place, specific inscriptions of classifications and orderings, and in the solidification of temporal conceptions and cultural and geographical entities. This 'being caught' in colonial epistemologies through the everyday use of the database permit the argument to understand colonial difference-making as *discriminating*. I use 'discriminating' in the sense that it distinguishes different entities from one another, charged however with particular value regimes and hierarchies that rely on convictions of Western superiority and colonial modes of ordering the world. Current museum infrastructures rely on historical orderings and names. Discriminating is therefore used in the present tense here: The data base not only inscribes *past* conceptualisation of difference via its *present* structure. It also provides a limited framework in which *present* and *future* (provenance) research would be integrated.

Troubling access: The asymmetries in writing histories of provenance

Beyond an analysis of the object's present status and the genealogy of the categories which inform and shape this status, provenance research is also associated with retracing the object's itineraries *before* it entered the museum. This research focus implies the identification, situating and analysis of historic sources. Among her different interests and projects, the curator Paola Ivanov asked me to join her research project in order to find out how IIIC 14966 had circulated between its likely location of production in Central Africa, its acquisition by the collector Werner von Grawert, and its arrival in Germany. Introducing me to this part of provenance research in the museum, Boris Gliesmann told me how he approached this "documentation of collections".

> This is my favourite thing to do, the documentation of the collection. In other words: the documentation of the collectors! The people. To enrich the database with information on them, this is my passion, my playground. But it is extremely time-consuming!

Being "time-consuming" indicates that the museum's collections are characterised by a significant lack of documentation, already lamented when the first items of the collection arrived around 1900 (Adolf Bastian, discussed and cited in Zimmerman 2001: 190). Despite the effort and recurrent requests on behalf of museum staff to document the incoming objects, colonial staff rarely provided information about what they sent to Berlin's museum. This lack of accompanying information indicate that Berlin's Africa collections were above all the result of colonial collecting; such practice contrasts notably with scientific collecting, which focused not only on *owning* but also on *knowing* the people by the means of their material culture.[9] The Africa Department's collection consists substantially of objects acquired by colonial staff during Germany's colonial rule in what were then called Togo, Cameroun, German East Africa, and German South West Africa. It can be estimated that about 64 percent of today's Africa collections, comprising approximately 75,000 objects, stem from what has been defined as "colonial contexts", be they governed by German or other European colonial powers (German Museums Association 2018: 16–23).[10] In the museum's Africa Department, the lack of sources was further compounded, for the object cards and photographs related to the objects burned, and were thus destroyed, during the Second World War.

Source work in the archive and the library

Apart from the lack of sources, however, Boris Gliesmann's quote points to a seemingly natural mechanism current in provenance research. In lacking other kinds of indications, the object is above all defined by the person who had *collected* it, not the person who had *produced, owned,* or *used* it. Provenance research was shaped by the presence of particular sources produced within, for, and in dialogue with the colony. This contrasted with the significant absence of local subjects, their voices, and perspectives in the museum's archives. To retrace the object's trajectory then means to identify sources retracing the coloniser's trajectories. In the case of IIIC 14966, this primarily meant the correspondence of the collector Werner von Grawert. Several files in relation to Werner von Grawert exist. In contrast to the historic inventory available as scans, the complete historic records are only physically accessible and stored in the museum's archive.[11]

In the archive, information on von Grawert was minimal regarding our research focus on the object's trajectories.[12] The correspondence only reveals that IIIC 14966 had been part of an important shipment of 108 objects that

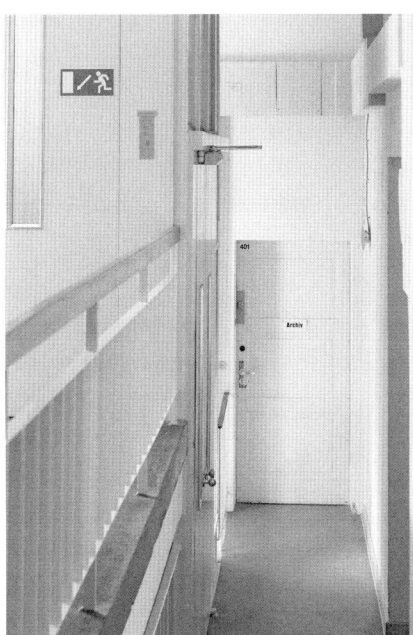

Fig. 2.5 The entrance door to the archive. Photograph by Marion Benoit, © Ethnologisches Museum der Staatlichen Museen zu Berlin – Preußischer Kulturbesitz

Fig. 2.6 The museum library. Photograph by Marion Benoit, © Ethnologisches Museum der Staatlichen Museen zu Berlin – Preußischer Kulturbesitz

arrived in Berlin in 1902 and 1903. Research on the collector indicated that he had probably not acquired the objects on the location of production, because he had not left German East Africa during his term in office.

The research in yet another of the museum's locations – the library with its primary and secondary sources – also led to insufficient evidence. When we consulted historians and anthropologists based in universities and museums, they confirmed Paola Ivanov's hypothesis that the object may have circulated via Swahili trade caravans or as diplomatic gifts or trophies, but none of them had come across specific sources that could confirm it. The archival fragments we identified, thanks to exchanges with other researchers, consisted of an image of a caravan which carried an "idol" (Cameron 1877, cited in Volper 2010), providing traces of how European colonial staff exchanged objects among themselves (Mayer 1913, cited in Plankensteiner 1998), as well as research on the circulation of artistic expertise and ideas within the region (Roberts 2013). The sources were from various times and places, however, and could only hint at possibilities rather than substantiate claims.

The research thus involved bringing together sources that were spatially dispersed and materially diverse, locating them in their historicity. We physically and virtually moved through offices, on computer screens, the archive, and the library. These movements enabled different encounters with the materials available: historic documents in their fragility; scans of the historic inventory, flattened on screens; digitally assembled information; printed scans of historic originals which turned into 'originals' themselves via the stamps and notes added to them. The time-consuming research process left us with archive transcriptions, a collection of publications, e-mail correspondence with external experts. We manoeuvred in the boundaries of the restricted sources and resources that the museum provided.

Access and gaps

These research results echo Arlette Farge's descriptions of what defines archival research, namely, as being "forever incomplete" (Farge 2013: 55). The archives were incomplete with regard to local voices in particular. This absence pointed to the denial of the locals' agency, presence, and even existence, as well as the omission of the function, production, or transaction of IIIC 14966. By contrast, what *was* documented were traces of a colonial apparatus of extracting the colonies from their material culture, which was logistically sophisticated and financially well equipped. The (minimal) documentation of shipping, transport costs, and the department director's appraisal and request for more objects shows the entanglement of colonialism with museums and academia. This documentation reflects the contemporary department director Felix von Luschan's ambitions to "systematically" collect, in order "to raise an inventory, as it were, of the complete cultural heritage" (Ankermann and Luschan 1914: 9).

For Farge, "today, to use the archives is to translate this incompleteness into a question" (ibid.). However, the search for such alternative interpretations is difficult when the Ethnologisches Museum's collections and archives remain largely inaccessible to outsiders. Only a small portion of the approximately 495,000 datasets that have been inventoried are freely accessible online, to be precise, only 71,500 of them (2019).[13] Moreover, crucial information is missing in the openly accessible database, including the date and mode of acquisition and, sometimes, the collector. Being available only in German, access is reduced to German speakers only. Whereas the archives are freely accessible on location, the access to the museum's complete database, and thus its collections, are reserved to museum staff. Functioning as gatekeepers, the museum curators' responsibility – among an overwhelming amount of other tasks – is to respond to requests addressed to the museum.[14] The fact that the curators' names and contacts are not identifiable on the museum's website further restricts access. An updated inventory catalogue, or a simple listing of the museum's collection does not exist. Access to the collection remains therefore reserved to those who already have or succeed to acquire the financial and symbolic capital to access the collections from within the museum.

Apart from underlining the museum's historical entanglement with colonialism, analysing this process of provenance research shows an *unequal distribution* concerning where and how knowledge about the object is and can be produced. In other words, conditions for producing knowledge depend on where the resources (financial, personnel) and sources (library, archives, collections) are concentrated. In view of the lack or limited (digital) access to both collections and archives, the disparity of access not only shows a *difference* but also an *inequality*, even *injustice*, of these politics of concentration. Pointing to unequal distribution here, I do not aim to question the validity of expertise in Western institutions, nor to reduce their position to their sole geographical location. Rather, I want to indicate the ongoing disparity of who is consulted, given voice, access and, thus, the right and possibility to write these histories and to own the resulting knowledge. The dissemination, accessibility, and sustainability of provenance research results was further challenged by the insufficiency of the museum's database system to record the available information at the time. Concerning the investigation into IIIC 14966, the research ultimately resulted in a paper folder, securely stored in the curator's office.

Disturbing attributions: The paradoxes of naming and colonial appropriation

Complementary to the research concerned with IIIC14966's trajectories before entering the museum, and its coming into being and present status as museum object in the museum, a final step of provenance research addressed its reception history.

Generally speaking, those who produced the objects remain anonymous in ethnological collections. Implicit in the lack of the contemporary documenting of producers, and individuals more generally speaking, was a denial of individual creativity in societies considered localised, collective, and isolated as cultural entities. A progressively established reaction to the anonymity has been the retroactive identification of "masters", "workshops", or simply "artists" – a practice which can be interpreted as a *resistance* to colonial modes of ordering and perceiving the world. III C 14966 was proof of one particular attempt to counter colonial epistemologies, as the data base's category "producer" ("Buli workshop") testified.

Anonymity, identity, and authorship

IIIC 14966 reflected the attempt to counter anonymity. The stool belonged to a group of objects, to which the Belgian anthropologist Frans M. Olbrechts had attributed a particular author since the 1930s, the "master of the long-faced style", also known as the "Buli Master". The author was named after the village where two sculptures were acquired (Vogel 1980: 133; Nooter Roberts 1998: 61). The naming practice therefore has its origins during colonial times, but continues to be used prominently, and progressively, in the ongoing 'invention' of 'masters'.[15] Such and similar processes of naming have had complex, and even paradox, consequences. Mary Nooter Roberts describes the politics of naming as "both an appropriation of identity and an imposition of it. To withhold a person's identity may be a form of protection or of subjugation. To impose a name may be a form of repression or of elevation" (Nooter Roberts 1998: 56). This paradox of naming was reflected in the reception history of IIIC 14966.

On the one hand, challenging the alleged anonymity of African artists and showing an interest in the artist's style and characteristics reflected a political standpoint. Frans M. Olbrechts built his reflection on anthropologist Franz Boas' concept of culture areas and his conviction of racial equality, a conviction which rejected evolutionist theories dominant at the time. This approach was paired with art historical methods aimed at identifying artist's "hands", such as established by the art historian Giovanni Morelli in the nineteenth century (Petridis 2001). The Buli Master was the first individual artist retroactively to be assigned to a group of African objects, followed by the invention of a number other 'masters', such as the Master of the Cascade Headdress or the Warua Master, all put forward by Western scholars, dealers, and collectors (Nooter Roberts 1998: 61). The recognition of an individual author contributed to counter dominant Western ideas of Africa, as well as recognise individual creativity and artistic genius within African cultures.

On the other hand, the reassessment of anonymous works as authored and singular pieces of art contributed to transform the museum's collection to "another exceptional resource of the colony" (Van Beurden 2013: 483). Objects identified as "Buli", and IIIC 14966 in particular, have been outstanding examples of processes of the production of value via the interlinked resource production of the museum, the market, and academia. The museum's historic publication and photo archives confirmed its exceptional reception. This reception started with its denomination as 'art' upon its arrival in the museum in 1902 and continued with a prominent international publication and exhibition history. The subsequent symbolic value encouraged the object's commodification and translated into financial value. The perceived rarity, both of the object and of the occasion to acquire such an object, is reflected in the record prices which caryatid stools associated with "Buli" reached on the auction market. In 1979, one object was sold for 249.000 GBP (Sotheby's 1979); in 2010, a similar stool attained at 5.4 million euros at auction (Sotheby's 2010).

Disputes over "Buli" have been ongoing. They concern the particularity of the artistic identity – Is it one artist, a workshop, a generation? – but also which object is considered to be "Buli", and thus exceptionally valuable or not.[16] The number of "Buli" objects has continuously risen from twelve objects identified by Olbrechts in the 1930s to twenty-nine being under scrutiny in 2011 (LaGamma 2012: 263). The disputes are also ongoing because naming as a practice is valuable in itself: The acknowledgement of an individual author accentuates the absence of an identified individual – an absence, Sarah Van Beurden argues, which was subsequently occupied by either the collector, scholar, or dealer who had 'discovered' the master, or the museum in charge of keeping it.

Naming and valuing

Beyond the value generated by and for Western institutions, assigning an individual artist to IIIC 14966 contradicts Luba definitions of authorship. The attribution reveals, on the contrary, a modernist Western understanding about the status of art. Mary Nooter Roberts, in her fieldwork about the Luba in the then Republic of Zaire, never came across court historians who mentioned individual artists (1998: 56). She demonstrates that during the conception and production of a sculpture, the Luba concept of remembrance was at play, which integrated several people and spirits. In contrast to the individual artist, Nooter Roberts refers to how Luba artists participate in a "transpersonal identity", that is, "the phenomenon whereby artists become subsumed by the larger network of relationships – both social and spiritual – of which they are part" (Nooter Roberts 1998: 67). As James Clifford (1988) noted, the Western understanding of individual artistry cannot simply be imposed upon non-Western cultures, as definitions of originality, authenticity, and authorship differ. He stated that "'culture' and 'art' can no longer be simply *extended* to non-Western peoples and things. They can at worst be *imposed*, at best *translated* – both historically and politically contingent operations" (ibidem: 236).

Understanding the naming of Buli as such form of imposition, the processes of naming and valuing can be considered colonial difference-making as appropriation. As Benoît De L'Estoile (2008) has argued, "colonial relations, often stamped by domination and violence, are however more aptly characterised by a multifarious process of appropriation than by the sheer negation of the colonised" (ibidem: 268). Whereas naming can be interpreted as an attempt to repair and engage in the nuanced and complex character of colonial relations, the appropriation seems to also result here in a second expropriation, since the generated symbolic and financial value ultimately continue to serve Western institutions.

Concluding discussion

Provenance research has been an important aspect of how decolonisation is discussed and practised in Germany. However, provenance research is complex, time-consuming, and limited. It also risks posing more questions than it answers. This chapter underscores the struggles that accompany working with infrastructures and epistemologies stemming from and relying on past colonial practices and knowledge production.

My account shows how my interlocutors in the museum and, in this regard, especially Boris Gliesmann, not only identify but also try to change the museum's epistemologies. These, as the deciphering of genealogy of the museum's inventory and ordering systems show, are the result of the historical complicity between colonial systems of appropriation and the discipline of anthropology. Museum staff engage with these epistemologies on a daily basis. They commit to provenance research with a number of consequences and intentions, which include rendering the museum's colonial entanglement transparent; adding categories to the data base grids in order nuance the object's categorisation; or changing the depictions of objects to avoid the further inscription and reproduction of the colonial epistemic violence, as reflected in the ways in which objects were documented, as well as described. While calls for the opening of inventories have been voiced publicly (Öffnet die Inventare! 2019), efforts to render the collections' histories transparent and accessible have been pushed further since my departure from the museum in 2015.[17]

At the same time, the deconstruction of different anthropological categories and imaginations in past and present knowledge infrastructures shows how their unstable, provisory, and fragile character continues to be solidified, materialised, and perpetuated within the database and, more broadly speaking, the museum's infrastructure. Whereas my interlocutors struggle with these categories and names stemming from colonial thought, they nevertheless form the differentiating and discriminatory grid and order which organise the museum. The ethnography of the research processes further points to the symbolic geographies and hierarchies of knowledge production that are sustained between the Global North and South, perpetuated through the imbalance of access to sources and resources available to research, analyse, and write provenance histories today. Problematising the paradoxes of naming finally shows how even the explicit search for alternatives to colonial modes of ordering the world risks faltering. The ethnography discusses how those systems of knowledge and value systems persist and how deeply the epistemological practices are engrained in the museum – both in the past and today.

Troubling the museum's coloniality, then, goes beyond telling the museum's histories, even beyond the possible restitution of particular artefacts. It encompasses dealing with the very words, categories, and place-making which name, order, and differentiate museums and collections.

Reconceptualising the storing, ordering, and digital documentation of collections offers the means to find new ways to engage the museum's knowledge infrastructures and epistemologies and, thus, to redefine the collections themselves.

Notes

1. The image on p. 106 is Figure 2.1 Boris Gliesmann working in the archive. Photograph by Marion Benoit, © Ethnologisches Museum der Staatlichen Museen zu Berlin – Preußischer Kulturbesitz.
2. I would like to thank Paola Ivanov for introducing me to the Ethnologisches Museum as a research fellow. Without her, this research would not have been possible. I am grateful for her continued feedback on drafts of my written-up work. Among other museum staff, I would like to thank Boris Gliesmann in particular for reading several versions of this text, and for always providing me with more fascinating details about the field and his work. Both my supervisors Sharon Macdonald and Béatrice Fraenkel, as well as Sophie Houdart, have been guiding and shaping my work consistently, and productively. Sharon Macdonald has continuously contributed to getting this text into shape, for which I am very grateful. I would also like to thank Magda Buchzyk, Duane Jethro, Tahani Nadim, Katarzyna Puzon and Jonas Tinius for commenting earlier versions of this text. I take responsibility for any remaining errors or misinterpretations.
3. The research that led to this piece was funded by the Alexander von Humboldt Foundation as part of my research fellowship and the research award for Sharon Macdonald's Alexander von Humboldt Professorship.
4. Object biographies have gained in popularity and have been widely discussed since *The Social Life of Things: Commodities in Cultural Perspective* (Appadurai 1986; Kopytoff 1986), in disciplines such as archeology (Gosden and Marshall 1999; Joy 2009), museum studies and anthropology (Hirschauer and Doering 1997; Förster and Stoecker 2016; Basu 2017), or the history of science (Daston 2000). For an overview, see Hoskins (2006).
5. In November 2013, I joined the museum apprentice Verena Rodatus in the provenance research on one object group, which the Africa department's co-curator Paola Ivanov had initiated. Verena Rodatus was the museum apprentice ('Volontärin') in the Africa Department and Humboldt Lab Dahlem since May 2013; Paola Ivanov had been employed as the department's co-curator since 2012. The three of us regularly met to exchange results of the research, and Paola Ivanov instructed us on how, who, and what to consult to trace the object's past trajectories.

6. All translations from German to English by the author.
7. Interview with Boris Gliesmann, 8 November 2016.
8. Notes from a conversation with Boris Gliesmann, 16 April 2018.
9. This distinction is not an exclusive one, but French museums for example, different to Berlin's Africa Department, acquired a significant part of their collections via scientific expeditions. For details on the different modes of acquisition concerning the *Musée de l'Homme*, see Sarr and Savoy (2018: 42–52).
10. The statistical estimation of 64 percent stems from the following calculation: Between 1884 and 1914 (German colonial rule), the African collections grew from 7,388 objects to 55,079 objects (Krieger and Koch 1973: 106). Given that today's Africa collection is estimated at 75,000 objects, the difference constitutes approx. 64 percent. Website Ethnologisches Museum, https://www.smb.museum/museen-und-einrichtungen/ethnologisches-museum/sammeln-forschen/sammlung.html (last accessed 16 April 2019).
11. In the long run, this will change as the museum will scan and make publicly available all of its archival files up until 1947, https://www.smb.museum/museen-und-einrichtungen/ethnologisches-museum/sammeln-forschen/bibliothek-und-archiv.html (last accessed 02 February 2019).
12. The information on Werner von Grawert in the archives is limited to the archival files E 1555/1902; E 1494/1902.
13. SMB-database consulted 11.02.2019, email from Boris Gliesmann 11.02.2019.
14. The curators are obliged to answer all requests, as they are the keepers of a public collection, but can *de facto* ignore requests just like any working professional can ignore emails.
15. In an interview with the art consultant and expert in the art market for African art Bruno Claessens, he confirmed the explosion of 'masters' in the last two decades, notably in relation to the auction market, Antwerp, November 2015. For scholarly explorations of the market of African art, see Steiner (1994) and Corbey (2000).
16. For a recent overview of the ongoing debate, see LaGamma (2012: 263–65). Different positions include the following (Neyt 1994: 216–17; Pirat 1996; de Strycker and de Grunne 1996; Pirat 2001).
17. Among other developments, the Stiftung Preußischer Kulturbesitz opened four positions explicitly devoted to provenance research in 2019, a research group devoted to "colonial provenance" across German-speaking countries has formed since 2017 ('Arbeitsgruppe Koloniale Provenienzen'), cross-university teaching on provenance has been advertised in Berlin, and several collaborative research and exhibition projects have been put in place, all of which include the research on the objects' trajectories, including with researchers and curators in the former German colonies Tanzania and Namibia.

References

Ankermann, Bernhard, and Felix von Luschan. 1914. *Anleitung zum ethnologischen Beobachten und Sammeln*. Berlin: Georg Reimer.

Appadurai, Arjun. Ed. 1986. *The Social Life of Things: Commodities in Cultural Perspective*. Cambridge; New York: Cambridge University Press.

Arndt, Susan. 2011. 'Ethnie', in: *Wie Rassismus aus Wörtern spricht: Kerben des Kolonialismus im Wissensarchiv deutsche Sprache. Ein kritisches Nachschlagewerk*, edited by Susan Arndt and Nadja Ofuatey-Alazard, Münster: Unrast Verlag, pp. 632–33.

Arndt, Susan, and Antje Hornscheid. 2004. 'Ethnie', in: *Afrika und die deutsche Sprache. Ein kritisches Nachschlagewerk*, edited by Susan Arndt, Antje Hornscheid, Andriana Boussala, Katharine Machni, Kathrin Petrow, and Marlene Bauer, Mumlunster: Unrast Verlag, pp. 124–27.

Bangma, Anke. 2013. 'Respondenz zu Susanne Leeb: Einige Gedanken über die unbequeme Aktualität Ethnologischer Museen'. *Texte Zur Kunst* 23(91): 62–71.

Basu, Paul, Ed. 2017. *The Inbetweenness of Things: Materializing Mediation and Movement Between Worlds*. London; New York, NY: Bloomsbury.

Bodenstein, Felicity, and Christine Howald. 2018. 'Weltkunst unter Verdacht. Raubkunst, ihre Geschichte und Erinnerungskultur in deutschen Sammlungen', in: *Deutschland postkolonial?: Die Gegenwart der imperialen Vergangenheit*, edited by Marianne Bechhaus-Gerst and Joachim Zeller, Berlin: Metropol-Verlag, pp. 532–46.

Bose, Friedrich von. 2013. 'The Making of Berlin's Humboldt-Forum: Negotiating History and the Cultural Politics of Place'. *Darkmatter Journal* Afterlives 11, http://www.darkmatter101.org/site/2013/11/18/the-making-of-berlin%e2%80%99s-humboldt-forum-negotiating-history-and-the-cultural-politics-of-place/.

———. 2016. *Das Humboldt-Forum. Eine Ethnographie seiner Planung*. Berlin: Kulturverlag Kadmos.

Bowker, Geoffrey C., and Susan Leigh Star. 1999. 'Categorical Work and Boundary Infrastructures: Enrichting Theories of Classification', in: *Sorting Things Out: Classification and Its Consequences*, Cambridge, MA; London: MIT Press, pp. 283–317.

BPA. 2019. 'Aufarbeitung der Kolonialgeschichte – Das Deutsche Zentrum Kulturgutverluste startet neuen Förderzweig. Pressemitteilung 41.' https://www.bundesregierung.de/breg-de/aktuelles/pressemitteilungen/aufarbeitung-der-kolonialgeschichte-das-deutsche-zentrum-kulturgutverluste-startet-neuen-foerderzweig-1576842 (last accessed 20 January 2020)

Clifford, James. 1988. *The Predicament of Culture: Twentieth-Century Ethnography, Literature, and Art*. Cambridge, MA: Harvard University Press.

Corbey, Raymond. 2000. *Tribal Art Traffic: A Chronicle of Taste, Trade and Desire in Colonial and Post-Colonial Times*. KIT Publications. Amsterdam: Royal Tropical Institute.

Daston, Lorraine. 2000. *Biographies of Scientific Objects*. Chicago: University of Chicago Press.

De L'Estoile, Benoît. 2008. 'The Past as It Lives Now: An Anthropology of Colonial Legacies'. *Social Anthropology* 16(3): 267–79.

Fabian, Johannes. 2014. *Time and the Other: How Anthropology Makes Its Object*. New York: Columbia University Press.

Farge, Arlette. 2013. *The Allure of the Archives*. New Haven: Yale University Press.

Förster, Larissa. 2019. 'Der Umgang mit der Kolonialzeit: Provenienz und Rückgabe', in: *Museumsethnologie. Eine Einführung. Theorien – Debatten – Praktiken*, edited by Iris Edenheiser and Larissa Förster, Berlin: Reimer, pp. 74–103.

Förster, Larissa, Iris Edenheiser, and Sarah Fründt. 2018. 'Eine Tagung zu Postkolonialer Provenienzforschung. Zur Einführung', in: *Provenienzforschung zu ethnografischen Sammlungen der Kolonialzeit. Positionen in der Aktuellen Debatte*, edited by Larissa Förster, Iris Edenheiser, Sarah Fründt, and Heike Hartmann, Electronic publication related to the conference 'Provenienzforschung in ethnologischen Sammlungen der Kolonialzeit«' Museum Fünf Kontinente, Munich, 7-8. April 2017, pp. 13–37.

Förster, Larissa, and Holger Stoecker. 2016. *Haut, Haar und Knochen koloniale Spuren in naturkundlichen Sammlungen der Universität Jena*. Kromsdorf: VDG Weimar.

German Lost Art Foundation. 2019. 'Frequently Asked Questions. What Is the German Lost Art Foundation and What Is Its Mission?' https://www.kulturgutverluste.de/Webs/EN/Start/FAQs/Index.html (last accessed 20 January 2020).

German Museums Association. 2018. *Guidelines on Dealing with Collections from Colonial Contexts*. German Museums Association, https://www.museumsbund.de/publikationen/guidelines-on-dealing-with-collections-from-colonial-contexts-2/ (last accessed 20 January 2020).

Gosden, Chris, and Yvonne Marshall. 1999. 'The Cultural Biography of Objects.' *World Archaeology* 31(2): 169–78.

Häntzschel, Jörg. 2018. 'Vertröstungen'. *sueddeutsche.de*, 12 April 2018, https://www.sueddeutsche.de/kultur/debatte-vertroestungen-1.4238454. (last accessed 20 January 2020).

Haraway, Donna. 2010. 'When Species Meet: Staying with the Trouble'. *Environment and Planning D: Society and Space* 28(1): 53–55.

Hirschauer, Stefan, and Hilke Doering. 1997. 'Die Biographie der Dinge. Eine Ethnologie musealer Repräsentation', in: *Die Befremdung der eigenen Kultur: Zur ethnographischen Herausforderung soziologischer Empirie*, edited by Stefan Hirschauer and Klaus Amann, Frankfurt am Main: Suhrkamp, pp. 267–97.

Hoskins, Janet. 2006. 'Agency, Biography and Objects', in: *Handbook of Material Culture*, edited by Christopher Tilley, Webb Keane, Susanne Kuechler-Fogden, Patricia Spyer, and Mike Rowlands. London; Thousand Oaks, CA: SAGE.

Joy, Jody. 2009. 'Reinvigorating Object Biography: Reproducing the Drama of Object Lives'. *World Archaeology* 41(4): 540–56.

Junge, Peter, Paola Ivanov, and Ethnologisches Museum. Eds. 2005. *Kunst aus Afrika: Plastik, Performance, Design; (... anlässlich der Ausstellung Kunst aus Afrika, eine Ausstellung des Ethnologischen Museums, Staatliche Museen zu Berlin eröffnet am 26. August 2005)*. Berlin; Cologne: DuMont-Literatur-und-Kunst-Verlag.

Koalitionsvertrag. 2018. 'Ein neuer Aufbruch für Europa. Eine neue Dynamik für Deutschland. Ein neuer Zusammenhalt für unser Land. Koalitionsvertrag zwischen CDU, CSU und SPD'.

Kopytoff, Igor. 1986. 'The Cultural Biography of Things: Commoditization as Process'. In *The Social Life of Things: Commodities in Cultural Perspective*, edited by Arjun Appadurai, Cambridge, Cambridgeshire; New York: Cambridge University Press, pp. 64–91.

Krieger, Kurt, and Gerd Koch. Eds. 1973. *Hundert Jahre Museum für Völkerkunde Berlin*. Baessler-Archiv : Beiträge Zur Völkerkunde. Berlin: Reimer.

LaGamma, Alisa. 2012. *Helden Afrikas: ein neuer Blick auf die Kunst (Museum Rietberg, Zürich, 26. Februar – 3. Juni 2012)*. Zürich: Scheidegger & Spiess.

Macdonald, Sharon. 2016. 'New Constellations of Difference in Europe's 21st-Century Museumscape'. *Museum Anthropology* 39(1): 4–19.

Neyt, François. 1994. *Luba: To the Sources of the Zaire*. Paris: Musée Dapper.

Nooter Roberts, Mary. 1998. 'The Naming Game: Ideologies of Luba Artistic Identity'. *African Arts* 31(4): 56–73, 90–92.

Öffnet die Inventare! 2019. 'Ein Appell, das vorhandene Wissen zu afrikanischen Objekten in deutschen Museen endlich frei zugänglich zu machen', Die Zeit online, 10 October 2019, https://www.zeit.de/2019/43/koloniale-vergangenheit-deutschland-afrikanische-objekte-museen (last accessed 20 January 2020).

Parzinger, Hermann. 2011. 'Das Humboldt-Forum. Soviel Welt mit sich verbinden als möglich. Aufgabe und Bedeutung des wichtigsten Kulturprojekts in Deutschland zu Beginn des 21. Jahrhunderts', edited by Stiftung Berliner Schloss – Humboldtforum, http://www.preussischer-kulturbesitz.de/meldung/article/2011/05/18/media-broschuere-das-humboldt-forum-soviel-welt-mit-sich-verbinden-als-moeglich.html (last accessed 20 January 2020).

Petridis, Constantine. 2001. 'Olbrecht and the Morphological Approach to African Sculptural Art', in: *Frans M. Olbrechts, 1899-1958: In Search of Art in Africa*, edited by Constantine Petridis, Antwerp: Antwerp Ethnographic Museum, pp. 119–42.

Pirat, Claude-Henri. 1996. 'The Buli Master: Isolated Master or Atelier?.' *World of Tribal Arts. Le Monde de l'art Tribal* 3: 54–77.

———. 2001. 'The Buli Master: A Review of the Case'. *World of Tribal Arts = Le Monde de l'art Tribal* 7(1): 82–95.

Plankensteiner, Barbara. 1998. 'Um den Tanganyika', in: *Austausch, Kunst aus dem südlichen Afrika um 1900*, Wien: Museum für Völkerkunde, pp. 120–21.

Reyels, Lili, Paola Ivanov, and Kristin Weber-Sinn. Eds. 2018. *Humboldt Lab Tanzania: Objekte aus Kolonialen Kriegen im Ethnologischen Museum, Berlin – Deutsch-Tansanische Perspektiven*. Berlin: Reimer, Dietrich.

Roberts, Allen F. 2013. 'Movement of Ideas and Forms between Central and Eastern Africa'. In *Shangaa. Art of Tanzania*, edited by Gary van Wyk, The City University of New York, pp. 197–224.

Roberts, Mary Nooter, and Allen F Roberts. Eds. 1996. *Memory: Luba Art and the Making of History*. New York: Museum for African Art.

Sarr, Felwine, and Bénédicte Savoy. 2018. 'Rapport sur la Restitution du patrimoine culturel africain. Vers une nouvelle éthique relationnelle'. http://restitutionreport2018.com/ (last accessed 20 January 2020).

Sneath, David. 2016. 'Tribe'. *Cambridge Encyclopedia of Anthropology*, http://www.anthroencyclopedia.com/entry/tribe (last accessed 20 January 2020).

Sotheby's. 1979. *Catalogue of Primitive Works of Art, Day of Sale 21.06.1979*.

———. 2010. 'Communiqué de Presse: Record for a Work of African Art at Sotheby's: €5.4m ($7.1m). Luba Caryatid Stool of The Master of the Buli One of Only Two Works of African Art Ever to Sell for over €5m ($7m).'

Splettstößer, Anne. 2019. *Umstrittene Sammlungen. Vom Umgang Mit Kolonialem Erbe Aus Kamerun in Ethnologischen Museen*. Göttinger Studien zu Cultural Property (15). Göttingen: Universitätsverlag Göttingen.

Steiner, Christopher B. 1994. *African Art in Transit*. Cambridge: Cambridge University Press.

Strycker, Louis de, and Bernard de Grunne. 1996. 'Le trésor de Kalumbi et le style de Buli'. *Tribal arts / Le monde de l'art tribal* (10).

Van Beurden, Sarah. 2013. 'The Value of Culture: Congolese Art and the Promotion of Belgian Colonialism (1945–1959)'. *History and Anthropology* 24(4): 472–92.

Vogel, Susan. 1980. 'The Buli Master, and Other Hands'. *Art in America* 68(5): 133–42.

Volper, Julien. 2010. 'Les cornes, la croix et les défenses. Essai sur trois masques du Moero'. *Afrique : Archéologie & Arts* 6: 9–24.

Zimmerer, Jürgen. 2019. 'Die größte Identitätsdebatte unserer Zeit'. *sueddeutsche.de*, 20 February 2019, https://www.sueddeutsche.de/kultur/kolonialismus-postkolonialismus-humboldt-forum-raubkunst-1.4334846 (last accessed 23 January 2020)

Zimmerman, Andrew. 2001. *Anthropology and Antihumanism in Imperial Germany*. Chicago: University of Chicago Press.

"Against the Mono-Disciplinarity of Ethnographic Museums"

A conversation with Clémentine Deliss

How would you situate your practice as a curator? How does it seek to transcend the kinds of distinctions we have proposed between the museum, contemporary art, and colonialism? When did you first come into contact with anthropology and, related to that, what is anthropology for you today?

My first point of entry, biographically, remains contemporary art *practice*.[1] I'm not an art historian. I studied contemporary art in Vienna at a particular period in time when certain forms of ethnographic writing, anthropological theory, post-structuralist philosophy, and ethno-psychoanalysis were being read by artists. And it's for that reason – as someone who wanted to become a curator at a young age – that I decided to take an interdisciplinary path and attend university to find out what information was filtering into conceptual art practice. I discovered that the intellectual material that formed a knowledge-base or an episteme for explorations in visual and performance-based art in the late 70s and early 80s was anthropology.

As for museums, yes, I did run a museum for five years, but my practice spans independent publishing, collaborative research, exhibition making, curating think tanks, with a particular focus on inquiry and therefore on the *backstage* dimensions to art practice. Right now, I view the relationship between three central civic institutions – the university, the museum, and the art school – as an issue that needs to be interconnected through the question of decolonial methodologies. I seek to transverse these venues in order to produce the necessary infrastructure for a critical process to take place. However, my starting point remains the field of advanced contemporary art.

If I took on a museum at a certain moment in my career, it is because I wanted to engage with the concept of the institution as a house, as a site of *domestic* research, in opposition to the corporatisation of most museums and forms of higher education. The house would be similar to what Michelangelo Pistoletto once described to me as the necessity for a *roof*. Today I recognise the need for institutions to offer *sheltering structures*. And if that can be provided through the reformulation of a museum, then I'm fine with that.

I first came into contact with anthropology when I was around eighteen years old, reading books as an art student. I didn't go to art school in London but I grew up there. As a child we didn't spend our holidays in Britain but were always camping in Eastern Europe. Everything that happened at home wasn't normative English. So I needed to find a discipline that was more culturally heterogeneous. Then I moved to Vienna and went to art school. With new friends who were all art students, I witnessed the tail end of Viennese Actionism and conceptual art. I decided to continue focusing on the art world and to study anthropology at the Institut für Völkerkunde. It was a fairly demoralising experience. I was in a social and educational environment that was very different to the art scene in Vienna, which I was already addicted to. The significant moments for me were watching endless ethnographic films from *Encyclopedia Cinematographica* and in the evening going to the Österreichisches Filmmuseum and looking at films by Peter Kubelka, Kurt Kren, Jonas Mekas, Stan Brakhage, and Kenneth Anger and then trying desperately in my student mind to form a dialogue between the two discourses of filmic representation.

Two years later, I returned to London and enrolled at SOAS (School of Oriental and African Studies). This experience was the complete opposite to my education at the ethnographic institute in Vienna and it gave me some faith in social anthropology again. In Vienna, the intellectual cut-off point in anthropology was Durkheim. In London it began with Durkheim and went straight into semantic anthropology. Today when I talk about anthropology, then it's the process of deconstructing categories and classifications in anthropology that is exciting for me and not some kind of fieldwork experience. I have always been deeply anti-territorial and anti-regionalist and more interested in reflexive and analytical forms of social and cultural anthropology.

And what is anthropology for you today?

It's a highly problematic, ailing discipline. There are some anthropologists for whom I have a huge amount of respect: Michael Oppitz, Paul Rabinow, and James Clifford, for sure. This goes without saying. But ultimately, it's really the first two with whom I have the most exchange. For me, anthropology is deeply disappointing. It's disappointing because it should be much more reflexive, much more open to disturbance, to fracturing. It could be more inclusive, more transversal, more polyphonic, formally as well as conceptually, on the edge and self-questioning. Since I moved to Germany, and apart from in depth dialogues with Michael Oppitz, I have not encountered this quasi-existential mise-en-cause of the validity of ethnographic research coupled with a critical view on the legitimacy of positions within anthropological discourse. And *that* I find deeply worrying.

How exactly would you describe or define 'museum anthropology'?
In London in 1988, the Museum of Mankind in Burlington Gardens still existed. We knew that it was going to 'upgrade' and become part of the British Museum. At the time, there was a lot of discussion about what to do with the museum's legacy. The DIY-approach to making exhibitions as an anthropologist was on its last legs. There was virtually no possibility any longer to position this amateur visual research against the authority of the interior designer, who basically took on the mediation and transmission of ethnographic knowledge. In many ways, it signalled the end of that form of ethnographic exhibition-making. Meanwhile, curatorial practice was beginning to define the question of the exhibition in ways that museum anthropologists knew nothing of.

After completing my PhD, I was invited to take part in a seminal conference entitled *The Poetics and Politics of Representation* held at the Smithsonian Institution in 1988. I showed photographs of current work by Jeff Koons, Haim Steinbach, Mike Kelley, Rosemarie Trockel, and Lubaina Himid, and spoke about the issue of the non-authored object in the context of ethnographic collections. At the time, these artists dealt with power relations in museum collections and the art market. By engaging with their work, I could develop a contrast medium with which to highlight the absence of a critical discourse around contemporary practices and phenomena within museum anthropology.[2]

What I noticed in '88, and what I noticed again to my horror only a few years ago, is that both then and now, there still exists a timorous polarity between the model of art-pedestal power in the exhibitions of artefacts from other parts of the world, and the so called contextualizing exhibitions that stem from an ethnographic approach. This antagonism which is really well-entrenched for a whole number of reasons that would take too long to debate, is not helpful. If you want to give the benefit of the doubt to museum anthropologists, then please insist that they become a little more informed about how to understand the notion of *context* and therefore the models of curatorial practice that inevitably inform the semantics of exhibitions in 2020. And likewise, let's recognise that in the art world, the question of pedestal-power and spot-lighting is really banal. Nevertheless, these dichotomies return all the time: context//no context; artwork//ethnographic object, and it's very numbing. At the end of the day, I prefer to return to the art world, where I find more interlocutors who are ready to engage in radical self-questioning. In the field of museum anthropology, I tested out such questions at the Weltkulturen Museum in order to emancipate existing interpretational models with regard to these collections. But this is not just about shaking up the notion of context, it's also about confronting the ideology of conservation, which overrides issues ranging from experimentation through to restitution.

Where do you think that critical knowledge production in anthropology takes place today?
If I'm frank with you, I don't believe there is this strain of critical knowledge production in museums. If I am going to read anthropology, then I want to be confronted with a clash between different fields of knowledge production, in order to recognise once again that anthropology is the *impossible* science. It is everything that it cannot be, and as such, it has to be much more inclusive and self-critical.

The question that we just asked leads to our discussion of the trans-anthropological as a term that we wish to engage with in this book. So, for you, is there any value in talking about trans-anthropological curating?
Paul B. Preciado, who recently wrote a text called "The Trans-Body is a Colony" for the offline print edition *Organs & Alliances* that I curated in Paris – is really vital as a thinker, as is Jack Halberstam.[3] This kind of intervention within classificatory systems of language and representation is not present within a museum anthropology. Lately, I've been very concerned with the formulation of the organ trade, and the relationship it is having on transborder communications and circulation. These issues can be read in the parallel light of restitution politics. Achille Mbembe is right when he states that while objects are purported to be going back, people are coming in, but are being stopped.

When I coined the terms *post-ethnographic* and *post-ethnological*, I was proposing a new paradigm for ways of working with the museum and its collections. At the start of my direction of the Weltkulturen Museum in Frankfurt in 2010, anthropologist Paul Rabinow came to visit us and gave a talk in the library. At the time, he said to me: "I don't want *ethnos*. I am prepared to work on the *anthropological*, but I'm not going to work with the *logos of ethnos*." And that's the point about the post-ethnographic. There are still majority positions in museum anthropology that continue to reify ethnicity and to qualify the works and designs of other cultures and nation states as *un-authored*. Instead, "ethnos" is the gathering point of everything and anything. So, when I speak about the post-ethnographic and the post-ethnological, I stake a claim to an alternative referentiality and modus operandi. In the framework of the Weltkulturen Museum, there was no way I could walk into that institution as if I had always played a role in German museum anthropology. I never had a role to play here in the first place, and I could not carry on doing exhibitions as they had been done until then.

The transformation I undertook was also about creating new spatial priorities in the museum: letting people sleep there, work in studios, use the library, employ the environment of a laboratory to do independent research, and have 24-hour access to all these facilities. We needed to be "post-ethnos", because the actual models of research and the accompanying representational processes would be altered. These subsumed inquiry, ways of working, and the necessary circulation of artefacts between depot, laboratory and exhibition. The laboratory turned into a third space that was neither private nor public. Our engagement with all forms of representation was experimental

Fig. 3.2 Weltkulturen Museum Storage Building, Frankfurt am Main. Photograph by Armin Linke, 2013

Fig. 3.3 Thinktank on photography at Weltkulturen Labor with (from left to right) Kokou Azamede, Otobong Nkanga, Martin Guttmann, Armin Linke, Jan-Philipp Possmann, Weltkulturen Museum, Frankfurt am Main. Photograph by Wolfgang Günzel, 2013

and purposely unresolved. Later I began to speak of the "post-ethnological", as constituting the core episteme within the deconstruction of ethno-colonial collections. For someone who grew up in a post-structural, postmodern period, the prefix 'post' indicates that you are creating a critical position in relation to a particular regime and discourse of power relations. You are positioning yourself in a complex relationship that is framed as the post-ethnographic and the post-ethnological in order to face problems taking place today. In my practice, that's what it takes to bring in a transversality of interpretation and to open the doors of these contentious world cultures museums in order to undertake concept work that is pluri-disciplinary and poly-cultural. Only in this manner, can one begin to dislodge what I see as the *intellectual plantation* of ethnographic museums. These monochannel everything around the logos of ethnos, thereby dangerously reinstating earlier forms of 19th century anthropology and 20th century identity politics.

So, where is the blockage, what's stopping more experimental work from being performed in so-called ethnographic museums? I believe one issue is the dominant ideology of conservation that supports the sequestration of these complex collections. Alpha Oumar Konaré wrote about this issue already in the 1980s, when he stated that it's up to every community in Africa to define what they mean by conservation. There is a generational issue too, but a lot has to do with notions that come from more general museological problematics, not only from ethnographic questions. One of these is the prioritisation of museum space, another of being in the service of a consumerist imperative built on an economy that forces people to walk as if swiping through exhibits without being given the opportunity to sit and study for longer periods of time.

Considering the different kinds of institutions that you have worked in many different parts of the world, – and we are thinking in terms of political, financial, and ideological framings too – what kind of curatorial practices did these institutions enable or prevent?
I've been an independent professional for nearing 30 years. Once I'd completed my PhD in 1988, I wanted to become a curator. In England, this role didn't exist. You had exhibition organisers and academics, who were consultants. But I came from the German-speaking art world, so I knew there were curators, and I saw that they had a kind of symbiotic role to play with artists, looking for what was being expressed and for platforms and ways to transmit this. For me the role of the curator has always been deeply connected to the way that artists conceptualise new systems, new forms of representation, new debates, new collectives as well as non-collectivist practices. When I work with an institution, I need support in order to develop a proposal that

Fig. 3.4 Clémentine Deliss and Metronome books, exhibition *Think with your feet* at Command N Gallery, Tokyo. Photograph by Masato Nakamura, 2006

emerges through the various discussions I'm having concurrently with artists as well as those issues that I'm observing around me. I need to find an institution that will provide a sheltering structure for what I want to do, to give me and the interlocutors I am working with the necessary freedom of movement.

In 1996, I turned to publishing in order to activate an alternative conduit between artists. *Metronome* and Metronome Press (1996-2007) enabled me to develop my position as an artist-to-artist curator. I sensed that the only way to run against the grain of institutional racism in the mid-1990s was to invent a conduit that was fundamentally *backstage*. At the time, I didn't feel that museums were the institutions that could provide this freedom of experimentation. Museums were entering the big bulimic phase that has continued until today, and were beginning to engage with the exploitation of *global* art. So I would find support from art schools in various European and non-European locations, managing to just about pay my rent in London through lecturing posts. My project *The Bastard*, for example, which I set up in 2000 in Scandinavia, was initiated in conversation with the *Laboratoire Agit'Art* in Dakar on the question of "magnetic speech" and produced together with art academies in Oslo, Bergen, Stockholm, Malmö, and Copenhagen. This was subsequently carried over to another long-term research project called *Future Academy*, which I initiated on all five continents and involved student cells in each location. Very often I was kept at arm's length by educational institutions by simply being given a consultancy rather than an academic position. In that way I could just about survive financially, and they didn't have to incorporate me within their respective, and often necessarily conservative, curricula.

What in your view produces an anthropological framing of an exhibition? Are there specific display techniques, modes of exhibiting that you would describe, for better or for worse, as typically anthropological? Is there such a thing as an anthropological or ethnographic exhibition?
Curatorial practice is a tool kit with which to articulate ideas visually and dialogically. In other words, the notion of trans-visual thinking needs to be at the basis of an exhibition. But monographic contextualisation and ethnological framing has continued since the inception of this genre of museum in the nineteenth century. Today this methodological intransigence has produced a lacuna between curatorial discourse and ways of working in an anthropology museum. That is the problem, because there is absolutely no connection. There's a class divide evoked through interior design. Ethnographic exhibits are like health food store displays in contrast to the high-end Gucci-style presentations of Nefertiti, for example.

And that's what we saw ten years ago with the exhibition next door to the Neues Museum redesigned by David Chipperfield. The one that dealt with the future Humboldt Forum was full of blown-up photos, decorative dots and wall patterns, and silly flags. And that was meant to be a serious exhibition to present the German State's largest cultural project!

... "Anders zur Welt kommen" (2009) ...
Exactly, and the problems were blatant with absurd displays such as bubble-jet prints of Native American chiefs fixed to easels. I mean, who comes up with this stuff? It's so mediocre. It puts you in a very difficult position because if you claim this is bad taste then you come across like some elitist. But frankly, there's an essential articulation missing. In my opinion, exhibitions are fields of inquiry. But their design appears like the big bad wolf in all of this. It doesn't help the process of emancipation, or the complexity of the decolonial process. It just makes it easier for a large audience to digest the Other, and that's a problem.

What I like about the Sarr-Savoy report on restitution is their notion of the emancipation of memory. Returns can trigger the latency of memory, something that we can recognise in every human being. And yet the debate continues to be framed through a notion of source, coming back to where the problem may have arisen. Restitution doesn't necessarily encourage the notion of contemporaneity that we badly need around these artefacts.

Contemporaneity, according to Rabinow, can only be activated through teamwork. You can't be contemporaneous on your own. And these objects can't be contemporaneous when they remain entrenched in the same disciplinary fields that they were placed in one hundred years ago. It doesn't make sense.

What we actually need today is a clash of the three civic institutions that I mentioned at the beginning. The university has to get inside the museum! The art school has to be in the collection!

How else can we engage with art histories that are more inclusive and contain a broader planetary dimension? The problem is that we don't see the material that is in storage and that constitutes these occluded art histories. It's easy to dismiss the importance of these collections today if you haven't got an author that's been recorded. At a moment, when art and art history students are becoming more and more diasporic, it is these collections that should provide the decolonial impetus for transformation.

I believe in creating a practice-based fieldwork inside the museum that can lead to a flourishing of transdisciplinary and transcultural approaches. If you're doing intelligent provenance analyses, you start to make real the presence of a different type of history. It's not about scratching around in filing cabinets for documents that were never written in the first place, but about enabling students from different disciplines and cultures to develop together contemporary meanings and identifications on the basis of these sequestered collections. It's also up to the art schools to demand access, so as to transform the canons of art history.

But you would call this endeavour 'art-historical' rather than 'anthropological'.
I would definitely see this as constituting new expressions of interdependent studies. For now, I tend to speak about the *art histories of the worlds* in the plural.

This kind of remediation process goes beyond the museum. The question is how can exhibitions create a decoloniality of art history? How can we go further? But there is another hindrance. Whilst we have to keep a focus on the inaccessibility of these vast collections of so-called ethnographic artefacts, we may run the danger of forgetting about twentieth-century art production in Africa, for example, with regards to painting. So there is a parallel issue around who is teaching art history where, and why there aren't more monographs being produced around essential named artists of the twentieth century who have worked and lived on the African continent, both male and female. I mean: Where are these monographs? How can we even begin to have an inclusive history of the past without this work? How can there be any kind of equity on a market level, if materials are not sent back and allowed to circulate? For me, this is a part of the issues we are facing today. On the one hand, one is creating an aura around iconic objects of restitution and, on the other, one is forgetting that there's a lot more in European ethno-colonial museums that needs to be brought into power. Meanwhile there is an absent concern about doing the difficult work of producing monographs on artists whose work has not yet hit the spotlight. In a few years, a generation of key artists will have passed in countries as different as Senegal and Nigeria. People of a certain generation, who lived through a lot, who experienced colonialism, independence, and post-independence, wars and transitions, will be leaving us. We don't need another Biennale at this point: We need an *infrastructural generator of memory*, a new kind of *museum-university* based on these collections.

Does it mean something to you to talk about curating as ethnographic and anthropological practice, or as a kind of fieldwork?
My PhD was on eroticism as a philosophical concept, eroticism as the intellectual and corporeal desire to go into something unknown, into something unforeseeable. I wanted to understand how eroticism featured within both anthropological and artistic discourses and interests. I saw eroticism as the connector that brings an artist close to that which anthropologists have also been fascinated with. It has more to do with the "avant-propos", or what I call "the *prelusive*" – in short, everything that is the *Vorspiel*, prior to the final production and experience or exhibit. It's that conceptual thinking that takes you on a route somewhere, replete with corporeal and epistemological violence that needs to be negotiated thoroughly and decentered.

When I took on the Weltkulturen Museum in Frankfurt, I knew that I was being ambitious, but I felt that at the age of 50, I had the right to put my stamp onto an institution, somewhere. I was the ninth director of this museum, and it was normal in anthropological circles to have a director who took a position, who held a stance. I couldn't just operate in municipal thin air. In a way, this was also my downfall: to insist on having a stance as a curator and museum director. It's probably why I don't get invited so quickly to debates about the Humboldt Forum because they know I won't be their handmaiden.

The idea of the Metabolic Museum-University that I am currently working on makes sense here. The museum-university states that the museum and the university are both places that have become stultified and normative. They're stuck in a rut. And the depot is the one area where everything is contained. It's the reservoir of future knowledge. So how do we create a new engagement of the publics? How does the visitor become a student?

For me, the museum-university is a sheltering structure where diasporic students of hybrid and diasporic disciplines can come together and research visual and conceptual routes into new meanings that are founded on the collections. Right now, we need more concept work that involves visual, heterogeneous, and polyversal thinking in relation to these materials that we have no right to occlude. European museums have no authority to stop people from seeing this material, even though they continue to exert this power. And it's our duty not to complain about whether the museums in the countries of origin are adequate or not. It's our duty to build working spaces, studying spaces, here in Europe, whilst restitution takes course over the next years.

The reason I work with artists is because they're the best transdisciplinary 'poachers'. But we need a lot more people from all sorts of studies and all sorts of backgrounds, without hierarchies. For this, there has to be a kind of commitment. The question is: "Can you give access to the *flâneur* as well as the specialist?" Yes, you have to. And you have to enable situations where you create fissures in regionalist studies. So you can no longer say: "This is an African issue, or this is a Sinologist's question, this is civilisation, or this is something else."

Note

1. The image on p. 130 is Figure 3.1 View into the Weltkulturen Labor, Frankfurt, with furniture designed by Mathis Esterhazy and various fish traps from the Weltkulturen Museum's collection. Photograph by Wolfgang Günzel, 2011.
2. See "Lotte or the Transformation of the Object", 1990, Styrian Autumn Graz at Stadt Museum Graz, Akademie der bildenden Künste, Konsthalle Malmo, Sweden. With works by Mike Kelley, Jeff Koons, Lubaina Himid, Haim Steinbach, and Rosemarie Trockel. Plus mass-produced items from Africa. Catalogue German/English with Isabelle Graw, Stuart Morgan, John Picton, Rasheed Araeen, Michel de Certeau, Georges Bataille. Catalogue published by Durch, Grazer Kunstverein.
3. "Organs & Alliances", limited edition portfolio of texts and image-works under the title EUROPE OR DIE with the participation of: Ismail Alaoui-Fdili (Morocco/France); Kévin Blinderman (France); Anne Dietzsch (Germany); Thibault Grougi (France); Seongju Hong (Korea/France); Paul-Alexandre Islas (Mexico/France); Rosalie Le Forestier (France); Philip Markert (Germany); Bocar Niang (Senegal/France); Jonas Roßmeißl (Germany); Araks Sahakyan (Spain/France); Clara Wieck (Germany). Presented at the Goethe-Institut Paris on October 17th, 2018. Produced in collaboration with the Ecole nationale supérieure de Paris-Cergy and the Hochschule für Grafik und Buchkunst, Leipzig.

Resisting Extraction Politics: Afro-Belgian Claims, Women's Activism, and the *Royal Museum for Central Africa*[1]

Sarah Demart

On 21 May 2016, at Brussel's Centre for Fine Arts BOZAR, the book *Créer en postcolonie 2010-15: voix et dissidences belgo-congolaises* ('To create in a postcolony 2010-2015: Belgian-Congolese voices and dissidence') was launched.[2] The edited volume is published by two cultural institutions: BOZAR and Africalia.[3] The book's point of departure was the absence of Congolese voices in the Belgian commemorations of the fiftieth anniversary of Congo's independence in 2010, in a context of long-term ignorance of Afro-descendants despite several decades of presence in Belgium (Demart 2013). As a reaction to this invisibility, the book brings together more than forty contributions from individuals with academic, activist, and artistic backgrounds to elaborate counter-narratives of the afterlives of the Belgian commemoration of Congolese Independence.

Just before entering the crowded room, the book's academic editors, Gia Abrassart and I, are discussing with the publisher and manager of the African desk of BOZAR. We are finally informed of the editorial pre-contract. Thirty minutes earlier, we threatened calmly but firmly not to go on stage and to boycott the book if we could not have access to the contract. The tension did not go down until we signed the contract giving four copies to each contributor and fifty to each of us for the promotion of which we were in charge.

When the moderator introduced us as the book's editors, in front of the two institutions' directors who funded the book, the director of BOZAR left the room. He would not give a speech. While this protocol transgression was labelled as a lack of professionalism by the institution, it is, for us, the culmination of several weeks of intense and exhausting negotiations with respect to the terms of the collaboration itself. It was a divergence of opinions concerning the book's spine (*la tranche*), which started this tussle. Only the book's title and the logos of the two sponsor-publishers would be apparent on the spine, which is the only visible part of a book when stored in a bookshelf. Neither of us, the journalist and the sociologist editing the volume, had paid any particular attention to this detail. Following the editorial process from afar, it was rather the book's contributors who interpreted the reductive labelling as part of rendering the 'diaspora' invisible for the umpteenth time.[4] The endless discussion about the spine of the book led to the similarly lengthy debate concerning an editorial contract on our request. The aim of the contract, as a third party, was for us to clarify the terms of the collaboration riddled with misunderstanding and divergences of views. Our request was perceived as a lack of confidence and therefore as a hostile act, while we saw the institutional call for confidence within this dysfunctional collaboration (editorial process, reviewing, authorship, intellectual ownership) as an injunction and a way to deprive us – as editors yet also as a collective of 64 contributors – of any agency.

Temporary inclusion and extraction politics

The quarrels around the book's spine and contract encapsulate a broader 'misunderstanding' between institutions and people of African descent as artists, activists, or experts, which is often framed as an experience of dispossession. The repeated testimonies of dispossession that I have more or less informally collected since 2004, as part on an immersion within different Congolese and then Afro-descendant circles of Brussels, show a wide range of temporalities and frameworks. This spectrum extends from occasional collaborations on the one end, characterised by either partial funding or logistical support provided to projects by people of African descent, to various forms of consultation on the other, intending to 'give' voice and visibility to people of African descent and their concerns. What these institutions have in common is that they need, produce, or circulate knowledge about Congo, people of African descent living in Belgium, or matters of race and racialisation, such as intersectionality, decolonisation, Afro-feminism, blackness, and so forth.[5]

In this chapter, I want to take seriously this dispossession experienced by people of African descent during collaborations or temporary inclusion within Belgian institutions. I will show that identifying misunderstandings or dysfunctions is not sufficient to explain why people of African descent, whether activist or not, consider that institutions appropriate their knowledge and sometimes bodies as part of more or less remunerated labor for/within Belgian institutions. I address these collaborations –which are seldom linked to long-standing inclusion or to diversity policies towards people of African descent leading to structural transformation of institutions (Ahmed 2012) – as instruments of 'temporary inclusion'. I will discuss the conditions under which the experience of dispossession that occurs through these devices can be addressed as an extraction politics (Foucault 1968; 1976; 1988).

Unlike major trends in Francophone social and political sciences addressing race as a subcategory of class, decolonial studies and black radical scholars consider that capitalism emerged from the outset as a racial and gendered regime (Andrews 2018; Davis 1982; Quijano 2007; Lugones 2007; Bhambra 2014). Extraction politics are at the core of racial capitalism and colonial regimes characterised by large-scale expropriation of natural resources, lands, as well as labour force, and bodies (Robinson 1983; Mbembe 2000; Tuck and Yang 2012). Looking at the difference between expropriation and exploitation, Fraser argues, in a conversation with Dawson, that while they are differentiated, these accumulation regimes are nevertheless interdependent. That means that exploitation and expropriation are differentiated categories of work (paid/unpaid) and of political status (free/non-free), which are historically and racially located, though they are intertwined in the global system of accumulation. In other words, the global logic of accumulation renders the political statuses of free – exploitable – working citizens and dependent – expropriable – subjects interdependent (Fraser 2016; 2017). In the post-colonial and neoliberal era marked by large-scale and intense circulations, the geographical distribution of economies of these different accumulation regimes based on exploitation and expropriation (North/South, centre/periphery) is becoming more complex. Fraser highlights the emergence of the figure of the worker-citizen, expropriable-exploitable, formally free but extremely vulnerable, which is no longer limited to peripheral populations and racial minorities. This refers to the notion of the "becoming-black-of-the-world" (*le devenir nègre du monde*), developed by Mbembe to account for the materiality of neoliberal policies (2013). Nevertheless, this evolution does not lead to an indiscernibility of the regime of accumulation as Dawson (2017) argues, and the expropriation remains closely linked to historical processes of racialization that need to be addressed in light with how black labor and bodies are rendered expropriable and disposable (Dawson 2017: 158–159). By contrast with the regime of accumulation of bodies, land, and labor within the global market and international circulation, knowledge is seldom addressed under the lens of expropriation, even as decolonial and post-colonial scholars have developed extensive research on the systemic destruction of local, native, and traditional knowledge and resistances strategies.

The scholarship on epistemic injustice is crucial for discussing the conditions under which knowledge can be rendered meaningless, disposable, and therefore expropriable. Following Fricker's seminal work on "epistemic injustice" (2007) – the notion by which she identifies the fact to ignore a knowledge because of the marginalised group of the knower or the incapacity of the concepts available to make knowledge understandable and to politicise experience – scholars have documented the epistemic effects of racial colonisation and colonial regime. In particular, they have shown that "epistemic exclusion" (Dotson 2014), "epistemic racism" (Grosfoguel and Cervantes-Rodriguez 2002), or "epistemicide" have been central to the imperial rationalities of domination and violence (de Sousa Santos 2014). While research has shown that traditional knowledge (such as medicinal plants) provide enrichment for multinational companies while being rendered worthless or invisible (Shiva, 2008 cit. by Godrie and Dos Santos 2017:16), the double-process of appropriation and devaluation of knowledge is less documented. On the other hand, the notion of "epistemic exploitation" is resourceful as it refers to the process by "which privileged persons compel marginalized persons to produce an education or explanation about the nature of the oppression they face" (Berestain 2016: 570). Looking at the position of women of colour in academia, Berestain shows how the social devaluation of the marginalised or the oppressed is raised as the very condition for an unpaid and unrecognised labor of epistemic production that is systemic.

Based on this literature, I will argue that resistances to epistemic exploitation brings to light the institutional economy of extraction based on temporary inclusion devices of the racialised others. I will focus on the resistance of Afro-Belgian militants – and, in particular, women – starting with the recent campaign for the return of objects stolen during colonisation. In particular, I seek to see how the different levels of Belgian, colonial and post-colonial, material and epistemic extraction policy are articulated from the point of view of Afro-Belgian women and Black subjectivities.

Researching activism

As a part of a study on Afro-Belgian activism (2011-2019), this chapter is grounded on a long-term ethnography within the organisation BAMKO-CRAN, which has led the campaign for restitution. My research initially focused on black social movements and post-colonial claims against the backdrop of a near total absence of public discourses on race and blackness. The social invisibility of black bodies in the institutional Belgian landscape led me to a more specific question about Afro-Belgian silencing in national narratives on colonisation and *living-together*. It is in this context that hybrid collaborations and publications took place, such as the book *Créer en post-colonie* co-edited with Gia Abrassard, as well as, in 2013, the special issue on the Congolese presence in Belgium in the journal *African Diaspora*, bringing together researchers and community activists (Demart 2013; Demart et Abrassart 2016; Demart and Robert 2018). This decolonial academic practice was motivated by the widespread epistemology of ignorance (Sullivan and Tuana 2007) and the obvious effects of colour-blindness and racial inequalities that I was approaching at that time as a mere lack of knowledge.

While I situate myself in a theoretical framework of feminist studies, decolonial/post-colonial studies, black critical studies, and cultural studies, my research is deeply rooted in an interactionist sociology of comprehensive and phenomenological inspiration (Goffman 1968; Becker 1982, Schütz 1987; Ahmed 2007). Accordingly, the research was 'on' activism and 'with' activists and was about creating an epistemic and material space at the edge of the academic and activist field, so as to bring into the conversation those who were experiencing Belgian coloniality in their daily life. At this point, it seemed crucial to me to break with the overhang position between researchers and activists, in particular in terms of theoretical framework (Weiner and Carmona Baez 2018; Jones 2018) – first, because the expertise seemed to me to be mainly located in the diaspora; second, because this expertise was linked to an experience of dispossession and to structural ignorance of 'African migrants', 'sub-Saharan', 'Congolese' in the field of knowledge production. Within this research framework, the tremendous transformation of the activist field since 2011 came to situate me within political and strategic divergences that happened to be gendered and within one of the most prominent organisations in terms of decolonial activism in the public debate. As an identified/designated member, I have been involved in a political praxis and a daily associative routine that led me, among others, to co-supervise and co-organise the publication activities of the BAMKO organisation and to provide theoretical and practical expertise without prejudging the purpose of this use. The political narratives and praxis *resulting* from obtaining this academic consultancy, however, belong to the activists and their rationales.

Against the backdrop of this research, I have collected the data on the campaign against the Royal Museum for Central Africa in Tervuren (henceforth: RMCA), led by BAMKO-CRAN in 2018, for the repatriation of human remains and restitution of cultural artefacts pillaged during colonisation, as well as for the recognition of the expertise of people of African descent used as means for gathering opinions.

While Afro-Belgian activism was part of a global mobilisation for restitution,[6] the Belgian campaign led to political recognition and resolution in a way that is unique in Europe. It is therefore crucial to report on the manner in which this activist praxis was carried out. I will show that behind this campaign for restitution, a double campaign was in fact at play: both for restitution – and the right of black nationals to take part in this conversation on the "Belgian national heritage" – and for the recognition of Afro-descendant expertise on a wide range of subjects including Congo, (de)colonisation, national identity and belonging, and the like.

Through the colonial genealogy of the RMCA and the long-term consultation process of 'diasporas', the collaboration institution/diaspora serves to magnify the tensions raised by a trans-anthropological project that would call into question the very foundations of theories, practices, and aesthetics inherited from colonisation (Ceuppens 2014; Rahier 2003; Macdonald et al. 2017). It also raises the question of post-colonial subjectivities in a highly racialised context. The number of people of African descent is estimated at 250,000; they face racialised patterns of integration that cannot be detailed here. Let me just outline a few significant figures: More than 80% of people of African descent consider themselves to have been the victim of discrimination, mainly in the field of employment and housing, while they are four times more likely to be unemployed than the national average, and while 56% report an overqualification (Demart et al. 2017)

This chapter provides information on how people who were not envisioned in the museum's reflection or institutional economics negotiated a place with stories that challenge the order of institutional representations and rationalities. Among them, some are actively engaged in a reflection on the conditions of possibility of trans-anthropological representations (see Toma Muteba Luntumbue, this volume). However, the primary aim of this contribution is to shed light on how people of African descent develop resistances and sometimes political action (Scott 1989; Martin Alcoff, 2008; Dorlin 2018; Vergès 2018) against institutional power. Accordingly, the renovation process of the museum (Wastiaux 2018; Van Beurden et al. 2018; Bevernage and Mesdagh 2019), which is at the core of this activism, is addressed through the gaze of activists or the experts of African descent designated by the representative organisation of the 'community'.

In a first part of this chapter, I explore the resistant practices of activist women against the consultation devices of the RMCA. I do so by considering the arguments of Mireille-Tsheusi Robert, head of BAMKO-CRAN, in the open letter she addressed to the museum at the beginning of the campaign for restitution and in response to a request for an interview. In the second part of this contribution, I look at how the campaign for restitution links with the colonial renovation process of the museum and the inclusion of black bodies within the institution by means of consultation.

The campaign for the recognition and remuneration of Afro-Belgian activists' expertise

In 2013, the RMCA, one of the oldest, and often depicted as 'the last remaining', colonial museums in Europe closed for renovation (Gryseels et al. 2005). In the following years, the renovation process was presented in the public discourse of the museum as part of a collaborative process of sub-'African diasporas' undertaken in the early 2000s. However, on the eve of the RMCA's reopening in December 2018, an intense media mobilisation took place for the restitution of property stolen during colonisation – conserved in the RMCA on an enormous scale – questioning the whole line of argumentation in the museum narrative, as expressed in the international sphere. The museum-diaspora collaboration came to be the subject of a public disavowal contesting the instrumentalisation of black bodies and the coloniality of the institution. The outdated and racist anthropological representations of the museum, the diversity policies (summoning Afro-descendant experts as external consultants), and the understanding of colonisation itself came to be the subject of public denunciation from Afro-descendant circles. The latter were informally organised around circumstantial alliances and through relations with a diverse range of actors, such as 'white allies', researchers and other academics, anti-capitalist political organisations, or decolonial movements rooted with a Moroccan heritage. While the museum (direction, curators, scientific boards) or activists may use the category 'diaspora' to name Afro-descendant voices, the social body of a sub-Saharan African diaspora is far from being a fixed and homogeneous category – nor is the full diversity of this diaspora represented in the Afro-Belgian organisations that took part in this campaign. Even so, the campaign showed unprecedented mobilisation developed during the museum's renovation process. The temporary inclusion of people of African descent through specific tools for representing 'the community', in addition to the lack of an agenda concerning restitution, refuted the museum's claim of any policy for genuinely cooperating with diasporas.

On 4 September 2018, the campaign for restitution had not yet been publicised, when Mireille-Tsheusi Robert, president of BAMKO-CRAN, published an open letter in response to a request for an interview she just received from the RMCA. The institutional request was as follows:

> I would like to interview you concerning your experience at the museum. I would like to know your vision for the functioning of the museum and, more particularly, what role the diaspora could play in the museum. This interview will not be made public; the aim is to get the opinion of members of the diaspora: What could it mean for Afro-descendant communities and for Belgian society in general?

The activist replied the next day with an eight-page pamphlet written down in one go that night, entitled "Open letter to the Colonial Museum of Tervuren. How dare you?". The pamphlet was published on the website of the BAMKO-CRAN association a few weeks later.[7] This letter explains why the consultation mechanism of this request cannot be understood in terms of a "peace offer" (Latour 2000) and why the request for an interview should have instead resulted in a contract that awarded expertise with adequate compensation.

> I notice that you suggest light-heartedly an "unpublished" and anonymous interview. In reality, your email is a request for structured but unpaid expertise by way of a meeting that is presented as informal and insignificant. In other words, you are asking me to give you a sociological analysis on the relationship between the [RMCA] and the African diaspora in Belgium for free, without any agreement regulating this knowledge acquisition. However, you will use the analysis in one way or another as part of your "employment contract" at the museum. Is the anonymisation of experts and the subsequent use of their knowledge production usually not considered plagiarism in our society? (...) You should have asked us to provide you with an external expert report on the basis of a contract. Based on an evaluation of the experience of the expert and partners involved, an appropriate payment would have been negotiated. To be sure, the diaspora does have expertise at its disposal, which needs to be valued and not exploited. (ibidem, pp. 2, 4)

The open letter took up the general points that had frequently been experienced by Robert and activists during processes related to means of 'consultation' (also briefly developed in a paper we have co-written), namely:

the activists' lack of control over the consultation process, the institutional racism within which these devices are developed, the way in which the consultation and the collected data are politically instrumentalised, the non-recognition of associative knowledge as expert knowledge (Demart and Robert 2018). However, the letter goes further by raising the question of the dispossession of activist expertise through different institutional mechanisms. Against the backdrop of the museum of Tervuren, this dispossession is from the outset subjectivated as an imperial formation.

> To a certain extent, it can even be said that thanks to Afro-descendants who would have a voice in the process, this last vestige of Europe's colonial museums seeks to be at the forefront of modernization policies. It must be said that, in recent years, European museums exhibiting their colonial capture have been in conflict with Afro-descendant communities who question the legitimacy of their cultural possessions, acquired in the context of colonial massacres. (ibidem: 1)

> It reminds me of the traditional black-and-white photos that any colonial tourist would take with the village chief and elders, giving the impression that they were in agreement when they were defeated. But this photo only relayed the colonist's story. The colonised person was relegated to silence while his skin colour and mere presence in the photo served as a moral guarantee for the colonist. (ibidem: 3)

The letter goes on by elaborating on how activist speeches are approached, considered, collected, and included in institutional narratives and policies. She starts with the anonymisation procedure.

> You will be looking for the best among us, those at the forefront of the diaspora's discourse, for important personalities – to then ask them to speak anonymously? You approach us as if we were mere "witnesses". But don't let our skin colour trick you, Madam, we are above all experts. (ibid.)

The activist diverts given categories to request subsequently a semantic and political requalification of the consultation. She aims at deconstructing a transaction which allows the (dis)qualification of activist knowledge, a transaction which risks creating conditions for the expropriation of activist knowledge. She suggests re-qualifying the object, terms, and subject of the transaction: This is not simply a collection of 'opinions ' or 'testimonies', she argues, but also 'activist expertise' (the subject matter) that is to be considered. The associative knowledge that will be collected cannot be reduced to an 'unpublished' and anonymous 'interview' while the real demand is for 'structured but free expertise' (the terms). Crucial to her argument is what qualifies the discourse: It is not the skin colour but political expertise constructed over time that is conveyed through expressions such as 'diasporic experts', 'the best among us', 'Belgian-Congolese voices concerned and competent', and so forth. This requalification requires denaturalising activist knowledge on blackness, race, and decolonisation, in addition to acknowledging the fact that activist knowledge is built alike.

By doing so, the activist affirms the interdependence of factual knowledge and expertise that institutional practices of appropriation dissociate when they delink expertise from their owner. The lack of structural change in terms of institutional policies which result from these tools for consultation explain activist reluctance to the reiterated request.

> I have also noticed that some institutions are not interested in actually implement[ing] the recommendations suggested by Afro-descendants, ignoring that their analyses have an impact on the institution's practices. At the most, the institution intends to give the impression of being open-minded and interested in their opinion. The experts should not be properly integrated in the mainstream organisation, otherwise they could exert their right to vote. (Ibidem: 7)

The eight pages of answers addressed to a 'simple' request for an interview must be understood in light of the requests that activists receive sometimes on a daily basis for unpaid/low-paid labor. Furthermore, the colonial shape of these consultation processes lies not only in the fact that activist or Afro-descendant discourses are not recognised as expertise or knowledge, but also in that institutional economy can be perceived as a coercive way to get access for free to epistemic labour. According to Berenstain

> A central feature of epistemic exploitation is that the labor demanded is unpaid and frequently unacknowledged and emotionally taxing. The coerce dimension of this labor is linked to a double bind which indeed raises the question of the more or less explicit institutional sanctions. (2016: 572)

As she states "marginalized persons often do not have the option to simply disengage from an epistemically exploitative situation without being subjected to harm as a result of their perceived affront" (ibidem: 576).

The second part of the open letter sets out a series of constraint techniques that facilitate the immediate and free access to this activist knowledge. She describes these techniques as reactions to the activist's absence of response or refusal to give access to her expertise. She states them as follows: "trial of ingratitude" (you are offered the opportunity to speak!), "accusations of narcissism" (who does she think she is to refuse our request?), "harassment" (repetition, insistence), "threat" ("her word will not be taken into account"). Their effect is to constrain the production of discourse.

Robert's open letter is an obvious narrative of epistemic exploitation that goes beyond the RMCA and the cultural landscape (as she comes from antiracist movements and is familiar with institutions involved in intercultural work). Even as this interaction and the offer of temporary inclusion occurs within the reference to the colonial history, however, it still raises the issue of a genealogy of expropriation.

She interprets the devalorisation of people of African descent as an economic system rooted in colonial times.

> The unpaid and unrecognised demands for "expertise" that provide an opportunity to treat specialists as "lambdas" or witnesses are rooted in the ancestral stereotype that Africans are not evolved, have not accessed knowledge and development, that they are not capable of abstraction, etc. Therefore, their expertise is regularly questioned or devalued. (ibid.)

This demand for re-qualifying the institutional request, contractualising the social and cognitive transaction underpinning the request, and eventually compensating the activist expertise brings to light a new mode of political resistance practices (Bassel and Emejulu 2017), as it imposes an *ad hoc* recognition of the expertise through the material.

It is not insignificant that the resistance to these racialised economies and ontologies are gendered. Women have not only reflected both in the private sphere and in their informal networks on the issue of free labour and the intersection of racial and gender domination, but they have also experienced male-dominated practices of subalternisation in Pan-African grassroots communities.[8] Likewise, the campaign for restitution led by BAMKO was organised around a constellation of women, while several experts mobilised within activist spaces attempting to build counter-narrative were constituted in particular by white men (researcher, journalist, lawyer). Pan-African associations were unexpectedly silent during this campaign that gave a collective dimension to the contestation of place consigned to Afro-descendant experts within institutional policies of knowledge production.

The campaign for the restitution of Congo's heritage: media and politics

Three weeks after the publication of this position paper, or *carte blanche* as it was referred to, on 25 September 2018, BAMKO-CRAN initiated a collective *carte blanche* entitled 'Belgium is lagging behind in the restitution of colonial treasures', launching the campaign in the media and public sphere (Demart 2018). Acknowledging the international dynamics for restitution, the letter calls for a restitution policy as well as a moratorium on the RMCA. To that end it additionally cites revelations by the journalist Michel Bouffioux[9] on the human remains from colonial expeditions and the almost 300 crates kept in various Belgian museums and royal institutions. Signed by some forty Belgian and foreign, including African, activists and researchers,[10] the letter generated unprecedented media upheaval.[11] On 3 October 2018, RTL-TVI organised a television debate as part of its Sunday programme on major social issues 'Giving back to Congo what belongs to Congo'. Mireille-Tsheusi Robert faced Julien Volper, curator at the RMCA, who was speaking on his own behalf; Yves-Bernard Debie, international art lawyer opposed to the idea of restitution; and the media expert for RTL-TVI, who was also opposed to the principle of restitution. Robert insisted on the legal concept of restitution, which does not necessarily involve the material repatriation of artefacts. She also called for an investigation into the origin or appropriation of objects and human remains, in order to repatriate unconditionally not only human remains but also stolen artefacts. Volper made claims for historical relativism regarding the "violence of the twentieth" century, whether it be Congolese or Belgian violence. As for Debie, he disputed the very separation between a "spoliated owner" and a potentially "illegitimate possessor", highlighting that the Belgian possession of objects ("thanks to the wonderful work of our museum and our merchants") has allowed for a transformation of the object from black art (*art nègre*) into one of classical art.[12] The illegitimacy of Afro-Belgian/diasporic voices in initiating and being part of this conversation came up through Volper ("Me, I know the artefacts, I'm not an activist") and would be reiterated privately on their way back from the TV studio, when the RMCA curator told the activist that if she wanted to be part of the national conversation on restitution, she should give up her Belgian citizenship.[13] In that line of argument, the material appropriation of artefacts not only operates through Eurocentric and racial hierarchies but also through a national lens that excludes black diasporic bodies from the conversation which basically revolves around: "What are *we* gonna do with *our* cultural objects/arts?"

In light of the debates that took place during this three-month campaign, this informal discussion is nothing but anecdotal. The RMCA, however, soon appeared to be polyphonic if not cacophonic. Researchers from within the museum published a paper on 17 October 2018, arguing that colonial crimes and expropriation cannot be relegated under the argument of "legal relativism".[14] Going against the museum's public voices, they demanded a research policy for advancing the precise information in regard of these objects and for implementing their restitution within set deadlines. They also argued that restitution should be considered as a physical matter that cannot be reduced to digitisation policies. It was signed by more than fifty researchers working in various Belgian institutions (cultural institutions, museum, universities), among them, several researchers who had signed BAMKO's *carte blanche*, despite the fact this new carte blanche did not call for a moratorium on the reopening of the RMCA.

The letter was published right after the conference 'Restitution of African cultural property: moral or legal question', organised by the Parliament's president Julie de Groote and BAMKO-CRAN. Clear-cut opinions had emerged between Guido Gryseels – the director of the RMCA, who proposed a 'USB key in hand' restitution policy, including the digitisation of artefacts – and the activists. Mireille-Tsheusi Robert began the conference by addressing restitution as a policy of reparation with respect to the material, but also in regard of the ontological, epistemic, and spiritual violence of colonisation. Meanwhile, Anne Wetsi Mpoma, a consultant for the museum and member of BAMKO-CRAN, went on to make people uncomfortable, pointing out the failure of the "concertation policies" that the museum was proud of having led. She emphasised the structural contempt on the part of the institutions for the Afro-descendant contribution.

Until the beginning of December 2019, BAMKO-CRAN went increasingly public with Mireille Tsheusi-Robert insisting on a moratorium of the RMCA's reopening, as well as making claims for the establishment of an expert commission on the collection's provenance, the unconditional return of illegally acquired artefacts, and ultimately a debate on the conditions of a return policy. This argument is also in line with the conclusions of the Sarr-Savoy report commissioned by the French president, following the activism of the CRAN led by Louis-Georges Tin, published in November 2018.[15]

At the end of these four months, the media effects of the campaign can be measured by the hundreds of pages of accumulated archives from the national and international press alone. Even so, the media sphere was only the visible part of the campaign, which at the same time was taking

Fig. 4.2 View of parliamentary debate with Mireille Tsheusi-Robert, Julie de Groote, and Anne Wetsi Mpoma. ©ASBL Nouveau Système Artistique

Fig. 4.3 Mireille Tsheusi-Robert during the parliamentary debate. © ASBL Nouveau Système Artistique

place in the political space and, on 11 March 2019, led the French-speaking Brussels Parliament to adopt a draft resolution launched at the instigation of Julie de Groote. With other activists, she met several times with the president of the Brussels Parliament but also with the office of the minister in charge of Equal Opportunities and with the socialist senator Simone Susskind, who introduced motions for resolutions in favour of the restitution of African cultural property into the Brussels Parliament and the Senate.[16]

Furthermore, given that Robert became the mediated figure of this struggle, the campaign could expand on strategic alliances within Afro-Belgian networks and beyond, thus involving the CRAN (Conseil Représentatif des Associations Noires / 'Representative Council of Black Associations') in France; the G6 (i.e., 'Group of the 6'), experts of Afro-descent involved in the concertation policies of African diasporas of the RMCA; the *Ateliers de la pensée collective*; and the collective *No Name*.

People of African descent and their networks: From national to international struggles

On 25 October 2017, BAMKO partnered with the international workshop 'Responsibility and post-colonial reparations' that we organised with Gia Abrassart from Café Congo, at the Théâtre National au Festival des Libertés in Brussels.[17] The workshop's objective was to question the notion of reparation from a transdisciplinary perspective. Louis-Georges Tin, president of France's CRAN, participated.

On 24 November 2017, a month later, Robert invited Tin to a conference entitled 'Enjeux post-coloniaux. Enseigner l'histoire, dé-raciser les institutions' (Post-colonial issues. Teaching history, undoing racism in institutions),[18] which she organised for the association BePax, in the context of a two-year mandate as an associate researcher and instructor.[19] The conference brought the two association leaders together. Tin took the opportunity to revive ongoing projects with the Afro-Belgian world, in particular the project on restitution. This rapprochement was symbolically reflected when the association changed its name to BAMKO-CRAN in early 2018. Fusing with CRAN meant that BAMKO's local engagement would be extended to a more international level. CRAN is represented is several countries all over the world and has put questions of reparation and restitution on the political, media, and legal agenda since 2012[20].

Furthermore, in June 2018, Tin was appointed the prime minister of the State of the African Diaspora[21] (he then left the presidency of the CRAN). Robert received a mandate to form the government of the African Diaspora in Belgium, while she did not communicate much on it. In the meantime, meetings were organised through legal consultation between the CRAN and Robert, and Tin remained in contact during the whole campaign. Significantly, the resolution project was drafted in Julie de Groot's office with Robert and Tin, right after the conference organised at the Brussels Parliament.

At the local level, as of 18 November 2017, just under a year before the launch of the campaign for restitution, BAMKO organised a series of conference on colonial museums and the role of diasporas in their decolonisation process, coordinated by Anne Wetsi Mpoma.[22] Monique Mbeka Phobam, cinematographer, was not directly involved in the organisation, though she has been very supportive and active in raising public awareness about the RMCA and the need for counter-narratives.

The aim of the first conference was to raise awareness of the representation and inclusion of people of African descent within the museum and to see how the community or the civil society could support them in their mission. Despite the confidentiality charter to which each Afro-descendant expert involved in the museum's renovation process was subject, several have taken a public stand to give an account of how their contributions have been rendered silent and ineffective. The consultation policies for the African diaspora led by the RMCA started in 2003 with the COMRAF (Comité de Concertation MRAC-Associations Africaines), which brings together different diaspora associations and museum representatives. Facing their limitations in following the renovation process, the COMRAF mandated in 2014 six experts of African-descent called the G6, the so-called 'groupe des six'. Among them was Gratia Pungu, who thought that the semantic blur of the appellation reflects the epistemological and political discomfort of the museum vis-à-vis the legitimacy of the experts of African descent. As Pungu put it:

> Some decide, others are "invited" to give their opinion. The relationship is clearly ambiguous, highly unequal and therefore opposed to any serious undertaking of decentralization, prior to the post-colonial approach. (2017: 2)

During the conference, Anne Wetsi Mpoma confirmed the theoretical vagueness surrounding the notion of decolonisation within the museum from the concrete negotiations undertaken with the G6 around the new exhibition (2017: 9–10), in addition to the fact that this notion came very later in the "modernisation" of the RMCA. The "concertation policy", she argues, is based on an epistemic violence opposing the researchers to the activists – though the latter are appointed for their expertise often based on an academic background – as wel as pitting the Diaspora against non-diasporic Africans. As she states later in an article published on the BAMKO website:

> African diasporas present in Belgium would lose their "authenticity" or legitimacy in comparison to Africans still living on the continent. A separation would suddenly appear between Diasporas and Others. This belief is strongly present and maintained among a majority of the [RMCA] staff. During meetings, experts from the diaspora often see objections that the Congolese in the country would be less demanding. This is a completely artificial categorization that reflects the difficulty of thinking of Afro-descendant nationals as nationals and not as foreigners. Or, put more simply, to let people be who they are, that is, cultural crossbreeds. As curators of contemporary art, historians or

black artists, we must deal with subjects related to Africa because we are absolutely not expected [to consult] on other subjects called "universal". At the same time, our legitimacy to deal with African subjects is systematically called into question because to have crossed the ocean and to be in contact with Western modernity would cut us off from our African origins.

According to Toma Muteba Luntumbue, also member of the G6, and contributor to this present volume, the museum's participatory museology is undoubtedly a "failure". He pointed to the lack of reversing the museum's "ethnographic gaze", as well as to the museum's opportunism and appropriation concerning the concept of decolonisation (Luntumbue 2018). As he stated,

> [i]t seems impossible to reconcile two visions: that of a management whose readiness to respect the reopening date, initially scheduled for October 2017, makes actions totally incoherent, and that of the African interlocutors who, discovering the theoretical void of the project, demand a complete overhaul (ibid.).

The year preceding the museum reopening, the 'diaspora' would no longer be involved in the renovation process. On 13 November 2017, a proposal from COMRAF was sent to the RMCA's direction to request being part of decision-making bodies and having the possibility of a daily presence in the museum (Billy Kalonji in Lismond-Mertes 2019: 37). On 8 December, the RMCA director responded by describing the request as unacceptable and threatening to change interlocutors if the terms of the collaboration did not suit them. The COMRAF and the G6 then suspended their collaboration with the museum for almost a year.

However, the G6 is far from being a homogeneous group, and tensions were perceptible from the first conference when one of the G6 members, Billy Kalonji, chairman of COMRAF, took to the floor. BAMKO had not provided a place for him in the panel as planned. The coordinator of the event, who is also a member of the G6, found her position towards the museum too conciliatory. After the round table, he stood up and addressed the microphone in front of the audience in a crowded room of about 70 to 80 people. He returned to the difficult integration of the G6 into the museum, while stressing that this was a major milestone in the history of the community: "We put a foot in the door, they didn't want us. We have come a long way… It took us ten years to get this foot in the door."

BAMKO and the Ateliers de la pensée collective

Robert's argument – as well as the policy paper, or *carte blanche*, released by BAMKO – is largely built on Martin Vander Elst's philosophical work, published on the BAMKO-CRAN website since 1 September 2018 (Vander Elst, 2018a; 2018b; 2018c).

Based on Michel Bouffioux's research and the legal proposals of the lawyer Christophe Marchand, Vander Elst considers the legal notions of "concealment" (of the remains of murdered persons) and "laundering" (*blanchiment*, which in French refers to laundering but also whitening) in framing the illicit and criminal appropriation of artefacts and remains of murdered persons as imprescriptible facts. By doing so, extraction practices are inscribed not only into the field of criminal law, but also into the long term of the history of artefacts: spoliation, displacement, classification, conservation, and so forth. By doing so, the ongoing economic benefit that derives from the institutional and scholarly practices is legally responsible (ibid.). Wanting to bring a collective conversation from outside the museum to what could become a restitution policy, he organised three workshops with Véronique Clette-Gakuba, a doctoral student in sociology at ULB within the Ateliers de la Pensée Collective at the Université populaire de Bruxelles. Robert was invited to present what was at the time a project of legal action against the RMCA to the first workshop held on 14 June 2018.[23]

Meanwhile, the ethnographic research of Véronique Clette-Gakuba has been looking at the disqualification of Afro-descendant experts as a component in the non-restitution policy of the museum. This disqualification, she argues, is epistemic, ontological, and political.[24] As mentioned by several members of the G6, she refutes the idea of a "concertation policy" as claimed by the museum while in fact it is a mere "consultation policy" that has been developed. Grounded on intensive fieldwork, she looks at how "diasporic subjects" are made subaltern within this consultation device through, on the one hand, an epistemological divide between the "neutral"/"objective" knowledge of the academics of the museum, and the "emotional"/"subjective" knowledge of the experts of African descent, and, on the other, a reduction of colonial and diasporic claims to an "equivalence system of subjectivities".[25] Finally, I build my own studies on Sarah Van Beurden's work, which shows how the language and practices of cooperation and development have not only depoliticised the Congolese claims for restitution but also the very notion of decolonialisation (Van Beurden 2015). Van Beurden argues that in spite of these developments, African experts – and in particular the Congolese elite, subjected to the cooperation and development policies – are the one and only interlocutor for the museum (see also Mpoma op.cit.10).

#NotmyAfricaMuseum#: The museum's reopening and No Name Collective

On December 8, the museum reopened its doors. Outside the museum, some twenty activists from various backgrounds gathered around the recently formed No Name Collective. No Name Collective is a satellite, artivist, and ephemeral group that reaches a younger militant population, both in terms of generation and militant engagement.

The core group is made up of Gia Abrassart, Catherine Moutoussamy, Aicha Achbouk, Amélie Umuhererezi, and Cindy Teme (who will later connect them with the Collectif Change asbl). Benjamine Laini Lusalusa aka Lili Angelou has just co-edited, with Jeanne Coppens, the first special issue of a *Zine Decolonial* on "Rethinking the museum". Completely self-financed, it brings together fourteen authors who have worked on counter-narratives to the discourse of modernisation and decolonisation, which the museum is developing with great support from the media. The meetings of the No Name Collective take place at CAFE CONGO, founded in 2013 by Gia Abrassart as a digital space, which, since May 2018, has been reorganising itself into an autonomous, cultural, and militant, decolonial and queer space.[26] The No Name Collective is composed of young black women of colour. Some of them are beginning their militant careers with this commitment to restitution – and will end it after the campaign. Mireille-Tsheusi Robert has not been able to respond to the request for guidance required by the desire for activist commitment and has proposed the creation of a group called the No Name Collective, which will in fact be coordinated by CAFE CONGO. Gia Abrassart is also a member of BAMKO, but is active on several activist fronts. A WhatsApp group has also been set up to bring together a larger group on a daily conversation although there were only a handful of persons actively mobilised on thinking and preparing an action for the day of the RMCA reopening. A protest t-shirt "NotmyAfricaMuseum–Stolen Artefact" was made by the young designer Imane Skaljac, inspired by the film *Les statues meurent aussi* by Chris Marker and Alan Resnais (1953). Not only is this t-shirt a symbol of protest, it is also an archive of that very moment of collective mobilisation.

The night before the reopening, they made hand pickets of cardboard painted in red to be planted in the ground as a symbol of colonial crimes that cannot be buried once for all. On 'D-Day', they distributed leaflets and planted dozens of red hands in the ground just outside the museum. The members of the G6 were outside and inside the museum where many members of the diaspora are gathered (artists, activists, civil society). Other activists joined them from the Collective Change asbl, Le Space, and Bruxelles Pantheres, Intal-Congo, while a few Belgian and international media channels covered the protestation.

In the following days, they intervened at the Palais des Beaux-Arts, disrupting an organised meeting on restitution between Congolese political and academic stakeholders and Belgian institutional leaders (notably the BOZAR and the RMCA), and pointing to the hypocrisy of the 'Afropean' politics of these institutions in the face of their diasporic public kept away from this meeting.

Fig. 4.4 Protest inside the museum. Photograph by Lyse Ishimwe,
© Lyse Ishimwe

Fig. 4.5 Protest outside the museum. Photograph by Lyse Ishimwe,
© Lyse Ishimwe

The COMRAF was inside the museum. A week before the reopening, the COMRAF made its presence during the inauguration conditional on a symbolic act. On the occasion of the conference organised by BAMKO at the Brussels Parliament on October 2018, the president of COMRAF, Billy Kalonji, and the director of the RMCA, Guido Gryseels, re-established contact. COMRAF then made the resumption of dialogue conditional on a symbolic apology and the installation of a commemorative plaque for the seven Congolese who died in 1897 during the human exhibition.[27] This was done a week before the museum reopened.

After only a month, the museum had already received about 45,000 visitors, with an average of 2,500 people per day. If the continued presence of militant protest in the media was unprecedented with an intervention of nearly a hundred representatives, it was nevertheless minor compared to the media power of the museum. A member of the G6 mentioned that more than 400 media representatives had reportedly covered the inauguration.

Robert withdrew from the public sphere and focused on the political lobby that appeared in the next few months. In May 2018, on the occasion of the visit organised by BAMKO to expose the new exhibition as well as confront curators and former G6 members, Robert was surprised to realise that RMCA curators were ignorant of and faced with the fact that the resolutions had already been voted in two parliaments, noting "we don't want to communicate too much about it until it's over, they could wake up". In the meantime, activists were invited to several conferences, including academic conferences, in Belgium and abroad to speak about the campaign. Given that constituting valid interlocutors who support the museum's policy of non-restitution and non-renovation operates as a subjection technique (Bennett 2004), one may ask whether the disregard of black diasporic voices is paradoxically what made the political lobby possible.

Conclusion

The Belgian campaign for the restitution of human remains and Congolese/African artwork stolen during colonisation has led to unprecedented political leadership. While activists and scholars have called for an implementation of these resolutions highlighting the risk of mere non-performative political action, the activist praxis leading to it needs to be underscored as well.[28]

In this chapter, I have shown that it was in fact a double campaign to redress historical injustices and to achieve social justice. The policies of material and epistemic extractions mark the juncture between these two campaigns, inscribed in differentiated temporalities and visibility regimes.

The highly publicised campaign for restitution took place over the course of a year, while the campaign for the recognition of expertise has been part of a long-term process and until then confined to a project of self-awareness.

The resistance that women of African descent developed to break with the means that silence and subordinate them shows that epistemic exploitation is deeply intertwined with the ontological and socio-political devaluation they experience. The demand for remuneration of activist expertise or contribution seeks to 'regulate' this racialised economy of knowledge circulation. Even so, the financial element appears more to be a tool for redefining the very terms of a social transaction and of a pattern of inclusion.

In Robert's open letter addressed to the RMCA request for an interview regarding her opinion of the museum, the requalification of the institutional request of "consultation" operates through a critique of institutional rationales, one that consigns Afro-descendants to an ontological and political exteriority. This is also what emerges from the narratives of the G6, structurally involved in a collaboration with the museum while the epistemic and material obstacles faced by G6 and which led to the dead end of "concertation" suggest an "epistemic oppression" (Dotson 2014: 2) rather than an epistemic exploitation. These different kinds of epistemic injustices should be explored further to better understand the institutional economy, yet in both cases vagueness occurs as the cornerstone and, by way of different techniques of institutional constraints, as the very expression of a racialised social contract.

Vagueness allows institutions not to be committed to the epistemic productions that they request of activists or experts of African descent. Instead, they are permitted to mobilise subjection techniques, from the de-qualification of epistemic production as 'opinion' or 'testimony' to more or less implicit requirements of epistemic labour (explanation, justification, education).

The feeling of expropriation is linked to this contractual vagueness and to the epistemic constructions and circulations it allows.

First, there is a supposed epistemological rupture between the 'subjectivity' of people of African descent on issues that concern them and the 'objectivity' of the knowledge produced by institutions. Then, there is the contribution requested of these same subjectivities in the form of unpaid/low-paying work. In other words, there is an epistemic exploitation under the guise of a 'recognition' policy, or even inclusion or diversity.

And it is precisely in this double movement that the process of making insignificant – that is, disposable – and expropriable knowledge takes place.

The entire concertation policy of the G6 and, by extension, the 'diaspora' relies on this principle and shows how temporary inclusion can work as a device of extraction. As a consequence, the expropriation does not refer not, or not only, to an individual experience of being exploited or silenced but more broadly to a device under which the epistemic production can be fragmented. This fragmentation not only makes knowledge disposable and expropriable but also depoliticises claims and forms of expertise. This is illustrated by the late arrival of the term 'decolonial' in the renovation process. The official RMCA discourse is disconnected not only from the G6 claims (regarding museography, methodology, temporalities, etc.) but also from a decolonial theoretical framework – all the while post-colonial or decolonial research are produced within the museum. This eventually leads to a capture of diasporic bodies in the museum narrative devices claiming for renovation and modernisation.

I conclude with the words of French artist and curator Olivier Marboeuf, formerly director of the independent space *Khiasma* in Paris, who put it as follows in an interview with Joachim Ben Yakoub:

> White cultural institutions – and here I include all the operators who constitute them; artists, curators, public and academics partners – understood that the capitalisation of knowledge has a limit, that they should be meant in different ways and that it would be necessary for them in the future not to only to capture the knowledge and experience of a body, but the body itself.

Notes

1. The first version of this article was submitted to the editors in February 2019. I would like to thank the two research centres of the Université Saint-Louis Bruxelles where I was invited to share my research on the basis of very preliminary versions of this text, namely the Observatoire du Sida et des Sexualités and the Centre de recherches et d'interventions sociologiques (CESIR). My thanks also go to Margareta van Oswald and Jonas Tinius for the quality of the editorial follow-up and the relevance of their comments on my article.
2. The image on p. 142 is Figure 4.1 #NotmyAfricaMuseum sketch. Image Imane Skaljac, © Café Congo.
3. Africalia is a cultural cooperation organisation, which intends to promote sustainable human development by supporting African culture and contemporary art. For a few years now, Africalia has opened the executive board to Afro-Belgians as a way to include diaspora concerns.

4. Here 'diaspora' refers to a critical position, given that not all the contributors are of African descent and only one of the editors has a diasporic background.
5. Institutions have their own historicity, and it is crucial to make it intelligible, in particular when it comes to the Afro-descendant or diasporic struggles for decolonising narratives and institutions. However, the experience of dispossession seems to transcends the historicity of the institutions themselves, even though cultural spaces have specificities. The historical centrality of the white gaze in the construction of Belgian expertise on Congo culture and artwork (Stanard 2019) is one of them, in addition to the material and discursive spaces that the cultural landscape has been offering over the past few years to the collectives of African descent. Around a whole series of issues – related to the representations inherited from colonization; the conditions for the possibility of new narratives; and new representations of history, blackness, or multiculturalism – these space-time dimensions bring together in a unique way a diversity of profiles (antiracist activists, artists, scholars, everyday people, etc.). The repeated collaborations and recurring (but not systematic) conflicts associated with the (temporary) inclusion of people of African descent into cultural institutions therefore need to be addressed with regard to this context, as well as in light with the commodification of culture, blackness, and even decolonial concepts.
6. See in particular the activism of the CRAN in France and abroad (http://le-cran.fr/); see also the *European Parliament resolution of 26 March 2019 on fundamental rights of people of African descent in Europe* (2018/2899(RSP)) and in particular point 8, 'Calls for the EU institutions and the remainder of the Member States to follow this example, which may include some form of reparations such as offering public apologies and the restitution of stolen artefacts to their countries of origin', http://www.europarl.europa.eu/doceo/document/TA-8-2019-0239_EN.html (last accessed 15 December 2019).
7. Lettre ouverte au musée colonial du Congo, à Tervuren. *Comment osez-vous ?*, https://docs.wixstatic.com/ugd/3d95e3_61db44196fa84233852196b4aa4552c5.pdf (last accessed 27 October 2019).
8. On the development of Pan-African grassroots communities in Belgium, see Grégoire, Nicole (2013), 'Faire avancer la communauté'. Diasporas africaines et associationnisme panafricain en Belgique. Thèse présentée en vue de l'obtention du grade de Docteur en Sciences politiques et sociales (PhD), Université Libre de Bruxelles, Bruxelles; on the exhausting of federative dynamic within grassroots communities, see Demart 2018.
9. 'Le crâne de Lusinga interroge le passé colonial belge', *Paris Match*, 21 mars 2018, https://parismatch.be/actualites/societe/129682/le-CRANe-de-lusinga-interroge-le-passe-colonial-belge. All his articles can be found on the website http://www.lusingatabwa.com/.

10. https://plus.lesoir.be/180528/article/2018-09-25/carte-blanche-la-belgique-est-la-traine-sur-la-restitution-des-tresors-coloniaux (last accessed 27 October 2019).
11. 'Faut-il restituer les objets sacrés du Congo aux Congolais?', Le Soir, 26 September 2018, https://plus.lesoir.be/180529/article/2018-09-26/faut-il-restituer-les-objets-sacres-du-congo-aux-congolais; Restitutions coloniales: pas si simple de renvoyer chez elles des antiquités bien intégrées..., Le Soir, 27 September 2018: https://plus.lesoir.be/180767/article/2018-09-27/restitutions-coloniales-pas-si-simple-de-renvoyer-chez-elles-des-antiquites-bien. The debate was also taken up by Flemish newspapers who only interviewed neerlandophone activists or experts.
12. See Silverman (2015) for a reading of the appropriation underlying this nationalisation of Congolese artwork.
13. Discussion with Mirielle-Tsheusi Robert, 3 October 2018.
14. 'Congolese kunst voor de Congolezen', De Standaard, 18 October 2018, http://www.standaard.be/cnt/dmf20181017_03852991/ Carte blanche: Le dialogue sur les trésors coloniaux doit l'emporter sur le paternalisme, Le Soir, 17 October 2018, https://www.lesoir.be/185112/article/2018-10-17/carte-blanche-le-dialogue-sur-les-tresors-coloniaux-doit-lemporter-sur-le.
15. On 23 November 2017, Macron expressed his desire for the temporary or permanent restitution of African cultural heritage throughout the next five years and he commissioned a few months later a report to implement the return of thousands of artworks. It was published on November 21, 2018, and two days later, Macron announced that Benin's 2016 restitution requests would be promptly answered with the return of 26 artworks that have been in France since the colonial period, cf. The Sarr-Savoy Report & Restituting Colonial Artifacts, center of Arts law, https://itsartlaw.org/2019/01/31/the-sarr-savoy-report/. The report is online: http://restitutionreport2018.com/sarr_savoy_en.pdf.
16. Motions for resolutions in favour of the restitution of human remains and cultural property from the colonial period introduced at the French-speaking Brussels Parliament: https://www.parlementfrancophone.brussels/documents/proposition-030571-du-2019-02-06-a-14-11-05 and to the Senate: https://www.senate.be/www/webdriver?MItabObj=pdf&MIcolObj=pdf&MInamObj=pdfid&MItypeObj=application/pdf&MIvalObj=100664026.
17. The workshop was supported by Bruxelles Laïque and Wallonia-Brussels Federation.
18. http://www.bepax.org/event/journee-d-etude-actualites-de-notre-passe-colonial-memoires-enseignement-et-discriminations,0000884.html (last accessed 03 December 2019).
19. http://www.bepax.org/ (last accessed 03 December 2019).
20. http://le-cran.fr/nos-avances/ (last accessed 03 December 2019).

21. The advent of an African diaspora state has gone almost unnoticed in the English-speaking press and is still little known to the general public despite official recognition. In December 2014, the president of the African Union, Mohamed Ould Abdel Aziz, mandated Louis-Georges Tin, then president of CRAN to set up the institutions of the African Diaspora State, and thus give substance to this project adopted in 2003 in the statutes of the African Union. With the support of His Majesty Tchiffy Zié, the secretary-general of the Forum of Kings and Traditional Leaders of Africa, Louis-Georges Tin formed a first government and set up development projects. The entire process was validated by the president of the African Union and the head-of-state of Mauritania, Mohamed Ould Abdel Aziz, who invited His Majesty Tchiffy Zié and the prime minister to formalise the state at the recent African Union summit in Mauritania.
22. « *Les diasporas décolonisent les musées royaux de Belgique?* (with Anne Wetsi Mpoma, Georgine Dibua Athapol, Bruno Verbergt, Véronique Clette-Gakuba) », 18 November 2017, Pianofabriek, Brussels; « *La restitution des trésors africains* (with Véronique Clette-Gakuba) » 15 September 2018, Pianofabriek, Brussels; « Restitution ! des trésors culturels volés en Afrique lors des massacres coloniaux (with Anne Wetsi Mpoma and Martin Vander Elst) » 22 September 2018, Pianofabriek, Brussels; « Restes humains en Belgique, témoignages de crimes coloniaux (with Michel Bouffioux), Saturday 10 November 2018: See the whole programme of conferences and publications on that issue: https://www.BAMKO.org/post-colonial (last accessed 03 December 2019).
23. De la restitution des objets culturels volés à l'Afrique 'le pygmée, le crâne et la place Lumumba', 14 June 2018; http://www.radiopanik.org/emissions/apc/apc-4-la-pygmee-le-CRANe-et-la-place-lumumba-/; Politique de non-restitution au musée de Tervuren Décolonisons!, 22 October 2018; http://www.radiopanik.org/emissions/apc/politique-de-non-restitution-au-musee-de-tervuren/; De la restitution des biens mal acquis inventer un nouveau droit, http://www.radiopanik.org/emissions/apc/de-la-restitution-des-biens-mal-acquis/.
24. In *les Ateliers de la Pensée collective* http://www.radiopanik.org/emissions/apc/de-la-restitution-des-biens-mal-acquis/ and in a conference organised by BAMKO-CRAN cf. V. Clette-Gakuba, Restitution des Trésors Africains, BAMKO-CRAN, 15 September 2018, Pianofabriek, Brussels.
25. Ibidem.
26. See: https://cafecongo.tumblr.com/.
27. Ibidem.
28. Restitution du patrimoine africain: appel pour un processus dé-colonial, *Le Vif*, 10/04/19, https://www.levif.be/actualite/belgique/restitution-du-patrimoine-africain-appel-pour-un-processus-de-colonial/article-opinion-1120145.html (last accessed 20 January 2020).

References

Ahmed, Sara. 2007. 'A phenomenology of whiteness'. *Feminist Theory* 8(2): 149–168.
Ahmed, Sara. 2012. *On Being Included. Racism and Diversity in Institutional Life.* Durham Durham, N.C.: Duke University Press.
Andrews, Kehinde. 2018. *Back to Black: Retelling Black Radicalism for the 21st Century (Blackness in Britain).* London: Zed Books
Bassel, Leah, and Emejulu Akwugo. 2017. *Minority women and austerity: Survival and resistance in France and Britain.* Bristol: Policy Press.
Becker, Howard. 1982. *Etudes de sociologie de la déviance* (trad. 1985). Paris: Editions Métailié.
Bennett, Tony. 1998. 'Pedagogic Objects, Clean Eyes, and Popular Instruction: On Sensory Regimes and Museum Didactics'. *Configurations* 6(3): 345–371.
Ben Yakoub, Joachim. 2019. 'Decolonial variations A conversation between *Olivier Marboeuf* and *Joachim Ben Yakoub*'. https://oliviermarboeuf.files.wordpress.com/2019/05/variations_decoloniales_fr_.pdf (last accessed 26 December 2019).
Berenstain, Nora, 2016. 'Epistemic Exploitation'. *Ergo: An Open Access Journal of Philosophy*, 3(22). Online publication: doi:10.3998/ergo.12405314.0003.022.
Bevernage, Berber and Eline Mesdagh. 2019. 'The Elephant in the room. How the AfricaMuseum has (not) shed its colonial "curse"', paper presented at the Congo Research Network, 29 May 2019, Vrije Universiteit Brussel, Brussels.
Bhambram Gurminder K. 2014. 'Postcolonial and decolonial dialogues'. *Postcolonial Studies* 17(2): 115–121.
Boast, Robin. 2011. 'Neocolonial Collaboration: Museum as Contact Zone Revisited'. *Museum Anthropology* 34(1): 56–70.
Ceuppens, Bambi. 2014. 'From Colonial Subjects/Objects to Citizens: The Royal Museum for Central Africa as Contact-Zone', in: *Advancing Museum Practices*, edited by Francesca Lanz and Elena Montana. Turin: Allemandi & C., pp. 83–99.
Davis, Angela. 1982. *Women, Race, and Class.* London: Women's Press.
Dawson, Michael. 2016. 'Hidden in Plain Sight: A Note on Legitimation Crises and the Racial Order'. *Critical Historical Studies.* Spring 2016:143–161.
Demart, Sarah, Schoumaker Bruno, Godin Marie and Adam Ilke. 2017. *Des citoyens aux racines africaines: un portrait des Belgo-Congolais, Belgo-Rwandais et Belgo-Burundais.* Brussels: Fondation Roi Baudouin. https://www.kbs-frb.be/fr/Activities/Publications/2017/20171121_CF.
Demart, Sarah. 2013. 'Congolese Migration to Belgium and Postcolonial Perspectives'. *African Diaspora*, 6: 1–20l; 136–152.

———. 2018. 'L'épuisement des dynamiques de fédération des association afrodescendantes: de la reconnaissance d'un sujet politiqu', *Analyse*, 31, Brussels: Edition Kwandika de BAMKO – CRAN asbl.

Demart, Sarah, and Gia Abrassart. 2016. *Créer en postcolonie: voix et dissidences belgo-congolaises (2010-15)*. Brussels: Bozar/Africalia.

Demart, Sarah and Robert Mireille-Tsheusi. 2018. 'Politiques de reconnaissance et tarification de l'expertise militante', in: *Dossier Diasporas, Analyse*. (21), special issue edited by Justin M. Ndandu and Sarah Demart. Editions Kwandika de BAMKO-CRAN asbl, Bruxelles: https://docs.wixstatic.com/ugd/3d95e3_fb20ddfb308b4d7f829a44f9526062b7.pdf.

Dorlin, Elsa. 2017. *Se défendre. Une philosophie de la défense*. Paris: la Zone.

Dotson, Kristie. 2014. 'Conceptualizing Epistemic Oppression'. *Social Epistemology* 28(2): 115–138.

Fraser, Nancy. 2016. 'Expropriation and Exploitation – A Reply to Michael Dawson'. *Critical Historical Studies* 3(1): 163–178.

Fricker, Miranda. 2007. *Epistemic injustice: power and the ethics of knowing*. Oxford: Oxford University Press.

Foucault, Michel. 1968. 'Entretiens avec Gilles Deleuze', in: *Dits et écrits*, T. II, pp. 312–313.

———. 1976. *La Volonté de savoir*. Paris: Gallimard, pp. 121–129.

———. 1988. 'La technologie politique des individus', in: *Dits et écrits*, T. IV, pp. 813–828.

Gillian, Mathys, Margot Luyckfasseel, Sarah Van Beurden, and Tracy Tansia. 2018. 'Renovating the AfricaMuseum. A conversation with Mathys Gillian, Margot Luyckfasseel Sarah, Van Beurden, and Tracy Tansia.' *Africaisacountry*. https://africasacountry.com/2019/04/renovating-the-africamuseum (last accessed 13 December 2019).

Godrie, Baptiste, and Marie Dos Santos. 2017. 'Présentation: inégalités sociales, production des savoirs et de l'ignorance'. *Sociologie et sociétés* 49(1): 7–31.

Goffman, Erving. 1974. *Les rites d'interaction*. Paris: Minuit.

Grosfoguel, Rámon, and Margarita Cervantes-Rodríquez. 2002. 'Unthinking twentieth-century Eurocentric mythologies: Universalist knowledges, decolonialization, and developmentalism', in *The modern/colonial/capitalist world-system in the twentieth century: Global processes, antisystemic movements, and the geopolitics of knowledge*, edited by Grosfoguel, Rámon and Margarita Cervantes-Rodríquez. Westport: Praeger, pp. xi–xxix.

Gryseels, Guido, Gabrielle Landry, and Koeki Claessens. 2005. 'Integrating the Past: Transformation and Renovation of the Royal Museum for Central Africa. Tervuren. Belgium'. *European Review* 13(4): 637.

Guido, Gryseels. 2014. *Towards the renewal and the renovation of the Royal Museum for Central Africa*. Africa Atlanta 2014 Publications. Georgia: Ivan Allen College of Liberal Arts, https://leading-edge.iac.gatech.edu/aaproceedings/towards-the-renewal-and-the-renovation-of-the-royal-museum-for-central-africa/ (last accessed 20 January 2020).

Latour, Bruno. 2000. 'Guerre des mondes—offres de paix'. http://www.bruno-latour.fr/fr/node/180 (last accessed 20 January 2020).

Lismond-Mertes, Arnaud. 2019. '"Comprenez notre deception"' *Ensemble!* 99: 37-38. http://www.asbl-csce.be/journal/Ensemble99.pdf (last accessed 20 January 2020).

Lugones, María. 2007. 'Heterosexualism and the Colonial/Modern Gender System'. *Hypatia* 22(1): 186-209.

Luntumbue, Toma Muteba. 2018. 'Tervuren: du musée empaillé au musée des illusions', in: *Bem* 297. Dossier: Bruxelles ville congolaise, edited by Mohamed Benzaouia, Thibault Jacobs and Andreas Stathopoulos, http://www.ieb.be/Tervuren-du-musee-empaille-au-musee-des-illusions (last accessed 20 January 2020).

Macdonald, Sharon, Henrietta Lidchi, and Margareta von Oswald. 2017. 'Engaging Anthropological Legacies toward Cosmo-Optimistic Futures?' *Museum Worlds* 5: 95-107.

Martin Alcoff, Linda. 2008. 'How is Epistemology Political?' in: *The Feminist Philosophy Reader*, edited by Alison Bailey and Chris Cuomo. New York: McGraw-Hill, pp. 705-718.

Mbembe, Achille. 2000. *De la postcolonie. Essai sur l'imagination politique dans l'Afrique contemporaine*. Paris: Karthala.

Mpoma, Anne Wetsi. 2017. *Quand le musée fait peau neuve*. Brussels: BAMKO, https://docs.wixstatic.com/ugd/3d95e3_86cdb150e1844154bc756110001487f6.pdf (last accessed 21 December 2019).

Pungu, Gratia. 2017. *N'est pas post-colonial qui veut*. Brussels: BAMKO. https://docs.wixstatic.com/ugd/3d95e3_e5ff44323157448283e04058bc9cf6ee.pdf (last accessed 21 December 2019).

Quijano, Aníbal. 2007. 'Coloniality and Modernity/Rationality'. *Cultural Studies* 21(2): 168-178.

Rahier, Jean Muteba. 2003. 'The Ghost of Leopold II: The Belgian Royal Museum of Central Africa and Its Dusty Colonialist Exhibition', *Research in African Literatures* 34(1): 58-84.

Robinson, Cedric. 1983 [1999]. *Black Marxism*. Chapel Hill: University of North Carolina Press.

Scott, James C. 1989. *La domination et les arts de la résistance. Fragments du discours subalterne*. Paris: Éditions Amsterdam.

Schütz, Alfred. 1987. *Le chercheur et le quotidien*. Collection Société. Paris: Librairie des Méridiens Klincksieck.

Santos, Boaventura de Sousa. 2014. *Epistemologies of the South. Justice against Epistemicide*. Boulder/London: Paradigm Publishers.

Silverman, Debora L. 2015. 'Diasporas of art: History, the Tervuren Royal Museum for Central Africa, and the politics of memory in Belgium, 1885-2014', *The Journal of Modern History* 87(3): 615-667.

Sullivan, Shannon, and Nancy Tuana. 2007. *Epistemologies of Ignorance*. Albany: State University of New York Press.

Tuck, Eve, and Wayne K. Yang. 2012. 'Decolonization is not a metaphor'. *Decolonization: Indigeneity Education & Society* 1(1): 1-40.

Van Beurden, Sarah. 2015. *Restitution or Cooperation? Competing Visions of Post-Colonial Cultural Development in Africa*. Global Cooperation Research Papers 12. Duisburg / Essen: Centre for Global Cooperation Research. https://www.gcr21.org/publications/gcr/research-papers/restitution-or-cooperation-competing-visions-of-post-colonial-cultural-development-in-africa (last accessed 13 January 2020).

Vander Elst, Martin. 2018a. '"Restitutions postcoloniales: de quoi parle-t-on?" Une interview de Mireille Tsheusi-Robert. Analyse n°1', in: *Musées coloniaux et restitution des trésors africains*, edited by Demart Sarah and Mireille Tsheusi-Robert, https://docs.wixstatic.com/ugd/3d95e3_d6100c6979f9470193d222cee21f3d78.pdf.

Vander Elst, Martin. 2018b. 'Restitutions postcoloniales belges: Comment "restituer" dans un contexte de recel et de blanchiment d'objets culturels spoliés. Analyse n°2', in: *Musées coloniaux et restitution des trésors africains*, edited by Demart Sarah and Mireille Tsheusi-Robert, https://docs.wixstatic.com/ugd/3d95e3_b5eb19aada2340a4b2c757eb77fc55a9.pdf.

Vander Elst, Martin. 2018c. 'Restitutions des spoliations coloniales: paternalisme, jeux de dupe et révisionnisme historique. Une interview de Mireille Tsheusi-Robert. Analyse n°3', in: *Musées coloniaux et restitution des trésors africains*, edited by Demart Sarah and Mireille Tsheusi-Robert https://docs.wixstatic.com/ugd/3d95e3_b5eb19aada2340a4b2c757eb77fc55a9.pdf.

Vergès, Françoise. 2019. *Un féminisme décolonial*, Paris: La Fabrique.

Wastiaux, Boris. 2018. 'The Legacy of Collecting: Colonial Collecting in the Belgian Congo and the Duty of Unveiling Provenance', in: *The Oxford Handbook of Public History*, edited by Paula Hamilton and James B. Gardner. Oxford: Oxford University Press.

Weiner, Melissa, and Antonio Carmona Báez. 2018. *Smash the Pillars: Decoloniality and the Imaginary of Color in the Dutch Kingdom*. Decolonial Options for the Social Sciences. Lanham, Maryland: Lexington Books.

"Finding Means to Cannibalise the Anthropological Museum"

A conversation with Toma Muteba Luntumbue

For this book, we have devised a set of interviews and position pieces with curators, since we regard curatorial practice as transversally agentive across the three main sections of this book: museums, contemporary art, and colonialism. We think that these are fields from which anthropology gets challenged and within which it is particularly mobilised in a generative way. Bearing this in mind, how would you situate your practice as a curator? Please elaborate with view to your involvement in rethinking (national) large-scale exhibitions and post-colonial and diasporic relations between Africa (esp. DRC) and Europe (esp. Belgium)?

I was the first non-white curator of Congolese origin to organise an exhibition in the former colonial museum in Tervuren (Belgium).[1] Symbolically, this is significant, given the context of requests to which the museum was paradoxically just beginning to be subjected, and which were lagging behind the dynamics of the museum scene in the United States and Great Britain. The preparation of the exhibition was an opportunity to take stock of the mutual ignorance of two worlds in Belgium: that of art and that of ethnographic museums. It was Boris Wastiau, for whom it was also the first exhibition to be curated in the Royal Museum for Central Africa in Tervuren, who invited me to organise a contemporary art section, while imagining a specific means for displaying about twenty objects from the collection. The Tervuren museum had not previously organised an art exhibition as such, but ethnographic exhibitions often resulted in ethnographic artefacts being reclassified as objects of art. The staging was often entrusted to freelance designers who used modes of presentation similar to art exhibitions. The particularly heavy physical setting – a neoclassical 'palace' of colossal proportions – was for me an opportunity to question the visual regime of this former colonial museum, a 'showcase' of colonisation according to Leopold II. The museum, in aesthetic terms, was the direct result of a universal exhibition organised in Brussels in 1897, and it employed modes of display characteristic of natural science museums. By confronting the works of contemporary artists with the means used in archaic demonstrations of objects, which often favoured a frontal relationship, I curated the exhibition *ExitCongoMuseum* (2000/2001) in a way to provide an opportunity for questioning the usual taxonomic presentations. More precisely, *ExitCongoMuseum* forced the Tervuren Museum to adopt a self-critical approach and to carry out an ideological decoding of its collection.

Fig. 5.2 ExitCongoMuseum, Johan Muyle, L'impossibilité de régner, 2001, © J.M.Van Dyck

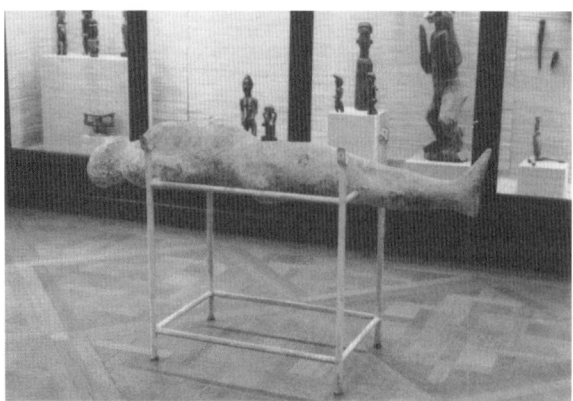

Fig. 5.3 ExitCongoMuseum, Philip Aguirre y Otegui, l'Homme de Tarifa, 2001, © Koen de Waal

More recently, as artistic director, I organised the 4th and 5th Lubumbashi Biennales in the Democratic Republic of Congo, my country of birth.

The theme of the 4th edition was entitled 'Meteoritic Realities' ('Réalités Filantes'). The exhibitions and events proposed for the Biennale questioned the diverse and complex way in which artists perceive a 'disposable' (*jetable*) reality, where nothing seems destined to last. This title was freely borrowed from the great Martinique poet, philosopher, and writer Edouard Glissant. The 5th edition was entitled 'Bedazzlement' ('Eblouissements'), which evoked both the wonders, seductions, fascinations, and blindness specific to situations of cultural, political, and economic changes as well as upheavals affecting the world. Preparing and presenting an exhibition in the DRC, one is exposed to various risks, to real limits, both material and conceptual, but it also provides opportunities to unknown 'elsewheres'. To show works of art in Lubumbashi asks you very seriously to imagine the representations, prejudices, and expectations of one's audience.

The 4th and 5th editions of the Lubumbashi Biennale took place in a climate of political tension in a country close to a state of emergency. Working in a large mining city like Lubumbashi required us to grasp the energy, movement, and rhythms specific to the city, unconscious choreographies of bodies that ignore or tame each other in the public space, and to integrate them as essential parameters for the exercise of the exhibition.

To sum up, the role of curator allows for confronting artistic as well as cultural otherness. It is a position from which it is possible to observe, on the one hand, the planetarisation of artistic gestures and the language of images as essential vectors of communication and, on the other hand, the singularity of each person's existential experiences confronted with a strong local context of a unique and irreducible reality.

Up until recently, art history and European art museums focused predominantly on (a history of) European art, while non-European art was mostly regarded and professionally constituted as the domain of anthropological research and anthropological museums. In what ways does your thinking and curatorial practice try to pervert or change the way we look at these distinctions of European/non-European, West/non-West? Could you perhaps expand on how the last Lubumbashi Biennale constitutes a case-in-point?

In 2003, I organised an exhibition of 28 contemporary artists, the vast majority of whom came from different African countries, at the Palais des Beaux-arts (BOZAR) in Brussels. The challenge for me at the time was to demonstrate that the meaning of 'African contemporary art' was obsolete and abusive. It had the consequence of denigrating artists by racialising the notion of contemporary art. This move also imposes a neo-primitivist and exoticist view of the productions of non-white artists, leading to the marginalisation of groups to which an artificial unity is attributed simply by their supposedly belonging to a 'Black Continent'.

Since 'Contemporary African Art' is perceived as synonymous with art from this so-called 'Black Continent', my selection of artists included artists living and working in Africa, but also others based outside the continent. I also invited an artist from the Philippines, Gaston Damag, and Keith Piper, a British artist of Afro-Caribbean origin. The title of the exhibition *Transfers* evaded the mention of 'Africa' or 'African' altogether in order to avoid the essentialisation of the participating artists. Abstaining from using the word 'Africa' in my title aimed at drawing attention to the works themselves, rather than to racial or geopolitical considerations. The management of the BOZAR in Brussels, by contrast, deliberately promoted a differentialist point of view, producing new posters with an explicit self-portrait of a Burundian artist, Aimé Ntakiyica, dressed in Scottish clothes and with the title *Transfers, African artists of today*. This conflict over the title of an exhibition is indicative of the permanent balance and tension of power in the cultural milieu at the time.

At the Lubumbashi Biennale, we asked ourselves how local artists could seize the opportunities for openness promoted by the Biennale without being victims of a form of homogenisation, neither of style nor of gaze. To this end, I imagined an experimental workshop to accompany young artists before the Biennale that took place between July and September 2017. Through this programme, the Biennale wanted to engage with ten young creators recruited in the country's four major cities: Kinshasa, Goma, Kisangani, and Lubumbashi. They worked on the implementation of their artistic projects, focusing both on practical tools (workspaces, content) and on dissemination tools (places, actors, networks). The workshop programme consisted of practical and theoretical seminars during which young artists worked with local mentors (artists, curators, critics, researchers) and invited guests. The principal aim was to reduce the distance between local artists and artists from other countries by allowing them to associate for a longer period of time than just the few hours before opening of the Biennale.

What does it mean for this art now to be collected at art museums rather than anthropological museums? Can you describe how you

regard these disciplinary divisions, and whether and to what extent you see or even participate in breaking down these divisions?
These disciplinary divisions do not mean much to me, since I remain optimistic about the changing perspectives in museums. It is necessary to challenge, or even break, the codes of hegemonic representation of anthropology museums by producing exhibitions of contemporary art that cannibalise their method. Often the presentation of ethnographic objects is marked by a special 'aura' when they are exhibited in an 'art' museum. While they are historically attributed a lower market value, they are, at the same time, being given a magical character. In addition, the discourse that accompanies their productions is often spiked with pseudo-anthropological remarks that deny them any contemporaneity. For a long time, the way we looked at artists and talked about them resembled the way we look at objects. By hybridising display techniques, it is possible to create a space that allows these visions to be questioned and to show complexity in order to produce new meanings.

This is essentially what I tried to propose with the exhibition *Ligablo*, which I organised at the Royal Library of Belgium in Brussels between November 2010 and January 2011. The context that gave rise to this project was the commemorative frenzy surrounding the celebration of the fiftieth anniversary of the independence of the DRC in Belgium throughout 2010. These commemorations irritated some Congolese nationals living in Belgium for the strange way in which it smacked of the rehabilitation of colonialism. The *Ligablo* exhibition began with informal discussions and meetings with members of the Congolese community living in Brussels and elsewhere in Belgium. It was decided that the experiences of this minority could become the exhibition's principal subject.

The title *Ligablo* refers to an object that is omnipresent in the urban landscape of Kinshasa. It is a stall, of variable size and morphology, made with

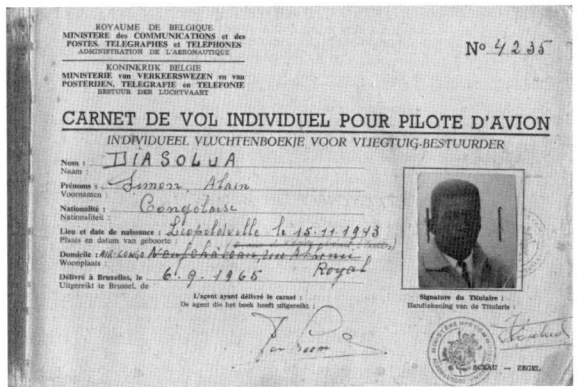

Fig. 5.4 Ligablo (personal document), © Toma Muteba Luntumbue.

wooden boards, on which various basic necessities are sold individually. More than an activity essential to the daily survival of the population, *Ligablo* is an act of resistance. It is the hallmark of the informal economy, a sign of an urban condition in which public deficiencies generate survival systems and alternative agents – particularly ingenious marginal agents. It is this polymorphic object that served as a model for the construction of the scenography, and which became the symbolic image of the exhibition.

A non-exhaustive corpus of emblematic objects – objects of everyday life, personal objects, video images, private photographs, and works by contemporary artists – were brought together with the idea of offering a kaleidoscopic vision through which nothing was spared: civil wars, years of dictatorship, criminal exploitation of resources, failures, dreams, and so on. This constellation of images, ways of thinking, desiring and dreaming was an attempt to respond to ethnographic narrative as a historically codified form of representation of an 'Other' that was privileged until then by numerous exhibitions. The *Ligablo* exhibition was neither linear nor chronological. The challenge was that discontinuity and heterogeneity become ramparts against a form of museum didacticism.

The constitution of the corpus of the exhibited objects went through several stages, methodical, disordered, fortuitous, lucky. The lenders were strangers, friends, intermediaries. During the preparation, it became very clear that Congolese networks, in general, were initially based on family networks. And that it was family ties that made it possible to keep the memory and transmit the identity of the community, an identity that was itself feverishly maintained thanks to a few – sometimes derisory – objects (identity documents, old bank notes, vaccination cards, school reports, driving licences from the country of origin, etc.) and an abundant private iconography.

How do you relate to anthropology's legacies in the present? Where do you grapple with anthropology today? We mean this in the sense of where do you think that critical and, in your view, interesting or new knowledge production concerning anthropology takes place today?

The study of transnational cultural processes, cultural globalisation, or urban anthropology are among the fields that interest me, especially in their methodological aspects. Anthropology is necessary to analyse the most urgent phenomena of our contemporaneity. Which grids for measuring the near and the distant coexist in the face of the telescoping scales produced by globalisation? Between "connectedness" (being in relation) and "contiguity" (being next door)? Which links exist between the places and territories experienced by individual or rather, collective identity? What importance should be given to local places and local times today?

To answer this question more precisely, Jean Bazin's words are helpful. He claimed that

> Ethnography, the writing and staging of differences, the manifest signs of an essential otherness, have now multiplied and universalised: Ethnography is no longer restricted to the West's gaze on 'its others' (...) – the indigenous peoples of its colonial empires who have become immigrants of its cities. Cultures are now just as much images of what these others manufacture and disseminate of their identity and that we consume. (...) Everyone acts as one's own ethnographer and tries to display and make have their cultural difference recognised as an indication, as proof of their essential otherness. There have never as many cultures as today. (2002: 88)

In view of the different initiatives attempting to decolonise museums and academia in Euro-American contexts, how do you consider the role of curatorial practice and institution building in the Belgian context? In what ways, if any, do you see these initiatives around decolonisation as continuing, rethinking, or expanding the work of institutional critique? Feel free to comment on these terms themselves.

In a Europe that is increasingly forced to transform its ethnographic museums into places of exchange and cultural integration, it was long awaited that a new exhibitionary regime would emerge in Belgium's Royal Museum for Central Africa in Tervuren. Many people thought that the new museum would review colonialism, while reinterpreting its own exhibition methods. It would, many hoped, subsequently commit itself to confront all kinds of taboo questions and, even if no answers could be found to the raised questions, at least enable the questions to be put at issue.

Since its reopening in December 2018, after a three-year closure for renovation, the Tervuren Museum has not ceased to be present in the media, due to the anxious expectations it had raised and to the opacity of its project management. The project's theoretical and epistemological void contrasts with the media activism of the museum's leaders: There is no real revolution, no project, no new narrative despite the museum's efforts to present itself as such. Beyond its patrimonial, symbolic, and memorial importance, Tervuren is just one symptom among others of a sly and complex Belgian unease about its policies for representation of cultural alterity.

Following the example of its many foreign counterparts, the Tervuren Museum wanted to define as a priority the involvement of six experts of

African origin to work closely with the museum's research department and the project team responsible for setting up the future reference exhibition. I was one of the six experts and witnessed how this collaboration – weighted of controversy, product of improvisation – developed over months in a climate of mistrust and rigidity. Overall, it is a failure, since the discussion space turned into a place of power struggles. It would therefore be inappropriate to talk about Belgian 'decolonisation' and even less so to talk about the advent of a 'post-ethnographic' or 'post-colonial museum'.

Many decolonial critiques are especially aimed at anthropological museums and collections. What, from your point of view, makes an 'anthropological framing' in an exhibition? Are there specific display techniques, modes of exhibiting, and framing, that you would describe – for better or for worse – as typically anthropological? Is there such a thing as an 'anthropological' or 'ethnographic' exhibition?

The fact that the visitor is *physically present* in a museum or exhibition space is the common denominator of most exhibitions. Exhibitions offer visitors a variety of opportunities to entertain different perceptive relationships. Visitors can evolve in the space as a mobile eye; they stop, look, read, listen to an audioguide, concentrate on an object, and so on. But in a classic anthropological or ethnographic exhibition, the presentation of objects is marked by the primacy of *discourse*, which sometimes even borders didacticism. The scientific law often dominates the museography.

Classic presentation devices reflect violence, translating an aesthetic of colonial domination. For me, the showcase represents the zero degree of exposure. These *dispositifs* remain stuck in some museums in the manner in which aesthetic objects were exhibited in the 1930s.

Current forms of museology are a compromise between different forms of presentation. There may not be or no longer be a form of pure ethnographic museography. Although it is necessary to mention the modes of display and techniques specific to anthropology museums, it must be noted that much effort has been made to break down these old models. And of course some museums remain prisoners of an ethno-stylistic, aesthetic, formalist presentation; with the showcase as a privileged device, which, in turn, influences the public reception of non-Western arts. This display *in vitro* condemns objects to live out of time. It is one of the oldest criticisms of ethnographic museums that are marked by classificatory thinking, because they are denying contemporaneity and historicity to non-Western objects and their producers.

In accordance with a paradigm of post-coloniality or post-modernity, different practices associated with the museums have developed in recent decades: 'xenophile' exhibitions, articulated through self-criticism, symposia, and publications in favour of the renovation of the anthropological museum, or the emergence of museums without objects. The recent development of participatory or inclusive museologies confirms this standardisation of practices – a practice of consulting, if not associating, any group which defines itself as a social or cultural entity corresponding to that which the museums represents.

But the question that recurs with great force is whether anthropological museums are the most legitimate places to address issues related to the representation of cultural alterity.

Do you recognise these kinds of framings also in non-anthropological museums? For example, in modern art museums that employ framings traditionally used in anthropological museums?
An exhibition of contemporary art can take the form of a pastiche, a quotation, an appropriation, or an archaeology of the *dispositif* of the 'museum of ethnography'. It can also seek to deconstruct the history of the gaze through an analysis of the exhibitionary regimes of anthropological museums. The possibilities are extremely varied. In 2017, the Palais de Tokyo in Paris devoted an exhibition to the diorama, a *dispositif* inherited from the nineteenth century. Coming from theatre, the diorama has been widely used in natural science museums as a means of staging knowledge about the world and in anthropology museums in their desire to contextualise objects. The Palais de Tokyo exhibition thus addressed the visual heritage of colonialism by problematising the diorama as an exhibitionary *dispositif*. The architect David Adjaye structured his *Geo-graphics* exhibition in Brussels in 2010 in a thematic subdivision according to geographical areas that characterise the African continent: Sahel, Maghreb, Desert, Savannah, Forest, and Mountains. This organisation encouraged the idea that the natural environment influenced cultural production. In doing so, David Adjaye paraphrased the ecological distribution of four sections – desert-prairie-valley-forests – suggested by the American Museum of Natural History in New York at the beginning of the twentieth century. At that time, similar to anthropology, the contextual approach affirmed itself with its tendency to place the object in its cultural environment in relation to its social organisation, religious life, political systems. I find it difficult to determine whether this approach is a conscious or unconscious borrowing from the museography of anthropological museums, but this aesthetic affinity surprises in its deterministic and primitivist character.

Related to this question, it is evident that terms and problems once associated with the difficult legacies of anthropological work (we are here thinking of notions like 'native', 'indigenous', 'subaltern', 'Global South', etc.) are increasingly 'en vogue' in contemporary, especially, post-colonial art discourse. How do you witness the transition and migration of such terminologies?

In the field of post-colonial contemporary art, there is a desire to build a theoretical apparatus in the face of an ever more complex world, a result of the numerous disjunctions of globalisation, imposing new openings as well as limits that question inter-ethnic or interracial relations. Language remains a crucial determinant in such a context, particularly with regard to the survival of the traces of colonial hegemonic order.

It seems to me that the term 'indigenous' as it has been used recently in the French cultural space, has been used as a metaphorical reference and for its political charge. But such terms, according to the researcher Pap Ndiaye (2008), are inappropriate to translate contemporary social situations. Even if contemporary problems have an obvious connection with the colonial past, they should be thought in their relative particularities.

A paradoxical situation is reached when an inflation or denaturation of these terms takes place in the contemporary art world and they become pseudo-concepts emptied of their initial meaning.

Note

1. The image on p. 174 is Figure 5.1 4th Lubumbashi Biennal, 2014, © Georges Senga.

References

Barthes, Roland. 1957. *Mythologies*. Paris: Seuil.
Bazin, Jean. 2002. *L'anthropologie en question: altérité ou différence?* Paris: Odile Jacob.
Ndiaye, Pap. 2008. *La condition noire. Essai sur une minorité française*. Paris: Calman-Lévy.

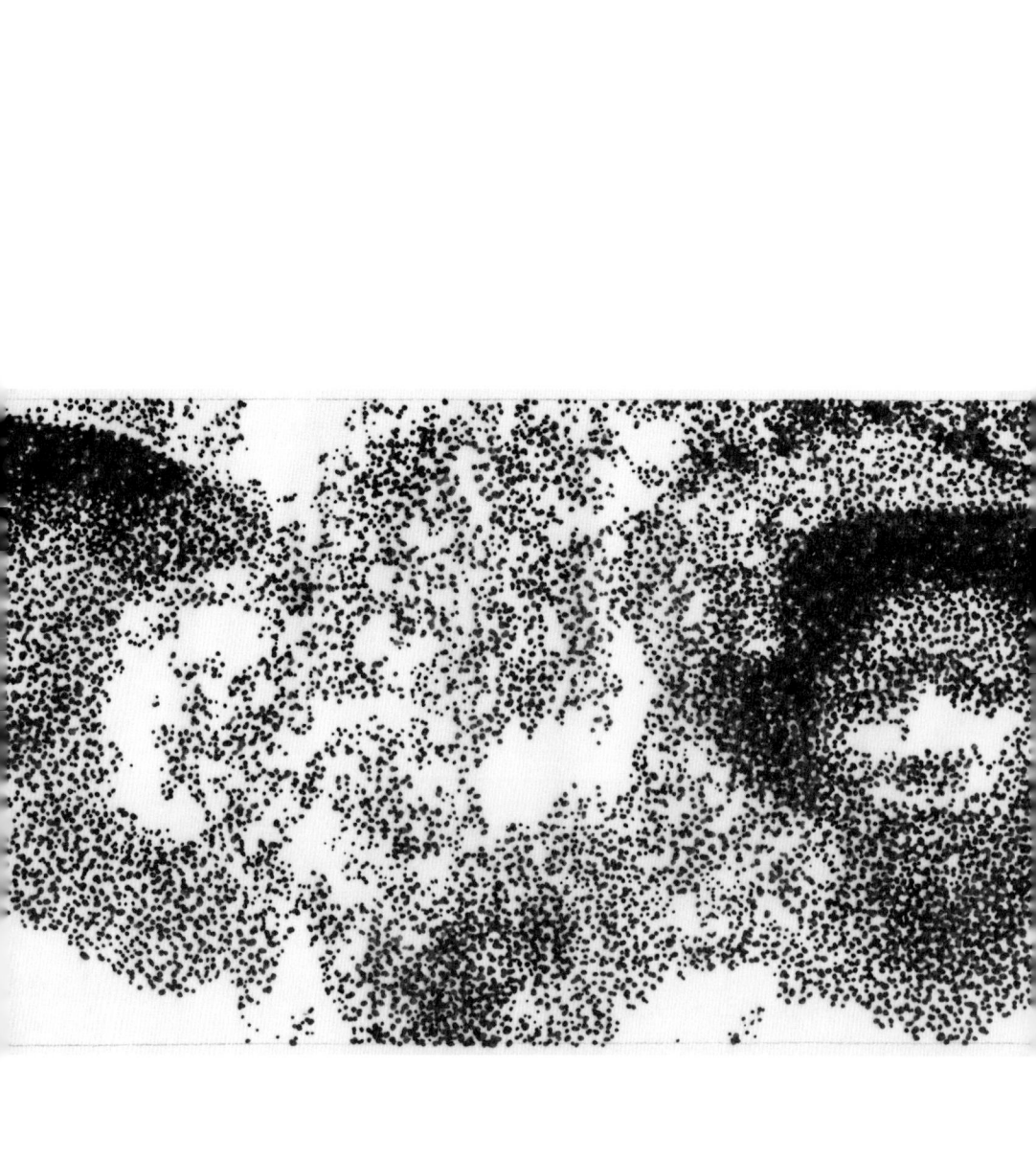

Animating Collapse: Reframing Colonial Film Archives

Alexander Schellow and Anna Seiderer

> We see the world through other eyes, while admitting that they might as well be our own. The same world has a different look, because it was at a different time that it was looked at. We contemplate it through an image that does not appear to be invented, but which confers a duration to the gaze through which we in turn become aware of it. (Belting 2004: 287)

In February 2016, the Brussels art school École de Recherche Graphique (ERG) held its annual conference in the historic Henry Leboeuf Hall at BOZAR in Brussels.[1] It was an opportunity for the ERG and the Royal Museum for Central Africa (RMCA, Tervuren, Belgium) to engage in structural cooperation for the purpose of granting access to colonial archives for artistic engagement. The RMCA's director, Guido Gryseels, opened the session by presenting the renovation project of the museum (it reopened on 8 December 2018). Next, the head of the history and politics department introduced the colonial propaganda film collection in the form of an alphabetical primer ("A" is for "Adventure", "B" is for "Bwana Kitoko", etc.). The atmosphere had already become charged when the director was speaking, but by the letter "B", the audience seemed to explode. They implored both speakers to stop their "unbearable" discourses, which were perceived as imbued with a tone of colonial paternalism. The interruption of the session by the audience offered, paradoxically, a great opportunity to open a discussion on the forms of disseminating and rewriting such highly sensitive archives. Unfortunately, the museum representatives engaged in the project felt personally targeted and offended by the incident and refused, at that time, to pursue any form of collaboration. The protest simultaneously addressed the visual material and the language and forms through which it was de facto disseminated by the museum. While the director's words appeared to the audience to be a kind of managerial (re)empowerment of a Belgian colonial past, the cheerful attempt by the head of the history and politics department disturbingly expressed the violence of writing history in the form of *one* story (Benjamin 2000: 441), claiming a neutrality for science, which might help one to get over the emotional charge of the images in question.[2]

If the productive critique of anthropological knowledge production engaged *by* as well as *in* the academy since the publication of *Writing Culture* (1986) has had any epistemological and political repercussions for the material collections in ethnography museums, it seems to be less relevant in regard to images. The currently contested anthropological representation to which the editors refer in this book's introduction is based mainly on the classification of cult and cultural objects as 'ethnographic' artefacts once they entered museum collections. The main debate since the Macron conference in Ouagadougou in 2017 and the publication of the restitution report by Felwine Sarr and Bénédicte Savoy (2018) is based on the political context of the objects' acquisition and their epistemological requalification as data for academic research.[3] By contrast, the colonial film collection produced over a period of fifty years in Belgian Congo, Rwanda, and Burundi, which we are discussing in this chapter and which was subject to the panel described above, has not been the object of any restitution request. It is worth mentioning, as was observed by a colleague, that the museum used the term 'restitution' for the first time[4] in the context of a project to digitise the films. In anticipation of the fiftieth anniversary of the independence of Congo (DRC), the Royal Museum for Central Africa, KADOC of the Catholic University of Louvain, and the Royal Belgian Film Library joined forces in a project to digitise some of the nearly 800 films. The aim was to 'restitute' to universities, national archives, and 'the general public' in Congo, Rwanda, and Burundi what they described as 'shared cultural heritage'. In two years, 150 films were digitised and were to be handed over solemnly to Joseph Kabila on 30 June 2010. He did not attend the reception, however, so the official 'restitution' could not happen.

Restitution was proclaimed for those objects that no one wanted back, as they are considered Belgian propaganda material. For the same reason, diaspora members and African colleagues contested the institutional designation of the films as a "shared memory" or an "asset of Central Africa".[5] On one side we have the rhetoric of the RMCA, now renamed Africa Museum,[6] and the self-proclaimed 'guardian' of Central African material culture. On the other, contemporary criticism is made manifest, expressed with vehemence by diaspora members who contest the identification of such representations with any kind of 'reality' in Congo, Rwanda, and Burundi. It is precisely this gap, that demonstrated the necessity to reframe the work on colonial films by transforming it into an artistic project, hosted by art schools and institutions. As Boris Wastiau wrote:

> In the specific cases of the Belgian museums, they have a responsibility as curators of a shared Belgian-Congolese heritage and a duty as 'public historians' to properly label and interpret the provenance of cultural artefacts acquired in the most inequitable context and to address in exhibition galleries all sensitive issues of colonial and post-colonial history. (2017: 461)

Wastiau reframes the idea of "shared heritage" to refer to the colonial violence that spawned the museum and its collections. The colonial violence mentioned by Wastiau denotes here the physical violence committed on the continent by Belgian soldiers and officers, which was doubled by the colonial rhetoric and the invention of the concept of "Congo", still defined in geographical terms today (Wastiau 2017: 463). The aim is not to challenge the reality that this concept became once it had been elaborated in 1884 at the Berlin Conference, but to observe that the fiction disseminated by the museum frames the colonial images within an ontological approach that, in our view, repeats the violence and conflict.[7]

In 'The Trouble with the Ethnological' (2015), Sharon Macdonald describes the presentation of an experimental prototype exhibit for an ethnological museum – a model exhibit that aimed to challenge stereotypes inscribed in particular exhibition frameworks. She quotes the curator, who faced many epistemological and political questions from the exhibit's visitors, as concluding that "it is so much easier if you are an art museum!" (Macdonald 2015: 211). The institutional migration of the film archive from the RMCA to African and European art institutions, which we address here in this contribution, is not based on the idea that colonial artefacts might become accessible once they are released from their historical context (such as the context of ethnography museums). Rather, their displacement from an ethnography museum into an art museum carries the risk of decontextualising and aestheticising the colonial past (Seiderer 2018). Regarding films produced in colonial contexts, the institutional displacement moreover changed how to handle and question the films and their conflictual memories.

With respect to the editorial proposal by Margareta von Oswald and Jonas Tinius (see the introduction to this volume), we observe how colonial images have been reformulated, rethought, and repractised once they moved from the institutional context where they had been framed as historical collections to an art project hosted by contemporary art institutions. This move complicates how we approach the images, as they are not mainly considered documents or representations but empirical and temporal objects involving the viewer's body and his or her memory (de Baecque & Delage 1998; Antoine & Perret 2015). Different to a historical approach searching for the unknown within the images and to a cultural approach focusing on their narrative aspects, the artistic based research we focus on here highlights the experience of viewing them today in the context of the field of contemporary art and within the framework of ongoing artistic methods that are collectively experienced (see also Binder, Neuland-Kitzerow & Noak 2008; Schneider & Wright 2013). The institutional migrations of the Belgian colonial film archives, generated by a collapsed collaboration between the ERG art school and the Royal Museum for Central Africa, epistemologically and politically reframed our study of them.

This chapter starts by observing how the RMCA's semantic ambivalence toward the visual material is embedded in the institutional frame of the images. They are considered as a collection that the museum has to 'take care of', and on which it is tasked to produce knowledge, yet without questioning and problematising the historical context on which the archives and collections build. Subsequently, we focus on the epistemological and political reframing of that semantic ambivalence of the colonial film collection within artistic practices, such as the drawings and animation Alexander Schellow has developed in the frame of the collective project GREYZONE ZEBRA.[8] In order to make this tangible we witness the changes that occur once the historical film collection is 'gleaned' within its silences, fragments, and heterogeneity. We continue the analysis with a description of the artistic gestures that took place in several art institutions in France, Belgium, and the DRC Congo. The invitation of the editors offers us the opportunity to build on reflections that we first formalised in *Critical Arts* (Schellow and Seiderer 2017). Here, we centre on Alexander Schellow's notes on two films shot during the colonial expedition in northern Congo led by Armand Hutereau between 1911 and 1913. Thus, the last part of this chapter is specifically dedicated to the drawings and animation developed with the same archival film material, and suggests how it leads us to an epistemological shift – becoming non-specular images of colonial past. This process, renewed by the practices initiated within the institutions hosting it, creates a singular context through which it becomes possible to apprehend the generative and troubling "awkwardness" (Tinius 2018) of the colonial films, as museum collection and as colonial representations.

Those processes highlight the reflexivity implied in the concept of the 'trans-anthropological', developed by the editors in their introduction. The institutional displacement of the research practices on the film collection and the specific artistic gestures – such as the notes, drawings, and animation developed within those particular frames – makes tangible the transformations of what has been stuck in a matter of representations of ethnic identities. As suggested by Oswald and Tinius, the prefix *trans-* enables a thinking "through, across, and beyond" the supposed represented identities, but it also overcomes the idea that they can only be studied as either anthropological or artistic material. The notes and the drawings, with which the animation films are made, are tools shared by both. On the one hand, the tools allow for overcoming their academic boundedness and, on the other hand, initiate a stimulating reflexive dialogue on the development of anthropological representations.

Institutional framing of colonial images: Ambivalent tropes

Belgian colonial cinematographic production remains fairly unknown to a broader international public and is a controversial subject in current discussions of the colonial past. Even if, from a scientific perspective, one could consider this field of production a significant document about Belgian colonisation, its narratives and mythology constitute a very sensitive matter. After all, Belgian cinematographic production presents an ideal image of the colonial project from which any kind of violence is erased. As pointed out by Ramirez and Rolot (1990: 6), the main goal of this cinema was to build an impressive image of the "*colonie modèle*". The erased violence, however, does not only result in sedimentation within the narrative structure of the images. That is, it is not reducible to the representation but is also inherent to the trope built on those images. Our argument is based on the fact that violent representations of the Belgian colony are already well-known and accessible in newspapers and on the Internet.[9] Freddy Mutombo's process presents an example of artistic responses to the digital circulation and availability of colonial images. Since 2009, he has developed his work on Belgian colonial photographs taken in the Congo Free State and in Belgian Congo between 1890 and 1960 and reinterpreted the images, by default, as a result of not having access to the photographs at the RMCA.[10] His first artistic gesture is thus of a methodological nature. It constitutes a 'second-hand' corpus by gleaning from historical or artistic sites and works that are accessible online or have been the subject of previous publications. His second artistic gesture consists of transforming the status of these colonial photographic archives, which become, in this artistic context, images of Belgian colonisation. Finally, his third gesture concerns the memory of the colonial past engaged by this practice.[11]

As the violent scenes recorded in photographs became accessible to civil society, political opponents saw an opportunity to stop Leopold II's diabolic invention of the Congo Free State (Ndaywel è Nziem 2009: 296). Thus, we align ourselves with the argument that the images of torture and mutilation perpetrated under the governance of King Leopold II had an important impact on the political opposition to the Congo Free State once they became reproducible and exportable to new political and social contexts. It is precisely these contexts which build a framework through which colonial exploitation is contested. As a consequence, we might say that the violence we explore in this artistic project is not so much focused on the narrative structures of the images – the represented violence – but rather highlights the frameworks into which images' meanings and resonances can be reflexively addressed. Therefore, the violence we are looking for in the project is invisible, it is the violence which desensitises us to the images, leading us to look at them as images of a distant past.

An other example that offers reflection on how the manipulation of the images radically changes our perception of them are the colonial photographic archives in *Congo belge en images* (2010) by Carl De Keyzer and Johan Lagae. They embedded aesthetically seductive images in the violent context of exploitation by restituting the historical context and giving voice to the protests that had occurred since the nineteenth century. As a filmic approach, we take as a reference Peter Kubelka's *Unsere Afrikareise* (1966). His extremely meticulous editing reveals the barbarism inherent to a hunting safari filmed by Austrian tourists along the Nile, transforming the meaning of the a priori hagiographical images into fierce criticism of what we can identify as colonialism and ethnocentrism.

These few examples point to the bivalence of tropes – and therefore the necessity to build specific critical frameworks – into which colonial archives can be perceived in their historical and memory thickness.

On a rhetorical level, we have already referred to certain ambivalent concepts such as "shared memory" and "shared heritage", as they were used in a contradictory sense.[12] In the same way, the notion of the "showcase" is also worthy of reflection. The museum's institutional position, publicly announced by the RMCA director in February 2016 at BOZAR, was to present itself as a "showcase" for "DRC Congo,", "Rwanda", and "Burundi". The ambiguity of the concept "showcase" is relevant to understand the conflict related to the film collection, insofar as it is used in different senses by the institution and its critics. The institutional rhetoric considers showcasing a metonymy, while it is perceived as a metaphor by those who contest the knowledge production that collections were supposed to serve.[13] As a metonymy, the museum's collections are supposed to stand for a direct link with cultural practices in the former colonies. As a metonymy, again, the colonial images are considered valuable witnesses of practices that were threatened by colonisation. As a metaphor, the collections are already considered in their fictional dimension, given that the concrete correspondence as such is impossible. Visual collections such as photography and films, like other colonial museum collections, are subject to criticism (Clifford 1997; Bouttiaux 1999; Couttenier 2005; Edwards, Gosden & Phillips 2006; Wastiau 2017). Unlike artefacts collected in the former colonies, visual collections were produced by the colonisers. In this regard, Belgian film production resembles cult and cultural objects that were classified as ethnographic artefacts once they entered into storage, even though they had mainly been collected by officers of the International African Association for Exploration and Civilization of Central Africa,[14] agents of the Force Publique[15] and, rarely, anthropologists (Couttenier 2005). Even when conducted outside explicit colonial frameworks, anthropologists collected within a positivist perspective, which gave rise to their self-criticism (Geertz 1973; Clifford & Marcus 1986). The links that the visual traditions of anthropology developed with the photographic medium, and later with film, changed from its early beginnings until the end of colonisation. The changes were linked to theoretical and singular apprehensions of the medium, which, at its very beginning, was considered a purely mechanical reproduction tool: "Because it was mechanical, photography was believed by many during this period to be a direct reflection of nature and reality" (Sherer 1992: 33). This relationship changed across contexts and over time, and even if anthropology may be considered to have distanced itself from visual mediums – when the research was dedicated to abstract themes such as myths, rituals, and social structures that were considered for their "immateriality" (Mauuarin & Joseph 2018: 6) – anthropology has always maintained a strong and complex relationship with film, photography, and drawing (Edwards 1992; Grimshaw 2001: 16; Guido & Lugon 2010; Mauuarin & Joseph 2018).

In our case, we want to underline that Belgian colonial film production was not created by anthropologists but, rather, by amateurs who progressively became professionals. Nonetheless, visual media, including photographs, offer insights for anthropological research and artistic practice (Edwards 2001: 27-50; Pinney and Peterson 2003). Artistic creations, such as those on colonial archive collections and family films, constitute a performative framework which renders explicit the interplay of various registers of memory and oblivion.

A gleaned archive. The GREYZONE collective's art project

As a consequence of the withdrawal of the RMCA, the work on the Belgian film archives of the former colonies of Congo, Rwanda, and Burundi shifted into the critical debate over colonial and ethnography museum collections and their history of domination and spoliation (Couttenier 2005; Edwards, Gosden, Phillips 2006; Bouttiaux 2009). Through the collaborative work on colonial film with a collective whose emergence we describe below, the aim is to go beyond the aporetic position of a radical self-reflexivity[16] and to turn these highly sensitive archives into material that elaborates aesthetic forms and gestures through which "other ways of doing memory, heritage and identity" are engaged (Macdonald 2013:3). In response to the conference at BOZAR, we proposed building on the incident through an experimental workshop dedicated to the film material at the Ecole de recherche graphique (ERG) art school in Brussels.[17] As expressed by the audience, tensions were partially generated by the lack of spaces dedicated to critical discussions on colonial past, and the art school offered such space.

At the same time, we discussed the space-aesthetic-political setup of possible workshops and performative screening sessions, and it became clear that the institutional framework of a school[18] or museum, with their defined spatial codes of screening, conference, or exhibition spaces, could not offer such a flexible experimental format.

It was partially this institutional migration which led us to redefine the project, status, and aims. What was initially a hybrid process between different frameworks (a description that remains somewhat relevant today) became an artistic project sustained by art institutions whose aims are no longer to produce knowledge about former colonies that might have been recorded in images, but to address contemporary perceptions of colonial images. The project involves several artists – such as Leila Burnotte, Milena Desse, Arthur Gilles, Sandra Heremans, Maxime Jean-Baptiste, Nelson Makengo, Freddy Mutombo, and Antje Van Wichelen – and is based on collaborative practices. It is structured around moments of exchange, which are constantly reformulated by the spaces and people involved.

In this respect, we would like to highlight a workshop held in the project space Khiasma in Paris (22-31 May 2018).[19] Recently closed because of budgetary restrictions, Khiasma was defined by its founder and director Olivier Marboeuf as a transitory space that made no distinction between artistic, scholarly, and various other forms of knowledge production. Instead, it was based on reflecting on artistic practice as a political, economic, and social tool. During this artistic residency, sustained dialogue with Marboeuf and the philosopher Catherine Perret provided a productive critical framework for the different artistic research projects.

The practice proposed by the GREYZONE collective is itself to a large degree based on an unstable position in relation to colonial film images. The non-availability of the film collections and their edited form intended for serving colonial propaganda led the collective to also become involved with private amateur films, which had been produced and mostly kept by private families. However, the project does not exclusively focus on the aspect of these films being made and kept by families, but rather more basically on their specification as non-edited film material created in a colonial context. These films – unlike the colonial propaganda film collection at the RMCA and the missionary films at Kadoc – do not constitute a collection responding to specific categories. They are not collected but gleaned, drawn together from various sources, such as individuals approached by members of the group, or found at flea markets or garage sales. Our practices developed in this context are based on three main axes: (i) collective (and partially public) film screenings, viewed also through the lens of note-taking, an exercise inspired by surrealist writing practices (Schellow and Seiderer 2017), (ii) long time residences during which artists engage more deeply with the film material by developing personal or collective artistic works, and (iii) the constitution of a digitalised archive hosted by several African and European institutions. It is through the lens of studying such family footage, that also readdressing specific films from the colonial propaganda film collection becomes possible for us – namely, footage such as the Hutereau film materials (more specifically, see below), which by their rather unclear category between amateur and professional, in their unedited form and time-related from a colonial gaze 'under construction', offer a particular porosity among this body of films.

Thus some members of the GREYZONE project, including us, aimed to constitute a reflexive device through which to understand how one views such kinds of films. We try to take into account the viewers' imagination of that past and the different ways one rewrites, remembers, and forgets. This resonates with Jonas Tinius' proposed mobilisation of the concept of "awkwardness", which "describes a state of self-conscious discomfort in response to things or practices perceived as improper or unacceptable" (2018: 145). The reframing of the colonial images within the artistic project, sustained by art institutions and schools, enables us to work with such "discomfort". Indeed, these images relay such discomfort, which is as such neglected or denied by the official institutional positions of the museum at the initial conference in BOZAR. The films we focus on are embedded in various frameworks, such as personal childhood memories, data for scientific researchers of colonial history, and ethical questions as witnesses of the unacceptable. The difficulty, and value, of the project is based on the process by which singular images are transmitted into a critical discussion on a colonial past.

The gleaned films disrupt the idea of a collection in which the images are implicitly embedded. In this regard, the footage shot by Hutereau[20] is of particular relevance to our reflection on the notion of 'trans-anthropological', as elaborated by the editors of this volume. Hutereau, a former military officer under King Leopold II, wanted to write a book on the people of the Uele region (Hutereau 1952). As part of our practice, Schellow created animation based on this particular body of films, which formed the first artistic proposal rooted in this stage of the project,[21] thus transversing the different steps proposed within the GREYZONE process. The specific practice of animation performed by him allowed us to shift the debate from questions of representation – where anthropology and animation share the same critical reflections – to those about memory. According to Hans Belting, such a praxis of animation as developed by Schellow might be considered to "confer [...] a duration to the gaze through which we in turn become aware of it" (Belting 2004: 287). This awareness is that of the symbolical and physical frames, which provides meanings to colonial images.

Towards non-specular colonial images

Our analysis of Schellows' animation films leads us to reconsider critically our own assertions of a critical work engaged with the images, once they migrated from their historical institutional context, such as that of the RMCA, into an artistic 'environment'. Methodologically, we look at the epistemological and political consequences of this migration of colonial images by focusing on two gestures: first, the impact of institutional displacement on our perceptions of those images and, next, their rewriting process through a specific practice of animation. We first try to understand in how far this displacement, 'facilitated' by the withdrawal of the RMCA, radically changed the form and the material of our research on images shot in colonial times.[22] Secondly, we focus on one specific practice developed in the framework of a project, as a continuity and singular answer to the critical approach on colonial images tackled by the artistic collective GREYZONE. The field of animation here builds an inestimable framework through which to reconsider the self-criticism engaged in by anthropology, insofar as it can offer a reflection on the ontological status in regard to photographic and filmic representations (Honess Roe 2013: 140). Having access to anthropological archives such as colonial films through the practice of animation, therefore, can transform the fetishist relationship we have in regard of visual collections, leading us to reconsider critically the notion of anthropological representation.

The animation films developed by Schellow on the expedition of Armand Hutereau in northern Congo are put forward in the continued exercise of note-taking that we have been exploring since the beginning of the project; they thus change the status of the colonial images. No longer considered documents of the past,[23] as they were for anthropology at the end of the nineteenth century (Edwards 2018: 33) – a reading to which Hutereau's images still refer – they now constitute instead a memory praxis.

Performing images

Alexander Schellow's animation can be discussed in reference to a debate initiated by Honess Roe, one of the most influential theoreticians in the field of documentary animation. She relates photography and drawing to memory, considering them "way[s] of accessing the past" (Honess Roe 2013: 139). While for anthropologists at the time, the images were produced in order to "rescue" and to proceed on "cultural excavation" (Edwards 2018: 33), animation as realised here plays with images in order to perform a past. In this regard, the past to which visual materials refer is considered a complex object that is always mimetic and mnemonic (Leslie 2003: 181). This notion, however, is contrary to Roland Barthes' indexical correlation between the image and the "pro-filmic", which Honess Roe reconnects to Benjamin's concept of the "aura", apprehending photographs instead as temporal objects, as "a record of a moment that would otherwise pass by, never to be seen and experienced again" (Honess Roe 2013: 140), Schellow's practice conveys memory as a simultaneously objective and subjective one. While the temporal object mentioned by Honess Roe still refers to a "frozen moment" that the work of animation might excavate and "revive" (Honess Roe 2013: 141), we argue that the complex conception of photographs as mimetic and mnemonic, to the contrary, leads us to consider them as "an act of imagination" (Edwards 2018:32). This concept refers to a new understanding of photography: no longer as a mechanical objectivity but as a complex one taking into account the ethnographer's body, in which the subjectivity at stake in the observation meets the distance implied by the gesture of observation (Edwards 2018: 54–55).

It is precisely from this perspective that we put forward Schellow's practice of animation to be a drawing *of* and *by* memory, through which the entanglement of his subjectivity at stake in the observation and the distance implied by his protocol materialise. Thus, the strict protocol defines the parameters of his practice in order to reproduce the mnemonic trace of a past experience: Set on the basis of a given situation on day 't', the artist sets a date t+1, when he undertakes to reproduce the event from memory; then again a date t+2,when he will repeat the act aiming for repetition, however, while de facto also referring to the first memory drawing; and so on until t+x, when the registered and (re)produced memory drawing will not trace any of the reference performed in t+1 any more (see Perret & Schellow 2015: 233).

In this process, countless image sequences are created from dots and shadows, building a gap between perception and memory. The protocol into which Schellow develops his drawing praxis does not create an image to remember, nor does it represent a memory. It draws the limits of its own body as an observation site. This physical limit experienced by the protocol is anchored in the incorporation of the past experience which his drawings explore progressively, frame by frame.

> In one who draws, that which does the drawing is not the effort to reproduce a representation of the externalised vision but rather the power and pacing of the memory that incorporates itself instantaneously into the physical act of drawing. By taking shape in movement, by investing itself in what, before being a drawing, is a performance, memory consumes its own trace. (Perret & Schellow 2015: 234)

This specific practice of memory paradoxically materialises forms of forgetting and erasing. The very performativity of the images is based on the fact that the mimetic gesture is emptied from its mnemonic reference. Consequently, each viewer is constantly reactivating the images and confronting them with his singular perceptions of a colonial past.

Collapsing representation

The drawings realised by Schellow on the Armand Hutereau expedition re-realise ethnographic scenes shot in northern Congo. For the first time, Schellow developed his praxis on a past experience of already framed images such as films. Therefore, the source and trigger of the mental images is different, while the process of materialisation follows the previously developed pattern of images referring to physically experienced sites.

Echoing such physical points of departure, however, as observed by Aleida Assmann, the resulting drawings and animation films ("Acheiropoieton") seem to have the peculiar character of not being handmade.[24] In fact, their time-based construction builds a tension between the mimetic aspects of an image anchored within its geometrical structure and the granulation and flickering of the multilayered countless dots whose superposition sculpts fragmented images within the visual surface perception.[25]

Even if Schellow reframes the images in order to reduce the distance with the filmed person, the animations reproduce – "as not being man-made" – the structure and the materiality of the very historical images. We may in fact ask what kind of criticality such realistic images can – or do not – provide in regard to the ethnographic representations that we precisely aimed to dismantle.

One possible approach would be to consider the reproducibility of the "colonial" framing by the drawings as leading us to dissociate the images from their representation. In this way, the images cannot be considered critical or colonial as such, precisely because the historical image cannot be structurally condemned or rescued. It is the *topos* framing the images, which provides (and renders perceivable) their political and epistemological meanings.

In this regard, we can state that our position has changed since we started the GREYZONE project. We were initially searching for the colonial violence within the images, convinced that they were reflecting the epistemological and political frameworks in which they were produced and which they had to serve. Due to this position, we were based in a functionalist perspective that Edwards deplores among anthropologists themselves, considering "the photographic technique only a crude metaphor of the colonial relationship, embodied for example in the relationship between focal length and cultural distance, or in the functionalist implications of the wide angle" (Edwards 2018: 53).

Schellow's animation facilitated the development of a critical position towards our own theoretical a priori. While we were still dealing with the structural construction of the colonial images in the works that we engaged in via the note-writing process published in *Critical Arts* (2017), his animation, created in the tension of the mimetic and mnemonic, emptied the representations of any substantial content. This sedimentation of ethnographic representations operates on the drawings as such, which are, taken individually, abstract deposits of points, as well as on their superposition building the three-second sequence.

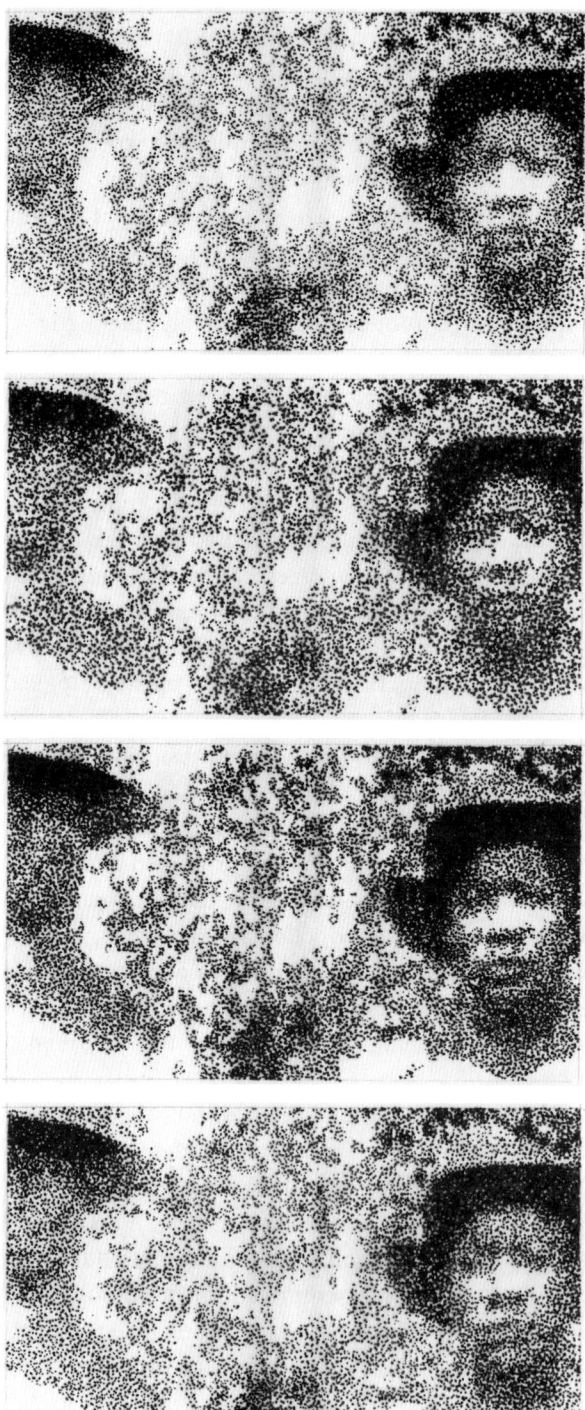

Fig. 6.2-5 Stills 007/021/044/061 [from: series of animations, work in progress / since 2015 / 3+3'' - loop / 16:9 / BW / silent. Each sequence: approx. 36 drawings, 29,7x42cm, ink on paper

This short time frame by which the images are visible constitutes fragments that articulate a temporal window of a short-term memory span, paradoxically transposed into permanence. The images can only be maintained by persistent enforcement of a permanent, constructive, and perceptibly artificial act, namely their representation. In other words, in the irreducibly interlocking of the various layers of such representational act to create what is remembered, the situation induces uninterrupted overstrain of one's own perceptual apparatus. It is this overburdening that sets in place, albeit on a minimal and temporary level, a controlled delay in our ability (and necessity) of objectification. Thus, by performing the collapse of Hutereau's ethnographic representations, Schellow confronts viewers with their own perceptual apparatus, triggered to rebuild representations of the fleeting images.

Conclusion

We developed the 'trans-anthropological' as a critical approach based on practices that layer representations within the ethnographic frameworks of the images.

The first workshop initiated in the ERG art school helped generate experimental approaches to the images and test some hypotheses we progressively elaborated, complexified, or abandoned. We started to explore the practice of note-taking during screenings, inspired by the "automatic writing" developed by surrealist artists. We took notes on silent film footage as well as on the edited colonial propaganda films and analysed the colonial ideology within the images. We screened some films by cutting up the sound in order to focus exclusively on the images, trying to understand if one could trace their embodied colonial representations or if they could not be identified with it.

We were stuck in an indetermination, balancing between our desire to dissociate the images from their colonial framework and our incapacity to get over the strong and oftentimes unbearable ideological narratives. We kept in mind Ramirez and Rolots' observation about the supremacy of the scripts that colonial images were supposed to illustrate. In some way, we secretly hoped that they would have recorded elements that could escape or even deny the colonial propaganda they were supposed to serve and legitimate. Therefore, the practices we developed in the framework of the experimental workshops – such as the note-taking during and after the screening – aimed to crystalise the relationship between the viewer, the visual archives, and the colonial representations. The workshop at Khiasma offered the possibility of experiencing other forms and practices for exploring the material. It offered the opportunity to engage in practice-based research whose first steps were publicly shared and collectively discussed. Contrary to the format of the BOZAR conference mentioned in the introduction, the Khiasma public event built an 'agora'[26] where experiences, doubts, and emotions could be shared without hierarchy or attempt to knowledge production. The strong political statement of the place offered the possibility to materialise the embodied memory engaged in the viewing process.

The collective experiences on that visual material within different institutional contexts – such as in ERG, Khiasma, the Mechelen Biennale CONTOUR, WIELS and Picha in Lubumbashi – enabled us to grapple with the concern over knowledge production on the colonial past through practice-based research. The notes, the ensuing discussions, and the artistic works engaged in these frameworks expressed a dystopian aspect of these images linked to their status as representations of the past.

Conceived in this way, the gestures engaged in by the collective have a performative character that prevents these specific images from making sense in and as representations.

Schellow's animation on the Hutereau expedition films prompted us to delve further into that epistemological and political rupture we pursue with the GREYZONE project. His work proposes a disconnecting of the images from their representations, emptying them of any substantial content, such as a past that should be 'excavated' and 'rescued'. The numerous 'abstract' drawings – sequenced as animation films that appear alternately with black frames also projected at the same length – provide critical elements to the research undertaken on the notes by materialising the process of memorisation and oblivion at work in our perceptions of such images of the colonial past. In this respect, we consider Schellow's animation on the Hutereau expedition a work that engages the viewer in a reflexive process through which we become aware of the act by which images are constantly reframed as colonial representations, serving thus quite different political discourses.

Writing those last lines of the chapter we might mention that the ongoing process of the collective work of the project brought up some irreconcilable assumptions. While the Khiasma residency enabled us to embed the experimental proposals of the colonial images within an artistic frame through its exhibition and the moderation of the discussion, the other venues appeared as much more problematic. The transposal of experimental gestures into public artistic events (modifying or at least specifying what was written above) generated tensions that were not only linked to the symbolic violence of the images. A general enthusiasm crossed with the different intentions of the various members of the project. Travelling around several places in the world, the latter considered the reproduction of the note-writing techniques on those colonial films to be problematic, echoing Hal Fosters' critique (1995: 302).

The way in which a development workshop of the Lubumbashi Biennale was framed, for instance, could have been read in perspective as replaying the staged categories of a 'we' turned into 'executioner expiators' and a 'them' as 'eternal victims'. It is also in this respect that Sandrine Colard de Bock, the curator of the Biennale, finally declined the participation of the collective at the event. In such context, the images seemed stuck in a colonial identity which the organisers precisely wanted to avoid – a process amplified by some of the artistic and social 'techniques' proposed to the participants.

The ambivalent positioning of being the reference by which to 'repair' the historical injustice and violence is strongly challenged by both of us. We do not consider ourselves as being *out* of history. In this sense – when for instance sharing Schellows' drawings and animation films within the winter school '*Arts and Anthropology*, Heritage-making, Uses and Museumification of the Past'[27] at the Iziko Museum in Cape Town – we focused our reflection on our different perceptions of Schellows' artistic proposal. The performed dialogue was not offering 'a solution' or 'empathy', nor did it follow any therapeutical intention, but instead it inscribed our position in an ongoing process that was theoretically and artistically enriched by the collective discussion with the participants of the school – only in such a mirrored way echoing matters faced and debated since the end of the apartheid regime.

Notes

1. The image on p. 186 is Figure 6.1 Still 1/021 [021 from: series of animations, work in progress / since 2015 / 3+3" – loop / 16:9 / BW / silent. Each sequence: approx. 36 drawings, 29,7x42cm, ink on paper.
2. This sovereign position of science, by which fight against affects and 'croyance', has recently been expressed at the conference 'De l'ombre à la Lumière. Pour une politique de gestion des collections coloniales de restes humains dans les universités', at the Université Libre de Bruxelles on 15 February 2019. Alain Froment, a doctor and anthropologist at the Musée de l'Homme in Paris, built his entire presentation on the argument that positivist sciences such as bio-anthropology – unlike human sciences like social anthropology, which are too deeply engaged with the colonial past – were able to deconstruct racial theories.

Maarten Couttenier, a historian and anthropologist at the Royal Museum for Central Africa, observed that, to the contrary, the heritage of physical anthropology is still embedded in emotions, which is important to take into account. In the meantime, he distances himself from what sometimes took the form of a sterile "process of intention".

3. https://www.lemonde.fr/afrique/video/2017/11/28/retour-sur-le-grand-oral-africain-d-emmanuel-macron-au-burkina-faso_5221665_3212.html (last accessed 27 October 2019).
4. We thank our colleague Damiana Otoiu for mentioning the irony of this semantic change.
5. "Central Africa" is the designation given by the institution (RMCA) to the Belgian former colony of Congo and the trust territories of Rwanda and Burundi.
6. The official name is still Royal Museum for Central Africa, but Africa Museum is used in all publicity and communications. The choice of the new denomination is quite paradoxical in that the institution decided to dedicate the 'new' permanent exhibition exclusively to its former colonial territories. This choice ignores research conducted in the museum concerning several African countries that have no links with the Belgian colonial past. As mentioned by Anne-Marie Bouttiaux, the former head of the ethnography division, this political choice was motivated by the need to disrupt the quite ambivalent relationship that Belgium continues to foster with its former colonial territories, as well as by the pretence that it could claim any kind of "expertise" regarding them. Given the institution claims to be confronting its colonial history, the new name is quite improper.
7. From this perspective, we refer to Valentin Mudimbe's deconstructivist conception developed in *The Invention of Africa* (1988), in which he insists, as Towa and Houtondji do, on the dynamics of imposed European knowledge on African colonies and the intercultural fictions it generated on the continent.
8. In 2017, by crossing our different practices, our primary research on note-taking protocols led to the foundation of the GREYZONE ZEBRA project. It builds a collective of various students, artists, and researchers, and at this point frames also our own collective work on those methods, among other things. At first, the project worked on official colonial and missionary propaganda films, ethnographic works, and private film archives, yet without regard to such categorisations, which were not always clearly distinguishable.
9. Michel Bouffioux's *Paris-Match* article on Lusinga's skull: https://parismatch.be/actualites/societe/144771/lusinga-et-300-autres-cranes-dafricains-conserves-a-bruxelles-partie-2-le-pauvre-diable-de-lulb; the well-documented amputation of hands: https://www.google.com/search?q=mains+coup%C3%A9es+du+congo&source=lnms&tbm=isch&sa=X&ved=0ahUKEwjlyOX2hsrgAhWG_qQKHUX-ARYQ_AUIDigB&biw=1920&bih=937.

10. Freddy Yombo Mutombo, born in Kinshasa in 1978, is a member of the group *Eza Possibles*. Since his residency at l'Ecole Supérieure des Arts Décoratifs (ESAD) in Strasbourg, he has focused on the Belgian colonial past and worked with colonial images. He worked despite the impossibility of accessing the visual archives of the Africa Museum. In April 2019 he secured access for the next two years.
11. This work has been presented by Anna Seiderer at the Journée d'Etude 'Contemporary artists and colonial photographic archives in contemporary art', organised by Sandrine Colard and Maureen Murphy, at l'Institut National d'Histoire de l'Art (INHA), Paris, 24 May 2017.
12. As mentioned in the introduction, the notion of "shared memory", which was used in the colonial film digitisation project, was highly contested by diaspora members, because it erases the very violence to which Boris Wastiau refers.
13. Wastiau uses the term as a metaphor when he defines the Congo Museum as a "showcase of a colonial system" (2017: 462).
14. International African Association for Exploration and Civilization of Central Africa (AIA) was founded by Leopold II in 1876 at the Geographical Conference in Brussels.
15. The Public Forces were Congolese police agents who served the Independent Free State of King Leopold II and after 1908 Belgian Congo.
16. We explicitly refer to the debate initiated by Clifford & Marcus in *Writing Culture* (1986), and while we acknowledge the theoretical self-criticism of anthropological research, we agree with Dawson, Hockey & James (1997) that the critical position should not be an end in itself.
17. From its beginning, the project had been linked with ERG (see, for example, the initial anecdote of this text), and in its development over time has integrated several actors connected with the school, from one of the initiators of the entire process, Corinne Diserens (previous ERG director); to the founding member and coauthor of this text, Alexander Schellow (currently a professor); to the president of the ASBL Laurence Rassel (currently its director); to more then fifty percent of the current members, who have entered the framework originally through their network as former ERG-students. As a consequence, we considered defining the ERG as our main partner institution. In the end, however, based on several doubts concerning the (in)stability of school structure (personal, institutional, and political frameworks), as well as the fact of its politically embedded structure as a public academic institution in Wallonia, we abandoned the idea.
18. That is, even if the ERG defines itself very much as a place for experimentation on pedagogical forms and functions.
19. http://www.khiasma.net/rdv/pratiquer-les-images-coloniales/?lang=en.

20. This, however, is not part of our gleaned film stock but forms a dimension of the primarily digitised body of films in the RMCA collection.
21. Since we started to work on the paper, a workshop was held at Picha in Lubumbashi, but the artistic proposals are still in process.
22. An important aim of the project is to build a digital artistic archive of films shared by several institutions that are already project partners. The institutions' aim is to reflect on differences in the perceptions of colonial images when situated within the former colonial museum or institutions dedicated to contemporary art in Belgium, France, Democratic Republic of Congo, Benin, and Senegal. In the European context the spaces hosting this project are specifically dedicated to contemporary art, i.e., in Belgium: École de recherche graphique (ERG), WIELS Centre d'Art Contemporain, Biennial Contours; in France: the Department of Plastic Art of the University of Paris 8, the Centre d'art Khiasma; in DRC: Picha and the Biennal de Lubumbashi 2019; in Benin: École du Patrimoine Africain; in Senegal: IFAN. The different perceptions will be realised in a multilayer indexical entry built through notes, images, and gestures proposed during the several workshops we plan to organise with the partners.
23. Elisabeth Edwards recalls the ambivalence that anthropologists of the early twentieth century still associated with the documentary capacity of photography, even if they expressed their doubts – as Haddon did – about the nature of proof and the role of ethnography embedded in natural sciences (2018: 31–57). The way Hutereau practiced ethnography is still embedded in natural sciences, and he did not provide, as did the authors to whom Edwards refers in her paper (Everard im Thurn, Maurice V. Portman and Alfred Haddon), any critical attempt to consider the supposed objectivity of the recorded images.
24. Personal communication by Aleida Assmann in 2010.
25. See, for example, the following link: https://vimeo.com/370506469 (last accessed, 20 February 2020).
26. We employ the term in the metaphorical sense for conveying the square from Antiquity, which is a political, religious, commercial and sometimes topographical meeting point, closely linked to the main traffic routes of the group.
27. https://heritages.hypotheses.org/doctoral-school-cape-town-johannesburg-2019 (last accessed 20 January 2020).

References

Antoine, Jean-Philippe, and Catherine Perret. 2015. 'Les artistes font des histoires'. *Le Genre humain* 55(1): 11–14.

Baecque, Antoine de and Christian Delage. Eds. 1998. *De l'histoire au cinéma*. Paris: Complexe.

Belting, Hans, 2004. *Pour une anthropologie des images*. Paris: Gallimard.

Benjamin, Walter. 2000. *Œuvres III*. Paris: Gallimard.

Binder, Beate, Dagmar Neuland-Kitzerow and Karoline Noak. Eds. 2008. *Kunst und Ethnographie. Zum Verhältnis von visueller Kultur und ethnographischem Arbeiten*. Berliner Blätter. Ethnographische und Ethnologische Beiträge 46. Münster: Lit Verlag.

Bouttiaux, Anne-Marie. 1999. 'Des mises en scène de curiosités aux chefs-d'œuvre mis en scène. Le Musée royal de l'Afrique à Tervuren: un siècle de collections'. *Cahiers d'Études africaines* XXXD (3-4): 595–616.

———. 2009. *Persona. Identités cachées et révélées*. Tervuren/Milan: Musée royal de l'Afrique centrale/Cinq Continents.

Clifford James, 1997. *Routes: Travel and Translation in the Late Twentieth Century*. Harvard: Harvard University Press.

Clifford, James, and George E. Marcus. Eds. 1986. *Writing culture: The Poetics and Politics of Ethnography*. Berkeley: University of California Press.

Couttenier, Maarten. 2005. *Congo tentoongesteld. Een geschiedenis van de Belgische antropologie en het museum van Tervuren (1882-1925)*. Louvain: Acco.

Dawson, Andrew, Jenny Hockey, and James Allison. Eds. 1997. *After Writing Culture. Epistemology and Praxis in Contemporary Anthropology*. London: Routledge.

Deren, Maya. 1946. *An Anagram of Ideas on Art, Form and Film*. New York: Alicat Book Shop Press.

Edwards, Elisabeth, Chris Gosden, and Ruth Phillips. Eds. 2006. *Sensible Objects: Colonialism, Museums and Material Culture*. Oxford: Berg.

Edwards, Elisabeth. Ed. 1992. *Anthropology and Photography, 1860-1920*. New Haven/London: Yale University Press.

———. 2001. *Raw Histories: Photographs, Anthropology and Museums*. Oxford / New York: Berg.

———.2018. 'Uncertain Knowledge: Photography and the Turn-of-the-Century Anthropological Document', in: *Sur le vif. Photographie et anthropologie*. Special issue edited by Camille Joseph and Anaïs Mauuarin. *Gradhiva* 27: 30–57.

Foster, Hal. 1995. 'The artist as ethnographer?' in: *The Traffic in Culture. Reconfiguring Art and Anthropology*, edited by George E Marcus and Fred R. Myers. Berkeley et al.: University of California Press, pp. 302–309.

Geertz, Clifford. 1973. *The Interpretation of Cultures. Selected Essays*. New York: Basic Books.
Grimshaw, Anna. 2001. *The Ethnographer's Eye. Ways of Seeing in Anthropology*. Cambridge: Cambridge University Press.
Guido, Laurent, and Lugon, Olivier, eds. 2010. *Fixe-animé: croisements de la photographie et du cinéma au XXe siècle*. Lausanne/Paris: l'âge d'homme.
Honess Roe, Annabelle. 2013. *Animated Documentary*. Basingstoke: Palgrave Macmillan.
Hosea, Brigitta. 2010. 'Drawing Animation'. *Animation: An Interdisciplinary Journal* 5(3): 353–367.
Hutereau, Joseph-Armand-Oscar. 1952. *Histoire des Peuplades de Luele et de Lubangi*. Brussels: Goemaere.
Keyzer, Carl de, and Johan Lagae. Eds. 2010. *Congo Belge en Images*. Brussels: Lannoo.
Leslie, Esther. 2003. 'Absent-Minded Professors: Etch-a-Sketching Academic Forgetting', in: *Regimes of Memory*, edited by Radstone Susannah and Hodgkin Katharine. London/New York: Routledge, pp. 72–185.
Macdonald, Sharon. 2013. *Memorylands. Heritage and Identity in Europe Today*. Milton: Routledge.
Macdonald, Sharon. 2015. 'The Trouble with the Ethnological', in: *The Laboratory Concept. Museum Experiments in the Humboldt Lab Dahlem*, edited by Martin Heller, Agnes Wegner, and Andrea Scholz, Berlin: Kulturstiftung des Bundes, pp. 211–226.
Mauuarin Anaïs, and Camille Joseph. Eds. 2018. *Sur le vif: photographie et anthropologie. Gradhiva*. Paris: Musée du Quai Branly.
Mudimbe, Valentin. 1988. *The Invention of Africa: Gnosis, Philosophy and the Order of Knowledge*. Bloomington: Indiana University Press.
Ndaywel è Nziem, Isidore. 2009. *Une nouvelle Histoire du Congo. Des origines à la République démocratique*. Brussels/Kinshasa: Le Cri/Afrique Editions.
Perret, Catherine, and Alexander Schellow. 2015. 'ELLE/SIE: une biographie.' In: 'Les artistes font des histoires'. '*Le Genre humain* 55(1): 225–240.
Pinel, Vincent. 2000. *Écoles, genres et mouvements au cinéma*. Paris: Larousse.
Pinney, Christopher, and Nicolas Peterson. Eds. 2003. *Photography's Other Histories*. Durham/London: Duke University Press.
Pinney, Christopher. 1992. 'The Parallel Histories of Anthropology and Photography', in: *Anthropology and Photography, 1860-1920*, edited by Elizabeth Edwards. New Haven/London: Yale University Press/Royal Anthropological Institute, pp.74–91.
Pöppel, Ernst. 2000. *Grenzen des Bewußtseins*. Frankfurt am Main: Insel.

Ramirez, Félix, and Christian Rolot. 1990. 'Le cinéma colonial belge. Archive d'une utopie'. *Revue Belge du Cinéma* 29: 63.

Roberts, Allen, 2019. 'Is Repatriation Inevitable?' *African Arts* 52(1): 1–7.

Sarr, Felwine, and Savoy, Bénédicte. 2018. *Rapport sur la restitution du patrimoine culturel africain. Vers une nouvelle éthique relationnelle.* http://restitutionreport2018.com/sarr_savoy_fr.pdf (last accessed 23 January 2020).

Schellow, Alexander, and Anna Seiderer. 2017. 'Writing Within Colonial Film'. *Critical Arts* 31(2): 87–101.

Schneider, Rebecca. 2011. *Performing Remains. Art and War in Times of Theatrical Reenactment.* London/New York, Routledge.

Schneider, Arnd, and Christopher Wright. Eds. 2013. *Anthropology and Art Practice.* London: Bloomsbury.

Scherer, Joanna. 1992. 'The photographic document: photographs as primary data in anthropological enquiry", in: *Anthropology and Photography. 1860-1920*, edited by Elisabeth Edwards. London: Yale University/RAI, pp. 32–41.

Seiderer, Anna, 2018. 'Empirical notes on the exhibition "L'Un et l'Autre" at the Palais de Tokyo.' https://blog.uni-koeln.de/gssc-humboldt/empirical-notes-on-the-exhibition-lun-et-lautre-one-and-the-other (last accessed 03 January 2020).

Tinius, Jonas. 2018. 'Awkward Art and Difficult Heritage: Nazi Collectors and Postcolonial Archives', in: *An Anthropology of Contemporary Art. Practices, Markets and Collectors*, edited by Thomas Fillitz and Paul Van der Grijp. London: Bloomsbury, pp. 130–145.

Wastiau, Boris. 2017. 'The Legacy of Collecting: Colonial Collecting in the Belgian Congo and the Duty of Unveiling Provenance', in: *The Oxford Handbook of Public History*, edited by Gardner Hamilton. Oxford: University of Oxford, pp. 460–478.

"Translating the Silence"

A conversation with *le peuple qui manque*

For this book, we have devised a set of interviews or position pieces with curators, since we regard curatorial practice as transversally agentive across three fields central to our thinking for this book: museums, contemporary art, and colonialism. We think that these are fields from which anthropology gets challenged and within which it is particularly mobilised in a generative way. Bearing this in mind, how would you situate your practice as curators and as a curatorial platform? Do you, in your practice, seek precisely to transcend these kinds of distinctions, and if so, how? Please elaborate with view to your emphasis on theory and research.

The expression you use – "transversally agentive" – is very accurate.[1] When considering the relationship between art and anthropology (or between art and something else), it is often assumed that art denotes a defined set of practices and discourses, that art is a discipline like any other, from which to build bridges (interdisciplinarity). There is obviously nothing more false and even absurd, since the ontological extension of art to the ensemble of fields of the possible has indeed taken place. As curators engaged in what you could call a 'research-based' turn, we consider the field of art as an "ecology of knowledge", borrowing from the "sociologist of emergence" Boaventura de Sousa Santos (Imhoff and Quiros 2014) – an ecology of knowledge from which to consider, together, artistic, indigenous, scientific, fictional knowledge, and more broadly, knowledge disqualified by the partitions of modernity. We consider this possibility for the (still largely vacuous) field of art as going against a certain hegemonic discourse on art, which has been predominant for two decades. It is one which thinks of art and its relationship to research as the realization of this "epistemological anarchism" theorised by the philosopher of science Paul Feyerabend, according to whom "everything is good" – any methodology "against the method", that is, against the uses accepted by the discipline (anthropology for example) would, in any circumstance, produce knowledge. To the contrary, we postulate that this 'anarchism', which nevertheless remains very interesting, does not take sufficient account of the historical possibilities and skills offered by the field of art and curatorial practice. More specifically, curating is an interstitial practice and a practice of translation between epistemological regimes – between different contexts, between discourses and practices, or, to use your expression, it is a "transversally agentive" practice. We thus suggest our *curatorial politics*, our ecology of knowledge, as first and foremost a *politics of translation*. Translation, however, in a sense that does not adhere to a principle of fidelity, but is always a poetics, a "listening to the continuous", as Henri Meschonnic put it, wherein the *subject* is fully part of the very process of translation between texts (or rather here, contexts and practices). There is this beautiful sentence by the Russian poet Boris Pasternak about the act on language produced by the translation of poetry, which we could transpose to curatorial practice: "Moving from one

Fig. 7.2 First Declaration of the Stateless Museum, film directed by Aliocha Imhoff & Kantuta Quirós, La Réunion: La plaine des Sables, 2017

Fig. 7.3 First Declaration of the Stateless Museum, film directed by Aliocha Imhoff & Kantuta Quirós, La Réunion: La plaine des Sables, 2017

language to another is more than just going from one region to another. It is rather a step from one century that did not exist into a century that is dreamt up" (Pasternak 1959).

The fields you suggest – museums, coloniality, and contemporary art – with the relations and divisions between them, are very pertinent for us. They evoke one of our projects that took the form of a film, entitled *The Stateless Museum*. This project inscribes itself in a certain genealogy of fictional museums and their bringing about of crises within art institutions. The notion of statelessness allows us to escape to the antiphony of a contemporary nomadology, which considers the art world as space of a fluidity that is travelling, happy, and triumphant, or exalting of a translating thought in which language renders itself at once global and entirely vehicular. This thought of translation conceives language only as a medium, a vector of communication – like 'globish', global English. In contrast to this perspective, which advocates an easy grip on language, we postulate, with Glissant, the irreducible "right to opacity" of languages. A language, among other things, is nothing more than an integral of equivocals that its history has allowed to persist, as Lacan said. On the contrary, the notion of stateless person, if it describes *par excellence* a figure of displacement, of exile, refers above all to the reality of blocked bodies, prevented because the stateless is the place of a radical heteroglossia: this irreducible remainder, this thick shadow which resides in translation. Translation therein remains an infinite process, burdened by the gravity of bodies, texts, and works to be circulated in the so-called globalised space, as well as by the conflictuality, especially post-colonial, which regulates the movement of artists, signs, and objects.

When did you first come into contact with anthropology, and what is anthropology to you today? How do you relate to anthropology's legacies in the present?

If we speak as actors from the art world, indeed, anthropology has been, for us, a very structuring base for thinking about the space of art. This has not so much been the case because of anthropology's relation to 'radical otherness', to supposed *Others*, but, for us, as a constant reconfiguration of the relationships between actors, producers, and viewers – in other words, as a political dislodgement (*déplacement*) from the modalities of enunciations and the formal *dispositifs* displacement that produce them.

Jean Rouch's filmography, for example, has been for us very significant. Deleuze later declared about Rouch's film *Moi, un Noir* (1958) that "the people are missing" – an idea that inspired the name of our curatorial platform (Deleuze 1985). It also was important for us regarding his theorizing of the figure of the intercessor for documentary cinema; and *Chronique d'un été* (1961, with Edgar Morin) as a prefiguration of a polyphonic writing of art (and here, of cinema). All of Rouch's filmography, like all the history of anthropology, testifies to a particular attention paid to a reconfiguration of the *dispositifs* of enunciation.

Despite these close ties (*filiation*) of attention with the formal *dispositifs* of enunciation, which remains very operative for us today, a particular misunderstanding about anthropology often remains. It is a misunderstanding between those who wrongly think that 'radical alterity' (which would be the subject of anthropology) has become the basis for a rethinking of criticism (to be reworked with regard to an Elsewhere, after the end of the ideologies and promises of modernity), and those who think, almost in the opposite way, but also wrongly, that the anthropological grid has been used in the art world exclusively (we underline) against or in spite of a certain politicization of art. The exhibition that is seminal in this respect, *Les Magiciens de la Terre* (1989), has often been criticised for having privileged the anthropological paradigm as a heuristic grid for approaching non-Western works of art, despite more directly political (left-wing, even revolutionary) approaches, in the context of the Tricontinental and the Non-Aligned movement discourses of the time.

However, neither of these two perspectives proved to be entirely accurate considering the importance of our first filiation, that is, the emergence of a *politics of enunciation* (often summarised far too quickly by *who speaks and from where?*) maintained and theorised by the history of anthropology. James Clifford specified its nomenclature of formal *dispositifs* of knowledge enunciation brilliantly in *The Predicament of Culture* (1988), analysing the different regimes of authority that have marked the history of anthropology – from monological authority to dialogical authority and then the polyphonic authority called for by post-modern anthropology, including participant observation.

The whole history of anthropology – and this it shares with art – manages, like no other discipline stemming from modernity, to escape its original framework, to extend to infinity (to become "post", almost from its origin and well before its postmodern shift), and to reconfigure the order of knowledge: From Lévi-Strauss' "writer's desire" to Eduardo Kohn's anthropology of the forest (and his anthropology beyond *anthropos*), via Bruno Latour or Viveiros de Castro, it became increasingly difficult to 'reduce' anthropology to a uniform discipline with fixed contours, and even less so as a 'filter' that could be applied to any *topic*. In other words, it is a poetic, formal, and political history of the configurations of enunciations, but also of exchanges, correspondences, and translations from which we must depart again (*repartir*) when it comes to the relation between art and anthropology. Either for art or anthropology, therefore, it is not a question of rebuilding criticism or escaping politics, but rather, together, of pursuing the formal exploration of the modalities and locations of speaking as much as of redesigning the ordering of knowledge and practices. This implies as much the spaces for the exercise of democracy as the spaces for the production of knowledge and the poetics that run through them.

Where do you grapple with anthropology today? Where do you think that critical and in your view, interesting or new, knowledge production concerning anthropology takes place today?
Regarding the above, our interest in the contemporary forms of enunciation – what we call *scenographies of speech* (scénographies de la parole), articulated in our work through discursive proposals in the form of mock trials, imaginary diplomatic congresses, or parliaments of things – meets an expanded understanding of the subjects in a contemporary anthropology.

If, for a long time, the question addressed to anthropology, both by its postmodern turn and by art, was the question of the authoritative position of the producer of knowledge (*scripteur du savoir*) pursuing the decentralisation dear to post-structuralist thinkers and 'standpoint' epistemologies (post-feminists, queer, post-colonial, ...) – today, it is the silent voice of the world that catches up with us. With the Anthropocene, all life becomes worthy of inhabiting a wider parliament, which opens itself up to animals, plants, machines, cyborgs, objects.

Indeed, the ecological, even cosmomorphic, turn in anthropology goes hand in hand with a great current gesture of broadening its subjects and objects, but also about broadening the recognition of subjectivities and enunciating subjects. We are thinking here, for instance, of Eduardo Kohn (*How Forests Think*, 2013)[2] and an anthropology that pays attention to the murmur of the living, the language of Earth (David Abram in *The Spell of the Sensuous*), the language of animals (the works of Vinciane Desprets, for example), and new entries into both the anthropological scene and the arena of political representation.[3]

Indeed, as identified by Pierre Montebello,[4] this *cosmomorphic turn* in anthropology, philosophy, and metaphysics joins the project of an extended attention to everything (Garcia 2011), without particular privilege granted to any of them, carried by new ontologies – "flat ontologies" – in a democratic gesture in the face of the sensitive where all objects would become worthy of equal interest (human and non-human, living and non-living, animated and inanimate, existing, having existed, to come, or imaginary, objects or works of art). In this respect, it also meets with the ecological concern for renewed political representation,[5] through the establishment of new parliamentary forms, and the necessity to make lakes, rivers, mountains, forests, oceans, and more generally, the land, legal subjects, able to claim rights and to bring to justice against those who are responsible for the great contemporary ecocide.[6]

Today, many of the most challenging projects in the field of art are at the intersection of anthropology, fictional diplomacy, and law – as, for example, Terike Haapoja and Laura Gustafsson with their *Museum of Non-Humanity* and *The Trial* – a fictional trial around non-human law, led from the case of the wolf Perho; or Bruno Latour and Frédérique Aït-Touati's pre-enactment of COP21; or Christophe Bergon and Camille de Toledo's *PRLMT*, the parliament stripped of its vowels. These projects work to rethink constitutions, forms of representation, rebalancing the rights of human and non-human subjects. These thought experiments developed on a 1:1 scale in the field of art, and which are part of what we call a "potential regime" (Imhoff, Quirós, and Toledo 2016), are concomitant with the work of legal retooling carried out in the real political space by indigenous, ecological, and political movements, and for which democracies provided space, particularly in Latin America.[7]

Such an extended anthropology, cosmomorphic and poetic, is then woven into a fragile place of the desire to restore the word, to translate unheard voices,[8] to make themselves diplomats (Morizot 2016), and to listen to silence – silence of land that has become inaudible, silence of birds after their tragic disappearance, but also the silence of disappeared languages (as in Susan Hiller) and the rarefactions of world views they represent. This anthropological expansion is therefore to be thought of as one of listening, as the theorist Marielle Macé clearly reminds us.[9]

As part of your reflections on Magiciens de la Terre, you claimed: "Global art has failed. Which other geo-esthetic regimes are to be invented and practised in the years to come? Which instituting gestures are necessary to provoke a shift? And finally, which museums and institutions to re-imagine?" (2015) How would you respond to these questions today and in view of the developments since then?
The main focus of the *Beyond the Magiciens-effect* ('Au-delà de l'Effet-Magiciens') meetings, which we organised in early 2015, was the question of how to overcome a certain globalism, or global turn, of the 2000s that to us seemed still widely accepted until this point.

While the nationalist reassertion of many countries around the world (Brazil, United States, United Kingdom, Turkey, etc.) invites numerous theorists today to identify, more locally, a set of contextual strategies, others are now more concerned with pursuing efforts towards an ecologisation of the art space, as the primary space for reflection and proposals towards a habitable and inhabited world. Bruno Latour, for instance, suggests speaking of "earthlings" rather than humans (not characterised by a necessary return to the earth, but caused by the return of the earth in the order of the present). The principal question is thus whether we can identify an "earthly *geo-esthetics*" today.

This last question is about what we might call disciplinary claims or disciplinary sovereignty. Up until recently, art history focused predominantly on a history of European art, while non-European art was mostly regarded and professionally constituted as the domain of anthropological research. Can you describe how you regard these disciplinary divisions, and whether and to what extent you see or even participate in breaking down these divisions?
Besides its reactionary margins, art history has for the most part opened its canon and its working methodologies (*world art history*, connected history, etc.). It has taken note, to a large extent, that modernity is to be conjugated in the plural. It is nonetheless regrettable that this revision took place out of sync with theories of art and the field of historiography itself. Rather, it has been done much more closely aligned with the development of new globalised markets. This asymmetry reflects another more profound problem, which could be considered to be the blind spot of art history. We are here referring to the lack of reflexivity on the very notion of art – that is, on the movements brought about by each of the agents of art (artists, institutions, theorists, critics, etc.) on what is or is not regarded as art. The subject of art history still remains art and is too little interested in the conflict, in the *war*, preceding the becoming of art. The anthropology of art, by contrast, has understood this quite some time ago; and, for example, the work of Alfred Gell – for whom any object (art, artefact, idol, ritual, functional, etc.) is a work of art – is always considered within a network of relationships between agents and patients, that is, as a set of elements between the *indice* (the object itself), the *artist* (or other producers), the *recipient* (the viewer), and the *prototype* (what is 'represented' by the work in a broader sense). It is the set of relations that constitute the 'art network', recognised as such by the various social actors, thus further expanding the ideas of art propounded by the work of Nelson Goodman and Howard Becker.

To understand the issue of restitution today[10] – and for which art historians (or museum directors) are regularly opposed to anthropologists (the former considering these objects *exclusively* as art and the latter as *something else* first of all) – it is also necessary to revisit the agency and social history of objects, at the expense of what, objects, run the risk of becoming renegotiated currency between Nations (we would of course take the side of the dominated Nations – this would be the minimum) – and thus reducing the intellectual and aesthetic scope, and the possible plurality of art narratives. The space of conflict – of interpretation, designation, displacement – must be ordered by a poetics. This is what John Peffer (2004) envisioned when he invited us to consider looted, displaced African art objects as being a diaspora themselves. He proposed to conceptualise a history of African art objects by thinking of them as vehicles, as time and space, for "diasporas of images", moving objects articulating disparate cultural histories. We also recall Jennifer Gonzalez's brilliant analyses, in *Subject to Display* (2008), of the material logic of objects in museum contexts and the way in which they are "epidermalised" therein as subjects of racist projections (Gonzalez 2008). Despite the stated desire for greater egalitarianism, some objects continue to occupy only limited spaces in museums: display strategies which nevertheless place a semantic hierarchy on the exhibited objects.

The question remains: how to reinvent forms of experimental museography without reifying tangible and intangible heritage? The will to reflect on the decolonisation of museums and the voice and life proper of the objects and communities from which they come, remains quite exemplary in this respect today. Do these diasporic objects have a voice? Can they cry and demand a "right to return"?

Notes

1. The image on p. 210 is Figure 7.1 'Beyond the Magiciens Effect', symposium performance curated by Aliocha Imhoff & Kantuta Quirós, scenography by Adel Cersaque, © Helena Hattmansdorfer, le peuple qui manque; 2015.
2. An "anthropology of life", an anthropology, he writes, that is not limited to the human being but is concerned with our "entanglements (...) with other types of lives" (see Kohn 2007).
3. "A metallic voice, tapering like a blade, trembling (...) with a cold rage ready to submerge them. Then there were words." Pierre Ducrozet tells the story of the *émergence* of the ecological children of the twenty-first century, of the voice, at COP 24 in Katowice, of the young Greta Thunberg, who is on strike from school. She stood in front of the Swedish Parliament with a "Strike for the Climate" placard, soon joined by tens of thousands of schoolchildren, high school

students, and university students – children of the twenty-first century – who took to the streets of their city. In Davos, in 2019, where all the world's CEOs gathered, Greta Thunberg came back on stage. Her power seized the assembly again. " 'I don't want your hope. I want you to panic,' whispered the voice", as Pierre Ducrozet writes in 'Nous, enfants du 21eme siècle' (*Libération*).
4. Montebello sees "cosmomorphic views" replacing old anthropomorphic patterns. A new geo-cosmic period eccentrates the human from his world. The human enjoins to redistribute to the non-humans a dignity of being without which the human will end up erasing himself or herself.
5. See how Bruno Latour was able to imagine in 2015, at the *Théâtre des Amandiers*, a pre-enactment of COP 21 (World Climate Conference), eight months before the real COP 21 in Paris took place. This way, he tried to find ways of 'alternative' representation to the given form of an addition of nations, and which is unsuitable, as representative entities, when it comes to considering the fate of the oceans or migrants. During *Make It Work*, it was no longer the states alone but cities, oceans, and land that were invited as political subjects to the negotiating table, thus extending Latour's past reflections on the establishment of a parliament of things.
6. Experiencing the 'idea of democracy' now seems to require a scene, even a scenography, for speech. The conditions for the exercise of the right to speak have been based in contemporary political movements, from the recent "Movements des places" (Syntagma, Nuit Debout, Occupy, …) to the dream of assemblist democracy of the Gilets Jaunes movement in France, which has highlighted the indistinction and equality in speaking out as a key claim.
7. On 15 March 2017, the Parliament of New Zealand granted the Whanganui River a "legal personality", giving it the right to defend itself in court. The Bolivian Constitution now recognises Pachamama (Mother Earth) as a legal subject. The Andean notion of Living Well has been incorporated into the Ecuadorian and Bolivian constitutions.
8. See the inter-species translator of the artist Tomás Saraceno; poets and bird translators such as Jacques Demarcq; the Quechua singer Luzmila Carpio, translator of birds; or the zoopoetics or bioacoustics of Bernie Krause.
9. Marielle Macé, for example, makes the poem's expertise – in the ability of poets to listen, not only to translate the speculated words of animals and plants, but also to listen to their unspoken voices – a possible future for anthropology (Macé 2019). Her 2019 lectures at the Maison de la Poésie are entitled *Poésie et anthropologie élargie*.
10. In this regard, we welcome the remarkable restitution report by Felwine Sarr and Bénédicte Savoy (submitted to the president of the French Republic in November 2018 and referenced below), which represents a turning point in the

history of restitutions, advocating the return of many African objects in French national collections which were stolen during the colonial period. Let us hope that, beyond the open acknowledgements of the French administration, this report will not remain a dead letter.

References

Clifford, James. 1988. *The Predicament of Culture. Twentieth-Century Ethnography, Literature and Art*. Cambridge, MA: Harvard University Press.

Deleuze, Gilles. 1985. *Cinema 2. The Time-Image*. Minneapolis: University of Minnesota Press.

Garcia, Tristan. 2011. *Forme et objet*. Paris: PUF.

Gell, Alfred. 1998. *Art and Agency. An Anthropological Theory*. Oxford: Clarendon.

Gonzalez, Jennifer. 2008. *Subject to Display. Reframing Race in Contemporary Art*. Boston: MIT Press.

Imhoff, Aliocha, and Kantuta Quiros. 2014. 'Curating Resarch, Pour une diplomatie entre les savoirs'. *l'art même* 64. http://www.lartmeme.cfwb.be/n0064/documents/AM64.pdf (last visited 13 January 2020).

Kohn, Eduardo. 2013. *How Forests Think: Toward an Anthropology Beyond the Human*. Berkeley: University of California Press.

Lettre de Boris Pasternak à Michel Aucouturier du 4 février 1959, publiée par Georges Nivat, dans 'Six lettres inédites de Boris Pasternak', *CMRS*, 15(12), 1974.

Latour, Bruno. 2017. *Où atterrir?: Comment s'orienter en politique*. Paris: La Découverte.

Macé, Marielle. 2019. *Nos Cabanes*. Paris: Verdier.

Meschonnic, Henri. 1999. *Poétique du traduire*. Paris: Verdier

Morizot, Baptiste. 2016. *Les Diplomates, Cohabiter avec les loups sur une nouvelle carte du vivant*. Marseille: Wildproject.

Montebello, Pierre. 2015. *Métaphysiques cosmomorphes*. Paris: Les presses du réel.

Peffer, John, and Thierry Baudouin. 2013. 'La diaspora des images de l'Afrique'. *Multitudes* 53(2): 4758.

Sarr, Felwine, and Bénédicte Savoy. 2018. *Rapport sur la restitution du patrimoine culturel africain. Vers une nouvelle éthique relationnelle*. http://restitutionreport2018.com/sarr_savoy_fr.pdf (last accessed 13 January 2020).

Toledo, Camille de, Aliocha Imhoff, and Kantuta Quirós. 2016. *Les potentiels du temps: art et politique*. 1 vol. Paris: Manuella éditions.

Art-Anthropology Interventions in the Italian Post-Colony: The Scattered Colonial Body Project

Arnd Schneider

Introduction

How do we intervene in the post-colonial landscape of Italy by means of an art-anthropology collaboration?[1] In 2017, this 'landscape' or cultural setting was still characterised by widespread, and partly wilful, amnesia concerning the histories and legacies of Italian colonialism.[2]

Symptomatic for this were the remains of the former Colonial Museum, scattered across various institutions in the Italian capital of Rome. For a considerable time, critical historians – notably, Angelo del Boca (2014, 2015) and Nicola Labanca (2002, 2012) – had debunked the myth of Italy being the 'good' and 'benevolent' coloniser, epitomised by the expression *italiani brava gente*, when compared to their British and French counterparts. Nevertheless, it was this nostalgic version of history that prevails to this day among the Italian public at large, but also, for the most part, among former Italian settlers and descendants of colonists, and, unsurprisingly, in an even more pronounced fashion among those on the right and far right of the political spectrum (see, for example, Bertella Farnetti and Dau Novelli 2017, Chalcraft 2018, Giuliani 2019; on Italo-Libyans see AIRL 2016a and b, discussed further below). In this chapter, I focus on Italy's entanglement with modern-day Libya, an Italian colony from 1911 to 1943.

It was in this general context and political climate that I developed a research and exhibition project with the artist Leone Contini, who had trained also as an anthropologist. This work was situated between art and ethnography, focusing on intercultural frictions and power-relations.[3] In my previous work, I had been exploring the possibilities of art-anthropology collaborations in rethinking canons and alternative histories (see Schneider and Wright 2006, 2010, 2013; Schneider 2011, 2013 and 2017).

Our chosen site was the Pigorini National Ethnographic Museum in Rome (part of the Museo delle Civiltà).[4] The museum was, and continues to be, home of a large part of the collection of the former IsIAO (*L'Istituto italiano per l'Africa e l'Oriente*), including the collections of the former Colonial Museum. In 2017, other parts of these collections were still scattered across Rome: in the National Gallery of Modern Art, the Zoological Museum, the National Library, and various military museums. These collections thus constituted a 'scattered colonial body', a metaphor which also lent the name to our exhibition *Bel Suol d'Amore – The Scattered Colonial Body* at the Pigorini Museum in late June, early July 2017. *Bel Suol d'Amore* is taken from the title of an Italian patriotic war song from 1911, "A Tripoli Bel Suol d'Amor" (literally 'To Tripoli, beautiful soil of love'), composed right before the Italo-Turkish War that commenced in 1911, as a result of which Libya – then part of the Ottoman Empire – became an Italian colony. *The Scattered Body* refers both to the 'body' of artefacts from the colony and scattered throughout institutions in Rome, and also to the 'bodies' of those subject to colonial violence, while at the same time standing for an exploration and critical re-assemblage of some of this material in an exhibition (see Contini 2020: 42–43 for a detailed discussion, also Contini 2019, Grechi 2019).

The encounter with these collections had been serendipitous. In fact, when we walked in our preparatory visits though the corridors of the museum, Leone Contini noticed under a tarpaulin the archaeological model of the famous Roman amphitheater at Sabratha in Libya, excavated by his grandfather, Giacomo Caputo, a superintendent of antiquities in Libya in the 1940s.[5] Contini himself is a descendant, on his mother's side, of Italian settlers to Libya. This project, originally meant to take a different path, revealed an unexpected and troubling connection between his biography and family history and their colonial entanglement. Taking this relationship –and the historical amnesia in Italy more broadly on this issue – as a starting point, we decided to probe further into this hidden and scattered colonial collection.

As our research continued, we realised that several employees in the Pigorini Museum were former Italian settlers from Libya or, in fact, their descendants. Through conversations with them, we got in touch with associations, interviewed other former settlers, and sought to engage them with our

Fig. 8.2 Corridor of the Museo Prestorico Etnografio "Lugi Pigorini" (part of Museo delle Civiltà), Rome, with model of Sabratha amphitheatre, and painting from colonial period. Photograph by Wolfgang Thaler

findings in the museum, so as to discuss the problematic status of and lack of awareness about colonial history in Italy.

Right above the model of the ruins of Sabratha (the archaeological site excavated by Contini's grandfather) hung a picture, displaying two Italian soldiers on motorbikes and an armoured vehicle driving at full speed through a Libyan landscape, conveying the idea of speed reminiscent of the futurist glorification of war machines, military efficiency, and colonial domination.[6] These encounters with the as yet unreflected and uncontextualised colonial past provoked our research interest and persuaded us to work with the collections of the IsIAO, in temporary storage at the Pigorini (more specifically, in its offices and laboratory division), in addition to being scattered across other institutions and depots in Rome.

Objects in transit

During the period of our fieldwork, a large part of the IsIAO's holdings were moved into a number of museums and other institutions in the Italian capital. This provoked great challenges in doing work on such a dispersed, indeed, 'scattered body' – as the title of our exhibition suggested.[7]

The transitoriness and dispersed assemblage of the IsIAO collections were made visibly and physically manifest during the removal of the remaining collections from the IsIAO premises in Via Aldrovandi 16, in March 2017. The intention of the institutional governing bodies from the Ministry of Culture and the Ethnographic Museum was to concentrate the material in one museum (i.e., the Ethnographic Museum), where it would undergo a critical re-examination and eventual display to the public in future exhibitions. While we witnessed the removal, a certain number of objects particularly caught our attention: bronze busts, green with patina. These were busts of Italian imperial generals and politicians connected to the colonial project, such as Rodolfo Graziani. Graziani, a fanatical fascist, had committed war crimes – including the use of poison gas and construction of concentration camps – both in the campaigns to pacify Libya in the 1920s, where he was also vice-governor of Cyrenaica 1930-1934, as well as in Ethiopia as viceroy

Fig. 8.3 Leone Contini mounting exhibition *Bel Suol d'Amore – The Scattered Colonial Body*, Museum "Lugi Pigorini", Rome, June 2017. Photograph by Wolfang Thaler

Fig. 8.4 Map of colonial Libya (detail), Italy, 1930s, collection of former IsIAO, Rome. Photograph by Arnd Schneider

from 1936 to 1937. The busts in the collections appeared to us, and indeed were, particularly brutal and warlike. During the transit, Graziani's bust was bandaged, thus somehow contained, to go to yet another storage facility (see Fig. 8.1). Yet at the same time, it was also prepared to move into a new display, eventually – into our exhibition, namely, where we would deploy it in a new unmasking and re-bandaging, and thus the beginning of a critical re-examination.

Another notable set of items were the large-scale relief maps of lands colonised by the Italians in Africa. These gave an idea of Italy's colonial pretensions, as well as the extent of toponymical colonisation. For instance, newly established colonial villages in Libya and Eritrea were given mostly Italian names, or indeed some Arab names, when some new villages were founded in Libya as a reward for Arab Libyan auxiliary troops in the colonial wars in Eritrea.[8] In the case of Libya, euphemistically called the 'fourth shore', *la quarta sponda*, the tight links to the metropole were meticulously indicated with frequent routes and the names of ocean liners and seaplanes. So that the idea of this 'fourth shore' would come into full relief, the large map of Libya was oriented North to South from the Italian viewpoint across the Mediterranean, with dotted lines and a miniature ship indicating the route Tripoli–Syracuse, on which several of our interlocutors would still have travelled.

The removal of the busts was a truly 'moving' event, both emotionally and physically. One witnessed the colonial regime quite literally coming out of storage, which otherwise received such scant public exposure. The move itself also seemed to us to take place almost in secret, as if hidden from the public eye – for there was, to our knowledge, no particular attention paid to it in the media. This was not least due to the overall lack of critical work on this past within Italy, except from that done by a few critical historians, cultural studies and film scholars, and activists.[9] The lack of attention to this move, again, underlined the lack of a wider public debate on Italy's colonial legacy, where critical discussion has been largely confined to the academic sphere.

While the library of the IsIAO was transferred to the National library, the bulk of the objects including the busts of Fascist officials, canons, and relief maps went into storage in the Pigorini Museum, where they awaited further cataloguing and eventual use in future exhibitions. From these objects, we chose a number of busts and canons to display in our exhibition.

Even during the move, there was an element of serendipity – and perhaps a sign of the continued entanglement of these collections with the colonial past – when one of the moving men told us that his grandfather lived in Libya during colonial times. He later lent for the exhibition the school registry book from right after WWII, where tellingly, the curriculum subject 'Fascist Culture' (*cultura fascista*) had been crossed out.

The move had other implications as well. What did it mean to 'move', or rather 're-move' objects imbued with history and memory? Indeed, we were dealing with a proper *re*moval in this context. The objects had already gone through various moves before, witnessing all the institutional changes and metamorphoses of the Colonial (1923-1947) and then African Museum (until 1972), and what was to become the, now defunct, IsIAO (cf. Margozzi 2005: 18 and Gandolfo 2014: 125–216). These were not only nominal changes, that is of *name*, themselves linked to ideological and political changes during the museum's history and its 'prehistory'. In turn, these changes related to the larger canvas of political and cultural history and the regimes acting within it: the liberal paternalistic democracy at the onset of the colonial empire at the beginning of the twentieth century, succeeded by Fascism (when the Colonial Museum was founded in 1923), and eventually the postwar period and its largely unchallenged entanglement with colonialism.

Through the move, the controversial objects experienced a curious defamiliarisation. They were now wrapped up, effectively bandaged, and rather than being obscured or hidden through this procedure gained in meaning through their status as historically complex indicators. In fact – though temporarily moved into a depot and hidden from view and scrutiny, until further curatorial and exhibition work – as material indices and evidence of past injustice, their meaning became heightened and emphasised, even before they would enter a new place in a new museum context.

Fig. 8.5 *Bel Suol d'Amore*: The Scattered Colonial Body, Preliminary exhibition design, section view, Museo Prestorico Etnografio "Lugi Pigorini" (part of Museo delle Civiltà), Rome, June 2017. Photograph by Cinzia Delnevo

Agency, re-enactment, and 'reanimation': Facial plaster casts in the Pigorini

One particular part of the collection (of the former African Museum/ISiAO) comprised the difficult heritage of the facial plaster casts made by Italian physical anthropologists. Among them were such created by Lidio Cipriani (1892-1962), a prominent anthropologist during Fascist times, the director of the Florence Museum of Anthropology (1937-1940) and a signatory of the Manifesto della Razza (1938) (*Manifesto degli scienziati razzisti*; Manifest of race, or Manifest of the racist scientists) (Landi /Moggi 2014: 26 – 27), which was followed by the introduction of the racial laws in October 1938 that stripped Jews of Italian citizenship as well as governmental and professional positions.

This collection consists of 40 plaster casts, busts, and heads stored in nine boxes in the Pigorini Museum/Museo delle Civiltà (Fiorletta 2012/13), nineteen of which were cast by Lidio Cipriani, primarily of Tuareg individuals.[10] Leone Contini and I decided to address this problematic part of the collection by engaging in a staged and technologically altered reproduction of select facial plaster casts as 3D copies, allowing us to render them and their colonial entanglements with violence and injustice visible. These became later the subject of discussions and an integral part of our exhibition. From the collection, we chose to work with the casts that were most probably part of a plaster collection consisting of twenty-two casts, created in 1929 in Libya by the colonial government of Cyrenaica.[11]

Although to date there has been no further evidence found in the catalogues and archives of the Pigorini – specifically on how the plaster casts came to IsIAO – it is possible that this particular expedition for the anthropometric research and execution of facial plaster casts might have been the one carried out between 1928 and 1929 by Nello Puccioni (1881-1937), the director of the Florence Museum of Anthropology (1931-1937) and predecessor of Lidio Cipriani (Surdich 2016, also Landi/Moggi 2014: 24–25). The results of this expedition were published in two volumes as *Antropometria delle genti della Cirenaica* (Anthropometry of the peoples of Cirenaica) (Puccioni 1934 I & II). In an introductory note on the collection of the material, Puccioni specifies the periods of research between mid-January 1928 to the end of March 1928, and from March 1929 to May 1929 (Puccioni 1934 I: 3; for extensive research on the provenance of the mask, see Schneider 2020).

The plaster casts were taken during the colonial regime from colonial subjects subordinate to the Italian administration, in the service of Italian physical anthropologists working for the colonial government, specifically the *ufficio studio* of the colonial government of Cyrenaica. In the late nineteenth century and the first decades of the twentieth century, taking facial plaster casts was common practice among physical anthropologists working for colonial governments in other contexts, too, such as the Dutch colonies in Indonesia (see Sysling 2016). The procedures in these contexts were time-consuming, intrusive, and painful (ibidem, pp. 90–91). Making moulds for the facial mask was particularly unpleasant, often violent and forced, as it involved the application of a wet plaster directly onto the face, leaving open only the nostrils for breathing (Puccioni 1934 I: 428). This act implied the danger, not to mention the fear of suffocation. In fact, signs of duress and pain experienced during this process were visible in the masks. Colonial officials and physical anthropologists sometimes even had to trick people or provide gifts to persuade them. One way or another, they were met with fear and resistance (Sysling 2016: 92–93). As Sysling writes, it is clear that "the making of plaster casts was much easier to do within the disciplinary structures of the colonial state" (2016: 93). For our exhibition, we decided to employ the technological means of a 3D reproduction and print not to recreate but, rather, to deconstruct the original violent act of appropriation from colonised persons. The scanning process itself was repeated, and thus defamiliarised and staged for scrutiny, as a performance during the opening of the exhibition. The 3D printing of the cast, on the other hand, invoked the possibilities and limits of 're-animating', or of giving agency to the cast as a kind of simulacrum. The repressed agency of the person whose facial features were cast, subjugated under a colonial regime and forced to be impressed into plaster to obtain the negative mask, thus became *subject* again of our process.

A new facial plaster cast

What, then, to do with such casts, including the ones we chose? We commissioned *Mnemosyne*, a Naples-based company specialised in 3D printing (that also worked for the physical anthropology department of the Pigorini Museum) to scan and replicate one of the skulls as a 3D copy. We documented the printing and scanning, part of which we repeated at the exhibition with the process simultaneously visualised on the computer screen. In many ways, this raised tricky questions about the possibility and impossibility of dealing with the products of such violence, as well as the possibilities and impossibilities of re-examining and re-contextualising them in a project aimed at addressing the amnesia about the Italian colonial past.

A key and problematic question for us was just what kind of agency is involved in the plaster mask and its 3D replication. In many ways, the process of scanning and printing reactivated in an uncanny way the persons and their agency behind the facial mask. Not only was the mask reproduced, but through various movements, layering, colours, and changes in pixilation, the representation on the screen seemed to animate more than just its sculptural representation captured in Leone Contini's video *Restolen' #2'* (2017).

The mask – a positive copy from the original plaster mould – is both a remnant of and a critical testimony to the original process of plaster-making. It also served as a tactile and haptic document and artefact for us in trying to engage with this violent history. The process of reconstruction through the 3D copy then comes into the middle of the two 'sides' of the mask: its inside, so to speak, showing the contours of the facial mould (now lost), and its outside being the mask taken from the mould (and reproduced as a 3D copy), which we see. The 3D copying then probes into this process and also constructs a new artefact – novel both in its virtuality on the screen and in its materiality. In fact, it was the austere material recreation – layer upon layer, in the 3D printing process filmed by Leone Contini – that really 'remade' the mask. The incessant machine-driven, almost robot-like process of 3D printing, embossed on the mind by the constant clicking sound of the 3D printer, was the minimalist score to which this 'resurrection' was being performed. Unyielding in this monotonous and repetitive layering, the arm of the printer was in stark contrast to the seemingly more individual procedure conducted by the physical anthropologist who had taken the mould (and "human" only when contrasted to the machine), yet without the possibility of being resisted or stopped by the subject on whom this act of colonial domination originally was performed.

Once completed, the 3D copy of the mask, in some ways, reverts the gaze and also holds the beholder captive, confronting him or her with their continued gaze upon a problematic history. For the exhibition, this capacity was mobilised by Leone Contini in placing the 3D copy on a wall and a photographic still camera with an auto-shutter at a right angle next to it, which would make the unmistakable clicking sound of the shutter when the viewer looked at the mask. While the current post-colonial context is different in this regard, and Julius Lip's work would have to be critically re-assessed in in its historical contingency (not least in the problematic title of his book), one is nevertheless reminded uncannily here of his old dictum that the 'savage hits back' at his or her colonisers (Lips 1937).

Background: Ambiguous status

Returning to the discussion of the Italian-Libyan context, it can be noted that these former Italian settlers have an ambiguous status in Italy. They are only partly comparable to others who returned from former European colonies in Africa, such as the French *pieds-noirs* or Portuguese *retornados*, since Italy did not face a war of decolonisation from the Libyans before their independence in 1951. Italy lost its colonies de facto during the Second World War after Mussolini's fall in 1943, and the process of formal decolonisation was only concluded in the early 1950s. The colonial Italian settlers and their descendants – still around 20,000 – had to leave from Libya only in 1970, after Gaddafi's coup d'état in 1969. Therefore, Italy's colonialism and subsequent decolonisation, while not entirely phenomena *sui generis*, and certainly not decoupled from global developments, are difficult to classify with the standard conceptual tools of post-colonial studies. In contrast with other colonial empires, decolonisation was *not* primarily the result of struggles for independence, although resistance movements put up a fierce fight against the Italian occupiers right from the beginning – especially the Senussi Order (cf. Evans-Pritchard 1949) and the Senussi rebel leader Omar Mukhtar.[12] Instead, Italian colonialism was brought to an abrupt end through Fascist Italy's defeat in World War II in 1943, resulting, in the case of Libya, from the German-Italian defeat in North Africa in 1943, and, in the case of East Africa, from the defeat of Italian forces by the British in 1941. Thus Libya is characterised by a long and drawn-out process of decolonisation, not marked by one single date (of independence in 1951, for instance). Rather there are certain turning points that put this process into relief and signify important stages, and which historian Pamela Ballinger addresses with her critical questions:

> [C]an we say that practical or de facto decolonisation came about between 1941 and 1943 and formal decolonisation in 1947 as a result of Italy's defeat in war? Does this even count as decolonisation in Le Sueur's terms, if decolonisation entails "hard-won battles between nationalists and metropolitan colonial powers"? Or, by this definition, can decolonisation in a territory like that of Libya (...) only be said to occur in 1951 with the achievement of independence? Or does decolonisation in a genuine sense occur in 1956, with the Italo-Libyan accords that laid out the terms by which Italian projects of demographic colonization would formally cease and remaining colonial settlers would assume the mortgages for their lands? Does 1970 instead signal the final act of decolonisation, with the expropriation of Italian property and the expulsion decrees issued

by Gaddafi's revolutionary regime and the flight of the approximately 20,000 Italians still resident in Libya? Or, rather, does the 2008 Italian and Libyan Friendship Treaty in which Italy pledged $5 billion compensation for colonial atrocities mark the true closing of the decolonisation era? (Ballinger 2015: 814–815)

The Italo-Libyan interviewees of our research are living remnants of this process in today's Italy, constructing a particular and nostalgic version of both their history and the current relationship with Libya, which ultimately defines their identity in contemporary Italy and contributes to the amnesia I mentioned earlier.

In the main, the community of mostly elderly Italo-Libyans preserves strongly nostalgic memories, both privately and through the communal activities of its associations. In order to understand their mainly positive evaluation of the (post)colonial past till 1970, one has to look at their structural position in terms of history and in relation to post-colonial society. Those still alive in 2018 were obviously born after the occupation of Libya following the Italo-Turkish War (1911/12) and the subsequent colonial administration and repression of indigenous resistance during the 1920s and 1930s. Only very few had been young children during the Second World War, and, in effect, they are *descendants* of original colonists. The majority of them have a conservative outlook, stressing the Italian contribution to the development of Libya, in terms of modernity, infrastructure, and agriculture, and emphasising overall good relations with the Libyan Arabic population, indeed along with an important Jewish community, as well as with Greek and Maltese settlers. This trope of positive nostalgic remembrance of the colonial and post-colonial past also gets ritually celebrated in regular meetings of their associations and at special cultural events – a phenomenon for which our exhibition provided an attempt at a different perspective. An example of this is the exhibition *Gli Italiani in Libia: il contributo allo sviluppo del paese*, held in Bologna in 2016 (AIRL 2006a).[13]

The positive and self-congratulatory evaluation of the Italian involvement in what is perceived as the 'development' of Libya is strongly evinced in this recent exhibition and catalogue produced by the Italian association of returnees from Libya. The invitation leaflet stresses, in ways that glorify and problematically recast the Italian colonial past, three types of memory that this exhibition intended to address:

> The Proustian, involuntary memory, which "reinvigorates in the heart of the Italians in the unforgettable perfume of life in Libya", the voluntary

memory which "causes the memory of forced and painful abandon of persons, places, and things to reemerge intermittently", and the "therapeutic memory which alleviates every suffering and which projects itself as a treaty of union, of brotherhood between the past and the present, between the Italians of Libya and the young Libyans of today ..." (AIRL 2016b, with variation AIRL 2016a: 9).

Over the years the importance of the impact of the work of the Italians in the former colony, before and after World War II has been forgotten. All of Libya benefited from a radical transformation which made it a modern country. (AIRL 2016b)

These tropes of memory, all of which paint a picture of a positive colonisation, also came to the fore in our conversations with Italo-Libyans. A significant number of Italo-Libyans whom we interviewed were enrolled in the 1940s and 1950s in Catholic schools (specifically, La Salle) and have childhood memories from this time and other communal activities, such as football clubs, organised by these schools. Most of them have a conservative outlook and only a very few among them have antifascist and socialist backgrounds. In other words, it is not just that the role of Italian colonials has been 'forgotten' (as suggested by the above-mentioned exhibition catalogue), but rather that the subject of Italian colonialism, its historical responsibilities, and legacy have not been fully addressed to date in Italian society. Clearly, it has been the subject of widespread amnesia.

In this context it is useful to draw parallels with other European settlers and their forced migration from former European colonies in Africa. Former European settlers and their descendants having 'returned' to the home countries (i.e., the former colonial powers) as diverse as the French *pieds-noirs* (as well as their allies, the native Muslim Algerian *Harkis*), Portuguese *retornados*, and the former Italian colonists of Libya in their present configuration, then, constitute communities of memory or 'mnemonic communities' (Francesca Cappeletto 2003, cited in Crapanzano 2011: 193). That is to say, they are not defined by the geographic place they currently inhabit (i.e., France, Portugal, or Italy) but, rather, by the place and society surrounding them. In this sense, they are also "part of and apart from their own nation", as Eldridge (2013: 121; also 2016) writes of the *pieds-noirs* in France.

As the anthropologist Vincent Crapanzano notes on the *Harkis*, the Algerian auxiliary troops who were fighting with the French in the Algerian War of Independence (1958 – 1962), "their communities are not founded on place, but on shared memories" (2011: 193). While their structural position regarding memory is similar, the Harkis' historical experience, of course, is highly diverse from the *pieds-noirs*. The 'white' French settlers fled *en masse* after 1962, protected and helped by the French army, quite unlike the Harkis who were offered no such protection, persecuted in Algeria as traitors, interned in camps, and treated as forgotten and underdogs in French society, while being equally ostracised by other Algerian immigrants in France. Similarly, the Portuguese *retornados* still seem to carry the stain of colonialism with them (David 2015), having become "internal strangers" in Portugal after 1974 (Lubkemann 2003: 76, 84).

By contrast, the position of the Italian settlers was quite different. The Italians in Libya, despite having lost the colony, kept a privileged status in society. They continued to hold positions as administrators, technical personnel, and agricultural technicians, and even as farmers, too, under the government of King Idris from 1952 forward, when Libya became a constitutional monarchy. After the coup d'état by Ghaddafi in 1969, and their subsequent expulsion in 1970, the Italians who returned from Libya lost their raison d'être and their memories became displaced in time and space.

As I observed at one of their gatherings, the Italians who settled in Libya look back to their time in Libya in idealised ways – they even share a strange sense of elation at these gatherings, since they have nowhere to return. No reference community is left behind. As a privileged and highly regarded community before expulsion, their case is also different from the many communities which, historically and in contemporary times, had to flee their homelands, or were displaced following a history of economic and social marginalisation, not to mention ethnic or other forms of repression.

All my interview interlocutors had nostalgic views of their past in Libya, encapsulating a timeless image in their memories apparently largely untouched by external events or problems. The stories show a clear pattern of an unusually happy childhood as part of a privileged settler society, which had lost the war but, under British rule and the subsequent King Idris regime, could continue to do business and stay in a superior position in respect to the Arab majority population. With few exceptions, however, such accounts also gloss over internal differentiation and stratification within the community, including attempts during the colony to 'civilise' and 'sedentarise' South Italians, often from precarious situations as landless workers, in addition to subsequent class differences between those working in Tripoli (in oil companies, for example) and those performing agricultural work in the countryside (cf. Ballinger 2015: 822–825).

Conclusion. The challenges and limits of art-intervention, or the ethnographic field as artistic laboratory

I describe our project as an art-anthropology intervention (see Schneider 2016), as part of which we interrupted the museum's process of uncovering, reassessing, and projecting towards the future the collection of the former Italian colonial museum. As I outlined in this chapter, this process was not without surprises, detours, setbacks, and serendipitous encounters. Not least, our positionality had important consequences for our research. My colleague, the artist Leone Contini, himself a descendant of Italian settlers in Libya, found himself often in uncanny and uncomfortably encounters with the Italo-Libyans we interviewed, relating to the broad cultural life-worlds, yet entirely at odds with their views on colonialism and their nostalgically idealised memorialisation of the Italian colonial project.

Particular challenges also arose from our roles and position in the field and from our specific research agendas. While museum staff were familiar with anthropologists in a narrow sense – that is, as assuming a role of researching the artefacts, archives, and the library – the ethnographic aspect of this role, including interviews and fieldwork in the museum, had to be carefully negotiated and contextualised. Similarly, while the museum had collaborated with contemporary artists before (for instance, the collaboration of the artist H.H. Lim within the SWICH project, cf. Lim /Paderni, di Lella 2018: 8-29), it appeared uncommon for an artist to work and do intensive research on the collections and, in fact, was not always appreciated and understood, not only by technical staff.

As I have shown in this chapter, research with the artefacts from the collection posed epistemologically and ethically complex challenges, as it raised complicated questions concerning appropriation and agency of colonial subjects in Italy's colonial and post-colonial contexts. Our research made these questions productive in the final exhibition where they were laid out for critical inspection, as was our ethnographic and interview-based work with Italo-Libyans and their descendants.

During the process of this research, the museum had become both an ethnographic field and an artistic laboratory for us not only to explore ideas but also to learn to tread carefully, so as not to upset the delicate balance of powers between our serendipitous process and the limitations set by the museum context. The museum, too, had evolved during this period, even partly through the process of our research. What in 2016 had been a hidden collection in the corridors and vaults of the museum, now, under new directorship and new curators, is planned to become a research collection and exhibit for a critical reckoning with Italy's colonial past and post-colonial present – and thus works towards the cosmopolitan aspirations of decolonisation (see Macdonald, Lidchi, Oswald 2017: 96, 97, 102).

Notes

1. The image on p. 222 is Figure 8.1 Bronze bust of Rodolfo Graziani during removal from IsIAO premises, Via Aldrovandi, Rome, March 2017. Photograph by Arnd Schneider.
2. This chapter, significantly rewritten here, is based broadly on an earlier version, different in form and emphasis, published as 'The Scattered Colonial Body: Serendipity and Neglected Heritage in the Heart of Rome' in *Art, Anthropology, and Contested Heritage: Ethnographies of TRACES* (Schneider 2020). Fieldwork was part of the *TRACES* project (www.tracesproject.eu), which has received funding from the European Union's Horizon 2020 research and innovation programme under grant agreement No. 693857. The views expressed in this chapter are the sole responsibility of the author and do not necessarily reflect the views of the European Commission. Fieldwork consisted of two short exploratory field trips to Rome in May and October/November 2016, and extensive fieldwork lasting almost six months, from the end of January through to the beginning of July 2017, and culminating in a final exhibition *Bel Suol d'Amore: The Scattered Colonial Body* (25 June – 9 July, 2017). I thank all museum staff for their collaboration, especially successive directors Leandro Ventura and Filippo Maria Gambari and curators Loretta Paderni and Rossana di Lella. Thanks are also due to the Italo-Libyan settlers interviewed for this research (eleven interviews between 2017 and 2018, transcribed by Giulia Livi), and for their hospitality at a number of community events. Not everybody can be named, but special thanks are due to the Calandra family and Giancarlo Consolandi.
3. For examples, see https://leonecontini.tumblr.com/ (last accessed 14 January 2020).
4. The full title of the museum is Museo Preistorico Etnografico "Lugi Pigorini", and it is now part of the Museo delle Civiltà (that comprises also the Museo Arti e Tradizioni Popolari "Lamberto Loria", the Museo d'Arte Orientale "G.Tucci", and the Museo dell'Alto Medioevo). In the current text the shorthand 'Pigorini Museum' will be adopted. For a historical note on the museum, see https://museocivilta.beniculturali.it/museo-pigorini/ (last accessed, 8 May 2020).
5. See, http://www.treccani.it/enciclopedia/giacomo-caputo/ (accessed 9 July 2018) and https://it.wikipedia.org/wiki/Giacomo_Caputo_(archeologo) (accessed 9 July 2018).

6. *Militari della P.A.I. in motocicletta* (after 1936), by Giuseppe Rondini (Palermo 1895 – Grottaferrata, Roma 1955). P.A.I. is the acronym for *Polizia dell'Africa Italiana*.
7. In the first half of 2017, our research would arrive at a particularly delicate moment. The executor of the estate of the IsiAO, an official of ambassadorial rank at the Foreign Ministry (whom we also interviewed), was awaiting an estimate on the nominal value of the collection and was in contact with various institutions as to the future allocation of the collections. In addition, some museums, especially military museums, were closed for renovation, and for admission we had to secure special clearance from the high command of the military district of Rome.
8. See by comparison also Todorov (1984), for a classic example of a critical discussion of toponymical colonisation in the Americas during and after the conquest; for a recent discussion in the African context, see Uluochoa (2015).
9. Notably, Angelo del Boca (2014, 2015) and Nicola Labanca (2002, 2012); more recently, for example, also Bianchi and Scego (2014), Bertella Farnetti and Dau Novelli (2017), Del Monte (2015), Di Carmine (2011), and Giuliani (2019).
10. Cf. internal catalogue entries at Pigorini Museum, inventories from 1938, 1964, 1987 and 1998.
11. As above.
12. Mukhtar was hanged by the Italians in 1931, as immortalised in the 1981 film by Moustapha Akkad *The Lion of Dessert*, where Mukhtar was played by Anthony Quinn. The film was financed by Gaddafi, banned in Italy in 1982, and not shown even on pay tv until 2009. His glasses – Italian war booty, long believed to have been lost or hidden and repeatedly demanded back by successive Libyan governments – were recently rediscoverd in the collections of the IsIAO held in the Pigorini Museum.
13. As of 2018 there were also plans to show this exhibition it at the Pigorini Museum, contextualised with a critical view of exhibits from the former IsIAO and further testimonies from the Italo-Libyans.

References

AIRL 2016a. *Gli Italiani in Libia: il contributo allo sviluppo del paese*. Exhibition catalogue. Bologna: Comune di Bologna.

AIRL 2016b. *Gli Italiani in Libia: il contributo allo sviluppo del paese*. Bologna: Comune di Bologna (leaflet without page numbering).

Ballinger, Pamela. 2015. 'Colonial Twilight: Italian Settlers and the Long Decolonization of Libya'. *Journal of Contemporary History* 51(4): 813-838.

Bertella Farnetti, Paolo, and Cecilia Dau Novelli. Eds. 2017. *Images of Colonialism and Decolonisation in the Italian Media*. Cambridge: Cambridge Scholars Publishing.

Bianchi, Rino, and Igiaba Scego. 2014. *Roma negata: Percorsi postcoloniali nella città*. Rome: Ediesse.

Cappelletto, Francesca. 2003. 'Long-Term Memory of Extreme Events: From Autobiography to History'. *Journal of the Royal Anthropological Institute* 9(2): 241–260.

Chalcraft, Jasper 2018. 'Beyond Addis Ababa and Affile: Italian public memory, heritage, and colonialism'. *EUI Working Paper RSCAS* 2018/69, European University Institute: Robert Schuman Centre for Advanced Studies, San Domenico di Fiesole (Florence), http://cadmus.eui.eu/bitstream/handle/1814/60274/RSCAS_2018_69.pdf?sequence=1&isAllowed=y (last accessed 24 May 2018).

Contini, Leone. 2019. 'The Palm, the Cuscus, the Face', in: *Art, Anthropology, and Contested Heritage: Ethnographies of TRACES*, edited by Arnd Schneider. London: Bloomsbury.

———. 2020. 'The Scattered Colonial Body il diario'. *Roots & Routes* IX (30). https://www.roots-routes.org/leone-contini/ (last accessed 5 December 2019).

Cooper, Frederick. 2003. 'Postcolonial Peoples: A Commentary', in: *Europe's Invisible Migrants*, edited by Andrea L. Smith. Amsterdam: Amsterdam University Press, pp. 169–183.

Crapanzano, Vincent. 2011. *The Harkis: The Wound that Never Heals*. Chicago: University of Chicago Press.

David, Isabel. 2015. 'The *retornados*: trauma and displacement in post-revolution Portugal'. *Ethnicity Studies* 2: 114–130.

Del Boca, Angelo. 2015 [1993]. *Gli italiani in Libia: Tripoli bel suol d'amore*. Milan: Mondadori.

———. 2010 [1994]. *Gli italiani in Libia: dal fascism a Gheddafi*. Milan: Mondadori.

———. 2014 [2005]. *Italiani, brava gente? Un mito duro da morire*. Trebaseleghe (Padua): BEAT.

Del Monte, Stefania. 2015. *Staging Memory: Myth, Symbolism and Identity in Postcolonial Italy and Libya*. Frankfurt am Main: Peter Lang.

Di Carmine, Roberta. 2011. *Italy Meets Africa: Colonial Discourse in Italian Cinema*. New York: Peter Lang.

Eldridge, Claire. 2016. *From Empire to Exile: History and exile within the pied-noir and harki communities, 1962-2012*. Manchester: Manchester University Press.

———. 2013. 'Returning to the "Return": *pied-noir* Memories of 1962'. *Revue Européenne des Migrations Internationales* 29(3): 121–140.

Evans-Pritchard, E.E. 1949. *The Sanussi of Cyrenaica*. Oxford: Clarendon Press.

Fiorletta, Serena. 2012/2013. *Il museo che non c'è: Il non luogo della memoria tra narrazione nazionale e postcolonialismo*. Università degli Studi Roma "La Sapienza", Facoltà di Lettere e Filosofia, Dipartimento di Storia Culture Religioni, Scuola di Specializzazione in Beni Demoetnoantropologici (unpublished thesis).

Gandolfo, Francesca. 2014. *Il Museo Coloniale di Roma (1904 – 1971): Fra le Zebre nel Paese delll'Olio di Ricino*. Rome: Gangemi Editore.

Giuliani, Gaia. 2019. *Race, Nation and Gender in Modern Italy: Intersectional Representations in Visual Culture*. London: Palgrave Macmillan.

Grechi, Giulia. 2019. 'The Scattered Colonial Body: Leone Contini e la collezione coloniale del Museo Pigorini'. *Roots & Routes* IX (30). https://www.roots-routes.org/the-scattered-colonial-body-leone-contini-e-la-collezione-coloniale-del-museo-pigorini-di-giulia-grechi/, (last accessed 5 December 2019).

Labanca, Nicola. 2002. *Oltremare: Storia dell'espansione colonial italiana*. Bologna: Il Mulino.

———. 2012. *La guerra italiana per la Libia 1911-1931*. Bologna: Il Mulino.

Landi, Mariangela, and Jacopo Moggi Cecchi. 2014. 'Colonial anthropology: 'from the peoples of the world to the Fascist man': Nello Puccioni, Lido Cipriani', in: The museum of natural History of the University of Florence: Volume V. The Anthropological and Ethnological Collections, edited by Jacopo Moggi Cecchi and Roscoe Stanyon. Florence: Firenze University Press, pp. 22–32.

Lim, H.H., Loretta Paderni, Rossana di Lella. 2018. 'H. H. Lim at the Museo Nazionale Preistorico Etnografico "Luigi Pigorini"', in: *Co-Creation Labs: Illuminating Guests, Artists and new Voices in European Museums of World Culture*, edited by Georg Noack, Inés de Castro. Stuttgart: Sandstein Verlag / Linden-Museum Stuttgart, pp. 8–29.

Lips, Julius. 1937. *The Savage hits back or the White Man through Native Eyes*. London: Lovat Dickinson.

Lubkemann, Stephen C. 2003. 'Race, Class, and Kin in the Negotiation of "Internal Strangerhood" among Portuguese Retornados, 1975–2000', in: *Europe's Invisible Migrants*, edited by Andrea L. Smith. Amsterdam: Amsterdam University Press, pp. 75–94.

Macdonald, Sharon, Henrietta Lidchi, and Margareta von Oswald. 2017. 'Introduction: Engaging Anthropological Legacies toward Cosmo-optimistic Futures?' *Museum Worlds: Advances in Research* 5: 97–109.

Margozzi, Mariastella. Ed. 2005. *Dipinti, sculture, e grafica delle collezioni del Museo Africano: Catalogo Generale*. Rome: Instituto Italiano per l'Afica e l'Oriente.

Puccioni, Nello. 1934. I. *Antropometria delle genti della Cirenaica*. Vol. I. Florence: Felice Le Monnier.

———. 1934. II. *Antropometria delle genti della Cirenaica*. Vol. II. *Tabelle e Tavole*. Florence: Felice Le Monnier.

Schneider, Arnd 2011. 'Unfinished Dialogues: Notes Toward an Alternative History of Art and Anthropology', in: *Made to Be Seen: Perspectives on the History of Visual Anthropology*, edited by Marcus Banks and Jay Ruby, Chicago: University of Chicago Press, pp. 108-135.

———. 2013. 'Contested Grounds: Reflecting on Collaborations with Artists in Corrientes, Argentina'. *Critical Arts* 27(5): 511-530.

———. 2016. 'Art/Anthropology Interventions', in: *Practicable: From Participation to Interaction in Contemporary Art*, edited by Samuel Bianchini and Erik Verhagen. Cambridge, Mass.: MIT Press, pp. 195-214.

———. Ed. 2017. *Alternative Art and Anthropology: Global Encounters*. London: Bloomsbury.

———. 2020. 'The Scattered Colonial Body: Serendipity and Neglected Heritage in the Heart of Rome', in: *Art, Anthropology, and Contested Heritage: Ethnographies of TRACES*, edited by Arnd Schneider. London: Bloomsbury, pp. 15-36.

Schneider, Arnd, and Christopher Wright. Eds. 2006. *Contemporary Art and Anthropology*, Oxford: Berg.

———. 2010. *Between Art and Anthropology: Contemporary Ethnographic Practice*. Oxford: Berg.

———. 2013. *Anthropology and Art Practice*. London: Bloomsbury.

Surdich, Francesco. 2016. 'Nello Puccioni', *Dizionario Biografico degli Italiania, Treccani*, vol. 85, http://www.treccani.it/enciclopedia/nello-puccioni_%28Dizionario-Biografico%29/ (accessed 21 August 2018).

Sysling, Fenneke. 2016. *Racial Science and Human Diversity in Colonial Indonesia*. Singapore: National University of Singapore Press.

Todorov, Tzetvan. 1984. *The Conquest of America: The Question of the Other*. New York: Harper and Row.

Uluocha, Nna O. 2015. 'Decolonizing place-names: Strategic imperative for preserving indigenous cartography in post-colonial Africa'. *African Journal of History and Culture* 7(9): 180-192.

"Dissonant Agents and Productive Refusals"

A conversation with Natasha Ginwala

What does the practice of curating mean for you? How do you describe your practice as a curator? When we first communicated about this conversation, you refused the initial label of the curator as a translator and wrote, "Why don't we also think about refusal?"
I think you are asking important questions for what trans-anthropological representation would imply – for the museum and the collection.[1] It is crucial though to consider how this realm of trans-anthropological representation and its intersection with contemporary art is also a space of productive refusals, as much as it is a source for the generation of vital debates and 'communing' in which we find ourselves. As a curator I'm particularly keen not to remain a translator between contextual realities but instead an 'actant' and dissonant agent, so as to continue thinking how the expanding toolset of anthropology may be applied in live exchanges with artistic trajectories and interdisciplinary analyses. I'm committed to sharing vulnerability – that allows for realignments toward a grammar of non-violence, elective affinities, and pathways beyond the muscularity of success, toward what José E. Muñoz has named the art of "queer failure".

"Dissonant agency" and "productive refusal". How central are these terms to you when thinking about your practice as a curator?
It feels as though I belong to a generation of curators who have been invested in a confluence of practices from the very beginning. We have not waited for institutions to reset their agenda towards a 'non-Western' compass or to craft a more inclusive dialogue between ethnographic/anthropological collections, literature, activism, social history, and contemporary art. As the author Arundhati Roy (2003: 75) has put it: "Another world is not only possible, she is on her way. (...) But on a quiet day, I can hear her breathing." This sort of attitude where shared urgency and radical hope co-exist in the mind and hand has shaped one's curatorial labour. Those of us who form this messy

diaspora of art workers, especially in today's Berlin but also elsewhere – come with our stories, bruises, and mixed accents – these conjoin as a subjective framework to add pressure upon institutional entryways, obligations, and discourse. Whether institutions eventually change in order to stay relevant after delayed reckoning – choosing progressive or regressive agendas – this is something one has limited control over.

I trust this gives you a sense of where I'm coming from ... the dissonance is inherent in my own academic background, too, which is actually in political science and journalism prior to visual studies. It stirs certain default responses towards a literary and investigative drive.

Could you situate and contextualise this "generation of curators" that you evoke?
In this generation of curators, I mean colleagues such as Vivian Ziherl with whom I co-founded the research platform *Landings* – investigating entanglements between landforms, extraction economies, rural conditions, and colonial modernity – in partnership with a series of artists, academics, filmmakers, and cultural institutions like, for example, Witte de With Center for Contemporary Art, Stedelijk Museum, Tropenmuseum, and David Roberts Art Foundation. This was a direct negotiation with a highly West-centric discourse around the Anthropocene. I would also add allies such as Bonaventure Soh Bejeng Ndikung, Candice Hopkins, and Övul Durmuşoğlu, whose wildly creative frameworks and ethics make this profession a worthwhile shelter for me.

Not waiting for institutions implies, it seems, that you do not want to wait on them to realise your projects. Where do you locate dissonant agency and refusal in this regard?
I think that refusal and collaboration can be coefficients toward staging a mode of cultural practice that remains agile and alert toward institutional codes. There can be several ways to journey through museological spaces – through biennale making, time-based programming, contemporary exhibits that challenge archival processes – which bring a range of voices to open up museum discourse by composing a kind of 'temporary occupancy' rather than the permanent co-habitation that the institutional preservation drive imposes. At times but not always, such artistic and curatorial 'ruptures' become resonant with the dissonant energies and current velocity of our macro-political climate paving the way for sustained shifts in the field.

Let's recall here a reflection from Toni Morrison that indicates how much pressure there is on a writer or we may say creative practitioner of colour in memory keeping and bearing witness to the present. She notes:

I SUSPECT my dependency on memory as trustworthy ignition is more anxious than it is for most fiction writers—not because I write (or want to) autobiographically, but because I am keenly aware of the fact that I write in a wholly racialised society that can and does hobble the imagination. Labels about centrality, marginality, minority, gestures of appropriated and appropriating cultures and literary heritages, pressures to take a position—all these surface when I am read or critiqued and when I compose. (2019: 322)

The precondition of coloniality is to continue offering the load of trauma and systemic violence to the next generations. The cycle is broken through re-writing these ingrained codes and inscribing methodologies within and beyond the power grid of instituting disciplinary regimes.

Having been an independent curator and writer this past decade, I realise that I'm certainly dependent on institutional environments. The attempt has been to evolve multi-site models for communal and critical inquiry. Processes of building intergenerational cultural dialogue and exhibition-making become longer commitments and broker alliances that impact the way we choose to play out our lives. I've been preoccupied with cultivating a set of relations among artists and public intellectuals that to me form a kind of collective brain to understand the state of things – our tumultuous era. My first loyalties lie with them and not to one particular institution. Over various projects I've brought together thinkers such as Denise Ferreira da Silva, Leela Gandhi, and Elizabeth Povinelli into conversation with artists such as Otobong Nkanga, Lawrence Abu Hamdan, Julieta Aranda, Ho Tzu Nyen, Shilpta Gupta, and Naeem Mohaiemen, among several others. While institutions have traditionally privileged the cult of the individual auteur, another sign of the times is a move toward polyvalent approaches that break this mould.

Where do you locate and encounter anthropology today?
Your question could be modified to how does anthropology perform between academic, museum, and civic spaces today. Personally, I'm interested in the experimental approach that certain anthropologists are taking toward expanding their research into mediums such as literature, film, performance, and arts pedagogy. Some of those I'm drawn to or have collaborated with include Rosalind Morris, Anand Pandian, Jill Casid, and Bhrigupati Singh. For example: Morris's long-term research on mining in South Africa has included visual dialogue with artist William Kentridge as well as cultivating a 'subterranean' cine-aesthetics for her film work with miners examining questions of labour, distress migration, and extractivism.

Fig. 9.2 Installation view, 'Double Lives' 8th Berlin Biennale for Contemporary Art, at Museen Dahlem, 2014, © Angela Anderson

Fig. 9.3 Installation view, 'Arrival, Incision: Indian Modernism as Peripatetic Itinerary', part of Hello World. Revising a Collection, Hamburger Bahnhof – Museum für Gegenwart, Berlin 2018, © Mathias Völzke

So, if you're asking, "Where do you find the kind of contexts for anthropology and curating to intersect?" then it is amid the non-conformative kinship of academia and artistic thinking where a mutation of forms can occur – and then bringing together institutional partners who are adventurous in animating frameworks for such exercises. Most often the ethnological museum is bypassed and other kinds of contemporary sites become the hub or laboratory for re-thinking anthropological inquiry in cultural terms. An essential aspect of the discipline is 'self-interrogation', and therefore museums must offer a self-reflexive character to be able to host such dynamic interplay between scholarship and cultural production. One of my earliest projects within a biennale framework was *The Museum of Rhythm* at the Taipei Biennale 2012. It involved rendering a speculative institution premised on principles of rhythm analysis, modernism's relation with time-keeping, and historical narrativisation through recursive and pulsating schemes of rhythm, labour, and sonority.

Two of my recent projects relate to these observations: *Arrival, Incision: Indian Modernism as Peripatetic Itinerary* in *Hello World* at Hamburger Bahnhof (2018) and *Double Lives* as part of the 8th Berlin Biennale (2014). The Ethnological Museum in Dahlem is among the first institutions I grew familiar with after moving to the city to join the Berlin Biennale team in 2013. The commute to Dahlem and learning about the collection became a sort of rehearsal for the biennale and informed our curatorial approach in relation to taxonomy and display architecture; historical becoming and fiction in narrating 'between the cracks'; false binary of nature-culture in the colonial enterprise. The invited artists did not disrupt the standing displays in Dahlem, instead the Biennale curator Juan A. Gaitán and the artistic team developed a trajectory by which interruptions could take place that in turn diverted, re-routed, and multiplied pathways and developed constellations inside the museum's genealogy.

It's interesting to see anthropology in an undisciplined way – not meaning that "anthropology is what anthropologists do". Rather, anthropology actually takes as its focus an undisciplined and deliberately unfocused way of the human being and their practice. It gathers a certain set of materials and practices and documents, and tries to make sense of them through these practices. By spending time in a field. Through embodied, time-intense being in a particular kind of field. This seems to also apply to your work, but you're describing your relationship to anthropology without any reference to the problematic legacy of anthropological work.
I think an endemic problem of Western anthropology is that it has thrived on deadening the flow of living traditions. There's a fundamental disparity

between one wishing to study active knowledge systems of a community in order to fixate meaning and transfer their potency for a constituency that has no regard for the everyday survival and embodied relatedness to the producers of that living practice. There is a need to acknowledge incompleteness in understanding, since the endeavour of arriving at total comprehension is an aggressive and entitled one – capturing the world as universal image has caused disasters. When working with cultural practitioners there is reconciliation with incomplete understanding, untranslatable expressions, and unfinished archives.

To explain, let me actually just mention a few things about the research exhibit that I organised as part of the 8th Berlin Biennale for Contemporary Art – *Double Lives*. The exhibition departed from the lack of visibility of agents: colonial administrators, early geographers, armchair naturalists, local guides, surveyors, and expedition aides who produced the ethnological collection as knowledge and as valued possession. I wished to expose the biographies of some of these 'collectors' alongside the samples, annotations, maps, exhibition items, and hand-illustrated manuals. This parallel gaze was meant as a way to underscore the feedback loop between colonial expansion, imperial conquest, early expedition history, and the professionalisation of the sciences as well as ethnology. The stereoscope – an analogue viewing

Fig. 9.4 Installation view, 'The Museum of Rhythm' at Muzeum Sztuki, Łódź 2017. © Piotr Tomczyk

device that provides dimensionality to pictures – stitching together faraway horizons into proximity became a leitmotif for this project. Stereoscopic vision creates an illusion of intimacy and desire between the observer and the perceived object or destination. I therefore felt this nineteenth-century instrument could provoke an inquiry into hyphenated characters such as the colonial administrator, geologist, and naturalist Franz-Wilhelm Junghuhn, also called the 'Humboldt of Java', and other such figures. They haunt collections built as part of the colonial enterprise, but their presence is often elided from the official narration surrounding museum artefacts. The larger agenda of repatriation, knowledge-sharing, and reconciliation can only grow by acknowledging these hybrid personas across colonial time.

You've worked with, against, and within different institutions, which have different kinds of framings. Whether its the framing through their name, through the collections, through a discipline – the Hamburger Bahnhof, the Ethnologisches Museum, Museum of Asian Art, Kunst-Werke, and so on. What do you feel that these different institutions enable or disable, specifically with regard to the non-disciplinary anthropological work that you're interested in?

Firstly, I feel that there's a re-shuffling of what used to be stable framings in cultural institutions today. Needless to say, this is further impacted by the massive sweep of far-right authoritarian rule in so many corners of the world. That is also why the anthropological museum *and* the contemporary art space are undergoing a crisis of language. Just look at the chapter that I was curating, *Arrival, Incision: Indian Modernism as Peripatetic Itinerary* as part of *Hello World* at the *Hamburger Bahnhof* (2018). Nearly the entire exhibition departed from a collection that was built by the archaeologist and Indologist Herbert Härtel, who was the founding director of the Museum für Indische Kunst in 1963. He did archaeological research in central India and was teaching South Asian art history at the Freie Universität Berlin in the 1970s. This special museum with collections of modernist Indian painting, which included seminal works of abstraction and tantric art especially, was eventually dissolved. So it is quite sad to see as that what you inherit is actually something of what the frames have dissolved and been erased. You then need to piece them back together in order to create an understanding for the present that is more complete. In museum anthropology, I've witnessed how the inventory is a messy site of erasure, haunting, and inaccuracy. And this is where that 'rear entrance' occurs, which is often ignored in debates on curatorial practice. As part of engaging with the Dahlem Museums, one has engaged in longer discussions around the politics of an inventory and how to add meaning to a collected object that is undocumented. Aspects of authorship, gender dynamics, social history can be enabled, literally switched on, by re-situating where and how the reading of collected fragments takes place.

In the chapter of *Hello World. Revising a Collection* there's a painted portrait of Jawaharlal Nehru from the 1950s by the artist Laxman Pai, and for some reason it was not listed in the inventory (of the Asian Art Museum) I received when starting to work towards the exhibition. It became an excavation while visiting the storage and re-contextualised the first section of the exhibition. What does it mean for this Nehru portrait to remain in the storage of an ethnological museum in Berlin today and how do we frame its broader relevance? This is why I feel like, unless we trigger conversations from *within* the institutions, it's going to become more difficult to access and dialogue around the work, conflicted histories, and translocation. Of course, there are curators who are taking a completely different approach of rejecting entirely the space of the anthropological museum. I'm not talking about an outright rejection because I'm constantly seeing that it is only through rigorous study from inside and from imaginative leaps – with older colleagues who are trained and became stakeholders of ethnographic collections – that a shift in contemporary cultural practice can be realised. This quote from Bénédicte Savoy and Felwine Sarr's report released in November 2018, *The Restitution of African Cultural Heritage. Toward a New Relational Ethics* has stayed with me:

> To fall under the spell of an object, to be touched by it, moved emotionally by a piece of art in a museum, brought to tears of joy, to admire its forms of ingenuity, to like the artworks' colours, to take a photo of it, to let oneself be transformed by it all: all these experiences—which are also forms of access to knowledge—cannot simply be reserved to the inheritors of an asymmetrical history, to the benefactors of an excess of privilege and mobility. (2018: 4)

It interests us that you seem to be suggesting that, if some of these museum and exhibition-making institutions dissolve, we would also lose track of some of the genealogies, some of the stories by which such collections came about.

There is such a ruthless history of dissolving traces of imperial violence, looting, and cultural erasure. Anthropology museum storage rooms become depersonalised, sleepy, and toxic depots that usually separate the narratives of mercantile quest, colonial administration, indigenous knowledge from the biography of objects. Herein lies the unfinished task of recuperation, resuscitation, reanimation, and recirculation.

However problematic and outdated some of the display systems were at the Ethnological Museum in Dahlem, that topography of display had within it an inherent logic and imagination that conveyed German museology's relation to the colonial project as well as its aftermath. For decades, it also played a role within the micro-history of West Berlin as a pedagogic interface for certain generations to reckon with the imperial economy of a global collection from a fractured western European city. On the other end of this spectrum is a project such as the Humboldt Forum that promises to re-brand as a 'place of discovery and worldly encounter' without the anchorage of this collection's history and has become a disputed internal migration across the city bearing a mammoth price tag. I think we have to be really careful in reading the public mission of such an endeavor – and whether it can eventually enable the de-centralisation of museum practice.

Terms like 'indigeneity', 'tribe', and 'native' are the subjects of much anthropological critique. They are also used as a challenge against anthropology while, at the same time, you see that the same terms are re-used in contexts of contemporary art. How can the migration of these terms from one context into another suddenly shift their value, meaning, and use?
It is problematic for indigenous knowledge to become commodified within the contemporary art landscape without agential performance. This process enables certain kinds of creative mobility, while the broader infrastructural and legal landscape keeps these very knowledges trapped, deteriorating, and incarcerated. However, let us also be conscious here of the immense power of indigenous movements and planetary solidarities that are taking shape in simultaneity.

It is a privilege to witness the expanded vocabularies that various communities are foregrounding through the arts and advocacy for representation in a longer struggle for survival. Recently, I've been meeting with Samí artists, poets and musicians in Sapmi, Maori, and Pacific Islander communities in Aotearoa, and shamans undertaking extended ceremonies in South Korea. While we need to remain conscious of terminologies and means of engagement, there are greater lessons to watch for, which are especially informing the research Defne Ayas and I are doing as part of the Gwangju Biennale 2020, lessons that attend to the role of the 'communal mind' and collective intelligence in mobilising modes of renewal, healing techniques, and addressing trauma in an age of anxiety.

During *Experimenter Curators Hub* 2018 in Kolkata, I had an interesting conversation with Persian-Samoan artist and curator Leuli Eshraghi, who was exploring ways to generate productive visibility, sharing of logistics, and re-coding the spatial grammar of institutional spaces with indigenous artists and art organisers. They spoke of the need for mourning and ceremonial practice as a process against the continuum of violence and networks of healing. In these actions there was an operation against translation such that the manifestation was geared toward the communal stakeholders and not 'white privilege' needing to be central to each story. We also considered how tools of 'reverse anthropology' are actively being deployed by indigenous artists and writers to explain the dominant culture to itself and treat it as minor within an embodied literacy.

Cultural anthropology and contemporary curating, both to different extents, must embrace opacity to cope with the psycho-social darkness and toxicity in our midst. When one enters a sacred architecture in several traditions from Shinto shrines to Balinese temples, there is a point at which not everyone is invited into the inner shrine. This is not about exclusion per se but about the interplay of factors connected with patterns of belief, preservation and manifestation. Contemporary cultural institutions assume a mandate of total access, while in reality there is an entrenched hierarchy that forms trajectories of rejection. Learning from models for assembling that provide a grammar of participation and access without alienation interests me greatly.

Note

1. The image on p. 242 is Figure 9.1 Karrabing Film Collective, installation view at Contour Biennale 8 for *Polyphonic Worlds: Justice as Medium*, Mechelen 2017. Courtesy of the artists and Contour Biennale 8. Image Credit: Kristof Vrancken.

References

Morrisson, Toni. 2019. *The Source of Self-Regard. Selected Essays, Speeches, and Meditations*. New York: Alfred A. Knopf.
Roy, Arundhati. 2003. *War Talk*. Cambridge, MA: South End Press.
Sarr, Felwine, and Bénédicte Savoy. 2018. *The Restitution of African Cultural Heritage. Toward a New Relational Ethics*. Translated by Drew S. Burk. Paris: Ministère de la Culture. http://restitutionreport2018.com/sarr_savoy_en.pdf (last accessed 20 February 2020).

Porous Membranes: Hospitality, Alterity, and Anthropology in a Berlin District Gallery

Jonas Tinius

Membranes are ambiguous.[1] They divide and connect. The gallery at the centre of this piece has such a membrane, and it is composed of its large, nearly five-metre high window front, covering the 180 square meters of gallery space. These windows allow for the exchange of glances, hushed and cramped, on a rainy November morning, or curious and playful, on warm July evenings. One side faces Müllerstraße, one of the central alleys named after the windmills that used to stand on this still windy and busy road leading from Berlin's north into its central business artery Friedrichstraße southwards. Bus drivers stop in front of the gallery at the 'Rathaus Wedding' stop of the 120, N6, and N20 lines almost every five minutes on a weekday. Doors open, twenty to fifty pairs of eyes glance at sculptures, paintings, installations, videos, photographs; many will not enter the gallery. Curators, assistants, artists, and, sometimes, visitors gaze back. The southern side of the gallery faces Rathausplatz, the Schiller Library, and Simit Evi, a small Turkish-run bakery and café, rescued from disappearance during the recent reconstruction of the square thanks to a neighbourhood initiative. On top of a building, someone has written a message in large letters: *angst fressen seele auf* (fear eats the soul), the title of a 1974 film by Rainer Werner Fassbinder on social oppression, projections of fear, and the precarious life of a Moroccan guest worker and his elderly working-class German partner.

The gallery is located in the bottom corner of the social services department of the district's municipal offices – *Bezirksamt Mitte, Amt für Soziales*. People step off the bus and walk past the gallery, on their way to the district, for forms on care, ageing, shelter, pensions, debt, unemployment. A membrane divides and connects all at once. It is a boundary, a vibrating tissue, a layer, a skin, a permeable film. Towards the gallery, this membrane is a kind of selective barrier, mechanical barrier, architecture, and curatorial element at the same time. For their exhibition *Circling Around Oneness* (shown between November 2016 and January 2017), the artistic duo Mwangi Hutter blackened out the windows with dark chalk. Soon, traces and carved lines were scratched into this porous boundary: Kids wrote their names; others carved hearts, dates, insults, questions. One reads, "Wedding ist cool", another, "*von wegen!*" ('as if!'). More and more erased lines in the chalk let the light in and allow viewers from the outside to discover the projections of a man and a woman sleeping in separate beds. Some stop, peer in, curious; one of the curators returns the gaze. The membrane becomes more and more porous, opens gaps, and invites, at least for a hasty moment, a look inside.

Prefigurative curatorial fields

In June 2016, after several years of studies and research in the UK, I had just moved to Berlin for a post-doctoral research fellowship at the Centre for Anthropological Research on Museums and Heritage (CARMAH).[2] As part of the larger research project to which I belonged – and from which, together

Fig. 10.2 View of the gallery membranes from Müllerstraße during the exhibition *Circling Around Oneness* (2016) by Mwangi Hutter, Galerie Wedding, © Fernando Gutiérrez Juárez

with Margareta von Oswald – this edited volume emerged, we focused on the ways in which museums, curatorial work, and heritage practices act as catalysts of 'differences', discriminating and otherwise, such that they not merely reflect as public theorisers, but, to varyingly deliberate degrees, help to constitute. We collectively studied the ways in which ethnographic research into and with exhibition practices can help understand how museums and heritage practices and also contemporary art and curatorial practices are involved in the complex "coordination of difference and identity" (Macdonald 2016: 4) within cities and nations. This concerned most urgently, as we present in the introduction to this volume, the ways in which anthropological museums are steeped in legacies of colonial ordering and knowing, which determine the past and future of objects as they transit through their negotiations as art, artefact, gift, or loot, valued or deaccessioned, stored or restituted. This debate moved across the scales of in-house curatorial discussions in such institutions to nationwide conversations about museums, heritage, and the role of the colonial past for contemporary European societies.

My research looked at how contemporary art institutions and curatorial practice deliberate *with* but, more interestingly, *across* such discursive formations. In particular, I attended to artistic and curatorial ways of dealing with alterity and othering, sociality and hospitality, diversity and discrimination in

Fig. 10.3 One part of the video projection, with visitors sitting on the radiators in front of the gallery membrane facing Müllerstraße, during the exhibition *Circling Around Oneness* (2016) by Mwangi Hutter, Galerie Wedding, © Fernando Gutiérrez Juárez

a city like Berlin. I conducted fieldwork on three galleries in Berlin, including the ifa-gallery of the Institute für Auslandsbeziehungen (Germany's oldest intermediary organisation for international cultural relations supported by the German Federal Foreign Office); the independent and project-based art space SAVVY Contemporary; and the district gallery of Wedding, or Galerie Wedding – Raum für zeitgenössische Kunst (hereinafter, GW). For my fieldwork, I sought out conversations with curators and contemporary artists who were addressing questions that Margareta von Oswald and I theorise in our introduction as 'trans-anthropological', that is, ways of addressing the legacies of anthropology as a discipline and its institutions. These forms of questioning and areas of problematisation that I traced thus included artistic practices addressing museums and forms of classifying European and non-European cultures, as well as practices that themselves took inspiration through methodological queries about fieldwork, or engaged themes that had long been part of the curricula and theoretical canon of different anthropological traditions, such as alterity, migration, hospitality, archives, object histories, and provenance.

While the Humboldt Forum and its creation – as well as its reception by critics and fellow anthropologists inside and outside the institution – served as a backdrop to my studies (see our introduction to this volume, and Zinnenburg and Tinius 2020), I was interested in following the rethinking of themes associated with this large museum and heritage project in the field of contemporary art and "contemporary creation" (Sarr and Savoy 2018: 24). In the light of well-rehearsed anthropological analyses of contemporary curatorial practice and contemporary art as constitutive and reflexive of politically *prefigurative* social forms (Ssorin-Chaikov 2013, and Sansi 2014; Blanes et al. 2016), I studied how such practices negotiate the thin line that reproduces some of the barriers they seek to break down (Tinius 2020). These included failing to move smoothly between the precarious boundaries between exclusive arts spaces while marshalling a quest for inclusivity, or claiming to be alternative to, while often embodying the hyper-productive model of a creative industry innovation logic (see Reckwitz 1995; Boltanski and Chiapello 2007; Canclini 2014).

Thresholds and ambivalences

This chapter speaks to this problematic by highlighting how two curators – and a number of artists with whom they collaborated – grapple with this ambivalent intersection and such membranes between 'inside work' in

Berlin's Galerie Wedding and the 'outside life' of the district and its cultural politics that mandates the gallery. I do so by focusing on how its curatorial team struggled to address the very limits and possibilities afforded with the porous membranes of the gallery – the negotiation of a threshold, whose varying porosity encapsulates and is constitutive of the gallery's ambivalent status in the district. Its large floor-to-ceiling windows, often incorporated into exhibitions, act as literal thresholds between the inside of the gallery and its outside.

The gallery itself is also a threshold as a contemporary art institution. It is situated in a largely migrant and working-class district – more precisely, in the district's social security office – with a public mandate to engage with this urban social context. And yet, the gallery is clearly articulated by the curatorial duo, and thus tasked by public cultural policymakers who appointed them, to be a contemporary arts space, connected to scenes of artistic production that are "based in Berlin, but not defined by their location", as the curators put it to me. Their curatorial programmes, called *Post-Otherness Wedding (POW)* (2015-2017) and *Unsustainable Privileges (UP)* (2017-2019) speak to this ambivalent process and task, which I unravel in this chapter.

How, then, can a reflexive, hospitable curatorial programme, which addresses the distribution of privileges for German and non-German citizens and challenges essentialisations of difference along race and class lines, offer a productive critique, in spite of being itself, broadly, a privileged white cube marked out from the otherwise different district?

Offering thus a case study of curatorial work on hospitality, alterity, and anthropology – and also, to some extent, of attempts and perhaps failures of doing so – I want to suggest that it is precisely the *curatorial grappling* with the porosity of the gallery that constituted it. The gallery's 'district curating' became a reflection on its limits, porousness, and the attempts and failures to transgress its thresholds. Over the course of their curatorial engagement with the public mandate, and their own professional networks and approaches to curating, the artistic directors struggled with, and in doing so, constantly redrew the thin line between interrogating, representing, and inadvertently constituting the often reified idea of diversity in a district like Berlin-Wedding.

Gallery transitions and curatorial reframing

Up until the start of the new artistic team and the beginning of their curatorial reframing in January 2015, GW had primarily been a for-the-community gallery with district-based artists, focusing on art production without competitive market values or any embedding in the contemporary art structures, mechanisms, criteria, and fields of the city. By the time I had begun fieldwork, the gallery had already shifted its institutional structure, planned outreach, style, and rhetoric, as well as curatorial-theoretical framing to address this wider field of international contemporary art. The framing was phrased, by the curators, thus as solo shows by "internationally-recognised but Berlin-based artists". The transition was enacted principally through the hiring of two Berlin-based independent artistic directors, Solvej Helweg Ovesen and Bonaventure Soh Bejeng Ndikung, who had established connections to international artists and fields in contemporary art production and theorising. Both curators worked closely with the district officer for culture, Ute Mueller-Tischler, who was in charge of publicly-funded artistic and cultural institutions in the city districts of Wedding and Mitte, and who oversaw this structural transformation.

Anthropology and Post-Otherness

The change of curatorial and organisational culture went hand-in-hand with the creation of two successive two-year overarching exhibition frameworks. The first, *Post-Otherness Wedding*, was conceived on the basis of a collaborative curatorial concept co-authored by Ndikung and my colleague, the Humboldt-Universität zu Berlin anthropologist Regina Römhild (see Ndikung and Römhild 2013). The programme sought to take difference (social, cultural, ethnic) as a starting point for thinking about the hospitality, and indeed hostility, of cities and public spaces, rather than articulating such difference, epitomised by migrants and refugees, as a negative foil against a mainstream urban civic society. This was followed by a second curatorial programming phase called *Unsustainable Privileges* (2017-2019), which investigated how it might be possible to change the 'unsustainable' distribution of privileges pertaining to race, class, and gender – if at all.

For this chapter, I draw on fieldwork conducted during the transition of the GW programme from its *Post-Otherness Wedding* to *Unsustainable Privileges* between the summer of 2016 through 2019, when the artistic directors shuffled again.[3] During this time, I had become a close observer and participant in the gallery's jour fixe, during which the curatorial team met with artists included in the programming, usually in the crammed kitchen hidden from view of the gallery visitors, in order to negotiate their planned projects within the often precarious budgets and time frames afforded by the gallery. In fact, some publications emerged from the conversations that spontaneously took off during such meetings, and which were recorded or transcribed by me. Other notes and deliberations of aspects pertinent to the gallery's everyday negotiations also resulted in a set of preliminary field notes in the gallery catalogue that I was invited to write (Tinius 2019a). The curators' invitation of my presence, perspectives, and contributions as co-author, moderator, and colleague, opened the conversations in the gallery to becoming a kind of 'para-site' (Marcus 2000) and field of trans-anthropological practice. This situation arose because we understood our conversation as a form of recursive collaboration, in which curatorial and anthropological positions were not subjecting one another to an overarching position, but rather overlapped and corresponded; these aimed instead at understanding, transforming, and generating the contexts within which they operate (see Macdonald and Tinius 2020).

There are further evident connections to anthropology beyond the initial programming inspiration from a text co-authored and published by an anthropologist and a curator, which served as the starting point of the gallery's transition into a new set of programming focusing centrally on the issues of hospitality and the negotiation of alterity in Berlin. Many layers of the subsequent concept work, the artistic and curatorial research, or the exhibition-making drew on anthropological publications; research assistants to artists employed a variety of qualitative, fieldwork-based approaches to the city – some of which are further discussed below – in ways of thinking about difference, and about collectivity and conviviality that correspond closely with those practised, for instance, at the Department of European Ethnology from which Römhild and I engaged with the gallery team. In that sense, the curatorial work could be described as trans-anthropological, in so far as it engages and grapples with anthropology without itself either rejecting or becoming fully anthropological itself. In what follows, I describe these forms of thought and will argue that they converse with a trans-anthropological form of research across anthropology and curatorial practice, leaving open challenges to both fields, which were left unresolved but opened up ways for further considering the possibility of a recursive anthropological curation. In the following analyses of selected artistic positions in the curatorial programmes, in particular, I will be looking at how the 'curation' of a district became a central problem for the gallery team, and how this articulated further the problematic and constitutive issue of the gallery as a porous membrane.

Deep curating

In their published catalogue *POW.UP – Post-Otherness Wedding & Unsustainable Privileges* (Ovesen and Ndikung 2019), the curators reflect on the emergence of their curatorial positioning with the GW. "The curatorial journey", they write, "has attempted to undo mechanisms of othering as well as to unlearn privileges (Gayatri Spivak) with the language and tools of visual art" (p. 26). Part of this project, in their words, involves using

> our own privilege and the possibility of working non-commercially in the communal Galerie Wedding to take the time to play out often-unresolvable conflicts of interest in future models of cohabitation and society building. (ibidem)

Despite their reflexive positioning, the transformation of the gallery remained ambiguous. Nora Sternfeld, in her contribution to this volume, speaks of curating as a form of "making conflicts liveable". She refers to conflicts between the institutional demands of a creative economy that values innovation and a neoliberal climate in which curators act as agents, on the one hand, of gentrification and, on the other hand, of curatorial projects seeking integration and sustainable conviviality. The two curators were positioned precisely in this pitfall: how were they to reconcile the evident attention-economy of a high-frequency and discursive, if not intellectualised performance exhibition economy with the harsh and precarious realities of a district public that has little to no exposure to the references and infrastructures of this economy?

Ovesen, on behalf of the GW artistic team, proposes thus a particular model of curating, which she expounds in the same introduction to the gallery catalogue as a form of "'slow' or 'deep' curating" (2019: 26). For her, such a slow or deep curatorial approach at the GW focuses on longevity and relations – "one artist and two curators, along with a gallery team" – extending from this relation also to other discursive partners and 'thinkers', over the course of a year or longer. "Deep curating means going wide socially (...) and allowing for discursive conflict while taking time", Ovesen adds (ibidem).

District curating and the post-migrant Other

The specific task given to the curators by the district gallery's situatedness and institutional position creates additional complexity. The gallery team was grappling with this issue, both among the curators and assistants, but also in response to audiences visiting the space, and embraced the location and institutional context of GW as a steady and recurring reference point for each new project. Ovesen, in her statement, continues to reason about the different perspectives from which the district provides for a particular kind of curating.

> Ideally, this [deep curating] allows an artistic oeuvre, vision, and an urban situation like that of Wedding to be lit up from within, above, and behind and to be shared among a group of people for a certain amount of time. (Ibidem, p. 27)

Summarising the GW stance on the relation between the local and the cosmopolitan, she states that "[w]e have invited artists from around the world, who live and work in Berlin, to exchange ideas with our audiences, and with us as a team, about how to reach out to each other across our differences" (ibidem). This "reaching out to each other across our differences" is not just a statement about differences across artistic or curatorial positions, but across and in spite of what the curators describe as the problem of homogenised hegemonic ethnic, social, and aesthetic purity that nation-states perform with regards to 'newcomers' and 'migrants' in Germany (see e.g. Borneman and Ghassem-Fachandi 2017). This reference to newcomers across the Global South echoes the initial impulse for the curatorial programming by Ndikung and Römild (2013), wherein they explain that the figure of the '"post-Other" does not just "bear the signs of historical Othering", but also represents and experiments "with unknown futures beyond it" that unfold "a cosmopolitanised reality of convivial struggles" (Ndikung 2019a: 35). This contribution draws on conversations initiated in the field of performance and theatre in Germany, most notably questions of Germany as a post-migrant society – a society that recognises migration as a starting point of social becoming, not a development thereafter (see Tinius 2016, 2019b). Cognisant, again, of the particular situatedness of the gallery's curatorial practice, Ndikung also recognises that

> [i]n the context of the Berlin district of Wedding, a traditionally working-class area with roughly half of the population made up of immigrants, the concept and figure of the Post-Other seems to be an omnipresent but unrealised concept and figure. (ibidem, p. 36)

As such, the task inevitably remained for the curators to craft programming that would be participatory and, at the same time, aspire to move beyond a mere mirroring or double authentication of the 'diversity' of the district by exhibiting that very difference in terms of race, class, and gender postulated by the curators. Additionally, the curators tasked themselves with their phrasing to elaborate a type of conceptual programming that moves beyond binarisms of 'migrant' and 'non-migrant populations', which Ndikung sets up in his own reflection on the post-Other figure. As Ndikung and Römhild write, "While historically, the colonial Other was integrated into the binary hierarchical relation between 'metropolis' and imperial 'periphery' across geographical distance, this spatial order of 'here' and 'there' is collapsing because of the past and present of migrations and mobilities" (2013: 213–214). In this regard, Wedding was a former Western district and thus at odds with the clichéd relation of both 'migrant' and the former East of Berlin to working-class areas of Berlin. In the following, I outline how several, but in particular two artists tried to face, and to some degree unearthed, conflicts of this kind, attending in my analysis to the anthropological dimension of their grappling with the presentation and construction of a Wedding district identity.

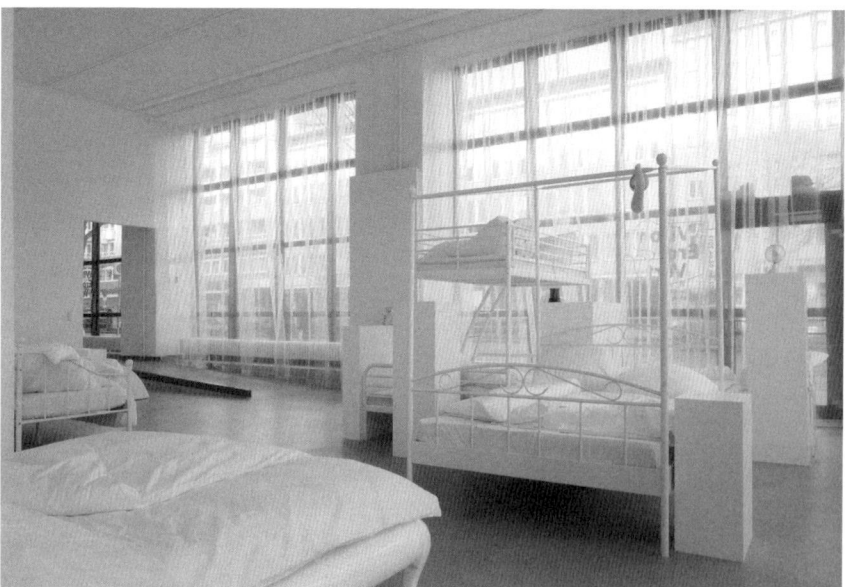

Fig. 10.4 Exhibition view of Viron Erol Vert's dreamatory, *The Name of Shades of Paranoia, Called Different Forms of Silence* (2017) in Galerie Wedding, © Johannes Berger

Dreamatories and hospitality

Artist Viron Erol Vert's exhibition was entitled *The Name of Shades of Paranoia, Called Different Forms of Silence* (shown at GW from February until April 2017). It was devised particularly for the gallery space and reactivated, in curious ways, the membrane as well as the tension between the inside of the gallery and its outsides, its porosity and thresholds. Upon entering the exhibition, a sleepy atmosphere engulfed visitors; the room set-up comprised twelve beds, white sheets, white wood; beds of different sizes, bunk beds, children's beds had been donated by district residents, following an open-call by the artist. Vert's exhibition spread across the entire space of the gallery. Veiled curtains shelter the space from view; the membrane is reactivated to create what he called a 'dreamatory' – a dream-laboratory, a social sculpture that invites visitors to sleep in the space during the day and to record their dreams in the notebooks provided by the gallery in lieu of a visitor's book. The artist invited visitors to narrate their dreams or record them in this way, offering, if they agree, their notes for analysis by *oneirocritics*, who are invited to the gallery space to interpret dreams on a regular basis.

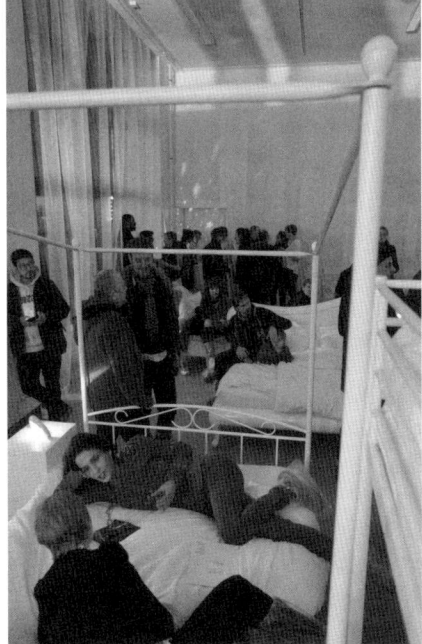

Fig. 10.5 Visitors during the opening of Viron Erol Vert's dreamatory, *The Name of Shades of Paranoia, Called Different Forms of Silence* (2017) in Galerie Wedding, © Johannes Berger

When I met Vert in his Kreuzberg studio-flat for an interview, he told me

> I want to collect these dreams, let people draw on what they've experienced – but I fear they might not dare. It's a tricky and for me very important task to create an environment that allows you to sleep, rest.

The curators elaborated Vert's thoughts on his dreamatory for envisioning the district and its relation to the gallery in the concept note for the exhibition: "It is also in sleep that our experiences are processed, and information taken on is processed and consolidated in short- to long-term memory. How can we consider sleep and dreaming as spaces and even as acts of/for unconscious political resistance?" (Ndikung 2019b: 188) They hoped that inhabitants of the district, marked by precarity and migration – thus also by the effects of social and psychosomatic forms of othering – would join the dream space. Ndikung even ponders the possibility of considering "taking the time to sleep" as an act of refusal; "especially within a neoliberal economic context of productivity and over-productivity, and within a social context wherein one finds drugs that allow one to go on and on for days without sleep" (ibidem). For him, the link between Vert's reflections on dream, sleep, and productivity and the gallery's social context – its relation to conviviality – become "a political choice" insofar as they offer a way to think about the rejuvenating process of sleep as "a mode of resistance that resuscitates society" (ibidem).

Prior to his exhibition opening, Ovesen and Ndikung had invited Vert to a jour fixe to plan a joint symposium on dreams and consciousness in collaboration with the Association of Neuroesthetics, organised by academic Jörg Fingerhut and curator Elena Agudio. "The beds are meant as an invitation", Vert began our conversation. "They function as propositions", the artist continued,

> [n]ot just to dream, but also to process: I just had a long conversation with a taxi driver, who told me of sleepless nights, trauma, because he fears for what happens in Turkey. But even here we are not safe: Many are paranoid to speak up. Much of this is invisible to the majority population, but I hear it.

Ndikung picked this up in the conversation during our jour fixe in the kitchenette behind the exhibition space: "These are invisible privileges: Who can rest and who cannot rest at night, who can speak and who cannot speak for themselves?" To what extent can a gallery become a space that speaks "for" others? It cannot, someone says, but we "speak nearby" as Trinh T. Minh-Ha

(1992) put it, for whom this indirect speaking is always "a way of positioning oneself in relation to the world."

"I don't want to talk about Germany, or Europe. I want to talk about humanity and to explode national frameworks, not redefine them", Ndikung adds somewhat disgruntled. "But we have to begin somewhere – with the local, with identification. We have to talk about freedom and competence of speech", Ovesen responded, "because it is a privilege and resource to speak." Someone turned on a laptop to show an online advertisement of the German Identitarian movement in Bavaria: "This debate on being rooted is highly charged – who is rooted where?", the production assistant Kathrin Pohlmann thinks out aloud.

Vert was born in Berlin but with a family background that stretches across Greece, Kurdistan, and Armenia – a series of relations that he has further fictionalised in his exhibitions, including *Born in the Purple* (2017, Kunstraum Kreuzberg/Bethanien Berlin) and the dreamatory invitations in GW. His popular opening of the exhibition attracted a significant amount of visitors as well as the usual suspects from the city's media and artistic circles, who filled the room and created a lounge club atmosphere. But the inscriptions in the visitor notebook, which he carefully prepared, read, analysed, and reproduced with permission in his catalogue, spoke of different stories – those of the youths, adolescents, and even children whose dreams were recorded, scribbled, or translated into drawings with Turkish, Arabic, and German annotations, suggesting an altogether more porous participation.

Wedding and the *Beast of No Nation*

Vert's white curtains and beds seeking dream-narratives contrasted, at first sight, with the search for a dark and dirty underbelly of Berlin, as suggested by artist Emeka Ogboh's project at GW. Ogboh, a sound artist and another long-term collaborator in Ovesen and Ndikung's 'deep curatorial network', frequently passed by the gallery for extended jour fixe, in which he presented a project that moved from oneiric to gastronomical queries of hospitality and conviviality. It was entitled *Beast of No Nation*, B.O.N.N., and shared with the public as part of the *Unsustainable Privileges* symposium with a book and beer launch in September 2018. His project was structured around the brewing of a beer that responds to the "taste of Wedding" (Ogboh, personal comment) – a notion that gave rise to much discussion among the gallery team, since it presupposed there could be such a thing as a 'taste' or 'character' of a district. "In fact", Ogboh added in our first conversation, "that is already the wrong idea; there is no character of a district, but I want to provoke people into bringing together their senses and their imaginations of place."

Already in 2015, GW, Vagebund Brewery, and Ogboh produced a dark beer that had explored dimensions of conviviality, the politics of race, and ethnic purity in reference to the German beer-brewing purity law, which was seen as an analogy to the predominantly white nation and continent (see also Tinius 2018). In 2017, the large-scale art fair documenta14, which was curated, among others, by Ndikung, popularised his critical Sufferhead brew, which was a direct outcome from this collaboration.

The project he proposed to GW, *Beast of No Nation* – a reference to beasts, that is, untidy and rough characters – attempted to think about the trans-national and post-national, about concepts beyond *Heimat*, through research into the taste and complex 'character' of Wedding. Carrie Hampel, Ogboh's research assistant, had gathered conversations with inhabitants of the district about their ideas on its character, sampling different imaginations of taste to be worked into a craft brew project (see Hampel 2019).

The project conjured up friction, however, forcing the gallery team in the project meetings to stop and think: the 'character' of a district cannot be grasped in its essence, because characters are about identity yet also about roles one assumes or is expected to perform. Wedding features as a district

Fig. 10.6 Emeka Ogboh's 'Beast of No Nation' beer bottle, on the railings of the subway station of the district. *BEAST OF NO NATION* (2018), © Emeka Ogboh

in the imagination of sociologists, artists, and the gallery itself, but it risks becoming a projection screen for characterisations of Berlin's new diverse and noble savage: working-class, ethnically diverse, rough, untidy.

"On the one hand, we say there's a strong drinking problem in Wedding, and yet we still do a beer project – that's ethically ambiguous", Kathrin Pohlmann, who had been production manager during my fieldwork in the gallery, adds to a conversation we had in the kitchen office during a jour fixe with the artist Ogboh. In a brief exchange between Ndikung and Ovesen during this meeting, it became evident that the curatorial framing of the gallery and its position in Wedding confront the same complexity as the beer project: Does it reveal or assemble, unearth or produce new ideas of what Wedding is?

"I looked for a pub and someone said 'Go there, and see the Yugoslavians!' They were all just known as 'the Yugoslavians'", Hampel recounted one meeting with interlocutors in the 'field' of Wedding. "But how does this represent Wedding?", Ndikung interjected. "It sounds to me like a stereotyped, even racialised, projection of 'a group of migrants.'" In the end, it became evident that the GW team itself was involved in projections of the district onto it, thus reproducing images of and projections of the district by speaking and working on its representation in artistic projects. When I articulated this critique within the jour fixe with Ogboh, he responded:

Fig. 10.7 A view of the gallery during Simon Fujiwara's exhibition Joanne (2018), Galerie Wedding. © Galerie Wedding.

No. It's not about representation but about provoking a discussion about Germanness, migration, subversion. If it's a beer, then it definitively cannot adhere to the German purity law (*Reinheitsgebot*). This district is 'impure'. So the beer cannot be 'pure' (*rein*) either.

As Hampel's research progressed, Pohlmann and others contacted local pubs who might be interested in serving the beer for free as part of the opening of the show by Ogboh. During this process, Hampel and Ogboh dug further into statistics and histories about the demographics, citizenship laws, and policies of inclusion in the district. While the beer ended up creating a small community of pubs and gathered reflections from inhabitants on the district and its inhabitants' perceptions of it, the most significant convivial performativity of the project took place among the artistic team and staff: Just how a gallery is able or unable to deal with its membranes – windows, publicity, public programming, and audience outreach – and the porousness and contentiousness of these became a subject of the gallery curatorial process.

Conclusion: Partial curatorial truths and district membranes

I often think of details about the kitchen office space in GW, in which most of the jour fix meetings took place that synthesised the shows, and the studio visit that inspired them. A few cupboards, a sink, no stove. A large fridge, a door leading to a storage room, a wall with posters. A staircase leading up to an office, assistants and interns typing. Programme direction, press and communication, everything else. In the main space: a make-shift table, a few foldable chairs, and a long heater with a wooden plank doubling as a bench. A classic white cube, one might think.

Yet the porous membrane at the heart of this chapter always breaks my isolated memories about this kitchen space. Milky windows above eye-level obscured my view onto the Rathausplatz of Simit Evi. Some sound outside came inside, however, in waves: construction site noise, alcohol-infused conversations, screaming voices, children, sirens. Inside remained isolated, the smell of used coffee cups, French press, croissants, the scratching of pens and notebooks. Newspaper reviews, and sketches for the next exhibition leaflet were usually stacked in boxes. A small flowerpot from an exhibition about food. The first copies of exhibition catalogues: I remember one of my last days of fieldwork, when a print preview of Viron Erol Vert's catalogue for his *Dreamatory* show lay on the able (2018).

The kitchen was thus less an office without connections and more of a transit zone, a thinking space, storage, archive, and meeting room, between the desktops and the exhibition space, with a threshold that opened more than it separated. Doors opened frequently; Laika, the gallery dog, would stroll in. A parcel delivery might arrive: the new programme leaflets for an upcoming show. In this space, the curatorial team met, week after week. Tuesday mornings, often well into the afternoon. Jour fixe – a loose term encompassing almost the entire planning of the gallery organism: laptops and Skype calls, budget plans, artist visits, drafting of texts, invitations to programmes, heated discussions, interviews.

Not seldom, ethnographic research, like the exhibition practice and curatorial work I described here, is less conclusive and fuzzier than the eventual results in a show or a publication may suggest. It is porous, ambivalent, and not isolated. This chapter discussed the ever-present negotiation and constitution of the thresholds, the membranes, and the distinctions between the in- and outside of an exhibition space and practice. These, I suggested, constituted the core struggle for the gallery, in addition to the significant ambivalence of the deep curating that the gallery team performed inside, outside, and across the porous membranes of the exhibition space.

And like the overall curatorial grappling, the notes that one first takes as an ethnographer often remain fragments of an incomplete struggle to capture – traces of experiences inside and outside, recorded on the spot, often composed by hand or typed into my phone, sometimes written up hastily after an event, or years later. Fieldnotes are recorded during or after an event or a meeting, and they are thus subject to memory, the unconscious bias of the note taker, and of course contingent on the inter-subjective and affective situations from which they arise. As such, they are palimpsests of lived experiences, covering former memories with new ones, records of collective atmospheres, yet also reflections and analyses of lesser-noted, behind-the-scenes, or seemingly marginal aspects of exhibition-making – fieldnotes as footnotes to a curatorial process. These notes are not objective records for documenting events but a quasi-archive of a collective curatorial practice written not from the desk but on the spot. They aim to translate and also to generate new gaps, new frictions – and to grapple with porosity. As such, my writing of notes during meetings became itself an initiating practice, rather than any passive documentation. Frequently, a conversation in a jour fixe got very heated, and after an hour and a half of immersion, one of the curators would stop, exclaim something like, "Shit, I wish we had recorded that." More often than not, I was able to smile and tap on my notebook in response, or show the little red bar on the top of my phone that said "Recording". In one case, these transcriptions led to a published conversation to accompany an exhibition that was in the process of being prepared during a jour fixe (Ndikung, Ovesen, Rizzi, Tinius 2017).

And yet, similar to the incomplete grappling with the district through the gallery membrane function, in seeking to grasp the working patterns and curatorial 'culture' of the GW, I tried to describe, and eventually was forced to recognise, the limitations of the anthropological presence; seeing and noting down always only a fraction of the shows and conversations that took place in the meetings, often leaving ten minutes before an important decision, or arriving just after it had been taken. Meetings often were dismissed and, as elsewhere, conflicts among curators and artists affect working cultures and taint the depth of a curatorial engagement. Yet these are not problems in the negative sense, in my view; rather, they offer a way to think curating *across* anthropology.

The curatorial challenges with the district of Wedding – its district curating – established by Ndikung and Ovesen as a longer-term engagement, and the 'slow' form of curating with a set of artists and thinkers offered no holistic rhetoric. Like anthropological research (see Thornton 1988), it grappled with the construction of partial truths (Clifford 1986), constant imagination, and creation of a district imagination, sometimes veiled and couched in what appears to be a claim to its representation. The curatorial programmes – along with their articulation in solo shows, symposia, and the deliberate inclusion of external observing perspectives, such as mine – all constituted a particular kind of curatorial conviviality that recognised its partiality and porosity. Rather than laying claim to represent the district, though, it opens the gaps and creates new frictions of this kind; as such, the gallery grapples – with no claim to a convincing solution – with the membrane porosity between its inside and the district outside.

District curating in the context of the gallery's porous membrane (and the gallery *as* porous membrane), then, became a form of thinking about how curatorial practice manages, and fails, to curate and gather complete, or even near complete, representations about a district. Rather than succumbing to this possibility, the projects – among which I discussed two of several multisensorial projects of this kind (others involving taste, imagery, and materiality to engage with the district) – offered a way to practise and try to grasp the complexity of a gallery with a public mandate in a district, in addition to coming to terms with its rendering in an artistic exhibition context, as well considering its failure to do so. This form of curating *across* membranes, I contend, is what spaces such as GW afford. It is what they offer by way of their particular situatedness, and the ambivalences that accompany them – that is, the history and change in an institution that comes to haunt the space, and the challenging public mandate which framed it. Taking time to work with small groups of artists, involving different kinds of reflexive agents, theorisers, thinkers, researchers, in a regular format and time frame crafted the porous membrane as a reference point over time. Such deep curating, then, is itself a form of conviviality, conflicted and heterogeneous, precarious and inconclusive, but interrogating and generative.

It offers, furthermore, in my view, a 'trans-anthropological' case study as it shows some of the limits but also possible ways of thinking anthropologically otherwise and beyond the confines of disciplinary or institutional anthropology. Diversity and conviviality are articulated and practiced – rendered perceptible and invited to break out in their messiness, rather than be contained in a clean curatorial or anthropological rendering. And these concepts did so across conversations with artists, who challenged anthropology but also enacted a multi-way interlocution. Rather than thinking about an anthropological curator-envy (Sansi 2020), it is precisely the uneven and often inconclusive grappling with each others' practices and ways of thinking and conceiving between anthropology and curatorial practice – the porosity between them – that can offer ways of getting closer to finding the tools and concepts for understanding the present both seek to grasp.

Notes

1. The image on p. 254 is Figure 10.1 A passerby peeking into the gallery during the exhibition *Circling Around Oneness* (2016) by Mwangi Hutter, Galerie Wedding, © Fernando Gutiérrez Juárez.
2. My research with Galerie Wedding would not have been possible without the trust and support of Solvej Helweg Ovesen, Bonaventure Soh Bejeng Ndikung, Kathrin Pohlmann, Nadia Pilchowski, and Jan Tappe. And it would have been half as fun and intense without the energy, poetry, and shared drinks with all the participating artists, in particular Viron Erol Vert and Emeka Ogboh, whom I highlight in this chapter. All of them read versions of my writings and I am grateful for their comments. Sharon Macdonald encouraged me to do my fieldwork in a manner that inspired and encouraged me. Her anthropological thinking and editorial criticality helped me refine not just this chapter, but all my writing that emerged during my fellowship at CARMAH. Margareta von Oswald was a relentlessly energetic co-editor of this entire book, and she also patiently read many different versions of everything I wrote for this volume. The research that led to this piece was funded by the Alexander von Humboldt Foundation as

part of my postdoctoral research fellowship and the research award for Sharon Macdonald's Alexander von Humboldt Professorship.
3. Since 2019, Ovesen directs the gallery with curator Nataša Ilić. Together, they devised a two-year programme entitled *SoS*, or *Soft Solidarity*, which, as they write, "connects Wedding's past and present as a workers district". They offer to focus on the gallery itself, writing that "[a]s an art institution that acts in critical correspondence to the local influences of demographic flows, xenophobia, acceleration of life and work experience, disembodiment of relations, neoliberal self-exploitation, and a split Europe, Galerie Wedding – Raum für Zeitgenössische Kunst will engage in a counter program to these life-compromising conditions with the new overarching curatorial concept of Soft Solidarity (SoS)." (see Curatorial Concept, 2019: http://galeriewedding.de/wp-content/uploads/2020/01/SoS_Konzept_concept_2019_20.pdf, last accessed 20 January 2020).

References

Blanes, Ruy, Alex Flynn, Maïté Maskens, and Jonas Tinius. 2016. 'Micro-utopias: anthropological perspectives on art, creativity, and relationality'. *Journal of Art and Anthropology* 5(1): 5–20.

Boltanski, Luc and Ève Chiapello. 2007 [1999]. *The New Spirit of Capitalism*. Trans. Gregory Elliott. London/New York: Verso.

Borneman, John and Parvis Ghassem-Fachandi. 2017. 'The concept of Stimmung: From indifference to xenophobia in Germany's refugee crisis'. *HAU: Journal of Ethnographic Theory* 7(3): 105–135.

Canclini, Néstor García. 2014. *Art beyond Itself: Anthropology for a Society without a Storyline*. Durham, NC: Duke University Press.

Clifford, James. 1986. 'Partial Truths', in: *Writing Culture. The Poetics and Politics of Ethnography*, edited by James Clifford and George E. Marcus. Berkeley: University of California Press, pp. 1–26.

Hampel, Carrie. 2019. 'A Taste of Wedding – On the Research for Emeka Ogboh's Beast of No Nation Beer Project', in: *Post-Otherness Wedding / Unsustainable Privileges. Galerie Wedding – Space for Contemporary Art Berlin*, edited by Solvej Helweg Ovesen and Bonaventure Soh Bejeng Ndikung. Bielefeld / New York: Kerber, pp. 164–176.

Macdonald, Sharon. 2016. 'New Constellations of Difference in Europe's 21st Century Museumscape'. *Museum Anthropology* 39(1): 4–19.

Marcus, George E. Ed. 2000. *Para-Sites. A Casebook Against Cynical Reason*. Chicago: University of Chicago Press.

Ndikung, Bonaventure Soh Bejeng, and Regina Römhild. 2013. 'The Post-Other as Avant-Garde', in: *We Roma: A Critical Reader in Contemporary Art*, edited by Daniel Baker and Maria Hlavajova. Amsterdam: Valiz, pp. 206–225.

Ndikung, Bonaventure Soh Bejeng, Solvej Helweg Ovesen, Mario Rizzi, Jonas Tinius. 2017. 'Bare Lives: A Conversation', in: *Bare Lives*. Berlin: Archive, pp. 68–75.

Ndikung, Bonaventure Soh Bejeng. 2019a. 'POW (Post-Otherness Wedding) and the Knowledge Embedded in an Object', in: *Post-Otherness Wedding / Unsustainable Privileges. Galerie Wedding – Space for Contemporary Art Berlin*, edited by Solvej Helweg Ovesen and Bonaventure Soh Bejeng Ndikung. Bielefeld / New York: Kerber, pp. 30–39.

———. 2019b. 'Viron Erol Vert, The Name of Shades of Paranoia, Called Different Forms of Silence', in: *Post-Otherness Wedding / Unsustainable Privileges. Galerie Wedding – Space for Contemporary Art Berlin*, edited by Solvej Helweg Ovesen and Bonaventure Soh Bejeng Ndikung. Bielefeld / New York: Kerber, pp. 184–191.

Ovesen, Solvej Helweg. 2019. 'POW-UP: Deep Curating', in: *Post-Otherness Wedding / Unsustainable Privileges. Galerie Wedding – Space for Contemporary Art Berlin*, edited by Solvej Helweg Ovesen and Bonaventure Soh Bejeng Ndikung. Bielefeld / New York: Kerber, pp. 24–29.

Reckwitz, Andreas. 2012 [1995]. *Die Erfindung der Kreativität*. Berlin: Suhrkamp.

Sansi, Roger. 2015. *Art, Anthropology and the Gift*. London: Bloomsbury.

———. 2020. 'Introduction', in: Sansi, Roger. Ed. *The Anthropologist as Curator*. London: Bloomsbury, pp. 1–16.

Sarr, Felwine, and Bénédicte Savoy. 2018. *The Restitution of African Cultural Heritage. Toward a New Relational Ethics*. Translated by Drew S. Burk. Paris: Ministère de la Culture. http://restitutionreport2018.com/sarr_savoy_en.pdf (last accessed 18 January 2020).

Ssorin-Chaikov, Nikolai. 2013. 'Ethnographic Conceptualism: An Introduction'. *Laboratorium* 5(2): 5–18.

Thornton, Robert J. 1988. 'The Rhetoric of Ethnographic Holism'. *Cultural Anthropology* 3(3): 285–303.

Tinius, Jonas. 2016. 'Authenticity and otherness: reflecting statelessness in German postmigrant theatre'. *Critical Stages/Scènes Critiques* 14 (2016). Open-access version: http://www.critical-stages.org/14/authenticity-and-otherness-reflecting-statelessness-in-german-postmigrant-theatre/ (last accessed 20 January 2020).

———. 2018. 'Alterity', in: Christine Gerbich, Larissa Förster, Katarzyna Puzon, Margareta von Oswald, Sharon Macdonald, Jonas Tinius. Eds. *Otherwise. Rethinking Museums and Heritage*. Berlin: Centre for Anthropological Research on Museums and Heritage, pp. 40–54. Open-access version: http://www.carmah.berlin/wp-content/uploads/2018/07/

CARMAH-2018-Otherwise-Rethinking-Museums-and-Heritage.pdf (last accessed 18 January 2020).

———. 2019a. 'Fieldnotes', in: *Post-Otherness Wedding / Unsustainable Privileges. Galerie Wedding – Space for Contemporary Art Berlin*, edited by Solvej Helweg Ovesen and Bonaventure Soh Bejeng Ndikung. Bielefeld / New York: Kerber, pp. 177–181.

———. 2019b. 'Interstitial Agents: Negotiating Migration and Diversity in Theatre', in: Bock, Jan-Jonathan and Sharon Macdonald. Eds. *Refugees Welcome? Differences and Diversity in a Changing Germany*. Oxford/New York: Berghahn Books, pp. 241–264.

———. 2020. 'Troubling Diversity and Iterations of Difference: Reflections on Curatorial Tensions and a Mapping Survey', in: *Beyond Afropolitan & Other Labels: On the Complexities of Dis-Othering as a Process*, edited by Kathleen Louw. Brussels: BOZAR, pp. 53–58.

Tinius, Jonas and Sharon Macdonald. 2020. 'The Recursivity of the Curatorial', in: Roger Sansi. Ed. *The Anthropologist as Curator*. London: Bloomsbury, pp. 35–58.

Trinh T. Minh-Ha and Nancy N. Chen. 1992. 'Speaking Nearby'. *Visual Anthropology Review* 8(1): 82–91.

Vert, Viron Erol. 2018. *The Name of Shades of Paranoia, Called Different Forms of Silence*. Berlin: Distanz.

Zinnenburg Caroll, Khadija von, and Jonas Tinius. 2020. 'Phantom Palaces: Prussian Centralities and Humboldtian Horizontalities', in: *Recentring the City. Global Mutations of Socialist Modernity*, edited by Jonathan Bach and Michał Murawski. London: UCL Press, 90–103.

"What happens in that space in-between and beyond this relation"

A conversation with Bonaventure Soh Bejeng Ndikung

Ndikung: How do we talk about the relation between curating and anthropology without having one usurp the other?[1] How do we avoid making the artistic, and in this case the curatorial, just another tool of anthropological research?

Our point of departure is the question posed the other way around: How do you make sense of the ways in which anthropology is negotiated within curatorial and artistic work? We're seeing that issues that we as anthropologists thought were traditionally associated with the discipline, not least issues around indigeneity – including problematic aspects of its colonial appropriation and knowing – are becoming the subject of curatorial projects.

This is an issue of claims, a question about who has the right – or to put it even more forcefully – the *audacity* to deal with these issues, including, for example, of indigeneity. In my view, first and foremost, one needs to question the role of the anthropologist. Underneath your question therefore is a more fundamental one: When did art not deal with indigeneity? Maybe we can unravel it from that direction. Just to complicate things. Underneath your question therefore is a more fundamental question. Because: When did art not deal with indigeneity? Maybe we can unravel it from that direction. Just to complicate things.

We are already unravelling things from the other direction. The issue you are raising about art, curatorial practice, and anthropology is also one of "epistemic jurisdiction" (Boyer 2008). It is a question about who – or which fields – assumes the epistemic jurisdiction over another field? And what happens when these claims overlap.

The issue of "epistemic jurisdiction" is what Lewis Gordon (2014) discusses as "disciplinary sovereignty" and "disciplinary decadence". The former being about the claiming of sovereignty over a certain territory – so as anthropologist, for example, to claim that *my* territory is the human being – while the latter is about ridding oneself of these imaginary boundaries.

The particular practice that I would like to imagine is one in which these disciplines and forms of jurisdiction don't matter. You don't have to be well-read or have studied in order to contribute to a conversation across art, anthropology, or curating. For me, the notion of studying is a very open one. Neither Harald Szeemann nor Okwui Enwezor *ever* went to a school of curating, and they are in the limelight. These disciplines should be open, necessarily. So the question for me is: How can we imagine, a kind of coming together of these disciplines – a co-existence – in which they inform each other, constantly?

Fig. 11.2 *Canine Wisdom For the Barking Dog – The Dog Done Gone Deaf* at the Dak'Art Biennale 2018; Ibrahim Mahama *No Time for Curation* (1966-2014-2018), © SAVVY Contemporary

You used a definition of curating as "the making of relations where there are none, or the underlining of relations where they need to be highlighted." In relation to anthropology, what is your understanding of curating in the sense of making those relations or highlighting them, or possibly even cutting them then?

If anthropology is also about understanding human relations, about situating humans *within* certain cultural spaces, and understanding the cosmogonies *of* these humans within certain spaces, then I think that this issue of relation-making is where art and anthropology come together. If anthropology is an attempt of analysing and deconstructing the ways in which societies function, then art is, for a lack of better words, a set of tools for understanding the ways in which we *find ourselves in the world,* be it in the form of myths or more consistent, real ways of acting in the world. But art is constantly there to make us understand those relations.

On the other hand, it must be there, too, to help alleviate certain burdens, in the sense of an aesthetics that takes you out of certain realms. At the same time, it must also be able to situate us within those realms, thus tackling what is at stake.

Fig. 11.3 *Canine Wisdom For the Barking Dog – The Dog Done Gone Deaf* at the Dak'Art Biennale 2018; Ibrahim Mahama *No Time for Curation* (1966-2014-2018), © SAVVY Contemporary

Taking this as a basis, there is hardly a way in which one can do an artistic practice – or, say, in this context, a curatorial practice – without situating oneself in something one can call 'the anthropological'. Having said that, when the anthropological then becomes a study of the Other, it becomes problematic. And the latter move is something we can witness in a lot of exhibitions that have been made in the past twenty or thirty years. Maybe one could even go back as far as *Primitivism* (1984) curated by William Rubin, Richard E. Oldenburg, and Kirk Varnedoe or back to the work of Susan Vogel – but I don't really want to name these key moments. In fact, I think we even need to skip over them. The key point is that artists have for some time been fascinated by the format of anthropology in its study of an Other, in presenting that Other in ways that sometimes reiterate and reproduce the epistemic violence of this form of representative governance. Art, too, is part of this complex.

I want to reiterate that, in expanding these ideas, I am not necessarily thinking about anthropology as a discipline. In fact, it doesn't matter to me. Anthropology is relatively insignificant in what I want to do, because it is again about tackling knowledge. It so happens that a lot of knowledge, or knowledges, that are out there have been brought to us through the eyes, the hands, the writings, of anthropologists. So be it – and if we want to get to this knowledge, it is difficult to do so without going through anthropology first.

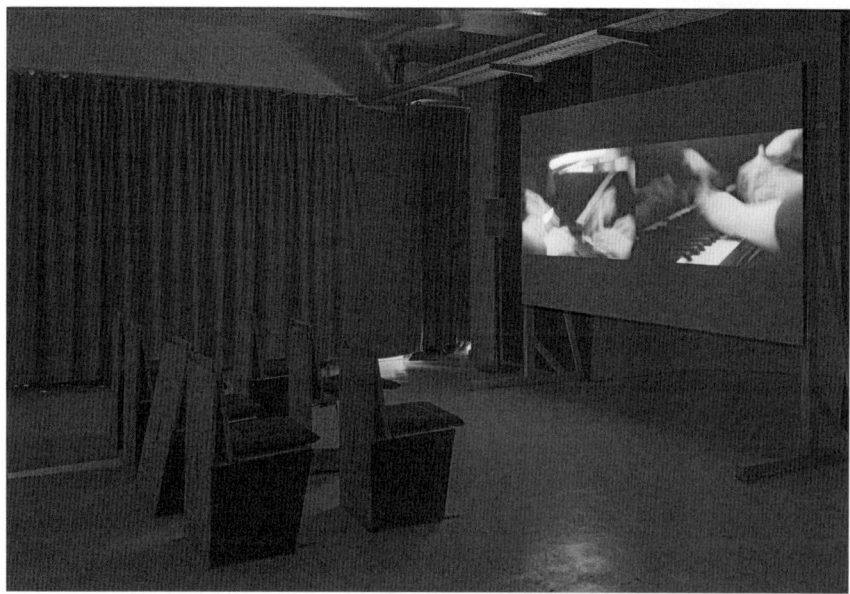

Fig. 11.4 *We Have Delivered Ourselves from the Tonal – Of, with, towards, on Julius Eastman* at SAVVY Contemporary, March 2018; The Otolith Group *The Third Part is the Third Measure*, © Raisa Galofre

But it remains just one path to go through these eyes. That is why in our work on the musicologist Halim El-Dabh (e.g., in its first instalment *Canine Wisdom For the Barking Dog – The Dog Done Gone Deaf* at the Dak'Art Biennale 2018), for example, we go and talk to people! We want to create additional and other spaces of knowledge production beyond anthropology, and that may mean finding the knowledge – as we did in the show on El-Dabh – through the sonic epistemologies embedded in textiles. Though anthropologists may have studied how textiles are worn or tried to understand what they might signify, we would rather want to 'overstand' the other ways they exist f.e. textiles as musical scores or notation systems. Though anthropologists may have done oral interviews, we want to talk to the people ourselves.

We are constantly engaged – not in a negation, but a form of contradiction – with the eyes of anthropologists, trying to circumvent them, or rather: situating them as *one* among other forms of trajectories.

Does it mean anything for you to speak of an anthropological framing in an exhibition, for example in terms of particular display techniques or modes of exhibiting – and if so, what?
First we have to understand what we mean by an 'anthropological framing'? Is it what we see in the ethnographic museum? Can we assume that the display in

Fig. 11.5 *We Have Delivered Ourselves from the Tonal – Of, with, towards, on Julius Eastman* at SAVVY Contemporary, March 2018; Eastman Archive, © Raisa Galofre

Berlin's Ethnological Museum in Dahlem, for example, was an anthropological framing? Or would you also call the presentation of Kader Attia's piece at documenta13 an anthropological display? If we understand by 'anthropological framing' the kind of display of archival materials that has in recent years come to be referred to as 'essayistic exhibitions', which demand the viewer to read into, not just to perceive, the objects on display, giving you multiple ways of reading an exhibition – then I don't have a problem with this kind of framing. It is simply one of the possible ways of framing exhibition-making. I think what is key, instead, is that whatever an anthropological framing may be, I think it needs to be negotiated. We need to find out what it is.

When I engage in exhibition-making – I do not think of these categories. To me, what is at stake is: How can I mediate what is being presented to the viewer? How can I set up a relation between that which is displayed and the person that comes into view? How can I set in relation the artists that *are* in the show with one another? Even to their own works. For me, curating is not unrelated to the practice of a DJ constantly listening to the people on the dance floor. Or rather, not even listening, but *feeling* them. The DJ has to be on his or her toes. As soon as the temperament on the dance floor changes, a good DJ has to feel that. What interests me in curatorial practice is that *possibility of feeling* what art brings with it, and what the person that comes in perceives through it.

There is one other thing which we can't overlook. In my last conversation with Okwui Enwezor, he mentioned to me that we do curating not just for the sake of curating. We watch history unfold and unravel. Curating is not necessarily just about *you* being witness to this unfolding. In fact, you're being *part* of it. You're *making* it happen. He was pointing, in other words, to the responsibility of the curator. Going back to modes of display, each one comes differently with each new question that is at stake. If I'm doing a show on Julius Eastman, for example, *We Have Delivered Ourselves from the Tonal – Of, with, towards, on Julius Eastman* (SAVVY Contemporary, March 2018) – then I have to think of a mode of display that carries sonicity, that carries this biography, that carries socio-political and racial issues. As curators, we should have a kind of a sensibility towards that.

Now, *if* you want to look at the anthropological display as a simple standardization of display within certain spaces irrespective of where the object comes from, then what I am proposing is the opposite of that. It cannot be that wherever the object comes from, it is the same light we use, the same box, the same mode of display. This kind of approach flattens the practices on which they focus. At some point, we have to make and mark those differences. One simply cannot just pluck people out of a geographical space as if they have no relations to particular spaces.

At the same time, one crucial question remains: How do we do this without limiting *these people* to *those spaces*? Another issue is: How can the space be cut off from properties of land, for example? Maybe we create other spaces, cognitive spaces, gendered spaces, racial spaces, or cultural spaces. The task is how we can de-couple our imaginations of being from fixed, physical spaces? Or put differently: How can we tell situated histories, like Donna Haraway and others said, that are not only bound to geography?

During a recent panel discussion with Arthur Jafa on the occasion of a show at the Julia Stoschek Collection in Berlin (12 February 2018), you asked a question that prompted this kind of thinking. You asked whether – or how – it was possible to translate the critique he was voicing in the context of the US-American, an Afro-American critique, into a geographic elsewhere. And how this exhibition could be re-situated, if at all, in Berlin.

When you go into the exhibition, and you see burned bodies, but nothing is being said about the burning of Oury Jalloh in his prison cell in Germany, then you think the curators didn't do their work. Connections have to be made. The same problem exists with travelling exhibition in general, because they are conceived in one place and often simply planted in another place. I think that this is very problematic. And we *need* to state this clearly.

The second question I asked at this panel discussion concerns the equating of Blackness to African-American-ness. Because *my* Blackness is a completely other experience than his. But just because American academia, the film industry, the publishing industries, the art industry, the music industry, and so on and so forth, is so powerful in terms of money, we tend to reduce a lot of things to its enunciations. But I disagree with its extrapolation. We need to open up to different geographies – again, not in terms of just another geographical space, like *Germany*, but in terms of experiences.

The issues you raise concern one of the key questions of our book, namely the 'trans-anthropological', understood as an adjectival modality describing the incorporation or negotiation of anthropology in fields beyond it. What we're interested in is how fields or practices or institutions take into account, as it were, that which we've been talking about as anthropology's legacies, but goes beyond it, or situates itself amidst it.

At the risk of not having understood your question properly, I would say we have to be careful (or you need to be careful) of creating an 'anthropologo-centrism', by which I mean seeing anthropology in everything, or making everything circulate around anthropology, making anthropology the sole *point de départ*. As if we go everywhere but always come back to the field of anthropology! I would beg to differ here.

What I appreciate in the term is that you are trying to think about what it means to become another anthropologist, to make another anthropology. In other words, you should be talking about the possibility of getting out, or going beyond anthropology, and to find out or even fight to see what that 'beyond' could be.

And yet, the issue with the idea of going 'beyond' or 'through' – definitional constituents of the prefix 'trans' – is that it denotes again the idea of being *in* or having to go *through* anthropology first before reaching anything *beyond* it. I am here thinking of Homi Bhabha's introduction to the *Location of Culture* (1994), in which he gets granular on this issue. The key thing at stake here is that for him the 'beyond' becomes about the space of 'in-betweenness'. Then the question would be: *If* we're talking about an in-betweenness within the field of anthropology, what kind of 'in-between' are we talking about? In-between anthropology and *what else*? In my case, the relation would be between the arts and anthropology, and I am asking myself what happens in that space in-between and beyond this relation. How is that space negotiated? Who claims territory or 'epistemic jurisdiction' over whom? At the end of the day, it comes back to a question of *governing*. *Who* governs? Under what terms? And who are the subjects of the governing? These are the questions that have to be negotiated in that space of the 'beyond' and the space of the 'in-between', or the ‚going through'. To me, the 'trans-anthropological' is an issue of governance. Who are subjects? How do you govern? Where do you govern?

Note

1. The image on p. 278 is Figure 11.1 'Monday' by iQhiya, installation view of *That, Around Which the Universe Revolves: On Rhythmanalysis of Memory, Times, Bodies in Space* at SAVVY Contemporary (2017), © Raisa Galofre

References

Boyer, Dominic. 2008. 'Thinking through the Anthropology of Experts'. *Anthropology in Action* 15(2): 38–46.

Bhabha, Homi. 1994. 'Introduction: Locations of Culture', in: *The Location of Culture*. London/ New York: Routledge, pp. 1–27.

Gordon, Lewis R. 2014. 'Disciplinary Decadence and the Decolonisation of Knowledge'. *Africa Development* 39(1): 81–92.

Material Kin: "Communities of Implication" in Post-Colonial, Post-Holocaust Polish Ethnographic Collections[1]

Erica Lehrer

"Objects, then, make subjects; subjects make objects."
Paul Basu, The Inbetweenness of Things[2]

"The tragedy and misery of things was comparable to the tragedy and suffering of people."
Rachela Auerbach, "Lament Rzeczy Martwych" ["The Lament of Dead Things"][3]

Introduction[4]

Contemporary museums of national culture – a broad genre that includes ethnographic museums, folk museums, *skansens* (open-air museums), and their ilk – are diverse inheritances: of colonial exploration and rule, empire- and nation-building, modernity, and industrialization. They bear the imprint of European epistemologies developed to make sense of and manage the anxieties of identity and difference, social and cultural change, and the demands of ethno-national politics. Their legacies of collecting, categorizing, displaying, and looking not only reflect but also continue to impact relations among groups of people, mediating differently-situated visitors' senses of connectedness to or distance from each other in the present day.

Such culture-focused museums tend to propose relationships between people and things – often in the language of 'heritage' – that fall on two poles: universalist/free-choice relationships (where anyone may claim as heritage the items that feel integral to them) and descent-essentialist relationships (where objects are understood as physical manifestations of the world views of the groups that created them – so-called 'material culture'). The latter, origins-based view – expressed in the notion that objects are uniquely linked to their 'source communities' – may be broadly politically progressive for groups attempting to re-claim items removed from their communities under colonial conditions. Yet this framework can also re-inscribe erroneous colonial categorizations of human collectivities, along with ossified stereotypes about them. The former, identification-based view, on the other hand, risks eliding the ways that people are unequally inscribed into more and less chosen cultural, historical, political, and affective entanglements with objects.

Betraying the insufficiency of these museum frameworks are what I will call "awkward objects",[5] items that bear traces of forgotten or suppressed social histories that both index, and link across communities in ways that raise questions about both 'source' and 'heritage.' These are not innocent categories. The materials in question reference enduring legacies of intergroup violence, some of which are sustained by ongoing museum epistemologies and curatorial strategies. Helping us think through these issues are three kinds of objects in particular, awkwardly linked to Jewishness in Polish ethnographic collections: the hybrid, the caricature, and the commemorative. These items point towards an alternative conceptualisation – "communities of implication" – that may prove useful for situating and interpreting a range of accessions in diverse museum contexts. I propose adding this term to a growing vocabulary that will be required to speak to the necessary decolonial social and cultural work of redress, repair, recovery, and reimagining that goes beyond (although does not replace) property restitution, which currently dominates the global conversation.[6] New language is needed both to grasp the full range of relationships and of injustices referenced by museum objects, as well as to develop both political and curatorial strategies to make these implications visible in museum spaces.

Colonial conversations

Recent debates about the status of colonial-era objects in European national museums (Hunt 2018) – think Benin bronzes or Elgin/Parthenon marbles – have grown out of post-World War II shifts in moral sensibility and attendant human rights discourse. These sensibilities and discourses remain biased, however, towards models of identity embedded in a national framework. In this framework, a group's claims to having a distinct cultural (and thus potentially national) identity are strengthened by the ability to point to a collection of 'our things,' or 'material culture.' National museums of culture have thus taken for granted particular notions of human-human and human-object relations that privilege the 'boundedness', 'homogeneity', and 'completeness' of groups, who are 'owners' of their cultural objects. These notions, in turn, help establish claims regarding the restitution or retention of what has come to be called "cultural property" (Barkan 2002) They also have consequences for curatorial practice; peoples who are characterised by cultures and possess objects expressive of these cultures are displayed together as a logical, self-evident set.

'Universalist' Western European museums have been increasingly pressed to publicly recognise the existence of complex and diverse meanings and social relationships that pertain to the objects in their collections, given the far-flung itineraries that led them there. Predictably, the administration and patronage of hegemonic museums are biased towards concepts that uphold the status quo of housing and managing collections in their current institutional homes, and they are correspondingly reluctant to embrace alternative notions of relatedness that might question these relations of power. These museums' elites focus on how objects originating in overseas colonies came to be the cultural property or heritage of the collectors' and museums' communities – becoming part of, say, British, French, or German patrimony – by virtue of the decades or sometimes centuries they have been in their care (ICOM 2004). While such a 'retentionist' idea is not without intellectual merit, it underpins conservative arguments that obscure the frequently unethical facts of the provenance histories in question. Indeed, European nations subscribe to juridical principles of property – for example the French principle of "inalienability" – mobilised today ostensibly to protect major victims of the post-colonial trafficking of cultural objects, such as multiple countries in Africa.[7] Still, national governments refuse to apply these principles retroactively, thereby all but ensuring that their own collections, even those partly based on colonial plunder, are now the legal property of their new (present) owners.[8] To correct such injustices, juridical innovation is needed.

The idea of "source communities" or "the people from whom collections originate" (Peers and Brown 2003: i) has been a progressive development in the debate about cultural property, strengthening claims for the return of objects from museums to their cultural (and typically geographical) contexts of their birth. The term relates to the indisputable notion that museum objects and collections can be crucial scaffolding that helps maintain the identity and support the survival of communities who have been historically marginalised, embattled, or oppressed – and from whom significant objects have been misappropriated. Yet the term "source" privileges an understanding of identity that is fixated on origins and risks replicating the historical classifications of social groups imposed by colonial institutions (Landkammer 2017: 278) (Modest 2012). It also naturalises the 'universal' museum and its conservationist regime as the given endpoint for objects no longer in everyday use (as opposed, for example, to natural decay, burial, or destruction). Further, while doing important decolonising work, the notion of a "source community" re-inscribes a dominant (and socially hermetic) Western idea of "one object, one culture, one progenitor".[9] While the 2018 Sarr-Savoy report, *The Restitution of African Cultural Heritage*, commissioned by French President Emmanuel Macron, is being heralded as a watershed, restitution is a narrow solution that overlooks a range of messier historical and contemporary injustices. Per some of the report's critics, restitution also risks both self-satisfaction and additional prestige conferred on the very museums that benefitted from the original wrongs, lacks a full moral accounting, and leaves fundamental colonial structures in place (Azoulay 2019).

Decolonising (post-Holocaust) Eastern Europe?

To portray restitution as the conclusive 'decolonising' response to colonial museum practice privileges post-colonial concerns related to Western Europe, specifically those contemporary nation-states that had 'new world' empires with overseas colonies to plunder. The spoils here accrued to one – the European – side. Poland provides an instructive counter-example. The country has been described as an 'internal' European coloniser, ruling over great swaths of today's Baltics, Belorussia, and Ukraine during the early modern era. Yet Poland was subsequently 'colonised' for over 120 years by Russia, Prussia, and Austria-Hungary beginning in the late eighteenth century until 1918, later by Nazi Germany, and then the Soviet Union during and (as a satellite state) after the Second World War for almost a half century, until 1989. Polish museums, in their epistemologies, collections, architectures, and *raisons d'être* reflect this complex legacy.

Colonialism, however, was not only a grand system of domination, theft, and redistribution, and its effects cannot be reduced to the vagaries of military, economic, or political aggression. It was also the highly successful attempt to replace a vast diversity of world views with a largely elite European-Christian perspective. Museums (along with universities, churches, and schools) played a key role in inculcating these. Eastern European national 'museums of culture' as a form were cut from epistemological cloth broadly shared with those in Western European metropoles – part of the wider heritage of European colonialism, empire-, and nation-building.[10] Such museums can be split into two main types: those based on *Völkerkunde*, or studies of faraway, exotic others, and *Volkskunde*, studies of the internal, peasant other, a class-based 'exotic,' celebrated as the source (and proving the territorial rootedness) of a distinctive, essential cultural self. If *Völkerkunde* museums naturally burgeoned in those countries with overseas colonies, *Volkskunde* museums were crucial in societies struggling for national recognition or liberation under nineteenth-century imperialism, and continued to be nurtured as part of the emancipatory ideology shaping the 'national sciences' under twentieth-century Eastern European socialist rule (see Lozoviuk 2005; Stocking 1982; Vukov 2011).[11] In Poland, the two types were blurred, with national culture privileged in permanent displays, and 'exotic' collections developed piecemeal from diverse sources at different historical moments.[12]

'Material culture' collections assembled by museums in nations without clear histories of imperial plunder may not be embroiled in current property restitution debates that focus on post-colonial nations vis-à-vis their former European rulers. Even so, the question of what such national culture museums are for, what roles they play, and how they frame 'culture' in general, as well as how they depict specific human groups, are complex, and still largely unasked questions in Eastern Europe. Polish ethnographic museums have also been largely spared the glare of critical attention directed towards their counterparts in the West in part because such attention often emanates from representatives of aggrieved communities who have historically been ill-represented by such museums. Poland, due to the combination of genocide, out-migration, and territorial shifts, has lost its historical multicultural character, and is today more than 96% White and Roman Catholic. Further, the link between today's majority citizenry and their largely peasant roots (as represented in these museums) has been effaced in Polish collective memory (Leder 2014; Lehrer and Sendyka 2019a).

While Eastern European nations have not escaped colonial legacies, their broad indifference to the divisive debates that wrack their Western counterparts are also a result of the additional aftermaths of their own that they must confront. In Poland, layered onto the shared European colonial epistemologies embedded in the museum form, are structures of thought, practice, and habitus that reflect both the country's particular historical experiences with feudalism, partition, dismemberment, and more recently World War II, a half century of communist rule, and the lingering and (at times officially) muffled trauma of the Holocaust. These are the controversial 'hot topics' in the Polish public sphere, where colonialism (and its range of attendant legacies – particularly in museums) is generally seen to be someone else's problem.[13]

Because of this palimpsest of historical injuries, attending to Polish ethnographic collections points to a range of issues not captured in the discourse of 'ownership' and 'source' emanating from restitution debates, but which are nonetheless relevant to thinking through the aftermaths of violence. These may, in turn, suggest a new vocabulary that can enrich our treatment of objects that have been 'museumised' in the wake of large-scale oppression and injury. Doing so will also help link discussions of post-coloniality and decolonisation with post-Holocaust and post-socialist conditions, as a number of prominent scholars have been calling for in recent years (Chari and Verdery 2009; More 2001; Rothberg 2009). The goal is not to collapse significant differences in historical experience, but to build broader solidarities around shared struggles against erasure, exclusion, and injustice in and via the treatment of material heritage in contemporary national museums of culture.

The murder of most of Poland's 3.5 million Jews during World War II and the Nazi occupation was a highly public cataclysm for their Catholic neighbours. As described by historian Irena Grudzińska-Gross,

> [t]he extermination of European Jews was happening mostly on Polish territory and in front of the eyes of Polish citizens – it was impossible not to notice it. One third of Warsaw was first walled off and then burned; across Poland Jews were expelled, assembled, transported, walked, and demonstratively humiliated before being murdered; tens of thousands escaped and tried to survive in cities, villages, and the countryside. (Grudzińska-Gross 2016: 41)

Public knowledge about this crime was censored during the subsequent decades of communist rule in Poland and even today is still a subject of "contentious heritage" (Macdonald 2016), in part because of disputes regarding the extent and quality of Polish complicity (Gross 2001, 2012; Grabowski 2013).

An enormous amount of tangible heritage was also left behind as a result. What are Poland's largely Catholic citizens today to make of the orphaned objects that survived the human genocide? The material traces of the lives of their prior compatriots – from synagogues and cemeteries to photographs, housewares, and religious ritual objects – range across local everyday landscapes (Auerbach 1946; Shallcross 2014). These objects beg some sort of relation with their remaining neighbours, who typically have deeply ambivalent associations with them, worsened by nationalist discourse that tends to whitewash the country's less-glorious historical episodes.

Much (particularly Eastern) European Jewish material heritage – albeit in immovable, sometimes monumental architectural form rather than objects in museum collections – may be seen as 'disinherited heritage'. It constitutes the built heritage that has become detached from its "source community" via genocide, out-migration, loss of knowledge or identification, or lack of resources for meaningful present-day stewardship. Objects perceived as conventionally valuable, especially those that had individual owners, have their legal claimants.[14] But what about the rest? In their radically changed demographic contexts, these material traces of the past have become "dissonant heritage", in that they do not fit the dominant national imaginary of the surrounding, non-Jewish population, and as such disturb the 'chosen' heritage narratives promulgated by many Eastern European national governments today (Ashworth and Tunbridge 1996).

Indeed, the sense that these dissonant objects are liminal, that they have been 'incompletely' inherited (and perhaps not entirely *dis*inherited), is suggested by the widespread term for such objects or properties that so many Catholic Poles personally or communally inherited: *pożydowskie*, or "post-Jewish."[15] While neglect, vandalism, or even destruction are unfortunate and common options for these misfit materials – as is simple appropriation – progressive Polish artists, culture brokers, and activist groups working since the first decade of the 2000s have illustrated the potential for 're-inheriting' post-Jewish objects, creating heightened awareness, and developing educational initiatives to foster new caretaker communities and create expanded, pluralistic identifications.[16] How may we describe the relationship between these people and objects? We also lack a term that captures the emergent communities that may 'newly' form around these kinds of objects and sites.

"Awkward objects", significant Others

A different category of awkwardly 'post-Jewish' things can be found in Polish ethnographic museums. These are remarkable objects made by non-Jewish Poles, but which in some way represent or register the memory of and imagination about Jews and testify to these two communities' long territorial co-presence. Examples of "awkward objects" drawn from the Kraków and Warsaw ethnographic museums defy single-origin stories and challenge the common terms of decolonising museology.

The Kraków museum is particularly fascinating, not least because it sits in the middle of the city's historical Jewish quarter. The neighborhood was emptied of its human Jewish culture-bearers by the Germans during World War II and its Jewish 'heritage sites' left largely derelict during the socialist period. Though over the past three decades an explosion of Jewish heritage revival activity has blossomed in the quarter, little of this has touched the museum's core displays or interpretive frameworks (Lehrer 2013). The museum's permanent galleries of Polish 'folk culture' remain largely, at times strikingly absent of Jews (10% of the pre-war Polish population) and lack context for understanding the awkward references to Jewishness that do exist, both of which I have described elsewhere (Lehrer and Murzyn-Kupisz 2019, Lehrer 2016: 49–51). This is in stark contrast with the fact that the museum's annex is named 'Esther's House' (*Dom Esterki*) for the legendary Jewish mistress of King Kazimierz the Great. Indeed, the main building's façade is adorned with a plaque depicting the king welcoming the Jews, who were fleeing persecution in German lands, to Poland in the Middle Ages – a key element in Polish national mythology. What is more, the building itself housed a Jewish school in the interwar period. The museum also stands across the street from the edifice that housed the offices, library, and kosher kitchen of the (tiny) local Jewish community from 1946 until 2015. The museum's wartime director, Tadeusz Seweryn (b. 1894), was posthumously awarded the Yad Vashem Institute's title of *Righteous among the Nations* in 1982 for his clandestine work to save Jews in World War II, and there is a (thus far undocumented) story that recently emerged that Jews were also hidden during the war in the building that would later become the museum's annex.

Despite this surrounding density of Jewish historical referents, attention to Jewish co-presence in Poland – either historically or in the present day, including as potential viewers of the museum's displays – has clearly not been a curatorial priority. The only interpretive material related to a group of ratchets (wooden noisemakers) on display in the "spring customs" room of the permanent exhibit of "Polish folk culture" in the Kraków museum 'reads' them as Catholic Polish *terkotka*s (or *kołatka*s) used in Easter ritual processions or in place of bells to call locals to church.[17] Yet they could just as easily be Jewish *groggers*, used by local children each time the villain Haman's name is said during the traditional reading of the Book of Esther on the holiday of Purim. (That is how they appeared to this author, having played with similar ones as a Jewish child in the USA.) Indeed, the relation of the Jewish *grogger* to the Christian *kołatka* – by way of the Polish springtime tradition of the burning of Judas, described below – adds an important element of socio-religious hostility and tension to the relationship of the 'two' objects (Kalman 2017).

From a curator's point of view, very small interpretive interventions could reframe the objects in terms not of simple provenance (and associated, normative function), but of "implication": the addition of an explanatory label connecting the two traditions that employ the same object, historical and contemporary photos of the two religious communities using them, and/or reminiscences from Jewish and Catholic individuals who played with them.[18] This kind of addition could remind museum visitors that, prior to World War II, Poland was (and to a very small extent is still today) a multi-ethnic, multi-religious society; doing so, it would place Jews within the story of 'Polish culture' from which they have, in significant ways, been erased. It would also challenge the common myth that Jews lived entirely separate social lives from their Catholic neighbours, a misconception held equally by Poles and foreign Jews. The display would tell a challenging story of cultural proximity, exchange, and hybridity – including a story of cultural boundary maintenance via mutual endogamy and prejudice, as well as anti-Jewish

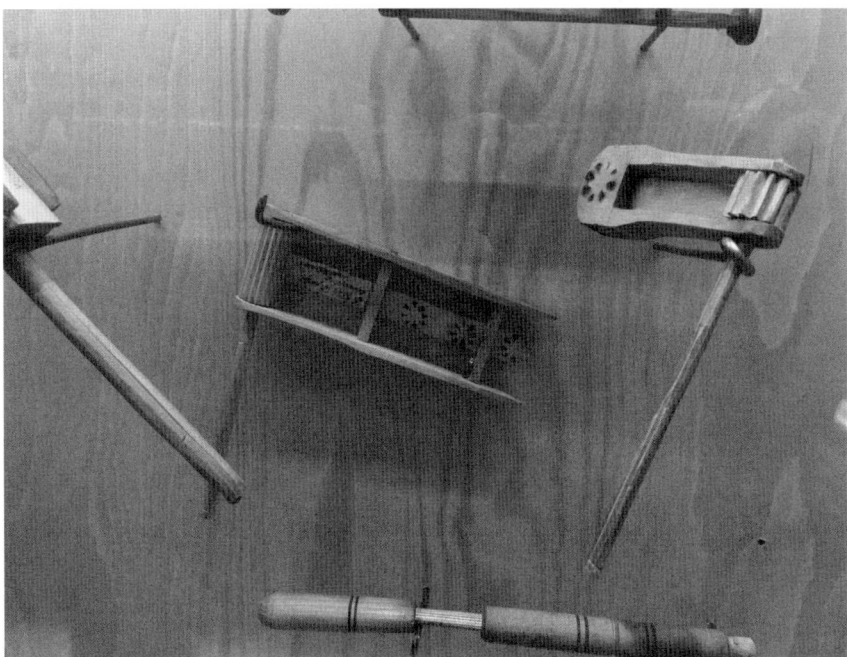

Fig. 12.2 Terkotkas on display at the Kraków Ethnographic Museum (Brzezowa near Myślenice, 1929), gift from the girl's junior high school. Object inventory no. 3764. © Erica Lehrer.

symbolic (and real) violence. An implication-minded approach would challenge both communities to understand 'their cultures' in more expansive ways than those that colonial-era ethnographic presentations and nationalist narratives have encouraged, and to acknowledge the contemporary political, educational, and emotional impact such museums have.[19] Similar treatments could be applied to many areas of social and cultural life that are or could be exhibited, from carpentry to papercutting, money-lending, and inn-keeping.

Also in the Kraków Ethnographic Museum (MEK) are objects that represent Jews through the eyes of Catholic Polish peasants, including masks, comical rocking wooden figurines, figural beehives, and a photograph of a straw effigy of 'Judas' hanging from a tree. These objects were used in Catholic seasonal rituals and strongly connected to the realm of magic, but they cannot be justly understood without reference to a broader European history of stereotypical and often anti-Jewish imagery, nor without attention to the contemporary affective responses of Jewish (and non-Jewish) museum visitors to them. Still, how are these objects 'related' to Jewish communities? The question points to a broader range of ways a community can be the 'source' of an object. Here Jews function as the precursors for a stereotype. The resulting artificial 'stand-ins' serve as proxies for the real community and are subjected to the out-group's feelings and fantasies about them. Similar to the proliferation of Jim Crow-era 'memorabilia' depicting Black people in racist ways (Patterson 2010) or the plethora of images and mascots of Native Americans in U.S. popular culture – legacies of colonialism and slavery – these Jewish caricatures also perform inter-group hierarchies and relations and thereby help keep them in place.

A black-and-white 1970s photograph on the gallery wall adjacent to where the masks hang shows local Polish men and kerchiefed women in colourful skirts from a provincial town laughing while another man, dressed as a Jew complete with mask, mounts a life-sized puppet depicting a traditional horned beast, or *turoń*. Clearly amused by the bawdy antics of this Catholic Pole dressed as a Polish Jew, what had been these local people's relations with their actual Jewish neighbours? And in the postwar period, what were their memories of them? In pre-war times, such costumes were often assembled out of clothes stolen from or forcibly demanded from Jewish neighbours, who were often required to pay a ransom for the Judas figure, hanging high in a tree near Jewish homes, to be cut down. Jews learned to stay indoors as much as possible during the Easter season due to threats of violence stirred up by such rituals, which can also be discerned in the lyrics of Christmas puppet plays featuring similar trickster Jewish characters (Tokarska-Bakir 2011).

Due to the traditional ethnographic style of display, these objects are presented as if they belong to a distant past and a bygone culture, divorced from contemporary concerns. Yet 'freighted' objects like these are not inert or outmoded. The stereotypical figurines can be purchased in updated forms – today holding shiny gold coins for luck in business – in shops just outside the museum's front door. These newer types of figurines, which draw still closer to explicit anti-Semitic stereotypes, have been viewed by the Kraków Ethnographic Museum curators as irrelevant to the 'bygone' culture on display in the museum, as I was informed when preparing my own exhibition in the museum in 2013. School children gaze up at these Jewish caricatures

Fig. 12.3-7 Left to right: Figural beehive (Zabierzów, late nineteenth century; archival photo); masks worn by "Jew" character in Christmastime carolling groups, (Silesia, 1956); Emaus Jewish figurine (early twentieth century). Photographs by Jason Francisco

on popular school trips to the museum. Many of them will never meet a real Jew, but it is hard to imagine that they would not connect the figurines in the museum's displays to those they see in their local stores. These objects are also political. The photo of the Judas effigy is no longer on display, removed from the "spring customs" gallery during renovation in 2011 (Kultura Ludowa 2015). If we are concerned with "implication", however, it should be. The climax of an anti-(Muslim) immigrant rally in the Polish city of Wrocław in November 2015 involved the burning of an effigy of a Hasidic Jew – a close kin of the one in the museum's 'Judas' photo – holding the flag of the European Union while the crowd chanted "God, Honour, and Fatherland."[20] In addition, on Good Friday of Easter 2019, inhabitants of the Subcarpathian town of Pruchnik revived the 'hanging of Judas' tradition, with members of the crowd (which included many children) shouting to deliver to the straw Jewish effigy an extra five lashes for 'reparations', referring to contemporary debates over Jewish calls for reparation for expropriated World War II property.[21] For a national museum of Polish culture, whose slogan is "my museum, a museum about me," the use of 'folk' traditions in xenophobic present-day politics offers much to be discussed.

A third type of object that begs pluralist contextualization can be found in the archives of ethnographic and other 'folk' museums across Poland, though my present example is from the collection of Warsaw's State Ethnographic Museum. Dedicated primarily to Polish rural culture, until recently the Warsaw museum obscured Jewish culture much as the Kraków museum had. Since 2014, though, a major re-installation of its permanent display, titled "Celebration Time",[22] has segregated it in an adjacent room (Lehrer and Murzyn-Kupisz 2019). The objects in question are part of a sub-genre of Polish 'folk art' carvings from the 1960s and 70s that represent the Nazi occupation of Poland and the Holocaust.[23] Rarely displayed and largely forgotten, these works are unsettling documents that in their symbolic constitution implicate multiple communities. An example is Polish carver Zygmunt Skrętowicz's *bas-relief* entitled *Gassing*, which is part of a series dedicated to the theme of Auschwitz, depicting the various forms of murder perpetrated by the Germans. Does it make sense to consider such a work as a part of 'Polish' heritage alone, as such works have typically been classified?

Jews are not a "source community" vis-à-vis such art objects; they did not create or own them. But they are 'implicated' in them. To the extent that such art depicts Jews or attempts to represent something of their historical experience – communicated via personal stories, news, or perhaps the few existing photographs documenting naked women being driven towards the gas chambers – we might say Jews 'inspired' it. The tombstone shape of the sculpture with the Lion of Judah carved on the top right panel suggests the artist had knowledge of Jewish symbols, and the work demands such knowledge to decode. Germans, too, are linked to this art, as it presents them, whether directly – here in the form of an SS guard and a Nazi death camp gas chamber – or invisibly, via the war, occupation, and genocide they perpetrated. Such objects open rich questions regarding bystander perspectives and the possibility of relations of witnessing via an artist's empathic, moral gaze on the suffering of an 'other' – albeit that a museum object may be experienced very differently for various viewers (Lehrer and Sendyka 2019b).[24]

Fig. 12.8 One of two panels (the lefthand) from Zygmunt Skrętowicz's The Gassing, from his Auschwitz series (1963). Warsaw State Ethnographic Museum. Photograph by Wojciech Wilczyk.

What were, are, and could be the relations among the groups implicated by these three kinds of "awkward objects"? Who were the real Jews that inspired such art pieces? What kind of contact did the carver have with the people he depicted? How to respond to the fact that the masks of Jews displayed until 2017 without any critical context in the Kraków museum (and still insufficiently so today) "are eerily similar to the forms of domination and violence associated with genocide" itself? (Feldman 2006: 265). And what is the relationship of Jews to these objects, and to the museums who hold and display them, to Jewish communities, today? Consultation with "source communities" regarding collections and displays of objects originating with them has become increasingly standard protocol in recent decades in North America, due largely to the activism and increasing empowerment of Indigenous people and post-colonial nations. To address the questions I pose above, protocols for engaging "communities of implication" must be developed and adapted to Poland's particular historical and contemporary reality.

Anthropologist Jeffrey Feldman writes about the "broad range of sensory experience that constituted the Jewish, German, and Polish encounter in the Holocaust", and develops a theory of "contact points" to move beyond James Clifford's widely cited use of Mary Louise Pratt's notion of "contact zones". Similar to the Khoisan facial casts in South African museums he discusses, these "awkward objects" in Polish ethnographic museums "are not just representations, but records of the process of encounter".[25] These, in turn, create a "lost body problem", in which "sensual products of unequal encounter" are "concealed by visual surfaces and routines of display" (Feldman 2006: 259). While Feldman's core attention is focused on Holocaust relics – objects that were separated from Jewish people (or bodies) in the process of genocide, like the now-iconic piles of shoes – "awkward objects" are a step, or sometimes two, removed from the bodies that inspired them. Feldman's critique is nonetheless generative: What is missing here are the "multiple aspects of agency" that gave rise to an object and brought it into the museum, and the stakes for the real people whose lives were (and, I would argue, still are) touched by them. If Feldman's critique is about missing bodies, I propose extending it to highlight elided relationships, around which ethical curatorial principles – principles of care and kinship – must be developed.

"Communities of implication"

How may curators simultaneously grasp the plural meanings of objects, constitute ethical stewardship, and allow for (or encourage) the emergence of future (-oriented) communities? What notions of 'inheritance' or 'kinship' might transcend the modern Western framework of "possessive individualism"[26] – that we are what we own – and address a range of circumstances within, but also beyond, Western post-colonial paradigms? And what approaches to display and encounter can museums use to open up such objects to their inherent plurality? Anthropologists Ivan Karp and Corinne Kratz invoke the variety of "links and claims" that define the relations that diverse "stakeholders"[27] may have to objects in museum collections, including "felt kinship, ownership, and rights" (Karp and Kratz 2014: 284). It is this range of possible relations – "relations of implication" – that might be enlarged, to bring a dynamic, pluralist gaze to bear on museum objects, one that accounts for the wounds of history of which such objects are traces. Such an expansion can help re-envision our relations not only to objects but also to each other.

Given the intensifying global migrations of people and things during the twentieth and twenty-first centuries, the grounds for 'cultural authenticity' – and the authority and analytical tools to determine it in relation to material culture – increasingly overspills the contours of any single national or cultural community. Quite simply, the language of ownership and property is insufficient both to theorise and to productively activate certain kinds of material culture present in museums today (Coombe 1993). Without eroding the fundamental ethical (and legal) achievement of recognising "source communities" and championing the restitution of "cultural property" to those groups from whom it was unjustly acquired, we must explore how museums can supplement and expand notions of object-community relations. Such a move would acknowledge that both colonialism and twentieth-century genocides destroyed more than property restitution can ever restore. Museums, however, are in a powerful position to help broker novel modes and terms of engagement with collections that enhance both our understandings of meaningful objects, as well as our ability to envision and call into being new, progressive communities and solidarities. Critical museum curators need a broader set of concepts, such as "communities of implication", that support innovative museum work in a range of social, cultural, and political settings, a vocabulary suited to complex past and present relationships of museology, object-making, and culture-building. The language of implication would also support new visions of identity politics and cross-group solidarity that help counteract our dangerously polarised world.

A starting point for conceptualising relations of implication is the notion of a "heritage community". The Council of Europe (CoE) defines a heritage community as "people who *value* specific aspects of cultural heritage that they *wish*, within the framework of public action, to sustain and transmit to future generations" (Council of Europe 2005, my emphasis). This conception brings a usefully flexible sense of agency, process, and change to people-object relations.[28] Even so, the idea of a heritage community is also limiting in its focus on 'desire' and 'choice' in relation to heritage. For this reason, I propose the term "community of implication", building on the CoE's definition to include people who are 'affected' by or can be said to be 'implicated' in certain tangible or intangible cultural products, in ethical terms.

A key concern with notions of heritage that construe material and intangible cultural traditions as freely chosen by anyone who comes to value them – as suggested by the CoE's definition – is the problem of cultural appropriation. That is, a simple desire on the part of Europeans to identify with, say, Jewish *mezuzahs* (doorpost prayer boxes) – or North American Plains Indian headdresses, for that matter – at minimum sidesteps the issue of what happened to the sources or former stewards of these cultural practices and objects; it risks simply replacing them and their narratives with new ones, and displacing these objects from their original owners a second time. Appropriation entails the loss of crucial historical and contemporary meanings – and thereby power – due to the choice by new individuals and groups to identify with, or simply employ or enjoy, objects or intangible heritage originating with other groups.[29]

The work of building ethical relations to material (as well as intangible) heritage involves building new kinds of human relations around them.[30] The idea of 'implication' highlights the need to reckon with the particular character of one's historical and contemporary connection to a given object. It means asking, "What other groups have claims to this object, and *how does my relation with it relate to theirs?*" In this way, identification takes on the quality of obligation, implying responsibilities as well as rights.[31]

I am broadly inspired here by Michael Rothberg's expanding on and complicating the standard victim/perpetrator/bystander paradigm via his theorization of "implicated subjects", which he defines as the "large and heterogeneous collection of subjects who enable and benefit from traumatic violence without taking part in it directly" (Rothberg 2014). He notes that

> [t]he category of implicated subjects emerges in relation to both historical and contemporary scenarios of violence: that is, it describes the indirect responsibility of subjects situated at temporal or geographic distance from the production of social suffering. It helps direct our attention to the conditions of possibility of violence as well as its lingering impact and suggests new routes of opposition...*implication* draws attention to how we

are *entwined with* and *folded into* ("im-pli-cated in") histories and situations that surpass our agency as individual subjects. (ibidem)

Debarati Sanyal's etymologically overlapping exploration of "complicity" in relation to cultural memory conveys a similar "gathering of subject positions, histories, and memories", which is both intimate and risky (Sanyal 2015). Both formulations resist the collapse of memory and identity, and both provide the grounds for 'ethical commitments' that push against the presumption that the proper containers of group memory follow ethno-cultural boundaries. Acknowledging one's implication and complicity in any history of victimization is the first step towards taking responsibility, helping to "foster a nuanced understanding of how power folds us into its mechanisms, of the institutional forces that mediate our agency, of the past's reverberations into the present" (Sanyal 2015: 13).

Finally, Gerald McMaster suggests that visual art and culture provides a basis for developing a historical perspective on cultural entanglement and interrelatedness, along with new curatorial approaches for juxtaposing objects (McMaster 2002). Olga Goldberg-Mulkiewicz's work on Jewish influences in Polish 'folk art' reveals such entanglements in the Jewish motifs that found their way into Polish domestic and public buildings via the Jewish craftsmen who built them – further disrupting mono-ethnic presentations of 'folk cultural' production (Goldberg-Mulkiewicz 2003).

In the present context, I am particularly interested in the lingering impact of violence, and the conditions of possibility for retroactively witnessing it, in ways that surpass our agency as individual subjects. How are we to not only redress but also 'account for' the wrongs perpetrated by the very museum institutions that purport to care for culturally-significant objects – from the misappropriation of such items, to the dehumanization of and implicit threats of violence towards marginalised groups embedded in offensive depictions and practices, to the ongoing erasure of these due to the absence of interpretive materials that would illuminate them? When regimes of display maintain modernist ethnographic priorities of hiving off the past, distrusting emotion, and presenting 'cultures' as if they are natural taxonomies rather than shifting, hybrid formulations, then colonial categories and ways of knowing endure, regardless of what objects museums return, what compensation they give, or what aesthetic risks they take to entice contemporary viewers by way of updated institutional identities. We must make objects' awkward implications visible if they are to be broadly and thoroughly addressed.

A move towards "implication" usefully decentres Europe as the space of definition and yet keeps European connections to the objects that have sojourned in colonial museums in full view without imputing any necessary or noble character to such custodianship. It also involves shifting the focus away from the agency of the 'subjects' – the idea that we always choose what aspects of heritage relate to us – and transposes it instead to the agency of the 'objects', recognizing the material world's ability to depict, to move, to connect, to remind, even to accuse.[32] Such a shift is particularly salient when considering complex recent histories involving both colonialism and other forms and catalysts of mass violence, forced migration, and subsequent mnemonic formations – so-called difficult heritage. "Difficult heritage", as defined by Sharon Macdonald, refers to that past that is meaningful but also contested, as it presents problems for positive, self-affirming identity discourses (Macdonald 2008). Yet as Macdonald herself notes, governments have in the last two decades become adept at using the museumification of past misdeeds to burnish their current national image, co-opting even this kind of history for self-affirming, exclusivist heritage projects (Ibid 2016). Chiara De Cesari, for example, describes how new, supra-national discourses of 'European heritage,' intended to counter exclusivist projects, are often deployed in museums in ways that draw on regressive nationalist paradigms (De Cesari 2017).

We must thus look beyond the notion of 'positive valuation' and a 'desire to protect and bequeath heritage' as a gift of identity that one hopes to see continued by one's descendants. There are simply too many tangible and intangible traces of the past that intrude on our social lives or consciousness unbeckoned, and often undesired, to allow us to think of heritage as always fully chosen and embraced. Such disturbing traces, too, may strongly contribute to our senses of self and others' ideas about us. Artist-researcher Paula Gaetano-Adi provocatively calls for us to consider objects not simply as artefacts, but as "essential members of the community in which they were created" and further that decolonisation requires not only material return, but also restoring these objects' abilities to enact their communal functions – and, I might add, new social roles proper to the changing historical context (Azoulay et al 2019).

While lawmakers do their necessary juridical work, museum scholars and practitioners can invent new concepts and devise new curatorial strategies that express material relationships otherwise. Indeed, thinking curatorially allows us to address crucial issues that processes of restitution risk overlooking. For example, if European museums want to claim and retain 'foreign' objects as their own heritage, should they not be required to account for the full biographical experiences of these objects since leaving their original homes? As Gaetano-Adi suggests, we should be radically opening the question of what these objects are evidence of, rather than limiting their meanings to illustrations of 'the culture' of the place from which they were long ago taken.[33]

To do this work of redress and repair, we must rethink the relations of people to material heritage in terms of not only voluntary identification but also involuntarily affectedness, or implication. I would suggest we consider this kind of relation as a form of kinship, those mutually constitutive entanglements we have with 'significant Others' whose own experiences of and reactions to us make up the other half of the dialogue that always co-constitutes our identities. These kinship relations form "communities of implication".

Conclusions

Histories of violence and oppression are inscribed in objects, which implicate us by proximity, symbolism, or other vectors of the past. The "awkward objects" I discuss often need at least Jewish, German, and Polish historical and cultural knowledge to unpack their full biographies.[34] Strategic curatorial approaches can frame objects to function as a source of ethical inspiration and empathy, spurring people to acknowledge and address those histories that are *un*chosen by national or communal authorities. Those authorities, as a rule, work to maintain an illusion of a singularly proud heritage they desire by effacing and rejecting, rather than embracing challenging pasts. Taking stock of, rather than expunging abject heritages provides the grounds to call into being new communities based on a sense of interrelation, mutual responsibility, and commitment.

There is important work to be done to help museums relate creatively to their diverse constituencies, even, as Steven Lavine proposed almost thirty years ago, "reimagin[ing] who those constituencies might be" (1992: 137). Colonial-era museums have inherent multicultural heritage. Their collections span the globe and contain evidence of cultural contact and heterogeneity elided by the very national boundaries that these museums were founded to underscore and legitimate. From continually-transforming American Indian totem poles (Jonaitis and Glass 2010), to Kenyan Samburu marriage beads (of nineteenth-century Venetian origin, coveted today by middle-class American women, see Straight 2002), to ubiquitous 'tourist art' created by cultural insiders but catering to visitors' desires (Phillips and Steiner 1999; Phillips 1999), the objects contained in museums embody and illuminate relationships among a wide array of cultural meanings and affects reverberating from a history of ambivalent inter-group engagements. Should not their galleries do the same?

This is not to collapse fundamental distinctions among various difficult histories nor among the differently constituted human taxonomies and hierarchies (cultural, ethnic, racial, class, gender) that underpin them. These historical classifications have contemporary corollaries and afterlives that inevitably distinguish the treatment of communities and objects in museums in ways that merit sustained consideration.[35] While a transcultural turn in memory studies has been forging important new ground, bringing histories of the Holocaust and colonialism into productive conversation (Partridge 2010; Rothberg 2009; Sanyal 2015), that work largely remains to be broached in the museum world.[36]

It is worth thinking – even if speculatively – across diverse cases to see what explorations of implication might illuminate. Like Indigenous objects in North America and elsewhere, Jewish-related objects were rendered mute, and were often misappropriated, in places where once vibrant source populations were destroyed, dispossessed, disempowered, and elided. However, due to political changes and associated global movements of people (via migration, tourism, or travel related specifically to museum collection-community re-engagement projects), such objects are being re-encountered and recognised by, re-acquainted with, and re-framed under the care of newly configured "communities of implication", setting the stage for attempts at their historical and cultural re-contextualization and social re-animation.[37]

These changes may – and do – proceed in progressive and regressive directions, towards increased social polarization, or go on to develop cross-group solidarity and social justice. Some projects of reclamation retrench ethno-nationalism: For example, Israeli youth tours that attempt to read Jewish and Holocaust history as hermetically sealed from its historical Polish (and broader Eastern European) surroundings, except as regards Polish violence against Jews, or Yad Vashem's spiriting of Polish-Jewish artist Bruno Schulz's murals to Israel by identifying them as the heritage of the Jewish people only (Paloff 2004). Such examples share characteristics with Polish right-wing discourses (including some that appropriate post-colonial discourse) that fixate on Polish oppression by Russian, German, or European power (blatant anti-Semitism like the 'Judas' ritual is simply one step further). New language is needed to resist the inscription of heritage objects into a range of pre-existing ethno-national and xenophobic formulations.

Museum practice is a highly political, overdetermined field. Ostensibly emancipatory terminology may elide the ongoing injustices perpetrated by European and Euro-colonial museums that continue to hold and misrepresent ill-gotten collections. The development of a notion of "communities of implication" must distinguish itself from the practice of "inventing conceptions and slogans that will protect [museums'] illegal holding of looted/stolen cultural artefacts of others" (Opoku 2015). Regressive formulations may hide under the banner of 'shared heritage,' 'world heritage,' and 'heritage of all mankind'. Difficult questions also arise about the divergent power relations surrounding Indigenous, Jewish, and further racialised, ethnicised, or otherwise 'othered' collections. Anthropologist Sharon Macdonald recently raised the question of whether the sort of "difficult heritage" she has long written about – for example Nazi heritage in Germany – is still actually difficult (Macdonald 2016). One cannot answer this question in universal terms, but it is worth asking. Holocaust memory, for example, has been popularly institutionalised to such an extent that it can in some locations and under some circumstances form a "comfortable horrible" that is *grievable* – and politically, socially, and emotionally 'safe' – in ways that colonial memory is not.[38]

With these caveats in mind, I offer the idea of "communities of implication" to expand the circle of voices that museums bring to bear on understanding objects, with plural, inclusive interpretation and exhibition, and new network-building in relation to these, achieved through the widest range of means. Further, the push to diversify the interpretive toolkit does not apply only to Indigenous or 'minoritised' cultural objects in majority, dominant-culture museums.[39] A Picasso painting inspired by African masks stands to gain as much from being viewed in the context of a multi-cultural, multi-national, multi-vocal "community of implication" as does a Benin bronze, or a Polish 'folk sculpture' depicting the German Nazi persecution of Jews. Arguments that such objects are somehow better exhibited in the British Museum, rather than in Benin or Brooklyn, are merely exercises in the perpetuation of colonial-era power politics. Rather, such contextual shifts – potentially achieved via rotating itineraries of custodianship agreed upon by the original owners, after restitution – would aid in the accumulation of perspectives on human-object, and human-human implication, and in building the envisioned caretaker communities, a new kind of inter-cultural, cross-group kin.

While my own work has long focused on Jewish memory in Poland, living and teaching in Canada has meant being immersed in discourses and practices emanating primarily from Indigenous people's struggles and negotiations with national and particularly ethnographic museums – institutions that have long unjustly collected and often misrepresented their material culture. I have found myself transporting, and working to translate, the progressive gestures of such decolonising museum methodologies into the Polish-Jewish context. There are risks in such a transposition, foremost among them repeating a colonizing gesture by imposing a 'Western' decolonising paradigm onto an 'Eastern' space with its own complex history. Yet the attempt to face and untangle these has been generative. Creative, critical interventions in museums by Indigenous and minoritised artists like James Luna, Fred Wilson, and Michael Nichol Yahgulanaas inspired me to work with Polish colleagues and students to develop a series of exhibitions and interventions in the Kraków Ethnographic Museum since 2013. These have moved from more external to increasingly collaborative projects vis-à-vis the museum, in a 'trans-anthropological' attempt to break out of problematic ethnographic tropes, while still finding value in the collections and the institution as a public platform. These include: exhibitions of ambivalent 'folk art' objects (and their contemporary corollaries)[40] displayed in an "interrogative" mode (Karp and Kratz 2014); "hacking" the museum with Polish university students[41]; working with a Jewish festival to catalyse local Jewish community attention to the museum's Jewish-related content[42]; and developing a critical tour of the museum.[43] It is hard to grasp the dynamics and directions of change in the museum, especially as since 2015 the radically conservative Law and Justice government, with direct influence on the museum's funding, has gained power. Yet overall our projects seem to have both paralleled and contributed to incremental changes at the Kraków Ethnographic Museum in relation to their depiction of Jews in the permanent exhibition. Some of the most troubling items have been removed – beginning in 2011, when a major renovation took place – and additional such work is being advanced. Whether such gestures signal increasing empathy, growing 'disidentification', or both, the result betrays the intense, multifaceted anxieties that "awkward objects" provoke for the museums that hold them (Lehrer and Murzyn 2019).

These material objects contain great affective potential that can lead to important inter-group insights. Talking with my Polish (non-Jewish) colleagues has been challenging and illuminating, and the museum's openness to experimentation has resulted in meaningful dialogues within and beyond its walls, and new audiences recognizing the institution's significance. MEK's director agreed to hold a public meeting at a recent Jewish culture festival to discuss the museum's treatment of Jewish themes.[44] He seemed genuinely surprised by the expressions of pain recounted by the audience members, mostly local and foreign Jews. After the event a friend of mine, an American Jew on a trip to connect with her Polish ancestral roots (and one of those people who spoke), bumped into the director near the museum. She had spent the previous day bushwhacking through blackberry brambles in a provincial cemetery to look for family tombstones; there was no way to connect with local Polish people there to discuss this ambivalently shared material heritage. But at the museum – where my friend had seen the masks and figurines and *groggers* – there was. The director clasped my friend's hand after the event and said, simply, "I'm sorry." She was moved, she said, and felt a little bit closer to home. Decolonising the museum here is not about restitution. These "awkward objects" are most valuable to us curated in ongoing, caring conversation wherever historical injuries still resonate, reminding us that we are tied together by our wounds.

Notes

1. Substantially shorter versions of the core idea in this text were published previously in Lehrer (2018) and Lehrer and Sendyka (2019a). Thanks to Aaron Glass, Shelley Ruth Butler, Cara Krmpotich, Nora Landkammer, Wayne Modest, Monica Patterson, Roma Sendyka, Jennifer Shannon, Jonas Tinius, Margareta von Oswald, Magdalena Waligórska, and Joanna Wawrzyniak – as well as the participants in the Museums and Public History Research Group at the University of Toronto – for their comments on prior drafts.
2. Basu, Paul. 2017. *The Inbetweenness of Things: Materializing Mediation and Movement Between Worlds*. London: Bloomsbury, p. 4.
3. Auerbach, Rachela. 1946. 'Lament Rzeczy Martwych'. *Przełom* 2: 6–8.
4. The image on p. 288 is Figure 12.1 One of two panels (the righthand) from Zygmunt Skrętowicz's The Gassing, from his Auschwitz series (1963). Warsaw State Ethnographic Museum. Photograph by Wojciech Wilczyk.
5. I am borrowing and building on the term "awkward objects", which originates in the research project 'Awkward Objects of Genocide: The Holocaust and Vernacular Arts in and beyond Polish Ethnographic Museums', led by Roma Sendyka as part of the European Commission Horizon 2020 grant *TRACES: Transmitting Contentious Cultural Heritages with the Arts* (grant agreement No. 693857), 2016-2019. Also see Tinius (2018), particularly his notion of approaching artworks as "relational prisms", made for a happy confluence that further strengthens the notion of awkwardness.
6. Collecting practices and policies as a discrete process (separate from interpreting or curating what has already been collected) also have implications for the notion of "communities of implication", as the act of amassing materials may itself make visible previously unseen cultural interconnections and raise new questions.
7. French cultural heritage code and the general code of the property of public personnel (CG3P) uphold a "general principle of the inalienability of publicly owned cultural objects – the founding principle of the legislation of French

museums". Sarr and Savoy (2018: 77). The 'inalienability rule' was originally written to protect the French crown's property but still today prevents individuals and other countries from taking possession of France's 'public goods' and monuments.

8. "France ratified in 1997 the UNESCO convention of 1970 concerning the illicit exportation of cultural property; but that this convention has no retroactive scope." Sarr and Savoy (2018: 21)

9. Handler (1991) calls this situation "fair play": Indigenous groups have no choice but to use outmoded and Western notions of cultural identity – as these are the dominant, politically persuasive categories – to make their case against the Western museum practice that would retain objects they understand to be rightfully theirs by genealogical connection.

10. In the nineteenth and early twentieth centuries, Poles were participating in Russian, German, American, and English ethnographic expeditions, and classical English-language evolutionist thinkers translated into Polish served as a theoretical base for the developing discipline as well as institutions of ethnography and ethnology. Polish professors who took up chairs in ethnography and ethnology were educated in Germany, France, Austria, and Russia. For a broad tracing of the impact of major political events on the history of these disciplines in Poland, see Jasiewicz and Slattery (1995). In the interwar period, influences came from France (Durkheimians), Germany (historical method), Great Britain (Malinowskian anthropology), and the United States (the Chicago school and Boasian school). See Linkiewicz (2016).

11. On peasant-based national mythologies, see also Baycroft and Hopkin (2012); Filipova (2011); Hofer (1990); Mihailescu (2004); Peer (1998); Thiesse and Norris (2003). Aaron Glass notes that in North America and other settler colonies, the two museum types were partially fused in the early twentieth century when Indigenous people, no longer a political threat, were appropriated as the source for an authentic, autochthonous, non-European source of national identity/culture (e.g. *American Museum of Natural History* and the *National Gallery of Canada* mounted exhibits of Native objects between 1915 and 1930 to promote growth of nationally distinctive art/design industries). [Personal communication, June 2019.]

12. Such 'non-Polish' collections in Polish ethnographic museums today were donated by or purchased from anthropologists (race scientists), ethnographers, other scientists, explorers, travellers, collectors, politicians interested in the issue of colonies, Catholic missionaries, and political exiles. See for example Rosset (2015) and Jacher-Tyszkowa (1998). Thanks to Olga Linkiewicz for direction.

13. There exists almost no literature on colonialism, post-coloniality, or decolonisation as it pertains to Polish or other Eastern European museums (*cf.* Bukowiecki

2019; Bukowiecki & Wawrzyniak 2019; Muthesius 2012; Muthesius & Piotrowski 2017; Piotrowski 2011). General discussion of colonialism and post-coloniality in Eastern Europe – as both a victim and perpetrator – has taken root in the past two decades in academic discourse on the region, offering new concepts but in piecemeal and uncoordinated fashion, and without any impact on mainstream postcolonial literature – see Głowacka-Grajper and Wawrzyniak (2019).

14. I do not mean to suggest the process is resolved; on the contrary, regarding the question of Jewish cultural property in postwar Poland, Cieślińska-Lobkowicz (2009: 143) described the "noteworthy absence of historical and provenance research concerning Jewish movable cultural property looted during the Second World War" in Poland.

15. For a discussion of the ambiguity of such sites among local communities in the early postwar era, and the gap between legal and personal relationships, see Weizmann (2017). Today the sites may be experienced by local Poles as haunted by Jewish ghosts, see Waligórska (2014). Sendyka (2019) calls for deeper attention to the available vocabulary for the treatment of another's belongings after mass violence, stressing the need for a term that at minimum retain a sense of trespass, that "reminds us always of loss, and recalls brutal deaths". She suggests that looting of 'abandoned' heritage is currently supported via the endurance in nineteenth-century property law of the medieval feudal latinate traditions of appropriation embedded in the terms *escheated* or *caducary* (along with a Slavic corollary *puścizna*).

16. Artists who have worked in this vein include Łukasz Baksik (*Matzevot for Everyday Use*), Natalia Romik (*Nomadic Shtetl Archive*), Wojciech Wilczyk (*There is No Such Thing as an Innocent Eye*), among others. For critical considerations of this form of identification, see Lehrer and Waligórska (2013), and Dembek (2019).

17. The quote inscribed on a nearby wall, next to a similar rattle, reads: " 'there is a custom in the countryside, that from Holy Thursday until the end of the week (...) boys race about the village clacking their clackers.' Buków (near Kraków), 1903." [In Polish: *jest taki zwyczaj na wsi, że od Wielkiego Czwartku do końca tygodnia (...) chłopcy biegają po wsi z kłapaczkami i kłapią. Buków (koło Krakówa), 1903.*]

18. The Kraków Ethnographic Museum's own collection contains original drawings, including one of a grogger [*grzechotka*] (inventory nr. IV/1343), for the renowned Judaica collector Regina Lilientalowa's book on Jewish children's culture *Dziecko żydowskie* [The Jewish Child]. Kraków: Nakładem Polskiej Akademii Umiejętności, 1927.

19. Recent additions to the Kraków Ethnographic Museum's website offer interpretive material in the direction I am suggesting in relation to another Purim object: a scroll of Esther. See http://etnomuzeum.eu/zbiory/-88. Similarly, on 17-18 March 2018 the museum organised a workshop for families focusing not on the traditional Easter celebrations, but focusing on Purim, in association with

local Jewish organisation Czulent. For one image see: http://etnomuzeum.eu/images/upload/edukacja/Etnokalendarz/03_2018/9.jpg.
20. The doubly-unfortunate imputation is that Muslims alone could not be responsible for overrunning Europe, and thus the Jewish conspiracy must be behind this perceived attack on the Christian heartland. See: JTA (2015)
21. An article with a video of the incident, and mentioning the extra "reparations" lashes, can be seen here: https://histmag.org/Kontrowersyjne-wieszanie-Judasza-w-Pruchniku-18609 (last accessed 25 May 2019).
22. Polish: *Czas Świętowania*.
23. As noted above, the category of 'folk' (*lud* in Polish, translated from the 19th century German idea of *Volk*) was highly political and manipulated by the Polish state. I do not mean to reproduce it uncritically (hence the scare quotes), but along with my co-curators, we often prefer to use the historically appropriate term to the other options like naïve, outsider, or vernacular, each of which comes with its own set of discourses.
24. It is a salient complication of this category of artwork that it is often unclear whether the victims of Nazi violence depicted are Jews or non-Jewish Poles.
25. Feldman (2006: 260) also raises the question of "whether or not the Holocaust is best understood solely as a process of destroying Jews through violence, or as an industrialized colonial encounter between multiple social actors, which produced a broad range of contact points."
26. Handler (1991) discusses how even Indigenous groups have today adopted – quite fairly in political terms – flawed Western notions of group property in efforts to regain their culturally-significant objects from Western museums.
27. The term 'stakeholders' is itself problematic, as it has economic and business-oriented resonances that work against a more humanistic notion and approach to the museum as a public good.
28. Or more broadly 'people-heritage relations', to encompass 'intangible' cultural materials like music, stories, specialised knowledge, ritual practice, etc.
29. The problem can be particularly egregious in a capitalist system where money is being made by dominant groups' use of marginalised people's creations.
30. Important work is being done in Poland to link the new, local caretakers of Jewish built heritage to living Jewish communities, sharing stories and experiences, and studying history. The work of the Warsaw-based Forum for Dialogue (http://dialog.org.pl/en/), for example, works with "the traces of ties that were ruptured in World War Two" and to "facilitate the formation of bonds between Jews and the country of their ancestors" via "people-to-people trust" and "difficult questions".
31. A consummate example of such an approach to curating is the recent *Americans* exhibit at the National Museum of the American Indian in Washington,

D.C. (see: https://americanindian.si.edu/americans/), which proposes that the difficult conversation is not so much about the genocide and violence against Indigenous Americans, but that "[settler-origin Americans] are all connected to Indians, even though [we] don't know it" (curator Paul Chaat Smith, personal communication, 24 April 2019).

32. Recent scholarship on the agency and affective force of objects includes: Navaro-Yashin (2009), Forensic Architecture (2014), Hoskins (2006), and Bennet (2010).
33. "Decolonising the Museum: A Teach-In." https://brown.hosted.panopto.com/Panopto/Pages/Viewer.aspx?id=a9f5b3f4-1ed1-4af9-bd2f-aa01011399e9 (Accessed July 10, 2019).
34. See, for example, Greenblatt's (1990) evocative consideration of potential curatorial strategies in relations to Prague's *Jewish Museum*.
35. The rise of Holocaust memorial museums, for example, is a phenomenon normalised in many countries for more than two decades, while there exists no museum dedicated to the trauma of colonialism (save for a recent online resource: https://www.museumofbritishcolonialism.org/ (Accessed 14 June 2019)).
36. Exceptions include Lawson (2013) and Moses (2012).
37. The attempts by Jewish Auschwitz survivor Dina Gottliebova Babbitt to obtain the paintings she made of a Roma woman during her time as a camp inmate were rejected by the Auschwitz Museum on the grounds they are today "part of the cultural heritage of the world" Friess (2006). In another case of the heirs of the Holocaust victim Pierre Lévi requisition control of their father's suitcase, the museum similarly cited a "risk of precedence", fearing similar suits demanding further deaccessioning of their collections. The museum also stresses "important documentary and educational functions" their collections play (see Riding 2006).
38. "Comfortable horrible" is Linenthal's (1995: 267) term for narratives of tragedy that have little social power beyond confirming what "we", as a pre-determined collectivity, already know, think, or feel. The idea of a "grieveable subject" is from Butler (2008).
39. "Minoritized individuals belong to groups that as a result of social constructs face prejudices and have less power or representation than other groups" (Smith 2016).
40. See The Ethnographic Museum in Kraków. 2019. *Terrible Close. Polish Vernacular Artists face the Holocaust.* www.terriblyclose.eu/ and www.luckyjews.com.
41. See Curating and Public Scholarship Lab. 2017. *My Museum, a museum about me!* http://capsl.cerev.ca/my-museum-a-museum-about-me/.

42. See FestivALT. 2019. "FestivALT: Pytając o "Widok zza bliska" (Event). *Facebook*. https://www.facebook.com/events/302698633768909/.
43. See FestivALT. 2019. "Alternative Tour of the Ethnographic Museum". *FestivALT*. https://www.festivalt.com/event/alternative-tour-of-the-ethnographic-museum-2/.
44. See FestivALT. 2019. "Every Museum is a Story: A conversation with the Museum director". *FestivALT*. http://www.festivalt.com/event/every-museum-is-a-story-a-conversation-with-the-museum-director/.

References

Art Institute of Chicago (Director), and others. 2002. 'Declaration on the Importance and Value of Universal Museums'. *Wall Street Journal* (12 December 2002). https://www.wsj.com/articles/SB1039660114241762793 (last accessed 15 May 2019).

Ashworth, G.J and Tunbridge, J.E. 1996. *Dissonant Heritage. The management of the past as a resource in conflict.* Chichester: John Wiley and Sons.

Auerbach, Rachela. 1946. 'Lament Rzeczy Martwych'. *Przełom* 2: 6–8.

Azoulay, Ariela, Yannis Hamilakis, and Vazira Zamindar (organisers). 2019. *Decolonizing the Museum: A Teach-In. Open Forum on the Sarr-Savoy Report on the Restitution of African Cultural Heritage.* (Conference). Providence: Brown University, USA. https://brown.hosted.panopto.com/Panopto/Pages/Viewer.aspx?id=a9f5b3f4-1ed1-4af9-bd2f-aa01011399e9 (last accessed 15 May 2019).

Barkan, Elazar. 2002. 'Amending Historical Injustices: The Restitution of Cultural Property— An Overview', in: *Claiming the Stones/naming the Bones: Cultural Property and the Negotiation of National and Ethnic Identity*, edited by Elazar Barkan and Ronald Bush. Los Angeles: Getty Research Institute, pp. 16–46.

Baycroft, Timothy, and David Hopkin. Eds. 2012. *Folklore and Nationalism in Europe During the Long Nineteenth Century: National Cultivation of Culture.* Vol. 4. Brill: Leiden.

Bennett, Jane. 2010. *Vibrant Matter: A Political Ecology of Things.* Durham, NC: Duke University Press.

Bukowiecki, Łukasz. 2019. 'Things of Warsaw and Things of the Past: Evolution and Priorities of the Museum of Warsaw'. *Museum of Warsaw Report #1*, ECHOES Horizon 2020 Grant Project: European Colonial Heritage Modalities in Entangled Cities. Grant Agreement No. 770248. University of Warsaw. http://projectechoes.eu/wp-content/uploads/Bukowiecki-Museum-of-Warsaw-Report-1.pdf (last accessed 2 November 2019).

Bukowiecki, Łukasz, and Joanna Wawrzyniak. 2019. 'Dealing with Difficult Pasts at the Museum of Warsaw: Implications of Curatorial Memory Practices'. *Museum of Warsaw Report #2*, ECHOES Horizon 2020 grant project: European Colonial Heritage Modalities in Entangled Cities, grant agreement No. 770248. University of Warsaw. http://projectechoes.eu/wp-content/uploads/Bukowiecki-Wawrzyniak-Museum-Of-Warsaw-Report-2_compressed.pdf (last accessed 24 November 2019).

Butler, Judith. 2008. *Frames of War: When Is Life Grievable?* London: Verso.

Cieślińska-Lobkowicz, Nawojka. 2009. 'Dealing with Jewish Cultural Property in Post-War Poland'. *Art Antiquity and Law* 14(2): 143–166.

Chari, Sharad, and Katherine Verdery. 2009. 'Thinking between the Posts: Postcolonialism, Postsocialism, and Ethnography after the Cold War'. *Comparative Studies in Society and History* (1/January 2) 51: 6–34.

Coombe, Rosemary. 1993. 'The Properties of Culture and the Politics of Possessing Identity: Native Claims in the Cultural Appropriation Debate'. *Canadian Journal of Law and Jurisprudence* 6(2): 249–285.

Council of Europe. 2005. 'Council of Europe Framework Convention on the Value of Cultural Heritage for Society'. *Council of Europe Treaty Series*, 199, article 2: Definitions.

De Cesari, Chiara. 2017. 'Museums of Europe: Tangles of Memory, Borders, and Race'. *Museum Anthropology* 40(1):18–35.

Dembek, María Magdalena. 2019. 'Archaeological fever: situating participatory art in the rubble of the Warsaw ghetto'. *Holocaust Studies* 25(3): 377–399.

Feldman, Jeffrey David. 2006. 'Contact Points: Museums and the Lost Body Problem', in: *Sensible Objects: Colonialism, Museums and Material Culture*, edited by Elizabeth Edwards, Chris Gosden, and Ruth Phillips. Oxford and New York: Berg, pp. 245–268.

Filipova, Marta. 2011. 'Peasants on display: the Czechoslovak Ethnographic Exhibition of 1895'. *Journal of Design History* 24(1): 15–36.

Forensic Architecture. Ed. 2014. *Forensis: The Architecture of Public Truth*. Berlin: Sternberg Press.

Friess, Steve. 2006. 'History Claims Her Artwork, but She Wants It Back'. *New York Times*, 30 August 2006, E1.

Głowacka-Grajper, Małgorzata, and Joanna Wawrzyniak. 2019. 'The Diversity of Postcolonialisms in Central and Eastern Europe: A Critical Review of an Emerging Research Field', in *Methodological Toolkit* [of ECHOES project], edited by Casper Andersen, Britta Timm Knudsen, Christoffer Kølvraa, pp. 102–119. http://projectechoes.eu/wp-content/uploads/ECHOES-MET-TK-FINAL-optimized-with-cover.pdf (last accessed 28 December 2019).

Goldberg-Mulkiewicz, Olga. 2003. *Stara i nowa ojczyzna: ślady kultury Żydów polskich*. Łódź Polskie Tow. Ludoznawcze.

Grabowski, Jan. 2013. *Hunt for the Jews: Betrayal and Murder in German-Occupied Poland*. Bloomington: Indiana University Press.

Greenblatt, Stephen. 1990. 'Resonance and Wonder'. *Bulletin of the American Academy of Arts and Sciences* 43(4): 11–34.

Gross, Jan Tomasz, and Irena Grudzińska-Gross. 2012. *Golden Harvest*. New York: Oxford University Press.

Gross, Jan Tomasz. 2001. *Neighbors: The Destruction of the Jewish Community in Jedwabne, Poland*. Princeton, NJ: Princeton University Press.

Grudzińska-Gross, Irena. 2016. 'Polishness in Practice', in: *Poland and Polin: New Interpretations in Polish-Jewish Studies*. Frankfurt and New York: Peter Lang, pp. 197–213.

Handler, Richard. 1991. 'Who Owns the Past? History, Cultural Property, and the Logic of Possessive Individualism', in: *The Politics of Culture*, edited by Brett Williams. Washington, DC: Smithsonian Institution Press, pp. 63–74.

Hofer, Tamás. 1990. 'Construction of the "Folk Cultural Heritage" and Rival Versions of National Identity in Hungary'. *Ethnologia Europaea* 21(1): 145–70.

Hoskins, Janet. 2006. 'Agency, biography, and objects', in: *Handbook of Material Culture*, edited by Christopher Tiller *et al*. London: Sage Publications, pp. 74–84.

Hunt, Tristram, Hartmut Dorgerloh, and Nicholas Thomas. 2018. 'Restitution Report: museum directors respond'. *The Art Newspaper* (November 27th). https://www.theartnewspaper.com/comment/restitution-report-museums-directors-respond (last accessed 15 May 2019).

Jacher-Tyszkowa, Aleksandra. 1998. 'Historia Działu Kultur Ludowych Pozaeuropejskich i zbiorów pozaeuropejskich w Muzeum Etnograficznym im. Seweryna Udzieli w Krakowie za lata 1911-1998'. *Rocznik Muzeum Etnograficznego w Krakowie* 14: 7–27.

Jasiewicz, Zbigniew, and David Slattery. 1995. 'Ethnography and Anthropology: The Case of Polish Ethnology', in: *Fieldwork and Footnotes: Studies in the History of European Anthropology*, edited by Arturo Alvarez Roldan and Han Vermeule. London and New York: Routledge, pp. 184–201.

Jonaitis, Aldona, and Aaron Glass. 2010. *The Totem Pole: An Intercultural History*. Seattle: University of Washington Press.

JTA. 2015. 'Polish anti-refugee protesters burn effigy of Orthodox Jew'. *The Times of Israel* (19 November 2015). https://www.timesofisrael.com/polish-anti-refugee-protesters-burn-effigy-of-orthodox-jew/ (last accessed 15 May 2019).

Kalman, David Zvi. 2017. 'The Purim Grogger's Christian Origins'. Paper presented at the *Association for Jewish Studies* annual meeting (December 2017). Washington, DC.

Karp, Ivan, and Corinne A. Kratz. 2014. 'The Interrogative Museum', in: *Museum as Process*, edited by Raymond Silverman. New York and London: Routledge, pp. 279–298.

Kultura Ludowa. 2015. 'Wieszanie Judasza'. *NaLudowo.pl* http://naludowo.pl/kultura-ludowa/wieszanie-judasza-ludowy-zwyczaj-wielki-czwartek-widowisko-kukla-palenie-kiedy.html (last accessed 15 May 2019).

Landkammer, Nora. 2017. 'Visitors or Community? Collaborative Museology and the Role of Education and Outreach in Ethnographic Museums', in: *Contemporary Curating and Museum Education*, edited by Carmen Morsch, Angeli Sachs, and Thomas Sieber. New York: Columbia University Press, pp. 269–280.

Lavine, Steven D. 1992. 'Audience, ownership, and authority: designing relations between museums and communities', in: *Museums and Communities*, edited by Ivan Karp, Christine Mullen Kreamer, and Steven D. Lavine. Washington, DC: Smithsonian Institution Press, pp. 137–157.

Lawson, Tom. 2013. 'The Holocaust and Colonial Genocide at the Imperial War Museum', in: *Britain and the Holocaust: Remembering Representing War and Genocide*, edited by Caroline Sharples and Olaf Jensen. London: Palgrave Macmillan, pp. 129–141.

Leder, Andrzej. 2014. *Przesniona Rewolucja*. Warszawa: Wydanie.

Lehrer, Erica. 2018. 'From "Heritage Communities" to "Communities of Implication" '. *Traces* (July 2018) http://www.traces.polimi.it/2018/07/26/from-heritage-communities-to-communities-of-implication/ (last accessed 15 May 2019).

———. 2016. 'Most Disturbing Souvenirs: Curative Museology in a Cultural Contact Zone', in: *Curatorial Dreams: Critics Imagine Exhibitions*, edited by Shelley Ruth Butler and Erica Lehrer. Montreal: McGill-Queen's University Press, pp. 46–63.

———. 2013. *Jewish Poland Revisited: Heritage Tourism in Unquiet Places*. Bloomington: Indiana University Press.

Lehrer, Erica, and Monika Murzyn-Kupisz. 2019. 'Making space for Jewish culture in Polish "folk" and "ethnographic" museums: Curating social diversity after ethnic cleansing'. *Museum Worlds: Advances in Research* 7: 82–108.

Lehrer, Erica and Roma Sendyka. 2019a. *Zróżnicowanie narodowego "my": Marzenie Kuratorskie*. Kraków: Wydawnictwo Uniwersyteckie Jagiellońskie.

———. 2019b. 'Arts of Witness? Vernacular art as a source base for 'bystander' Holocaust memory in Poland'. Special issue *of Holocaust Studies*, edited by Larry Ray and Sławomir Kapralski. 25(3): 300–328.

———. 2020. *Diversifying the National "We": Curatorial Dreams for the Seweryn Udziela Ethnographic Museum in Kraków*. Kraków: Exhibiting Theory series, Jagiellonian University Press.

Lehrer, Erica and Magdalena Waligórska. 2013. 'Cur(at)ing History: new genre art interventions and the Polish-Jewish past'. *East European Politics & Society* 27(3): 510–544.

Linenthal, Edward. 1995. *Preserving Memory: The Struggle to Create America's Holocaust Museum*. New York: Columbia University Press.

Linkiewicz, Olga. 2016. 'Scientific Ideals and Political Engagement: Polish Ethnology and the "Ethnic Question" Between the Wars'. *Acta Poloniae Historica* 114: 5–27.

Lozoviuk, Petr. 2005. 'The pervasive continuities of Czech naordopis', in: *Studying peoples in the people´s democracies. Socialist era anthropology in East-Central Europe*, edited by Chris Hann and Peter Skalnik. Münster: Lit Verlag, pp. 227–36.

Macdonald, Sharon. 2008. *Difficult Heritage: Negotiating the Nazi past in Nuremberg and beyond*. New York and London: Routledge.

———. 2016. 'Exhibiting Contentious and Difficult Histories: Ethics, Emotions, and Reflexivity', in: *Museums, Ethics and Cultural Heritage*, edited by Bernice L. Murphy. London and New York: Routledge / ICOM, pp. 267–277.

———. 2016. 'Is 'Difficult Heritage' Still 'Difficult'?'. *Museum International* 67(1-4): 6–22.

McMaster, Gerald. 2002. 'Our (Inter) Related History', in: *On Aboriginal Representation in the Gallery*, edited by Lynda Jessup and Sharon Bagg. Ottawa: Canadian Museum of Civilization, pp. 3–8.

Mihailescu, Vintila. 2004. 'The Legacies of a 'Nation-Building Ethnology': Romania', in: *Educational Histories of European Social Anthropology*, edited by Dorle Dracklé, Iain R. Edgar, and Thomas K. Schippers. New York and Oxford: Berghahn, pp. 208–219

Modest, Wayne, and Helen Mears. 2012. *Museums, African Collections and Social Justice*. London and New York: Routledge.

Moore, David Chioni. 2001. 'Is the Post- in Postcolonial the Post- in Post-Soviet? Toward a Global Postcolonial Critique'. *PMLA* [The Journal of Modern Language Association of America] 116(1): 111–28.

Moses, Dirk. 2012. 'The Canadian Museum for Human Rights: the 'uniqueness of the Holocaust' and the question of genocide'. *Journal of Genocide Research* 14(2): 215–238.

Murawska-Muthesius, Katarzyna. 2012. 'Love of Beauty in the Tsarist Colonial Capital: The Museum of Fine Arts in Warsaw (1862-1916)'. *Centropa* 12(2) (May): 179–193.

Murawska-Muthesius, Katarzyna, and Piotr Piotrowski. 2017. 'Introduction', in: *From Museum Critique to the Critical Museum*. London: Routledge, pp. 1–14

Navaro-Yashin, Yael. 2009. 'Affective spaces, melancholic objects: ruination and the production of anthropological knowledge'. *Journal of the Royal Anthropological Institute* 15: 1–18.

Nycz, Ryszard. 2013.'PRL: pamięć podzielona, społeczeństwo przesiedlone'. *Teksty Drugie* 3: 6-10.

Opoku, Kwame. 2015. 'Looted/Stolen Cultural Artefacts Declared Shared Heritage'. *No-Humboldt 21* http://www.no-humboldt21.de/wp-content/uploads/2015/08/Opoku_SHARED_HERITAGE-4..pdf. (last accessed 15 May 2019).

Paloff, Benjamin. 2004. 'Who Owns Bruno Schulz?' *The Boston Review* (1 December 2004). http://bostonreview.net/benjamin-paloff-who-owns-bruno-schulz-poland-stumbles-over-its-jewish-past (last accessed 15 May 2019).

Partridge, Damani. 2010. 'Holocaust Mahnmal (Memorial): Monumental Memory Amidst Contemporary Race'. *Comparative Studies in Society and History* 52(4): 820-50.

Patterson, Monica Eileen. 2010. 'Teaching Tolerance Through Objects of Hatred: The Jim Crow Museum of Racist Memorabilia as "Counter-Museum', in *Curating Difficult Knowledge: Violent Pasts in Public Places*, edited by Erica Lehrer, Cynthia Milton, and Monica Eileen Patterson. New York: Palgrave, pp. 55-71

Peer, Shanny. 1998. *France on Display: Peasants, Provincials, and Folklore in the 1937 Paris World's Fair*. Albany: State University of New York.

Peers, Laura, and Alison K. Brown. 2003. *Museums and Communities: A Routledge Reader*. London and New York: Routledge.

Phillips, Ruth, and Christopher Steiner. Eds. 1999. *Unpacking Culture: Art and Northeast, 1700-1900*. Montreal: McGill-Queen's University Press.

Phillips, Ruth, and Christopher Steiner. Eds. 1999. *Unpacking Culture: Art and Commodity in Colonial and Postcolonial Worlds*. Berkeley: University of California Pres.

Piotrowski, Piotr. 2011. *Muzeum Krytyczne*. Poznań: Dom Wydawniczy "Rebis."

Riding, Alan. 2006. 'In a Holocaust suitcase, a question of memories – Europe – International Herald Tribune'. *New York Times*, 13 September 2006.

Rothberg, Michael. 2009. *Multidirectional Memory: Remembering the Holocaust in the Age of Decolonization*. Stanford, CA: Stanford University Press.

———. 2014. 'Trauma Theory, Implicated Subjects, and the Question of Israel/Palestine'. *Profession* (Archive) https://profession.mla.org/2014/05/02/trauma-theory-implicated-subjects-and-the-question-of-israel-palestine/ (last accessed 15 May 2019).

Rosset, A. Kluczewska-Wójcik, A. Tołysz, Warszawa. 2015. 'Polskie kolekcje artefaktów afrykańskich. Między zbiorem pamiątek a kolekcją sztuki'. *Kolekcje polskie XX i XXI wieku*: 115-135.

Sanyal, Debarati. 2015. *Memory and Complicity: Migrations of Holocaust Remembrance*. New York: Fordham University Press.

Sarr, Felwine, and Bénédicte Savoy. 2018. *The Restitution of African Cultural Heritage. Toward a New Relational Ethics*. Translated by Drew S. Burk. Paris: Ministère de la Culture.

Sendyka, Roma. 2018. 'Caduca, or es(cheat)ed heritage'. *TRACES Journal*: A Research Beacon 5: 1–4.

Shallcross, Bożena. 2011. *The Holocaust Object in Polish and Polish-Jewish Culture*. Bloomington: Indiana University Press.

Smith, I. E. 2016. 'Minority Vs. Minoritized: Why the Noun Just Doesn't Cut It'. *The Odyssey*, (16 September 2016) https://www.theodysseyonline.com/minority-vs-minoritize.

Stocking, George. 1982. 'Afterword: A view from the center'. *Ethnos* 47(1-2): 172–186.

Straight, Bilinda. 2002. 'From Samburu Heirloom to New Age Artifact: The Cross-Cultural Consumption of *Mporo* Marriage Beads'. *American Anthropologist* 104(1): 7–21.

Thiesse, Anne Marie and Sigrid Norris. 2003. 'How Countries are Made: The Cultural Construction of European Nations'. *Contexts* 2(2): 26–32.

Tinius, Jonas. 2018. 'Awkward Art and Difficult Heritage: Nazi Collectors and Postcolonial Archives', in: *An Anthropology of Contemporary Art: Practices, Markets, and Collectors*, edited by Thomas Fillitz and Paul van der Grijp. London: Bloomsbury, pp. 130–145.

Tokarska-Bakir, Joanna. 2011. '"The Hanging of Judas"; or, Contemporary Jewish Topics'. *Polin* 24: 381–400.

Vukov, Nikolai. 2011. 'Ethnoscripts and nationographies: imagining nations within ethnographic museums in East Central and Southern Europe', in: *Great Narratives of the Past. Traditions and Revisions in National Museums*, edited by Dominique Poulot, Felicity Bodenstein & José María Lanzarote Guiral. EuNaMus Report No 4. Linköping University Electronic Press, pp. 331–343. (http://www.ep.liu.se/ecp/078/ecp11078.pdf).

Waligórska, Magdalena. 2014. 'Healing by Haunting: Jewish Ghosts in Contemporary Polish Literature'. *Prooftexts* 34(2): 207–231.

Weizmann, Yechiel. 2017. 'Unsettled possession: the question of ownership of Jewish sites in Poland after the Holocaust from a local perspective'. *Jewish Culture and History* 18(1): 34–53.

"Suggestions for a Post-Museum"

A conversation with Nanette Snoep

For this book, we have devised a set of interviews or position pieces with curators, since we regard curatorial practice as transversally agentive across the main sections of this book: museums, contemporary art, and (post)colonialism. Bearing this in mind, what for you is the practice of curating? Would you describe your practice as curating and if so, how would you describe it?

Although curating has just become a small part of my job since I became a museum director in 2015, when administrative tasks, programming, and strategic thinking have taken the largest part of my time, I still consider myself to be a curator, too.[1] My challenge is in finding a balance between directorship and curatorship.

Curating enables the generation of interactive situations with objects and actors. Curating to me is combining the 'language' of anthropology with the 'language' of artistic reflection and the 'language' of exhibitions. It generates associative critical and inquisitive thinking in three dimensions with the idea of simultaneousness. This differs from linear thinking on a flat surface, which is the case when it comes to writing an article. Anthropological curatorial praxis distinguishes itself from a work of art or from a scientific article. An artist who creates a work of art with anthropological insight must not necessarily take into account the visitors of the institution. In the context of a scientific paper, its form or its structure is clearly predefined. And here again one must not necessarily take into account the reader as long as your paper is correctly written.

Curating is more like composing a musical score or a film where rhythm and emotion and the consideration of the spectator are important components. That's why I like curating; to put on stage anthropological perspectives in a setting of constraints. This personal definition of curatorial praxis, this idea of three-dimensional thinking, a form of 'applied anthropology' has certainly something to do with the fact that during my study in anthropology in the mid-nineties in Paris, I was earning my money with theatre design for theatre companies and did ceramic design on a quite professional level. I think that the theory taught at the Ecole des Hautes Etudes en Sciences Sociales (EHESS) and my work as designer at the same time influenced how I became a curator and why I define myself as a kind of 'applied reflexive anthropologist'.

Exhibition-making inside an institution is determined by the moment of time, by space and the architecture framing the exhibition. In a certain way, form guides content. The same content can become completely different depending on the space. That's why I define my curatorial praxis as a kind of 'applied anthropology' permanently facing and circumventing bureaucratic systems, local political webs, institutional legacies, and habits. The final outcome of an exhibition is the result of all these constraints. The place in which I have to curate an exhibition has a profound influence on how I conceive an exhibition. It is different to conceive one exhibition, for example, for the HKW in Berlin, the Museum für Völkerkunde in Dresden, the Rautenstrauch-Joest-Museum in Cologne, or the Quai Branly in Paris. Those are different spaces, with very different institutional backgrounds, different *actants*, legacies, and habits, with or without collections. It is not an idea conceived solely in a library. A publication is non-spatial; an exhibition is. The role of the reader and the role of the visitor aren't the same. When you write an article, you are addressing scholars, often people from the same discipline who have consciously decided to read your article. When you are an artist and create a work of art, you do not necessarily think whether the spectator will entirely

Fig. 13.2 Open Space *Die Baustelle*, Rautenstrauch Joest Museum, Cologne, 2019, © Vera Marusic

understand your intention. As a curator you have to take into account all kinds of aleatory visitors (and particularly in ethnological museums where your audience is, I think, more heterogeneous compared to a contemporary art center): visitors of all ages, education levels, political opinions, or biographical backgrounds, descendants of colonisers and colonised, people who are merely 'urged' to visit (like children, a friend ...), visitors who come 'by accident' to your exhibition, because they have to cross the gallery in order to reach the exit. There are opening and closing times, rules for behaving like not being allowed to speak loudly, to lie down on the floor, to eat or drink ... When you curate an exhibition with anthropological questions, these surroundings of constraints define the way you think and create. Curating enables the involvement of the spectator in ways that are inaccessible to an academic paper.

When you conceive of anthropology, are you thinking about its legacies, its present-day practice? How do you relate to anthropology's legacies in the present? Do you agree that anthropological critique now takes place increasingly outside the discipline and museums, i.e., in what we call trans-anthropological fields? If so, where and how?
Anthropological critique was central to my studies of cultural anthropology at the EHESS in Paris. For my master's thesis, I worked on the representation of Africa in European ethnographic museums and its crisis. After my MA, I did doctoral research on the relation between colonial violence, ethnographic collecting in the Congo Free State, and the production of ethnographic knowledge. In particular, the seminars in 'Anthropology of the Object' by Marc Augé and Jean Bazin have notably influenced my way of thinking. Seminars in Historical Anthropology, Anthropology of the Event, Anthropology of the Object, Anthropology of the City, but also Anthropology of Art, Sociology of Art, History of Africa ... All those multi-disciplinary seminars you were free to follow, and one could build one's own research programme without having to worry about credit points. Unfortunately, that time of intellectual creativity and brainwork is over. Anthropological critique was present in almost every seminar (or at least the seminars I was attending). The grappling with objectivity, and the eventual renunciation of claims to the rhetoric of holism by anthropology at the time was informed by the idea that, at its core, ethnographic practice is about points of view and interpretations – in short, about poetic and literary writing. James Clifford, George Marcus, Johannes Fabian, Clifford Geertz, and Hal Foster were discussed in almost every seminar. This led me to consider so-called ethnographic exhibitions also as poetic and self-reflexive installations that address questions of colonial legacies, coloniality, alterity, anthropological representation, and identity.

Anthropological critique was 'put into practice' at that time at the Musée d'Ethnographie in Neuchâtel (CH) with exhibitions like *Objets prétextes, objets manipulés* (1984), *Le Salon de l'Ethnographie* (1989), *La Différence* (1996), or *Derrière les images* (1998) by Jacques Hainard, Oliver Gonseth, and Roland Kaehr. Those exhibitions were heavily discussed in seminars in those years at the EHESS in Paris. They really left their mark on my subsequent curatorial practice. All of these are surprisingly unknown outside French speaking countries, but those exhibitions already testified to a highly self-reflexive and critical take on anthropological representation and the ambiguities of imperial ethnography in the 1980s and 1990s. And all of this took place long before the much more well-known exhibition of Jacques Hainard in *Musée cannibale* (2002), which received international recognition. In fact, these exhibitions would still very much be regarded as avant-garde if they were put on today. Some years later, in 2008, I had the honour to curate an exhibition with Hainard on migration in the 1930s in the new Museum for Immigration in Paris. It is a pity that this type of curatorial praxis, which was initiated by Hainard and his two colleagues Oliver Gonseth and Roland Kaehr, has faded away.

At the same time, the project around the future Quai Branly Museum was nourishing highly polemical debates. Interesting discussions and research about the future and the past of ethnographic museums and of anthropology were in their heyday then, but were vanishing soon after the opening of the Quai Branly in 2006. Despite those many new anthropological studies on museums, curating, and the production of anthropological knowledge, most of the ethnographic museums in Europe have never opened their doors to this new generation of scholars. From the point of view of museums, it has been mostly argued that it is because of a lack of vacancies and money, but I am not so sure if this is really the case. Fact is that the gap between university or academic knowledge production and ethnographic museums has been amplified. Since I am based in Germany, I've also noticed this. Today in Germany, the Humboldt Forum again stimulates anthropological critique and exhibition-making. A new generation of global scholars familiar with post-colonial theory has arrived on the scene, joined by more and more artists inspired by the ethnographic turn, as well as those from the Global South. That's why perhaps this new wave of global anthropological critique and cross-disciplinary curatorial praxis rather takes place outside ethnographic museums, in editions of documenta, Venice Biennales, and contemporary art centres. My aim is to put this kind of trans-anthropological practice at the heart of my 'ethnographic museum'. I've tried this with this range of exhibitions in the Grassi Museum für Völkerkunde, *Grassi invites #* (2016-2018), and more specifically in the experimental exhibition *Prolog #1-10 Stories of People,*

Things, and Places, which I organised in Dresden. I realised this in adapted form in the Grassi Museum in Leipzig under the title *Werkstatt Prolog* (2018). One can generally perceive that ethnographic museums are slowly opening their doors, or that they are forced to do so because of increasing public pressure.

Is there any value for you in talking about "trans-anthropological" curating, that is, as a practice that engages with such anthropological issues, but not within the classic domains or institutions of anthropology?
As the disciplines are blurring, I am not sure if "trans-anthropological" curating is the appropriate terminology. The term risks reducing 'trans-curating' only to anthropology. Why does anthropology have to be the starting point? I would rather prefer 'transdisciplinary curating', which blurs all boundaries.

I think all cultural institutions are in a kind of crisis, and we have to undo and rethink those structures. It is just that in ethnographic museums, it seems more striking. I think we will go more and more in the direction of a cross-disciplinary curating – whether it is in an art museum or in an ethnographic museum. They just have different collections, different legacies, which influence the final outcome.

Up until recently, art history focused predominantly on a history of European art, while non-European art was mostly regarded and professionally constituted as the domain of anthropological research. Can you describe how you regard these disciplinary divisions, and whether and to what extent you see or even participate in breaking down these divisions?
The disciplinary boundaries between art history, cultural anthropology, and history seem to me more rigid in Germany and by consequence curatorial praxis is defined by those somehow hermetic boundaries. In France, this categorisation is more open, as symbolised by the Pavillon des Sessions devoted to ancient non-Western art in the Louvre, inaugurated in 2000. I also taught African art history for ten years at the University of Nanterre, as well as at the somewhat traditional Ecole du Louvre, mixing up anthropology, art history, and theory. In Paris, between the late nineties and the early 2000s, I was member of a research group of anthropologists and art historians, called "Anthropologie, Art, Objets et Esthétiques". In France, I always conceived and curated interdisciplinary exhibitions, like for example *Recettes des Dieux. Esthétique du Fétiche* (2009), *Exhibitions. L'Invention du Sauvage* (2011) or *Maîtres du Désordre* (2012) at the Musée du Quai Branly. Nobody asked me whether these exhibitions were anthropology, art history, philosophy, or history.

The Quai Branly has been heavily criticised, particularly by German, British, and American scholars and journalists, because of its aesthetic approach. I don't think that this was and still is the most critical point of this institution, especially if we take into account its general exhibition programme and twenty hours of ethnological films, which accompany the permanent collection. Since I have been in Germany, I feel that these disciplines in universities and museums are more hermetic. The ethnographic museum is expected to make 'ethnographic exhibitions' and not so-called 'art exhibitions'. Ethnographic museums and art museums in Germany are two very distinct museum landscapes. One observe that this is slowly melting together.

Fig. 13.3 *Maîtres du Désordre (Masters of Chaos)*, Musée du Quai Branly, Paris, 2012, © Nanette Snoep

Fig. 13.4 *Megalopolis – Voices from Kinshasa*, Grassi Museum für Völkerkunde, Leipzig, 2018, © Mo Zaboli

This is the case not least because of an upcoming generation of scholars and curators who are interested in crossing the disciplines, and because of audiences expecting that such institutions change.

Considering the different institutions you have worked with, what kind of curatorial practices did these institutions enable or prevent? What did you have to change in institutions to realise your kinds of curatorial interests?

While there were no objections from the side of the management team at the Quai Branly, for instance, to mix categories and to combine ethnographic objects with modern or contemporary art, post-colonial critique was much less tolerated. In this context, curatorial freedom was restricted. We weren't enabled to include post-colonial critique in an exhibition, or at least it was very difficult. I experienced this with the exhibition *Human Zoos. The Invention of the Savage* (2011). Since I have been in Germany, I am in a different role that I can hardly compare, because I am director of a museum now. In my role of director of three ethnographic museums in Leipzig, Dresden and Herrnhut (2015-2018), and subsequently as a director in Cologne (since 2019), I could theoretically do what I would like as long as I found the money and an audience. Yet one must not underestimate that the political environment, museum structures, and institutional legacies and habits can restrain your actions even as a director. I was quite surprised to observe how somwhat refractory one could be in German ethnographic museums concerning mixing disciplines, working with artists, or dealing with anthropological critique in temporary and permanent exhibitions. It is quite a long process to open up museum institutions and making possible the destruction of boundaries between disciplines, the mixing of genres, and the opening of museum doors for anthropological critique and reflexive exhibitions in a permanent way. Surprisingly, the 'ethnographic turn' in contemporary art practice has scarcely influenced ethnographic museum praxis.

What, in your view, makes an "anthropological framing" in an exhibition? Are there specific display techniques, modes of exhibiting, and framing which you would describe – for better or for worse – as typically anthropological? Is there such a thing as an 'anthropological' or 'ethnographic' exhibition?

Yes, I think there is a specific and even typical ethnographic exhibition grammar and aesthetics, which has been repeated for more than a century. It is surprising to note that 'ethnographic display' has hardly changed over time – as if its institutions, its objects, as well as its display has been frozen, as if contextualisation can only be done through dioramas. This is actually very fascinating. Even museums of natural history did much more to transform their design than anthropology museums: Wall display cases, dioramas, mannequins, the use of very specific colours, which one can only see in ethnographic displays, and even in how objects and costumes are mounted, in the way a group of objects in showcases is displayed, in the way of protecting them, the way of displaying text, the use and the status of photography as illustration. All of these are part of this typical ethnographic design heritage, which has its roots in the nineteenth century. One can witness some changes in ethnographic design during the time of the early 1930s, such as in some French institutions like the Rivière-Rivet at the Musée de l'Homme, or for example in the Julius Lips exhibition about masks at the Cologne Museum, and later on in the 1960s in the GDR, for example at the Grassi Museum für Völkerkunde. But these transformations never lasted very long and haven't been spread throughout Europe and often returned rapidly to a received prior routine.

Perhaps it is also due to the actors within ethnological museums, who are surprisingly often quite reluctant toward modern and contemporary art and design.

However, I wish to tackle this question about the 'anthropological framing', and give a new meaning to such museums, to their design as well to their content. That's why I often speak of museums as places of *conVersation* among objects and actors, instead of museums as places of *conServation* – as territories of exchange, contradiction, interaction, and experience. As places that generate various kinds of 'conversations'. This could become this new anthropological frame.

Some critics have described the use of contemporary art in ethnological museum contexts as a quick and easy but unsustainable remedy for the institution's problems. How do you see the role of contemporary art in the ethnological museums, and in relation to its collections, that you have worked in before, especially in Leipzig and Dresden – and what do you intend to do in this regard in Cologne?

I understand this criticism, because anthropology museums have often worked with artists, since they did not know how to deal with their own colonial legacy. This work was then simply *left* to artists – in a certain way out of despair perhaps. I consider my collaborations with artists as curating *with* and around a specific question. Rather than delegating difficult and problematic questions exclusively to artists, in order to avoid these questions that museums should ask themselves. It is a matter of *collaborating* in order to better face problems and not to avoid the confrontation.

If you think of the ground-breaking exhibition *Mining the Museum* curated by Fred Wilson at the Maryland Historical Society in 1992, and you consider the incredible influence of this exhibition on further exhibitions and theoretical works, it is evident that artists play a very important role in the transformation and the decolonisation of anthropology museums. Sometimes artists are simply better skilled to *communicate* ethnographic findings. I am myself a director and curator who has worked a lot with artists, and I consider the museum not just as a repository for scientific production, but also for artistic production. The museum offers a wide range of interesting material for an artist, starting with the collection, the archives, the museum rituals, and also the institution itself. The progressive strengthening of links between anthropology museums, anthropological critique, and artistic practice could also be seen as a further confirmation of the emergence of a new transdisciplinary field that operates across art, museums, and collections.

In Leipzig and Dresden, due to a persistent lack of funds, I had to improvise and work with the means at hand. When you don't have a penny, you have to be inventive. As a result, one is forced to drop the 'museographic rules', whether they concern the quality of the rails or walls, the printing of exhibit labels, or the lighting, to name just some examples. This took place against the backdrop of a very complex political context in Eastern Germany with the extreme-right movement *Pegida* (founded at the end of 2014) and the arrival of refugees in the post-2013 summer of migration to a region with the lowest percentage of non-German citizens in the country. This was the situation with which I was faced as director of three Saxonian anthropology museums between 2015 and 2018.

Despite the unfortunate infrastructure and financial situation, I was tasked by the former general director of the SKD, Hartwig Fischer, who invited me to come to Saxony, to create a new permanent exhibition. In Dresden, the museum had been closed and was entirely empty. By contrast, the permanent galleries in Leipzig (inaugurated in 2007), as I encountered these at the beginning of 2015, were stuffed with thousands of objects, highly naturalistic puppets, and plenty of dioramas, accompanied with texts that hierarchised cultures, and people stuck in a frozen time. I called upon students from art schools and universities, artists, and designers to work with my team on our collections and our museum so that we could collectively start a kind of analysis of this museum and to show the transformation processes we would like it to undergo. Of course, this caused a lot of critique, because I worked with students and non-professionals, instead of professional museum ethnologists. I must say that most of the people I involved did very serious research in our archives and collections and realised amazing productions, which revealed aspects of the museum's history that would otherwise never have been shown. In parallel, I curated in Dresden in this empty and abandoned museum an experimental and growing workshop and laboratory exhibition (Werkstattausstellung) called *Prolog #1-10 Stories of People, Things, and Places* (December 2016 – April 2018). In it, we built up a reflexive exhibition in ten steps/ten stations. Every month, we opened an installation with a specific reflexive anthropological topic. Among those ten stations, several were conceived in close collaboration with artists.

For the last show in Leipzig, *Megalopolis – Voices from Kinshasa* (November 2018-March 2019, see Fig 13.4), I gave *carte blanche* to a collective of twenty-four young artists from Kinshasa who curated an exhibition about the megacity Kinshasa in the Democratic Republic of Congo. Among individual art installations, films, fashion, performances, and photography, they produced a collective art work, the so-called "Restitution-Box", based on the historical museum collection from Congo (Republic of Congo and DRC). In matters of restitution, I think it is crucial to let people, artists, scholars, spiritual experts from these regions express by themselves where the objects come from. The method of the *carte blanche* was more important to me then the final outcome; I gave priority to having the intensity of their rich exchanges on this historical collection merge, which took place mainly in the storage areas of the museum, and in their discussions with visitors and my museum staff.

During my time in Cologne at the Rautenstrauch-Joest-Museum, I will certainly do things differently, because it is an entirely different museum institution with a different legacy and institutional habits with one of the best permanent exhibitions among European anthropology museums. However, the debates on anthropology museums will unfold, the process of decolonisation of anthropology museum institutions will provide strong inputs for rethinking our institutions in the years, if not decades to come. This is our chance. I would like to develop this idea of the museum as a place of "ConVersation", a polyphonic museum where we further experiment with the method of the *carte blanche*, the creation of sovereign spaces inside our permanent galleries, but also the idea of collective dialogical curating. We will experiment with this in the exhibition *Resist! Die Kunst des Widerstands (Resist! The Art of Resistance)*, to be opened next autumn 2020, an exhibition about colonial and post-colonial resistance from the perspective of the colonised. This means offering space for external curators from all kind of disciplines, artists, dancers, musicians, students, activists, and communities from the regions where our collections come from, but also diasporic communities in the German federal state of North Rhine-Westphalia, where we are based. I would like for my museum to become a laboratory for scientific, artistic, and spiritual production.

Above all the museum needs to become less authoritarian. For me, this is one of the main issues. Who has the authority to define a culture? Who is controlling? Transforming museums means taking away some of their own authority and giving back to people from outside in order to try to transform the museum as hegemonic institution into a democratic one, into the famous 'third space'. Museums need to be challenged to step out of their comfort zone, to take risks, to break with their traditional authority. Through methods such as the *carte blanche* or 'autonomous spaces', could we break this rigid structure and perhaps achieve a 'post-museum'?

Note

1. The image on p. 324 is Figure 13.1 *Prolog #1-10 Stories of People, Things, and Places*, Museum für Völkerkunde, Dresden, 2017, © Vera Marusic.

Representation of Culture(s): Articulations of the De/Post-Colonial at the *Haus der Kulturen der Welt* in Berlin

Annette Bhagwati

Preliminary remarks

Across Anthropology – the title of this book – could not more accurately describe the conceptual frame, or the challenges of this essay.[1] This text deals with the question of how to represent cultures, a central question of anthropological inquiry, and – at the same time – one of the core questions of curatorial practice in a 'transcultural' context.

> Footnote 1: The term "transcultural" is closely linked to a specific understanding of culture or a specific discourse on art and culture. As the discussion will show, 'transcultural' has come under increasing scrutiny from the perspective of an entangled history approach, especially over last ten years. Nevertheless, it was of central importance for a certain period of curatorial work, especially in the 1990s and 2000s. Thus, when the term is used in the following text, it is placed in quotation marks to refer to this discursive context of practice.

But how do you write when you are both the recording ethnographer and the ethnographic subject, both the observing participant and the participant observer? This essay is, firstly, an (ethnographic) approach to and an account of a specific cultural institution, the Haus der Kulturen der Welt in Berlin.[2] Founded in 1989 as a forum for contemporary international arts and cultures with a focus on Africa, Asia, and Latin America, without a collection, conceptual mandate, or disciplinary and theoretical affiliations, the Haus der Kulturen der Welt seems – at first glance – an odd choice for a discussion that deals with the "where, what, and how of anthropology" as a discipline (see introduction, this volume), an institutional framework, and a mode of inquiry. And yet, as we will see, in any institution that situates itself in a 'transcultural' context or is engaged with global entanglements, internal and external perspectives, action and critical reflection have been and remain inseparably entangled. The 'anthropological' is both content and method at the same time.

Secondly, the 'anthropological' defines much of my own personal history. In the early 1990s, as a student of social anthropology, geography, and art history, I completed an internship at the department of Exhibitions, Film and New Media. After completing my studies at SOAS (University of London) with a PhD in African Studies, I then returned to the Haus der Kulturen der Welt in 1999, for a further seven years as programme coordinator of the Visual Arts Department.

Given the high frequency of projects and exhibitions – often realised under considerable time and financial constraints in the context of the highly dynamic artistic and discursive environment of contemporary global arts – there was scarcely any time for a critical revision of my own, and the institution's, practice. The moment for a more theoretical reflection came when I joined my husband in Montreal and became Affiliate Professor in the department of Art History at Concordia University in 2008. In my research, I focused on questions of transcultural curating, curatorial studies, and global art history. In 2012, I moved back to Berlin. As project director at the Haus der Kulturen der Welt, I led long-term curatorial research projects that explored artistic positions, scientific concepts, and spheres of political activity amidst profound global and planetary transformations. By virtue of this decade-long connection with the Haus der Kulturen der Welt, lodged between practice and theory, my biography is also deeply anchored in the anthropological, both as the content and the horizon of reflection.

So how can and should we write from this mesh between inside and outside, between personal experience and institutional practice? In the following I will examine the notion of cultural representation at the Haus der Kulturen der Welt and trace its impact on programme-making and curatorial practice. How has the Haus dealt with this complex – and highly political – issue over the past thirty years? What was the discursive environment, which policies, strategies and formats have been developed in reaction to de- and postcolonial criticism? How can the conceptual approach be described today?

The vantage point from which I explore these questions must by necessity be a radically subjective one. In my account, I substantially draw on personal experience and memory. Theoretical considerations alternate with personal memories and accounts of key moments in my own practice as well as with the institutional history, as I experienced it.

> Footnote 2. Given my own long-standing affiliation with the Haus der Kulturen der Welt, one should expect source material that reveals the most inner workings of the institution: correspondences, conceptual sketches, or emails, which allow insights into programmatic thinking, reflective processes, and conceptual developments. Unfortunately, the data situation is more difficult than one might expect from a public institution. The Haus der Kulturen der Welt was founded as a cultural institution without a collecting mission. Due to its project orientation, increasing digitisation, a heavy workload, and a comparatively high fluctuation among the staff, neither systematic documentation nor the building of an institutional memory were accorded any priority. This was particularly true for the early years, when the focus was on the realisation of programmes, not their archiving. Consequently, many letters and documents were lost or are now stored in the Federal Archives in Bonn. Email correspondence, especially from the first decades, is no longer accessible or has been deleted following numerous server migrations and system updates. Even visual material from the early years is difficult to obtain. It was only in the mid-2000s that the Exhibitions Department began, for example, systematically to document openings and exhibition views as well as record and archive accompanying events such as conferences or workshops. The situation fundamentally changed with the start of long-term projects from 2013 onwards, when the practice of archiving became an integral part of the institution's practice. In terms of my first years at the Haus der Kulturen der Welt, I must therefore largely rely on personal memories, supported by publications, oral history, and reports by third parties – colleagues, artists, curators – or personal recollections of former staff members, the latter published online on the occasion of its twenty-fifth anniversary.

The early years: Genealogies of representation

I came to the Haus der Kulturen der Welt as an intern in 1994. I had just completed my Master's in Social Anthropology and African Art at SOAS. The Haus der Kulturen der Welt had been founded only five years earlier in

1989, the same year that the Berlin Wall had come down, heralding a new era of global relations and worldwide mobility. It was the same year in which the exhibitions *The Other Story* at the Hayward Gallery in London and *Magiciens de la terre* at the Centre Pompidou challenged the canon of Western modernism, changing the understanding of contemporary art forever.

The foundation of the Haus der Kulturen der Welt followed the successful festival of world cultures *Horizonte*, organised by the Berliner Festspiele. The 'cultures of the world' were accorded a permanent home: the former Congress Hall in the Tiergarten, a 'propaganda' building designed by American architect Hugh Stubbins in 1957, and a gift from the USA to Berlin. Situated in immediate proximity to the Berlin wall, the building was intended to promote democracy and liberal values and signal freedom across the border.

Funded by the City of Berlin, the Ministry of Foreign Affairs, the Ministry of the Interior and allied with the Goethe-Institute, the HKW (or HdKdW, as it was initially known) was one of the first institutions that spearheaded the systematic engagement with contemporary non-Western arts, with a special focus on Asia, Africa, and Latin America. Its mandate was to provide a forum for contemporary and emerging arts and cultures from regions which had hitherto largely been ignored or excluded by 'the West'. This understanding defined the programme well into the mid-2000s. When I left the Haus in 2006, the introductory paragraph of my reference letter read: "The mandate of the Haus der Kulturen der Welt is to present non-European cultures in the visual arts, dance, theatre, music, literature, film and media and to place them in a public discourse with European cultures. The programme of the Haus der Kulturen der Welt is dedicated to the contemporary arts and current developments in the cultures of Africa, Asia and Latin America."

From the onset, the Haus der Kulturen der Welt was designed as a multidisciplinary institution. Instead of being committed to a specific understanding of art or a theoretical approach, it highlighted the diversity of contemporary artistic, intellectual, and cultural expression around the world across all genres and subject matters. This holistic approach was reflected in the working structure of the Haus der Kulturen der Welt. It was divided into three programme areas led by three sections: the department of literature, humanities, and science (today: Literature and Humanities); the department of exhibition, film, new media (today: Visual Arts and Film); and the department of music, dance, theatre (today: Music and Performing Arts). In its conceptual approach, it combined ideas of multiculturalism with principles of foreign cultural policy.

A number of pages from the programme brochure, the so-called *Pixiheft*, which appeared twice a month, gives an idea of the outstanding diversity and

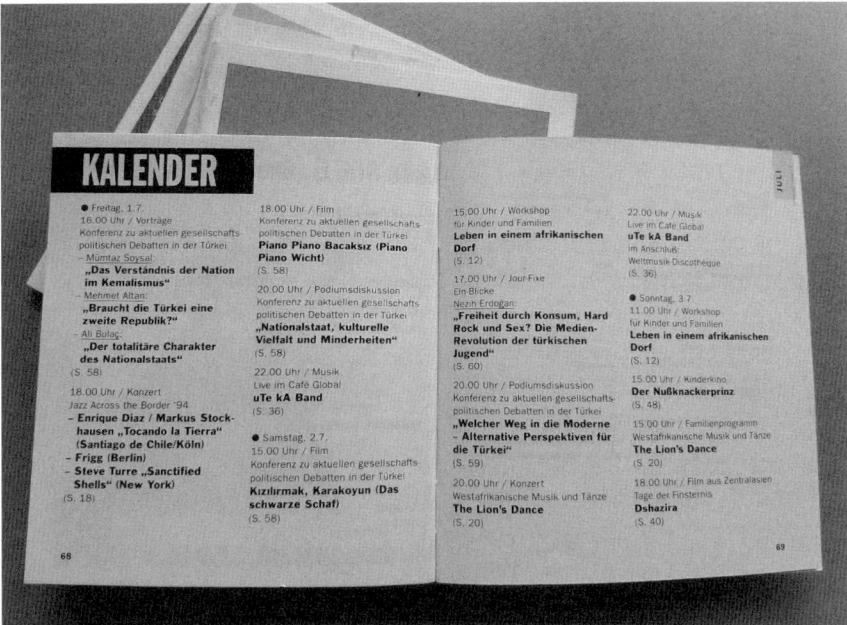

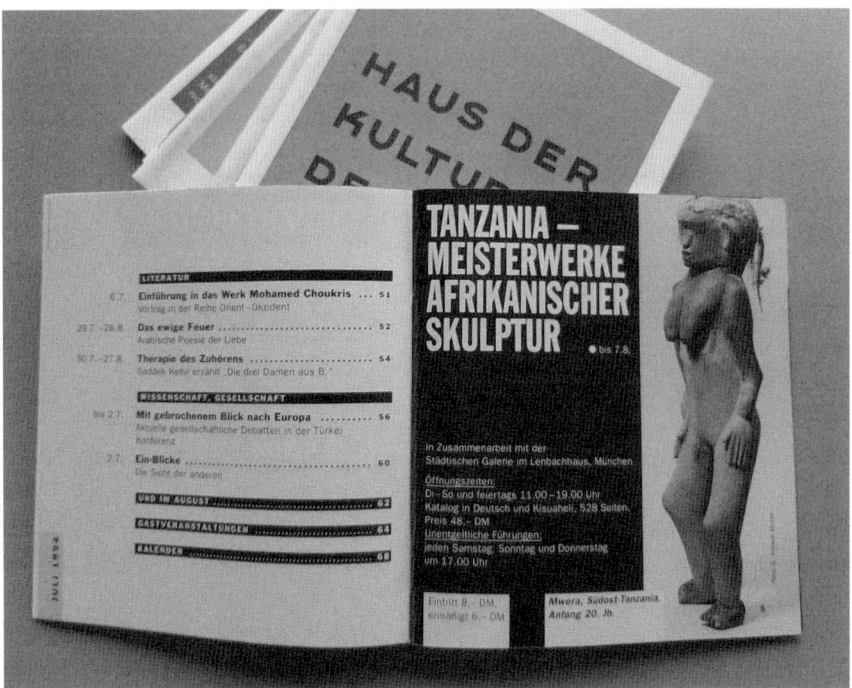

Fig. 14.2 Sample pages from the programme brochures (so-called *Pixihefte*), which appeared monthly. Photographs by the author

topicality, as well as frequency, of the programming of these early years. The teams were small, the responsibilities comprehensive. As an intern of the exhibition department, I had a wide variety of different tasks: On my very first day, I was asked to develop a guided tour concept through the newly opened exhibition *Tanzania. Masterpieces of African Sculpture* (1994) from the Marc L. Felix Collection. Next, I was to set up a showcase with Ukrainian headscarves from the collection of the wife of a German ambassador, write texts on an exhibition of Kanga fabrics and the meaning of proverbs in East Africa, and file correspondence from the landmark exhibition *China Avantgarde*.

With its commitment to contemporary international arts and cultures, the Haus der Kulturen der Welt soon acquired a considerable reputation: as a platform for 'non-Western' arts and cultures in Berlin and Germany, as well as an entry point to the Western art world and art market. Soon the diverse programme attracted more than a quarter of a million visitors a year (1992). Yet, given the lack of an overarching theoretical approach and conceptual framing, it was also criticised as being inconsistent, exoticising, and naïve.

What united the programme was a commitment to 'cultures' (plural), whereby culture was understood as a rather indiscriminatory term including all forms of contemporary artistic and aesthetic expressions of 'a nation' or a 'cultural region'. The scope was nothing less than 'the world', more specifically, the 'world out there' (as opposed to the 'Western' world). The idea at the time was to make visible those arts and cultures which, from the institutional point of view, were regarded as subaltern and therefore largely ignored by the 'Western' art world. The HKW was to counter these exclusion mechanisms and to decolonise the Western art's canon. Consequently, the notion of representation was considered primarily in positive terms. It was not after contemporary artists, academics and intellectuals, and 'entire art scenes' had been put on show for many years already, that the cultural assumptions driving this representational approach, this type of curating began to be criticised. Similarly, the concept of "culture", which was then essentially defined by national or ethnic affiliation, remained virtually unquestioned at the time. Terms from cultural diplomacy such as "encounter at eye level", "dialogue", and "understanding between nations/people" were part of the rhetoric, and inspired me and many visitors at the time.

Furthermore, the idea and practice of curatorial authority remained equally unquestioned in these first years. Affiliated to the Goethe-Institute, the Haus der Kulturen der Welt drew on the former's administrative structure. Both the director of the HKW – first called "General Secretary", later "Artistic Director" – and the department heads were employees of the Goethe-Institute. They were advised by a programme board which was composed exclusively of Germans, two of whom were directors of ethnological museums. Many of the department heads had served abroad on the executive level, before applying for their five-year tenure at the Haus der Kulturen der Welt as part of the Institute's rotation system. It was the Goethe-Institute reversed. The department heads curated the programmes, supported by a project team. In addition to their management experience and professional expertise, they brought regional knowledge and their global network. The programme reflected the diversity of their interests. The first head of the exhibition department, Wolfgang Pöhlmann, was a trained art historian; he was succeeded by Alfons Hug, who had studied linguistics, comparative literature, and cultural studies and later became a well-known curator in Latin America; succeeding Hug was Michael Thoss, a journalist and translator, interested in photography and contemporary arts from Africa. Topics dealt with under these directors ranged from the art-artefact debate and political art to art-theoretical discourses and canonical questions, such as the critical inquiry of a 'non-Western' modernity.

From today's perspective, it might sound problematic to fill curatorial positions with generalists and civil servants. Yet for a true assessment of this decision we must recall the level of knowledge and academic training in Western academia. In the early 1990s, it was not possible to study art ethnology, art history, or contemporary art from Africa, Asia, or Latin America as separate subjects in Germany. Neither did post-colonial discourse play a role in the teaching of art history. Regional or indigenous art historie(s) were taught by assistant lecturers, if at all, and – if so – mostly in the department of ethnology, not in the department of art history. As for myself, the only option I had was to enrol at the School of Oriental and African Studies in London, where I majored in African Art, African Literatures, and Social Anthropology.

In addition, the HKW was founded the very year in which the Berlin Wall came down. The end of the Cold War ushered in a new era of global networking and of worldwide artistic activity. Residency programmes for young artists from all over the world were established; the international art market began to reach out for art production beyond the Western centres; biennials or art fairs offered a platform and an infrastructure for worldwide contemporary art production. Young contemporary art scenes began to form worldwide at a rapid pace. For many of us, including the department heads, it was not easy to keep track of emerging artists and new developments. Overall, the atmosphere at HKW was marked by great excitement and a sense of 'discovery'. There was no binding canon, no established framework to discuss, assess, or select art works from contexts other than the Western canon.

Despite or perhaps just because of this openness – or: lack of conceptual framing – many exhibitions of these early years, including *China Avantgarde* (1993), *Other Modernities* (1995), or *Colours: Art from South Africa* (1996) turned out to be highly influential, contributing significantly to art discourses and artistic developments of the time. At the same time, however, cultural misunderstandings and differing expectations of curators, artists, and the audience shaped the Haus' early years.

I will never forget an anecdote that one of my colleagues told me during my internship as a warning: A group of Aboriginal women from Australia had been invited to perform a ritual chant. The performance was supposed to start at 8 p.m., and the time had been communicated to the performers. The hall filled up and the audience waited. When at 8:15 still nobody was to be seen on the stage, a staff member ran backstage and frantically signalled to the performers that they were late and had to get on stage. The women looked confused. They *had* started on time, at 8 p.m. sharp, with a ritual that was part of the singing but had to be performed in secret. This story stayed with me for a long time. To me, it highlighted the inner contradictions of a transcultural work environment, where differing perceptions, practices, and expectations needed to be reconciled. My way of thinking was still strongly influenced by my studies of *Ethnologie* in Germany, which was organised around the notion of culture, then understood as ethnically, regionally, and nationally distinct units. Curating in this environment – a Haus der Kulturen der Welt, that is, a House of the Cultures of the World – thus meant translating the 'outside' to the 'inside' – 'Curating Outside-In'.

Curatorial shifts: The Contemporary (capital C) art turn

Despite its successful programme and international recognition, the Haus der Kulturen der Welt began to face mounting criticism in the late 1990s. It was accused of a naïve and uncritical, if not neo-colonial, attitude. To be sure, the questions were numerous: Does ritual flute music by indigenous musicians from the Amazon belong on a *stage*? Is it an event, a performance, or a ritual? How is everyday culture from Ghana altered by the exhibition context in a Western art institution? Who has the right and the authority to classify, to value, and to judge these questions?

Another criticism was directed at the programming itself. In the eyes of many visitors, it lacked conceptual orientation. Were all events, exhibitions, and performances to be understood according to the same theoretical framework? What was praised by some as the greatest possible openness – and therefore as a significant challenge to the Western concept of art – for others was simply a programmatic and aesthetic confusion, an artistic 'supermarket'. These controversies were consequential; political pressure grew.

It became increasingly obvious that the HKW had begun to diverge from the objectives of the government's foreign cultural policy, which increasingly led to irritations. The metaphor politicians frequently used to describe their approach towards cultural policy was the "two-way street".[3] This was supposed to convey the idea of a two-way rather than a one-way cultural transfer. Yet, it failed to acknowledge the growing importance of dialogue and exchange and the expansion of international cultural networks after 1989. Other politicians considered the HKW "too intellectual" and not as attractive as a Carnival of Cultures, for example. Also, it lacked support within the German cultural scene. With exhibitions or film festivals such as "Die anderen Modernen" (Other Modernities) or FESPACO the HKW had questioned the judgement of well-known critics and art institutions which denied modern and contemporary art outside of "non-Western cultures" quality and equal status.

> Footnote: A much-discussed dispute between the HKW and the music critic Peter Müller highlighted how the media at the time struggled with their limitations when it came to understanding non-Western contemporary art and music. In a review of a concert of contemporary gamelan music, curated by Dieter Mack, Müller criticised the inability of Javanese musicians to play modern music. Musicians of the "third world", who were not familiar with modernity, should instead concentrate on their traditions.[4]

With the arrival of a new director, Hans-Georg Knopp (in 1996, general secretary; from 2002-2005, director of the Haus der Kulturen der Welt), the curatorial approach changed radically. Anything 'ethnographic', 'traditional', 'folkloric' – whether contemporary or not – was dismissed in favour of a rather narrow, very specific understanding of 'contemporary art'. It was contemporary art in a generic or canonical sense, with a capital C. The main cooperation partners and points of references were now global institutions of contemporary art, their networks, and infrastructures, meaning museums, biennials, independent curators, and so forth. Curators and artists including Danny Yung from Hong Kong, Els van der Plas (Prins Claus Fonds), Ong Keng Sen (Singapore) Margerethe Wu (Taipei) and Moon Ho Gun (Seoul) were invited as international advisors. A further and decisive step in the reorientation of the house consisted in the complete dissociation of the HKW from the Goethe-Institut and the Federal Foreign Office and thus also from the guidelines of foreign cultural policy.

> Footnote: The reorientation also marked the end of the cooperation with the "Heimatklänge" ("Homeland Sounds") channel, in residence at the HKW since its inception, which had broadcast so-called "world music" via the RBB (Radio Berlin Brandenburg). In the eyes of the director, the colourful mixture of cultural sounds from the so-called Third World was benign and well-intentioned, but not on a level playing field and devoid of political commitment.[5]

Upon completion of my studies at SOAS, I rejoined the Haus der Kulturen der Welt, first as a coordinator of the two exhibitions *Photographic Positions of a Century* (2000) and *Heimat Kunst* (2000). Then, a year later, I became the programme coordinator and deputy head of the exhibition department. Knopp's conceptual restriction to "Contemporary Art" made the work much easier. The playing field was much more clearly defined. It greatly facilitated the communication of the programmes to the press and the general audience, as well as received more critical attention from art historians, critics, and other art institutions.

The following years saw a series of so-called *Verbundprojekte*, collaborative and multidisciplinary projects, which were developed jointly by all three departments. They were dedicated to contemporary developments in the arts, literature, music, dance, film, or intellectual discourses of a particular 'nation-state' or 'cultural region', such as China, the Middle East, Iran, India, Central Asia, and others. The regional focus and this kind of geographical and cultural mapping was proposed by the artistic director or by a department head who would also chair the project team.

Even though the focus on contemporary art had brought conceptual clarity and defined a common frame of reference, a central dilemma remained: The curatorial concept and the selection of artists was still the responsibility of the department heads, that is, it was made from the 'outside' of these fields. So, while contemporary art had replaced the vague and more inclusive notion of 'culture', the Haus der Kulturen der Welt still remained committed to a cultural-geographical outlook or, to its critics, a world view of center and periphery.

At the beginning of the 2000s, this practice of mono-centric curating came under increasing attack from post-colonial theorists, who targeted a culture of exhibition-making in which the world was practically divided into *curating* and *curated* cultures. The practice of curators in the institution thus relied on the implied "acceptance of the curator's capacity to make transcultural judgements and, from here, the belief in the universality of art" (Mosquera 1994: 136).

To remain faithful to its mission – the celebration of cultural and artistic diversity – the Haus der Kulturen der Welt adjusted its approach once again. Not in-house staff, but, rather, 'local' curators from the region itself were assigned to develop a curatorial concept and select the artists. The Haus der Kulturen der Welt hoped it could thereby avoid the fallacies of misrepresentation, and feature the 'truly local', 'undistorted' by Western perception and judgment. This change of strategy raised a new set of questions, though. This became particularly clear to me during an exhibition that I coordinated between 2002-2003. It was entitled *subTerrain. Artworks in the cityfold (2003)* and part of the collaborative programme *body city* dedicated to contemporary arts and culture in India.

subTerrain (2002/2003)

As early as 2000, the then head of the exhibitions department and my direct superior, Michael Thoss, had travelled to Bombay and Delhi together with colleagues of the other departments. Together, they attended concerts, readings, performances, visited museums, studios, and art galleries and met with artists, writers, intellectuals, musicians, art historians, and curators. The aim was to get an overview of the contemporary art scene in India and identify a local curator for the exhibition. Local and international critics, museum curators, intellectuals, artists, and members of the local Goethe-Institute suggested names but no decision was made. A second stay was planned for autumn 2002. Several days before the planned departure, Michael Thoss had to cancel his trip and asked me to jump in and travel to India instead. I accepted, hesitatingly; I was certainly not an expert on Indian art, and I only had a few days to prepare. I trusted that my general understanding of contemporary art would help me understand the Indian art scene. I was wrong. During studio and exhibition visits and in conversations with collectors, artists, or curators, a complex picture emerged that became ever more confusing. Among our interlocutors, contemporary art seemed to be considered more as a temporal rather than a canonical category. Among other things, this became obvious to me on the cover of the standard work *Contemporary Indian Art* (2006) by art historian and curator Yashodhara Dalmia, where popular art, traditional sculpture, modern painting, as well as installation art share the same cover page.

Despite this holistic view, what became also evident was the outstanding role of modern(ist) painting. When I asked local artists and critics which contemporary artists they would select, I was repeatedly referred to painters such as Tyeb Mehta, Nalini Malani, Sayed Haider Raza, Bhupen Khakar, or M.F. Husain. By contrast, local staff of the Goethe-Institute and Indian interlocutors with a more international background recommended then emerging installation or performance artists. So, what was 'representative' of the Indian art scene?

During a studio visit to the artist couple Subodh Gupta and Bharti Kher, I understood that these two seemingly separate art worlds not only co-existed but also were both important reference systems, even for a younger generation of artists. While Bharti Kher had already attracted international attention with her sculptures and installations, Subodh Gupta was then still at the beginning of his career in terms of his international recognition. First, he showed me metal castings of milk cans for a planned installation, as a commentary on the complex of popular culture and the holy cow. In the following years such large-scale works would earn him worldwide fame and turn him into one of the most celebrated Indian artists in the international art circuit. When I asked him which work meant the most to him, though, he pointed to an early self-portrait that he had painted, partly with cow dung. As he explained, he had been trained as a painter. Even if he experimented with contemporary techniques, he still drew his strength and focus from painting.

Arriving back in Berlin, I wrote, somewhat perplexed, a memo in which I summarised the outcome of the trip. If one were to curate an exhibition from an Indian perspective, I argued, then painterly positions would have to dominate. In terms of both content and aesthetics, however, the works might not be received as contemporary art in the same terms by an audience in Berlin. How to convey the subtleties and specificities of Indian modernist painting to an audience which was neither acquainted with the modernist tradition in Indian art nor able to read and decode the many symbols and allusions to myths, religious narratives, or contemporary politics? It seemed hermetic. Much more familiar to me were young contemporary artists whom we had also met, and who were also recognised, though not by the majority of art connoisseurs, but by an internationally trained Indian elite. What exactly would such an exhibition then stand for? For India? For global art?

After extensive discussions within the team, the artistic director of the Haus der Kulturen der Welt invited the internationally acclaimed Indian critic and art historian Geeta Kapur to develop a concept for the exhibition. As author of the seminal book *When Was Modernism* (2000) and an internationally acclaimed curator, she was trusted to navigate the pitfalls of cross-cultural curating, while mapping out the local canon.

For her exhibition, entitled *subTerrain. Artworks in the cityfold*, Geeta Kapur followed up on the theme of 'politics of place' and 'the artist as citizen-subject', which she had begun to explore in her contribution to *Century City: Bombay-Mumbai 1992-2001* at Tate Modern (2001). *subTerrain* featured the work of sixteen artists from the then younger generation (such as Subodh Gupta or Anant Joshi) to internationally renowned artists (including Atul Dodiya and Nalini Malani). Equally familiar with Indian contemporary art and the expectations of a Western audience, Kapur was aware of her role as an interlocutor in a 'transcultural' exhibition context. In her curatorial selection, she opted for works that could transcend local references and inscribe themselves into the vernacular register of Contemporary Global art, or, as Terry Smith (2012) calls it, a "cosmopolitan aesthetics".

This became particularly evident in the selection of works by those artists who navigated between a national Indian and an 'international' context, and worked in different vernaculars. Nalini Malani, for example, was known in India primarily for her painterly work – watercolours, painting behind glass, and oil paintings. For *subTerrain*, however, Kapur chose the video work *Hamletmachine* from 2000, a two-channel video projection. Based on a text by Heiner Mueller, the work addresses the issue of fascism in light of the Gujarat Massacre. While the text by Heiner Mueller connected the work to the German context, the contemporary rendering moved the work even further beyond its local points of reference. The same could be observed with the selection of works by Atul Dodiya or Subodh Gupta.

The exhibition was a great success. Several of the participating artists soon became household names in the international art circuit. To me, however, the question remained: What exactly had been conveyed to an audience in Berlin? What had become visible and what not? The audience could rightfully assume that what they saw was representative of contemporary art in India. And in a way, it was. The audience, however, would be surprised if they visited India and expected to encounter the same canon. My Indian father-in-law was indeed quite irritated when he visited the exhibition in Berlin: "This is Indian contemporary art? Where is Husain? Or Raza?"

What could be concluded for the institutional practice of the Haus der Kulturen der Welt? The transfer of conceptual responsibility to local curators had been an attempt to redress the power imbalance between curating and curated cultures. The responsibility for representation had been reassigned from 'the outside' to the 'inside', from 'the etic' to the 'emic' perspective. And here, the same criterion applied: the criterion of 'connectivity' and

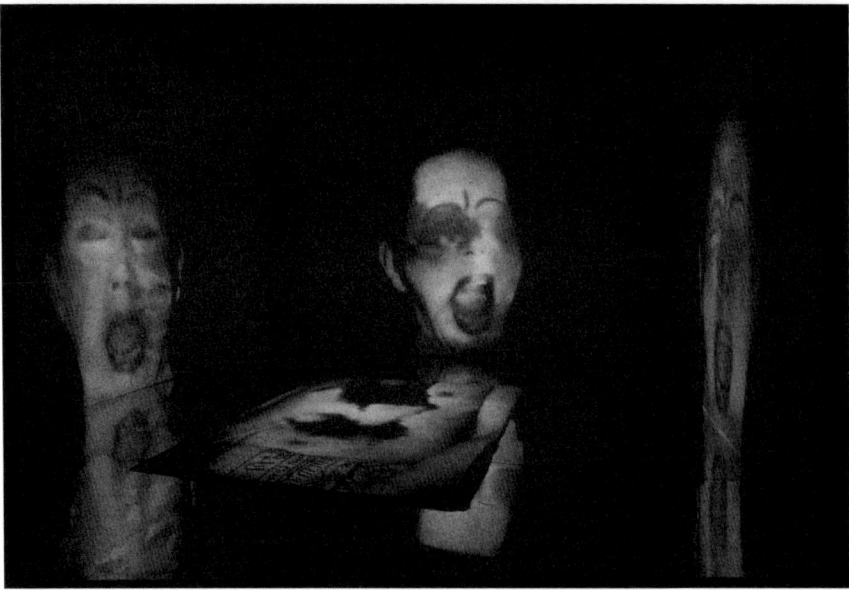

Fig. 14.3 Nalini Malani, Titel: Hamletmachine, 2000. Video installation with four lcd projectors, four dvd players, amplifiers, speakers, salt, mylar, mirror. Installed as projections on three walls and salt-bed (variable). Closed room 1100 x 800 x 400 cm (variable). Video loop 20 minutes, © Nalini Malani, Mumbai

'translatability'. Nevertheless, on closer examination, the problem had not been solved. It had just been moved. Western curators might no longer select the art, but they still chose the curator.

Spaces and Shadows (2005)

Despite all these unresolved contradictions that arose from the tension between curated and curating 'cultures', the regional exhibitions enabled a hitherto unknown overview of current developments, artistic networks, and emerging art scenes. Still, the focus on a 'region' also fostered the notion of a cultural identity and cultural representation.

National or cultural geographic boundaries explained the curatorial selection and demarcated the frame of reference. The subtitles of the exhibitions read as follows: *Off the Silk Road: Art and Culture from Central Asia* (2002); *DisORIENTation: Contemporary Arab Artists from the Middle East* (2003); *Distant Proximity: New Positions of Iranian Artists* (2004); or *Spaces and Shadows: Contemporary Art from Southeast Asia* (2005).

However, the more 'global' the artists became, and the more complex their biographies, the more problematic this approach became. One of the areas in which I blatantly felt this contradiction was catalogue production. For some years, it had become common practice to dedicate one or two pages to each artist, hence highlighting their artistic personality and celebrating their individuality. Each page began with their name, followed by place of birth or the current place of residence and work. While in the 1990s, there was apparently still a great conformity between place of birth and 'cultural'/'national' identity, this representational claim became increasingly difficult to maintain in the early 2000s.

How would such a convention translate, for instance, to an artist like Rirkrit Tiravanija – born in Buenos Aires to Thai parents; educated in New York, Chicago, Banff, and Toronto; resident in Bangkok, Berlin, and New York – if he participated in an exhibition of contemporary art from Southeast Asia? What justified his inclusion? Was it the origin of his parents, his family, the fact that he had spent his youth in Thailand, which influenced his thinking and artistic practice? What role did his cosmopolitan lifestyle play, his education in the USA and Canada, or his residence in Berlin? Or was it his pad thai series, in which he transformed a popular Thai dish into a contemporary art experience, thereby prompting a new theory and discursive turn (relational aesthetics)? Would it then not be justified to expand the circle of participants to include non-Thai artists, whose work engaged with Thai practices? And wasn't the celebration of a common meal, such as pad thai, a clever strategy to combine the two conflicting criteria of global art: authenticity, on the one hand, based on ethnic 'foreignness' or 'neo-ethnicity'; and global connectivity, on the other, as in his contemporary practice, relational aesthetics, concept art? What role did the regional framework serve?

Black Atlantic (2004)

The reality of global interdependence increasingly challenged the idea of regional exhibitions. A year before the project *Spaces and Shadows*, another project had already challenged the idea of cultural demarcation and thus also the distinction between 'one's own' and 'other' culture. The joint project *Black Atlantic: Travelling Cultures, Counter-Histories, Networked Identities* (2004), focused, for the first time in the history of the Haus der Kulturen der Welt, on the history of cultural entanglement.

The project was inspired by Paul Gilroy's *The Black Atlantic: Modernity and Double Consciousness* (2002 [1993]). Gilroy, one of Britain's leading post-colonial critics, describes the Black Atlantic as a space that has developed over the centuries of the slave trade as a cultural area in its own right, and that cannot be described by established attributions of cultural or national identity. As he puts it, the

> Black Atlantic is perceived as a complex unit, as a space of transnational cultural exchange beyond the bodily, economic, and material toward hybridity, across and beyond the nation-state identity. Through forced displacement new identities and relationships are forged, defying cultural constructions of national identity. It forms a distinct black Atlantic culture that incorporates elements from African, American, British, and Caribbean cultures. (ibidem)

Like other collaborative projects, *Black Atlantic* (2004) also was developed by the heads of the programme areas: Shaheen Merali took care of the exhibition area; Johannes Odenthal focused on the music, dance, theatre area; and Peter Seel took care of the literature, society, science area as the project leader –all three working closely with Paul Gilroy and the black feminist theorist of visual culture and contemporary art, Tina Campt.

With this project, the Haus der Kulturen der Welt brought the Black Atlantic into public awareness in Germany. It also addressed a persistent blind spot in the cultural and social consciousness among a German public at the time, namely, the history and present of the Black Diaspora. In contrast to Great Britain, where the Black Atlantic had long become an integral part of national consciousness through the writings of W.E. B. Du Bois and others, this recognition was still missing in Germany. At the time of the project, for instance, no German translation of Gilroy's book existed. In his introduction to the accompanying catalogue (2004), Peter Seel and Hans-Georg Knopp explained the project's motivation:

> The temporal shift in the reception of Du Bois' thought and work points to the difficulties in dealing with, the lack of awareness of, indeed the negation of, one's own history, in which German colonial rule is just as repressed as the contribution of the black population to German history, culture and German self-image as a whole. To this extent, any preoccupation with the Black Atlantic, with the history and present of the Black Diaspora in the world, also requires a critical understanding of history, demands that history be read against the grain and related to power relations and surviving colonial (thought) structures. (ibid: 6)

Leading post-colonial artists and theorists participated in the project, including Stuart Hall, Paul Gilroy, Edouard Glissant, Olu Oguibe, Koyo Kouoh, Tiago de Oliveira Pinto, Celia Quiarox, James Clifford, Fatima El-Tayeb, and Michel Rolph-Trouillot. Across a series of lectures, performances, talks, a music programme, films, and visual arts, the programming addressed issues of racism, colonialism, exploitation, identity politics, belonging, memory and counter-memory, image politics, history writing, and historicity.

The project focused on historical interrelationships but also opened up a space of transcultural relations and entanglements. From this point of view, the concepts of cultural 'demarcation', of 'representativity', and cultural 'representation' no longer made sense. What was 'self' and what 'other' could no longer be separated. They were inseparably interwoven in history and the present. This understanding also informed the exhibition *Black Atlantic* as curated by Shaheen Merali, then head of the exhibition department, himself a Black Indian British artist. The exhibition centered on the nature of image politics and cultural representation, both from a historical and a contemporary perspective. For the exhibition, Merali invited the artists Isaac Julien, Keith Piper, Lisl Ponger, and Tim Sharp. Julien explored the imaginative charge of black and queer identity in two large scale video-triptychs entitled *True North Series*. Keith Piper's *Sounding Gallery* was devoted to the situation of Afro-Germans under National Socialism. Ponger and Sharp's work somehow troubled me: In a free association, the video work *Passages* (1996) linked the ship of the middle passage as a central topos of formative migration to the experience of Central European Jews fleeing the Third Reich to Asia. Private recordings of holiday trips and cruises contrasted the idea of freedom and leisure with slave ships. While, in my view, Piper and Julien's positions represented an important step towards revising an 'ethnic-national' concept of culture and returning the gaze to the 'other' back to one's own, Pongers and Sharp's work made me question the extent to which one's 'own' narratives may and should dominate in the context of an entangled history.

Once more: Conceptual turn at the Haus der Kulturen der Welt

As this brief institutional history has shown, the self-understanding of the Haus der Kulturen der Welt has been anchored in and deeply influenced by de- and post-colonial positions. Over the years, however, it had to repeatedly adjust its curatorial approach. In the first years, the aim was to challenge Western art canons and to give artistic practices and developments international visibility; in the following years, the programme was more profoundly shaped by post-colonial thinkers and writings. As a consequence, we questioned our individual, institutional, and German social reality. Furthermore, the Haus der Kulturen der Welt attempted to de-colonise its curatorial practice by collaborating with local curators.

Despite all the efforts and improvements, however, it seemed impossible to free oneself from the post-/de- of post-colonial entanglement. Ultimately, as Mosquera (1994) put it, these contexts posed questions of power, the sovereignty of interpretation, the division of the art world into curating and curated, into representing and represented cultures. This imbalance did not appear to be resolvable by any curatorial practice, no matter how well adjusted and reflected upon. One reason for this lay in the inner contradictions of a public cultural institution operating in both local and international contexts: Who curated exhibitions, why, and for whom? What becomes visible, who decides on and according to which canon? Who are the addressees and what are their expectations?

We all, myself included, used the terms "inter-" or "trans-culturation", which had been so formative for many years, with more and more hesitation. They presupposed distinct 'cultures', between which one should translate. But how could this be done in a globally entangled world? Had the terms ever been justified? Had we not, despite all our efforts, always translated in just one direction?

This unease was heightened by the fact that contemporary artists were increasingly hesitant to exhibit at a Haus der Kulturen der Welt. More and more frequently, I received rejections of invitations to participate in exhibitions. The artists justified their refusals by saying that participating in a regional exhibition at a Haus der Kulturen der Welt would reduce their artistic personality to being representative of a 'culture'. Also, many of the artists who had been exhibited at Haus der Kulturen der Welt, had by that point embarked on international careers. They had become present in the art scene of Western biennials, art fairs, art galleries, and museums of contemporary art. In some sense then, the Haus der Kulturen der Welt had achieved one of its goals, namely, to challenge the Euro-American canon and help to fold it into a global art world. The Haus der Kulturen der Welt seemed to have become superfluous. Should it dissolve? What was the next step?

Crisis and reorientation (2005)

During this time of crisis, a new director arrived. Bernd Scherer took over the Haus der Kulturen der Welt in 2005. He knew the Haus well from his time as head of the Department of Literature and Humanities and had served as the director of the Goethe-Institute in Pakistan and Mexico.

One of his first initiatives was to organise an internal workshop, to which he invited the entire staff, amounting to more than sixty people. The questions he posed were vast: Where does the Haus der Kulturen der Welt stand today? What is its self-understanding and mission? Where does it want to head in the future?

One of the most animated debates centered on the name of the institution itself. It summed up the unease which was felt by many of us. Was the name Haus der Kulturen der Welt still appropriate in the context of a globally connected world? Had it ever been appropriate, quite apart from the fact that in the English version 'House of World Cultures' – instead of 'House of the Cultures of the World' – this translation had led to misunderstandings anyway? Shouldn't it be changed and a new name be chosen, once the future mission had been agreed upon?

In the weeks following the debate, Scherer and his head of communications decided on a compromise. The name itself would remain, but it would be only ever used as an acronym: HKW. This was an expression of recognition for the institution's founding idea. At the same time, a new beginning was marked, a paradigm shift, which would have been unthinkable without the history of the institution.

The programmatic shift, which was to shape the programme in the following years, was based on the understanding of global interconnectedness. The point of departure was the unprecedented speed and extent of planetary transformations that affect the world today and which caused an epistemological and ontological crisis; a crisis of representation. All certainties, concepts, world views, and strategies have been put to the test. On the methodological level, this change of perspective meant a break from the notion of representation. Global issues can since then, in this logic, only be tackled jointly. Reflecting the self is no longer an option or a programmatic decision, as it was with *Black Atlantic*, but a necessity.

The Anthropocene Project (2013-2014) // 100 Years of Now (2015-2018) // The New Alphabet (2019-2021)

In 2006, I moved to Canada with my family, where I taught as professor of exhibition history at Concordia University in Montreal. In 2012, I returned to Berlin, again to the HKW. My new task reflected the programmatic change of direction that the HKW had taken since 2006. I became director of projects at the office of the artistic director, which had evolved into a programme unit in its own right. In this function, I was responsible for the long-term curatorial projects that shaped and structured the HKW programming from 2013 onwards. The projects were based on each other: *The Anthropocene Project* (2013-2014) was followed by *100 Years of Now* (2015-2018) and by *The New Alphabet* (2019-2021). All the projects were designed as long-term curatorial research and were funded by the Bundestag.

Former methods and contents were subjected to a critical revision. The first major shift came with the Anthropocene Project. It was conceived as a joint project (Verbundprogramm). Over a period of two years, it determined most of the programme of the HKW. Curatorially, it differed substantially from earlier projects. The programs were openly curated in-house and communicated accordingly. The overall conceptual and curatorial responsibility lay (and still lies) with the artistic director Bernd Scherer. The department heads Katrin Klingan, Anselm Franke and Detlef Diederichsen were (and still are) responsible for the individual projects. Unlike earlier programmes, however, the project did not begin with a theme, but with a series of questions – in this case questions which addressed current planetary transformations and their cultural implications. In this way, a space for collaborative thinking and experimentation was opened up which was (and still is) explored and researched together with experts, scientists, artists and curators worldwide.

The curatorial approach was as radically specific as it was open. By inviting and moderating worldwide constellations of knowledges the question of representation becomes obsolete.

In another project, the exhibition project *Wohnungsfrage* (part of *100 Years of Now*), curated by Hila Peleg and the architects and critics Wilfried Kuehn, Nikolaus Hirsch, and Jesko Fezer the concept of the expert was reformulated and radically expanded: Those living and using houses – senior citizens, students, etc – worked together with architects and were actively involved in the research and conception process of a sub-project. Together with theoreticians, artists, and activists, they participated in discursive events and had their own publication in the twelve-part publication series. For the team and myself, this was one of the most enriching, and also one of the most demanding projects from a curatorial point of view, since we had to navigate the additional languages of experience and knowledge of the apartment users.

This and other projects were defined along thematically, and no longer cultural, national, or geographical parameters. Over a period of several years,

Fig. 14.4 Anthropozän-Projekt/ Anthropocene Project, 2013, Eine Eröffnung/An Opening, Haus der Kulturen der Welt, Jan Zalasiewicz. Photograph by Sebastian Bolesch

Fig. 14.5 Wohnungsfrage, 2015, Haus der Kulturen der Welt, Berlin, urban model, housing model, Kooperatives Labor Studierender (Kolabs) und das Architekturbüro Atelier Bow-Wow, Tokio/ and the Tokyo architecture office Atelier Bow-Wow. Photograph by Jens Liebchen, © HKW

these projects proposed thematic thinking frameworks that could examine the far-reaching transformation processes of the present. They interrogated planetary changes as well as global-technical and social transformations. They investigated historical conditions and looked at the cultural implications and epistemological ruptures in their global interdependencies. Every way of knowing, every expertise and perspective, was required to grapple with these changing times and to act within it.

As a result of the speed of these contemporary transformations, established categories and epistemologies, disciplinary methods, and convictions seem increasingly insufficient. The inquiry mode replaces the representative approach. Projects are conceived as experimental arrangements, as changing constellations of artists, curators, scientists, experts from all over the world, as curatorial and artistic research at the interface of art, science, and knowledges. Not the *representation* of knowledge, but *formats of knowledge production* in the sense of curatorial or artistic research moved into the centre of what could now be called processual and relational curating. Classical formats, such as exhibitions and concerts are thus redefined. In essay exhibitions, lecture performances, discursive concerts, experimental arrangements, conversations, art, science, and expert knowledge are brought into an exchange. The HKW of today searches for questions, initiates debates, and develops new frameworks of thinking by enabling new constellations of knowledges and enable trans-disciplinary exchange.

For me, this reorientation meant a shift from content-driven to method-driven work. Whereas previously the focus was on specialist knowledge, now other anthropological skills came to be of paramount importance: compiling, mediating, translating, moderating, stimulating, asking questions between cultures, between cultures of knowledge – anthropology across cultures.

Concluding remarks

In October 2019, I left the HKW and took up a new position as the director of the Museum Rietberg in Zurich. As a collecting institution, it differs, in many respects, from the conceptual approach and curatorial practice of the HKW. Yet in many ways fundamental questions remain the same, most importantly the issue of cultural representation.

Looking back at the years at the HKW, it seems to me to be a sequence of conceptual 'morphing' that emerged from the one basic question about the representation of cultures in a transcultural context: Who speaks for whom?

Is it possible to translate between different traditions of art and reception in such a way that misunderstandings are kept to a minimum? Are such translations possible in the first place? How do we reckon with the power imbalance between curating and curated subject? In the course of this morphing, categories such as 'culture', 'art', 'world', 'representation', or 'trans-culturality' have been questioned, formats were adapted, and a struggle for an institutional self-image maintained. This was possible because the HKW, as a multi-part building without a collection mandate, was conceptually and programmatically much more flexible than, for example, a museum.

The movements that the HKW has undertaken since its foundation can be described as a development from a representative to a research-driven, process- and topic-oriented approach. Differentiations between one's 'own' and 'other' have given way to dynamic, moving networks of relationships and knowledge constellations. With thematic projects such as the *Anthropocene* or *Wohnungsfrage*, some power structures seem to have been overcome – at least in theory. If one looks at curatorial practice, here, too, mechanisms of inclusion and exclusion, audibility, and invisibility affect different groups, such as the non-academic, non-English or German-speaking, or non-art communities.

Current projects address these inclusions and exclusions as well – not in the cultural sphere but in the participation in intellectual and discursive environments. *The New Alphabet School*, for example, is a collaborative self-organised school with the aim to explore critical and affirmative research practices. Over the course of three years, it will function as a colloquium to engage in discussions and develop ideas in the fields of the arts, archives, poetics, and activism. It is conceived of as a space for research approaches outside of academic, disciplinary, or genre constraints, seeking different methods of learning and unlearning in order to rethink the idea of criticism as a practice of shared responsibility and care.

To curate, to shape a program, always means to include and represent and thereby, by definition, also to exclude. Every curatorial attitude is based on a narrative. Even if this narrative is only a horizon, and the curatorial self-image is a moderating, rather than a determining gesture, the HKW still remains a particular institutional framework to which curators are committed. Whatever efforts are made to share or abolish interpretative sovereignty, and thus overcome colonial structures or discursive affiliation, each project will produce new inclusions or exclusions. What is needed is a radical transparency, a disclosure of selection criteria and curatorial choices, which lay open the narrative, while at the same time also serving as references to other practices, other communities, other languages, and horizons of experience that might remain hidden. An authoritative truth might thus become a narrative position, which can be discussed and challenged – until it is changed again.

Notes

1. The image on p. 336 is Figure 14.1 Anthropozän-Projekt/ Anthropocene Project, 2013, Eine Eröffnung/An Opening, Metabolic, Kitchen, raumlabor Berlin, Haus der Kulturen der Welt. Photograph by Joachim Loch
2. I would like to sincerely thank Hans-Georg Knopp and Bernd Scherer for their insightful and extensive comments on the first draft of this text.
3. Personal communication with Hans-Georg Knopp, 16 February 2020.
4. Personal communication with Hans-Georg Knopp, 16 February 2020.
5. Personal communication with Hans-Georg Knopp, 16 February 2020.

References

Gilroy, Paul. 2002 [1993]. *The Black Atlantic: Modernity and Double Consciousness.* London/New York: Verso.

Knopp, Hans-Georg, and Peter C. Seel. 2004. 'Vorwort', in: *Der Black Atlantic*, edited by Haus der Kulturen der Welt in collaboration with Tina Campt and Paul Gilroy. Berlin: Haus der Kulturen der Welt, pp. 6–9.

Mosquera, Gerardo. 1994. 'Some Problems in Transcultural Curating', in: *Global Visions: Towards a New Internationalism in the Arts*, edited by Jean Fisher London: Kala Press, pp. 133–139.

Smith, Terry. 2012. *Thinking Contemporary Curating.* New York: Independent Curators International.

"How Do We Come Together in a World that Isolates Us?"

A conversation with Nora Sternfeld

How do you understand the role of curating and the figure of the curator?

"The role of the curatorial figure" – already in your expression, there is an ambivalence.[1] Is a figure a practice, or is it a subject position? By doing these interviews for your book, you relate to 'subjects' and concrete personalities more than to collective subjectivities. And yet, since I am now in Kassel, and have worked for many years *as* a curator and *in* the field of curating, I find myself reflecting increasingly on the *subject position* of the curator. It seems to be my role now – not just being one but also researching them. I am trying to understand right now how the figure of the curator is constructed. And the more I look at it, the more I think that there *is* indeed a certain curatorial role, which has something to do with the transformation of institutions from public to privatised institutions.

When I look in the field of art, I would say that classically, the Western – or let's say *even* – the Western, white modern art, but also, of course, the Soviet modern art, has been brought forward by *collectives* rather than individual curatorial subject positions. These have furthermore been collections that work against received ideas of what we think an exhibition, a design, a display can be. These collectives have been forged around the idea of inventing an exhibition as a place where different artistic positions would come together and challenge each other. Classically, we can draw examples from the collective exhibition projects of the avant-garde movements, such as Dada or the Russian futurists – or even Impressionism. Many of these collectives worked against an academic understanding of what happened before. And within them, individual figures would not be so important. Some of them would be organisers, some would be theoreticians, some of them would be not very involved, and *some* of them would be well-known.

But very often these distinctions were not so clear. And if we look back, we see that who we remember now might not have been the main figure in these projects.

In short, we can trace back a collective beginning of what we call the curatorial today. And at some point this became a subject position. I look now at the materials and at the ways these curators describe themselves. And I see that what comes together is an intersection that takes on a contradictory function. First, a contradiction, I would say, between the artist and the bureaucracy. If you look at how the French sociologist of art Nathalie Heinich, for example, has very beautifully described the discourse of Harald Szeemann, whom she interviewed: She shows that his subject, who defines himself very much as an artist, suggests that "I do what I do for affective reasons! I don't have to describe. I don't have to explain why I do it. Because it makes sense for *me*. And as I know it, it will work, it will make sense. There will be something interesting in there." At the same time of *course* he has a bureaucratic role! He has the role of the manager. So, we could say that there is, classically, a contradiction between the artistic questioning of the management and the *policing* of the artists by the manager. But when these two functions come together, what does it mean? I would say it means that something that could become a conflict, is liveable, *without* breaking out.

After Szeemann, who himself is situated at this intersection between an artistic subject position and the managerial, bureaucratic subject position, this development continues. We see curatorial teams involved in the processes and, more and more, the subject position is one between activism and bureaucracy, communities and bureaucracy. In a sense, this is the position of the curator-mediator within the educational turn. This figure, classically at the intersection between activism and institution, I would call "the public programmer".

My hypothesis is that the role of this subject position of the curator as we see it emerging is to make conflicts liveable. Conflicts that might break out in all these places, because, as we know, institutions for contemporary art play a significant role in processes of gentrification. In other words, there is potential for conflict everywhere. And I am asking myself if we are not *most* of the time acting as 'organic intellectuals' – *not* of the counter-hegemonic forces but, rather, in a process of maintaining hegemony as it is.

My own role in this is not just as a curator, but also as someone who analyses this process. I am, myself, caught between the roles of educator, curator, and public programmer.

To give an example, could you expand on your experience as co-curator of the Bergen Assembly (2016) in Norway, especially with regards to the curators' self-presentation as a collective?

I'm part of a collective called *freethought* that has been, I'd say, brought into being by Irit Rogoff. Together, we are six people. Irit Rogoff calls herself "theorist, educator, and organiser", and she founded the Department of Visual Culture at Goldsmiths, University of London. She has shaped how we understand what we mean when we talk about the curatorial. Then there's Stefano Harney who founded, first, "Critical Management" as a department at Queen Mary, University of London. Then he left for Singapore, where he is at the Singapore Business University and wrote a fantastic book with Fred Moten called *The Undercommons*, linking questions of logistics and infrastructures with questions about Black struggles and anti-racism. Then there is Louis Moreno, a Marxist urbanist, living in London, who also teaches at Goldsmiths. Adrian Heathfield is a performance theorist, dramaturg, and curator, who is very interested in the affective dimensions of the infrastructural, let's say. And then Massimiliano Mollona, who is an anthropologist, a Marxist anthropologist.

All of us came together around the concept of infrastructure. Irit, Stefano, and Adrian proposed it to all of us, I think, seven or eight years ago, but it took me a while to understand what they mean. Now I understand that what they wanted to think about is how we are not mainly governed by *representation* any more, but by *infrastructures*. Infrastructures here include mathematics and algorithms, in addition to grant applications and budgets, time frames, and so on and so forth. This is really important for our discussion – it's just a footnote, but nonetheless interesting – because, as museologists, we used to refer to texts that analyse institutions through a critique of representation. If I look at the main texts that I am referencing here and also teaching, they speak of a critique of representation. We could think of those by Henrietta Lidchi, Stuart Hall, or Donna Haraway. If I look at these texts, we could clearly say that the critique of representation is not there just to understand representation. It is there to understand power!

In fact, the critique of representation is actually a critique of society *through* representation. What does it mean for us, when we are not anymore mainly governed by representation? It would imply that we would also need to analyse other things – other than representation – in the world *and* in institutions. And what I understood now, more and more, as we work on this topic of infrastructure, is that it makes absolute sense to analyse and change the structural level *as much* as the representational one.

But to come back to the project: All of this, I was only able to understand, because we established a context in which we could think together. And at some point, we were invited to apply for this Bergen Assembly, a triennial in Norway, to which we responded with a concept around infrastructures. One part of it was a city and infrastructure seminar, which we started two years before the opening. So, we would go to Bergen every month, or every two months in pairs of two, and we would propose a topic for a seminar to do with infrastructures. Usually, we would read texts, think about them, discuss them. This gave me the chance, in these two years, also – together with my colleagues whom I admire and respect a lot – to understand what we are actually talking about. And I think it was the same for them. It was a very intellectual process. Between us, but also with the people in Bergen – and of course other people from around the world, because people started to join the seminar, even to fly in for it. So it was ongoing work on trying to understand what infrastructure could mean. Because it *is* a way to understand how we are governed. And not only to understand it, but also to find ways *not* to be governed thusly. Or, as Stefano Harney put it in one of the seminars, not to be *accessed* thusly. Because infrastructures and its logistics, he says, access us, from every side. We are governed by being accessed.

Within this context, our idea was to try to understand together what our own topic could be and mean. Or what it could mean in relation to the world. We wanted each of us to enter with a research question and then to follow it through during the years of preparation so that at the *official* opening of Bergen Assembly, there would be something we could offer, present, materialise, discuss there, or whatever. During this time, Judith Butler's book *Notes Toward a Performative Theory of the Assembly* (2015) came out. It was a very important book for me, and it made total sense within our discussions. So it was from this book that I developed my research question: How can we *act* together, in a world that isolates us?

All my life, I was interested in thinking about the possibility of acting together, to learn from each other, to shape another possible world. To unlearn this one and to show each other another possible world, already here and now. And by doing so, collectively change this current one. Now, to respond to this question, I proposed to move further with my question not only in the format of the city seminar, but also to find and create a coffee house in Bergen. This idea of having a coffee house related to the history of a coffee house in the 1950s in London, which Stuart Hall did together with Raphael Samuel and Eric Hobsbawn. It was in Soho, and it was called *Partisan Café*. For them, who later were described as pioneers of cultural studies, thinking and learning did not take place on an ideological level. For them, culture *is* infrastructure, not superstructure or ideology. They were convinced that if we changed culture, we could change the world, since they came, more or less, from Gramsci. In this sense, a coffee house was for me a place where we can assemble. Where we can do exactly this: thinking together, imagining another world in the here and now that, in doing so, could begin to materialise bit by bit.

Now, we liked the idea and everybody was happy, but then we started looking for a space. And this was the interesting moment when the subject position of the curator as making conflicts liveable becomes relevant. So at this stage, the city shows us two different spaces. Both spaces had been something else before. One was a former prison. And the other one was the former fire station. And of course we already realise that we are shown places where there was something before and where, in this reasoning, there will be something afterwards. And in-between, we would be allowed to do our little thing there. Obviously, we were aware of our subject position. You don't say, "Ah! This is a scandal! I am part of gentrification process!" because you know that, if you are a curator of a Biennale, you are implicated in many different gentrification processes.

We rejected the proposal of the former prison – which would too heavily define our approach to the questions of prisons and deportation. So we moved to the fire station, which seemed very interesting. We went, got a tour, and it was beautiful. We could immediately imagine doing something there. But it was during this tour that we realised something was already there – beautiful historical objects, as well as vitrines – and we started asking ourselves what was going on. It was at this point that we were told: "Go ahead, we can make it work, it may just be a bit difficult … because there are people occupying the fire station!" And we were surprised! Basically, the fire station had to move out of the city centre due to larger new fire engines, but the former, retired fire chief and other retired firemen decided to occupy the station so that it could not be capitalised and turned into a private property! And what's so fascinating: they don't occupy it with their bodies but with their collection of huge historical fire engines. And many other things. Not only from Bergen or Norway, but from the all of Scandinavia. They put it inside there to keep the police from evicting them, since these things are just too huge and difficult to move. So these firemen already staked a claim – to have a fire museum in the city of Bergen with all this historical material. In other words, what we entered was an occupied place – a temporary amateur museum – that we were shown by the city to help them get rid of these occupants. So *here* is the subject position of the curator: brought in to change an existing conflict – the firemen and their economic tensions – with another one, exchanging one player with another one.

So we were faced with a dilemma. It was complicated and we were already implicated. But for me it was quite clear: My question was: How do we come together in a world that isolates us? Here we have a perfect example of two actors in society that are played against each other in order to be isolated. So the only possibility *I* saw was to find a way to relate, or to step out of the process. I proposed to meet the firemen, who came together, and we agreed on a joint project because I respected the occupiers, more than anyone else, to own the space in the moment. The project was called *The Museum of Burning Questions*, being aware that "burning questions", in a dialectical sense, is not just about fighting fires, but also about *making* fires. *Feuer legen.* I was honest about the fact that this would not be in any way *only* supporting their struggle, but it would be a temporary alliance. Respecting them as the occupiers and using the space in a solidary way. After some discussion, there was a clear majority on our side, and our *Partisan Café* could take place in the *Museum of Burning Questions*, in the occupied fire station of Bergen, during Bergen Assembly 2016.

Fig. 15.2 Nora Sternfeld, Isa Rosenberger, and the Retired Firemen of Bergen, THE MUSEUM OF BURNING QUESTIONS. The Partisan Café (at Bergen's historic fire station) with Jenny Moore, Freja Bäckman, Kabir Carter, Tora Endestad Bjørkheim, Johnny Herbert, and Arne Skaug Olsen. Educational and Performative Cafe designed by Isa Rosenberger, in collaboration with Heidi Pretterhofer, Bergen Assembly, 2016. Photograph by Thor

Does "making a conflict liveable" then not also mean that it became manageable for players like the city-government?
This is exactly what it means. But in this very case: I don't think so! It was actually a threat for the city of Bergen, and perhaps I brought the conflict further to a point. Maybe you're right! Maybe I'm wrong! But what's obvious is that there was a conflict: People occupy a space as others are in the process of changing this space into a hotel. So, *I* have seen it as a way of temporarily making this impossible. But, *yes*, of course, you are also right. On another level, you economise (monetise) *this* conflict. And we don't know where it is going now. What we know is that the retired firemen got a letter from the city a week before we opened, stating that they would allow them to use the space and to turn it into a fire museum. Now, is this managing a conflict? Maybe. But, in a sense, they won their struggle.

Since the book is developed from within anthropology, could you relate your thoughts to how you encountered anthropology for the first time. And what kind of relation you entertain with the discipline?
I don't feel either responsible, or willing, to build up on this discipline. This discipline is not interesting for me. Having said that, together with people coming from anthropology, and who align with social struggles, of course we would do something fantastic.

In 2005, I started to work on a project within the Vienna Mozart Year called *Hidden Histories – Remapping Mozart*, and, again, I found myself as part of curatorial collective that the artist from Vienna, Lisl Ponger, brought together. Part of the collective – besides the curator Luisa Ziaja and me, there were also the two anti-racist activists Ljubomir Bratic and Araba Evelyn Johnston-Arthur. Of course, part of our project was to completely reshape the aim of the Mozart Year. It was a one-year curatorial project with different – as we called them – configurations. Araba's approach was to build a research group for Black Austrian history, and it would work parallel to our curatorial collaborative practice. They went into the archives and researched possibilities of counter-writing the racist imagination of this celebration. They assembled a very heterogeneous group: musicians, pupils from school, scholars from university whom Araba always called "conservative studies people". All very very intelligent, reflective, and radical people. And together, they tried to find a way to – as they said – tell history themselves, instead of being told.

This was my first encounter – or conflictual encounter – with anthropology. Anthropology was exactly *not* a place where they found a lot to work on the history – histor-*y* and histor-*ies* – that seemed important for them. At that time, there were few people fighting against the racist 'normality' of anthropology departments in Austria. And this was how I encountered it, more or less. Then I became, of course, interested in the history of anthropology. And we were *diving* into the eighteenth century, at that time, because this was the time of Mozart. From his birth to his death, we could tell all the stories we wanted, we knew every year, more or less! How anthropology began was, of course, an important question for us. How did it work? How did it make itself work within a racist world? How could it survive, seemingly being critical, but without really changing existing structures? This is how it felt, to me. I wanted to analyse these discourses that seemed to themselves to be critical, but actually helped existing power relations to remain, rather than to break up.

Of course I knew that there was a tradition of criticality in anthropology. I was just asking myself: Is this a criticality in order to maintain existing power relations? Or to agitate them? This is a question I ask myself in many fields, also in relation to curators. I guess it's a question for all of us. I think there's a very problematic and specific problematic history of anthropology. But within this history is a certain criticality, and now, we should ask ourselves: Can we align to use it to agitate?

Related to this migration across fields, we would like to talk to you about the ways in which certain terms and concepts, which for us as anthropologists are associated partly with the negative and problematic colonial legacies but also with the critical and progressive aspects of the discipline – terms like "native", "indigeneity", and "source community" – are resurfacing and coming back into contemporary art discourses that are trying to work with these terms positively. We are asking you this not least because you have been active in the coinage of new terms, such as the "para-museum", for example, and wondered if this was a way to avoid dealing with the baggage of concepts?

My question in relation to some of those terms would be: How do we fight racism instead of avoiding it? Very often neologisms, or the avoiding of certain terms, maintains existing power relations. It's exactly what I said, and it might be the part of the transformism of this discipline of anthropology: You see a problem, and you change the name. But by changing the name, you don't change the problem. I *could* imagine that in a certain instance, you could *use* names and *refill* them with, let's say, an agitatoric potential, and thus to make them work, in conflictual ways. This would be interesting.

I am not saying that art is *more* able than anthropology to do that. In fact, you have very problematic and divided inscriptions in both fields. I think that people like Bonaventure Soh Bejeng Ndikung, people like you, asking: How can we come together, by playing with the inclusions and exclusions of the different fields, by playing them *against* each other, breaking something up, opening something up. *Aufbrechen*. This would be more interesting for me. Regarding words, I would just in the same way not leave one thing for something else. This even seems to me a rather capitalist practice. "This iPhone is old, let's get a new one." Instead, I would be more interested, or I would rather want to work together on understanding the sedimented conflictual potentials in the historic. How can they break out? And how can they work within the conflicts of today, in order to imagine another possible future?

And as a last note on this: We all know that racist terms have been appropriated by the communities of people discriminated against – in critical or other ways. Of course, we cannot, for example, take this appropriation away from the people who appropriated it. That would be absurd.

In view of different initiatives to 'decolonise' museums and academia across Europe, and Euro-American contexts, how do you consider the role of curatorial practice and institution-building? In what ways, if any, can such initiatives for the decolonisation of institutions continue, rethink, or expand the work of institutional critique? And how do you see your own work on the continuities of institutional critique, decolonisation, and decanonisation, as part of that?

The most important aspect of your question is that the *critique* of institutions – if we want it to work – has to have an effect on the *structures* of institutions. Not only on the representation, but also on the structural dimension of institutions. Put concretely, the decolonisation of an institution would mean that the people working in this institution would be less white and less bourgeois. But it's almost ironic how easy it seems that they *remain* white and bourgeois. And if they are *not* white anymore, they remain bourgeois. We need to rethink these structures in a much more radical way. I think that the word "decolonial" is helpful when it works in that way. And we can make it work in that way.

Of course, there's good sides and bad sides. You can also say, "Yeah, anthropology was a context in which some small critiques about slavery were articulated." But is this enough in a discipline that has brought racism forward as a functioning idea that killed people?

Institutional critique, decolonisation, and decanonisation all have to do with struggles. Is decolonisation an institutional critique? It wasn't at the beginning. But sometimes it can be part, or can be *just* an institutional reaction to existing social struggles that arrive in certain forms that cannot be denied any longer. And then – only when they can't be denied anymore – somehow academia or the institutional react. Many of these struggles were feminist struggles and anti-racist struggles. Historically, these addressed institutions not because institutions are so super-interesting per se, but because they are part of a society that governs people through representation.

Your own role within academic institutions – and contexts of institution-building – is associated with power structures. How do you make such positions work in the way you proposed?

Power is something that you don't have. It is something that is given to you. You cannot counter-act it from a position of power. You will immediately lose your power. But this is what I chose. I do not only occupy a classic academic position. I also have a position that will be central to a new institutional framework in Kassel called the documenta institute.

I am very sure that I will not be at the base of this new institution. At the moment, I am struggling to make concepts of a radical democratic institution hearable. And I collaborate with the Kunsthochschule, because the process, as it seems, is far away from not only criticality but also from art! I chose not to make compromises from a position of power. But to counter-act from a position of lesser power.

My contract is for another three more years, but I know that it is not smoothly going into the director position of the new institution. This also makes totally sense, and it was clear at some point. But I decided to propose a counter-concept. This counter-concept was done together with the Kunsthochschule – concretely with Alexis Joachimides, Dierk Schmidt, and Joel Baumann – and it is very likely that this counter-concept will remain only as a history, a legacy, of a counter-concept that is not realised.

Note

1. The image on p. 362 is Figure 15.1 'Fires need audiences' (tote bag), 2015. Photograph by Sarah Peguine, © Ariel Schlesinger

References

Butler, Judith. 2015. *Notes Toward a Performative Theory of the Assembly*. Cambridge, MA: Harvard University Press.

The Trans-Anthropological, Anachronism, and the Contemporary

Roger Sansi

While I was reading the chapters of this book, I attended the presentation of a film by Ariella Aisha Azoulay, *Un-documented: Undoing Imperial Plunder* (2019). Azoulay explicitly recognised her indebtedness to *Statues Also Die*, the 1953 film essay by Alain Resnais and Chris Marker, undoubtedly a great work of art and a fierce critique of the colonial plunder of Africa. Yet Azoulay also found it problematic in retrospect; she did not agree with the grand opening statement of the film: "When men die, they enter history. When statues die, they enter art." Yet statues do not simply die, says Azoulay: "When they are uprooted from their communities in which they are made, when they are forced to leave the people to whom they belong and who belong to them, they are placed under death threat (…) And of course, it is not only they who are threatened with death. It is their people too." (Azoulay 2019:122) In fact, her film, in her words, is an attempt to make coincide the two regimes that imperialism seeks to keep separated: the treatment of objects (as "well-documented") and maltreatment of people (as "undocumented").[1] In other words, the claims for justice and restitution of post-colonial objects should be inextricably related to post-colonial subjects, the "undocumented", the "illegal" immigrants that keep coming from the former colonies to their former colonisers.

Watching the film, I couldn't help but wonder what these undocumented immigrants would actually have to say about these objects. Perhaps some of them do not particularly identify with these things; many immigrants today may be Christian, Muslim, or even agnostic and may view these objects as relics of an ancient witchcraft or 'fetish' to which they may not particularly relate and do not feel that they belong to them. The identification of these objects from colonial or pre-colonial times with contemporary people, as 'African', may be yet another form of objectification. It may be possible that these objects are indeed dead, in the sense claimed by Marker and Resnais. Because the "communities in which they were made" may have changed substantially; they may have been buried in a colonial museum for too long.

Of course that was just a supposition. But that is precisely one of the recurrent problems with these collections: that they are premised on ignorance. Many times there is not much information about them. This ignorance may be voluntary of course, a form as misrecognition, of not wanting to know, of disavowal, in Freudian terms. Still, this misrecognition has effects. These objects have indeed been silenced for a long time. It may be not possible to undo what has been done, to go back to the past. All that is left are the objects themselves, in their immanence.

Years ago I worked on a Police Museum in Bahia, Brazil (Sansi 2005). This was not explicitly a colonial museum like the ones mentioned in this book but, rather, the result of internal colonialism. Many objects in the collection originated in relation to the Afro-Brazilian religion Candomblé, which had been repressed and persecuted for decades. As Candomblé was finally recognised as a religion in recent decades, a group of practitioners and scholars sued the museum for the undignified display of its collections in a museum of crime surrounded by weapons, drugs, and human remains of criminals. Yet they did not request their restitution. It was impossible to trace objects back to their original owners. There were no records. As such, the question of what to do with these objects remained. Is it really possible to make a 'dignified' exhibition of objects that have been violently taken away and whose origins we can't trace back? The museum was ultimately closed, some of its Candomblé objects made its way to other museums, and some were just withdrawn from public view. But they are still there. After all arguments, the objects are still there.

The paradox of the immanence of objects, however, does not question whether the claims for restitution and reparation are justified in political terms. Of course followers of Candomblé who sued the museum did the right thing, and we should all be happy that they succeeded. Furthermore, Azoulay's argument is also very valid: The restitution of colonial objects should not make us forget or cover up the very contemporary question of immigration. Colonial museums are an anachronism – perhaps that is the whole problem. Can there be a 'contemporary' reinvention of ethnographic colonial collections, though? This very question may lead us to understand that not only the colonial is problematic but also the constitution of the 'contemporary'. In Azoulay's proposal to connect the two regimes that imperialism seeks to keep separated, she shows that they are coeval, contemporary problems. We cannot address one if we do not address the other. But is it really possible to make contemporary a whole body of things built on anachronism? Is it possible to bring the dead back to life?

Reading the chapters and conversations in this volume, I felt I have acquired a privileged perspective on the complex and contradictory 'contemporary' landscape of the transformation of ethnographic collections in continental Europe, a landscape with many contradictions I am afraid I will not be able to summarise thoroughly in this afterword. Still, I can point to some of the questions that caught my attention. On the one hand, the revamping of ethnographic museums in different countries could be greeted as a positive cultural investment in a landscape of austerity. And yet, the investment in these infrastructures is extremely controversial, because the renovation of the displays seems far from overcoming the colonialist ideologies upon which they were premised. On the other hand, decolonial critique seems to finally be making a breakthrough in public institutions, although in many cases it is questionable if such critique really transforms them deep down. Some European institutions and governments are starting to recognise colonial legacies as a 'problem' and even systematically consider and realise restitutions, something few and far between only decades ago. And yet, at the beginning of 2020, it is unclear if this growing uneasiness with the colonial past will ultimately have any consequences. The future is uncertain, in particular, because there are also strong indications of a cultural, ideological, and political backlash in the radically opposite direction. In many European countries, souverainism, nationalism, white supremacism, and European nativism are a growing presence in their many different forms. This radical nemesis, the 'return' of fascism, looms large behind these apparently liberal and well-meaning debates between activists, artists, experts, politicians, and bureaucrats.

One of the most shocking cases for me is the Humboldt Forum in Berlin's reconstructed City Palace. The argument of an 'aesthetic coherence' with its neoclassic surroundings cannot overshadow the obvious political symbolism of a building that was the very embodiment of Prussian militarism and imperialism, even if defending such values seems taboo in contemporary Germany – or maybe no more? The very idea of the reconstruction of the City Palace is so obviously, explicitly anachronistic that it seems difficult to accept anyone could believe that filling it with 'contemporary', 'politically correct' content may counterbalance its (misplaced) temporality. It may appear as a clearly postmodern project. Anachronism was amply used in postmodern architecture, but in ironic terms. There seems to be no irony in the reconstruction of the Berliner Schloss. Here is the paradox: We seem to live, still, in postmodern times, but without the irony of post-modernity as an art movement in the late twentieth century. We no longer find anachronism funny. We live in anachronistic times, in which claims to return to the past seem perfectly valid. We may be too far from modernity, when it was obvious that time was moving forward, that it was not possible to return, the horizon was always the future. The opposite would be a joke. But the future is no more, it seems. Anachronism is no longer a joke but, rather, the sign of our times.

What, then, constitutes the contemporary at a time of anachronism? There is a form of practice that claims explicitly to be contemporary: contemporary art. One of the questions that emerges clearly from this volume is that contemporary art is often summoned to confront, repair, re-arrange the problems of the colonial ethnographic collection, especially the problem with its anachronism. Contemporary art is seen to have the power of bringing the past to the present. In that sense, it establishes a particular relationship with anthropology, the discipline that is institutionally in charge of these collections. This book is making a bold argument by proposing that the problems and questions that historically, in modern times, would belong to the discipline of anthropology have expanded beyond it in a "trans-anthropological" uneasy encounter with artists, curators, and activists. The different conversations with curators in this volume show well the uneasiness of this encounter, in which curators often distance themselves from anthropology's disciplinary claims of ownership. Situated within the field of contemporary art, many of these curators take a transdisciplinary or, perhaps better, anti-disciplinary approach. The claim for "the curator as ethnographer" made, among others, by Okwui Enwezor (2012) is part of a long list of "as"-forms of expertise and disciplines that contemporary curators can add to their "transversally agentive" practice, as this volume defines it: the curator as scientist, the curator as historian, the curator as ...

The extended field of the curatorial in which the curator takes the form and role of any other specialised expert is, for Irit Rogoff (2013), a manifestation of the epistemological crisis of our times – a crisis that the curatorial would be in a privileged position to address. For her, the role of the curatorial would be to bring together knowledges, sensibilities, and insights, assembling them, enacting the event of knowledge, rather than illustrating it (ibidem: 43). The act of assemblage, of bringing together, of enacting the event of knowledge, is to make it present, to make it contemporary. That is what the contemporary seems to mean: enacting an event that brings together difference.

Why does the "transversally agentive" curator come from contemporary art? First, because it is art that has vindicated its position in the 'contemporary', this horizontal space that brings together different knowledges. Modern art was built in radical opposition to disciplinary knowledge and practice, as an anti-disciplinary practice. In modern times, the anti-discipline of art was a prophecy of the utopia, of a future world where work and life would be reunited, where there would be no professionals or specialists but just people. Contemporary art has inherited the anti-disciplinary ethos of modern art, but it withdrew from its epochal ambitions and has redrawn its practice by addressing the here and now, the contemporary, not the future – the contemporary as a space in common, a space of "composition" (Smith 2016).

As opposed to art, the concept of the contemporary in anthropology has only recently been used. The post-modern self-critique of anthropology, as strongly formulated by Johannes Fabian (1983), questioned the "denial of coevalness" upon which classical modern anthropology was premised. Anthropology should be radically coeval and address the problems of and in its time. But only much later did anthropologists consider what would be 'contemporary'. For Paul Rabinow and others (2008), a contemporary approach, or rather, an anthropology of the contemporary, requires an acknowledgement that the object of study of anthropology is no longer a given singular community, located in a singular space for a particular time, but an assemblage of different parts: people, places, objects, concepts, and agencies of different sorts that constitute contemporary assemblages. In these terms, they propose to replace ethnographic fieldwork with "assemblage-work". This notion of assemblage-work is related to George Marcus' para-site (2000), participatory spaces where multiple divergent agents and agencies discursively interact across geographic, temporal, and disciplinary boundaries. Working with this assemblage, the role of the anthropologist would resemble that of the curator (Elhaik 2016). And yet it seems that anthropologists are arriving late to the museum assemblage. Contemporary art curators have often already taken this "trans-anthropological" role.

Another question is if this assemblage is indeed possible, if it can overcome the immanence and anachronism of colonial ethnographic collections and establish new relations, make them contemporary. As we see in this volume, this enterprise is often difficult, sometimes because the immanence of the institutions is too strong to overcome, but sometimes because the same narrative of the contemporary assemblage has its limits. I was particularly interested in the case of the Royal Museum for Central Africa in Belgium discussed especially by Sarah Demart in her contribution. Activists were invited to participate in discussions and to express their views in what could be described as a participative process. They explicitly refused, however, and requested instead for their expertise to be acknowledged, to be offered a contract, and to be remunerated. This attitude may go against the very principles of participation, collaboration, free exchange, and the commons that underpin the discourse of contemporary participatory practices (Sansi 2015); but precisely because of that, these claims are legitimate. Museum officials with their official roles and jobs and expertise ask people to participate without remuneration in a discussion, but what do they get in return? Recognition? It may be easy from a position of power to propose alternatives, other forms of working, relating and exchanging knowledge, reshuffling the assemblage, but from the external position of the powerless, to be invited to participate without pay may just be another form of oppression. Overcoming the institution and its anachronism may come to be a very difficult task, even accounting for the powers of art to build contemporary assemblages.

In these terms, this afterword cannot really offer any clear views on what comes 'after'. The contemporary is a time of anachronisms; and anachronism is nothing but disjuncture, the opposite of the desired assemblage. This disjuncture can lead in many different directions: perhaps the triumph of decolonial critique and the final dismantlement of the old colonial museums, accompanied by a dismantlement of the empires and borders that still endure. Perhaps it will come to a withdrawal towards a past that never existed, and the whole of Europe will become a museum fortress, a cemetery of dead statues and people. Probably none of the above. Still, it is ironic that the colonial ethnographic museum, such an anachronism, can become an emblem of our troubled times.

Note

1. https://fundaciotapies.org/en/exposicio/ariella-aisha-azoulay-errata/ (last accessed 27 December 2019).

References

Azoulay, Ariella. 2019. *Potential History Unlearning Imperialism*. New York: Verso.
Elhaik, Tarek. 2016. *The Incurable-Image: Curating Post-Mexican Film and Media Arts*. Edinburgh: Edinburgh University Press.

Enwezor, Okwui, Mélanie Bouteloup, Abdellah Karroum, Émilie Renard, and Claire Staebler Eds. 2012. *Intense Proximity: An Anthology of the Near and the Far [La Triennale 2012]*. Paris: Artlys.
Fabian, Johannes. 1983. *Time and the Other*. New York: Columbia University Press.
Marcus, George E. Ed. 2000. *Para-sites: A Casebook against Cynical Reason*. Chicago: University of Chicago Press.
Rabinow, Paul, George E. Marcus, James D. Faubion, and Tobias Rees. 2008. *Designs for an Anthropology of the Contemporary*. Durham, NC: Duke University Press.
Rogoff, Irit. 2013. 'The Expanded Field', in: *The Curatorial: A Philosophy of Curating*. London, edited by Jean-Paul Martinon. London: Bloomsbury, pp. 41–48.
Sansi, Roger. 2005. 'The Hidden Life of Stones: Historicity, Materiality and the Value of Candomble Objects in Bahia'. *Journal of Material Culture* 10(2): 139–156.
———. 2015. *Art, Anthropology and the Gift*. London: Bloomsbury.
Smith, Terry. 2016. *The Contemporary Condition*. Berlin: Sternberg Press.

List of contributors

Arjun Appadurai is a social-cultural anthropologist. He is Goddard Professor of Media, Culture, and Communication at New York University, where he is also Senior Fellow at the Institute for Public Knowledge. He is also Senior Professor of Anthropology and Globalization at The Hertie School (Berlin). Appadurai has published a number of seminal books within the field of globalisation studies, such as *Modernity at Large* (1996), *Fear of Small Numbers: An Essay on the Geography of Anger* (2006), *The Future as a Cultural Fact: Essays on the Global Condition* (2013) and, more recently, *Banking on Words. The Failure of Language in the Age of Derivative Finance* (2015). His most recent book, co-authored with Neta Alexander, is *Failure* (2019).

Annette Bhagwati is Director of the Museum Rietberg, Zurich. Between 2012 and 2019 she served as the head of projects at the Haus der Kulturen der Welt (HKW) in Berlin, where she oversaw long-term curatorial research projects including The New Alphabet, 100 Years of Now, and The Anthropocene Project. After studying social anthropology, geography, art history, and African art, she served as the programme coordinator and deputy head of exhibitions at HKW (1999-2006). Between 2009 and 2012 she was affiliate professor of art history at Concordia University, Montreal. She has lectured and published widely on topics related to curating, museum studies and exhibition history, global art, and African art.

Clémentine Deliss is a curator, publisher, and cultural historian born in London of French-Austrian parents. She studied contemporary art and semantic anthropology and holds a PhD from the School of Oriental & African Studies, London. Between 1996 and 2007, she published the itinerant and independent artists' and writers' organ, *Metronome*. From 2002 to 2009, she ran "Future Academy" with student cells in London, Edinburgh, Dakar, Mumbai, Bangalore, Melbourne, and Tokyo. From 2010 to 2015, she directed the Weltkulturen Museum in Frankfurt, instituting a transdisciplinary lab to remediate collections within a post-ethnological context. Exhibitions she curated at the Weltkulturen Museum include *Object Atlas – Fieldwork in the Museum* (2011), *Trading Style* (2013), *Foreign Exchange (or the stories you wouldn't tell a stranger)* (2014), and *El Hadji Sy – Painting, Politics, Performance*. In the academic year 2015-2016 she was a fellow at the Institute of Advanced Study in Berlin (Wissenschaftskolleg zu Berlin). In 2016, she curated the "Dilijan Arts Observatory" in a former electronics factory in Armenia. This interdisciplinary fieldwork was presented in "Hello World. Revising a Collection" at the National Galerie im Hamburger Bahnhof, Berlin (April-August 2018). In 2017-2018, she curated four international roundtables on "Transitioning Museums" in Southeast Asia for the Goethe-Institut. She is a member of the Scientific Council of the Musée du Quai Branly in Paris. In 2017-2018, she was Visiting Professor at the Ecole Nationale Supérieure d'Arts Paris-Cergy (ENSAPC) and held an international chair at the Laboratoire d'Excellence des Arts et Médiations Humaines, Université, Paris 8. In 2018-2019, she was Interim Professor for Curatorial Theory and Dramaturgical Practice at the Karlsruhe University of Arts and Design (HfG). She is currently Guest Professor for Theory and History at the Academy of Fine Art, Hamburg, Associate Curator at KW Institute of Contemporary Art, Berlin, and faculty-at-large in Curatorial Practice at the School of Visual Arts, New York.

Sarah Demart holds a doctorate in sociology from the universities of Toulouse-le Mirail in France and Louvain-la-Neuve in Belgium. Originally, she focused on African migration and the genealogy of political-religious struggles, both in the Democratic Republic of Congo and Congolese diasporic areas (mainly France and Belgium). Since 2011, she has been exploring Belgium's anti-blackness policies in the light of Afro-Belgian activism, and in particular women's activism and practices of resistance. She has published on issues related to religious transnationalism, black presences in Belgium, postcolonial controversy, and decolonial militancy. She is also the coordinator of the first large-scale survey on people of African descent living in Belgium (with Bruno Schoumaker, Marie Godin, and Ilke Adam, King Baudouin Fondation, 2017). One of the originalities of this study was to explore postcolonial claims related to historical justice by both activists and 'everyday' people. She is currently working on a book on Afro-Belgian activism and its intersection with decolonial dimensions. Her current research looks at how racial politics operate in the field of sexual health and the fight against HIV/AIDS.

Natasha Ginwala is a curator and writer. She is Associate Curator at Gropius Bau, Berlin, and Artistic Director of Gwangju Biennale 2020 with Defne Ayas. Ginwala has curated Contour Biennale 8, *Polyphonic Worlds: Justice as Medium*, and was part of the curatorial team of documenta14 (2017). Other recent projects include *COLOMBOSCOPE Festival 'Sea Change'* (2019); *Arrival, Incision. Indian Modernism as Peripatetic Itinerary* in the framework of "Hello World. Revising a Collection" at Hamburger Bahnhof – Museum für Gegenwart, Berlin (2018); *Riots: Slow Cancellation of the Future* at ifa Gallery Berlin and Stuttgart (2018); *My East is Your West* at the 56th Venice Biennale (2015); and *Corruption: Everybody Knows...* with e-flux, New York (2015). Ginwala was a member of the artistic team for the 8th Berlin Biennale for Contemporary Art (2014) and has co-curated *The Museum of Rhythm* at the Taipei Biennial (2012) and at Muzeum Sztuki, Łódź (2016–17). From 2013–15, in collaboration with Vivian Ziherl, she led the multi-part curatorial project *Landings* presented at various partner organizations. Ginwala writes on contemporary art and visual culture in various periodicals and has contributed to numerous publications. She is a recipient of the 2018 visual arts research grant from the Berlin Senate Department for Culture and Europe.

Emmanuel Grimaud is an anthropologist, film maker, curator, and researcher at the CNRS, Paris. His research explores the borders of human experiences, communication, perception, technologies. Following the intuition that anthropology is an experimental science ignoring itself, he designed creative ethnographic protocols to take Mori's 'uncanny valley' further. He has been especially interested in the way people deal with the undetectable, enigmas, or perceptive dead angles (*Les Plans-Limites d'Expérience*, 2018). Among the intriguing experiments he designed, *Ganesh Yourself* (2016) was a robot conceived to enable anybody to incarnate God and have a conversation; his film *Black Hole* (2019) comprised a transcommunication experiment involving an Indian hypnotherapist and ghost hunters. His earlier works explore religious animatronics (*Dieux et robots*, 2008), a Gandhi lookalike (*Le sosie de Gandhi*, 2007), Japanese robotics (*Le jour où les robots mangeront des pommes*, 2011), Indian astromorphology (*L'étrange encyclopédie du docteur K*, 2014), archaeology (*Archéologie et ventriloquie*, 2013), beetle fighting (*Insect magnetism*, 2012), ocular movement (*Le point de vue de la pupille*, 2015), aura-measuring machines (*La face obscure de la clairvoyance*, 2019), and the limits of perspectivism (*From the squid's point of view*, 2015). He coordinated many collective volumes, curated the *Robo-Garage* exhibition (Enghien Les Bains, 2007) and *Persona, strangely human* (Quai Branly Museum, 2016).

Aliocha Imhoff and **Kantuta Quirós** are curators, art theorists, and filmmakers based in Paris, as well as founders of the curatorial platform le peuple qui manque – a people is missing. For several years they have been developing a research project that calls for a new ecology of knowledge, based on curatorial formats that present contemporary thought (diplomatic fictions, mock trials, staged controversies, assemblies, and thought experiments on the subject at a scale of 1:1). Among their latest curatorial projects are *What Does It Desire to Be? To Become Something* (Biennale de Lyon, 2019), *A Debt of Times* (Konsthall C, Stockholm, 2018), *The Trial of Fiction* (Nuit Blanche, Paris, 2017), *A Migrant Constituent Assembly* (Centre Pompidou, 2017), and *A Government of Times* (Rebuild Foundation, Chicago & Leipzig, 2016). Their most recent publications are *Les Potentiels du Temps* (Manuella Editions, 2016), *Géoesthétique* (B42, 2014), *Afropolitan Histories of Art*, (Multitudes, 2014). They are currently developing Les Impatients, a film-essay and a chronopolitical series. They are also part of the editorial board of the journal *Multitudes*. Kantuta Quirós is Associate Professor at the Ecole Nationale Supérieure d'Architecture in Nantes. Aliocha Imhoff teaches at University Paris I – Pantheon Sorbonne.

Erica Lehrer is a sociocultural anthropologist and curator. She is currently Professor in the departments of History and Sociology-Anthropology at Concordia University, Montreal, where she also is Founding Director of the Curating and Public Scholarship Lab (CaPSL). She is the author of *Jewish Poland Revisited: Heritage Tourism in Unquiet Places* (Indiana University Press, 2013); and co-editor of *Curatorial Dreams: Critics Imagine Exhibitions* (McGill-Queens, 2016); *Jewish Space in Contemporary Poland* (Indiana UP, 2015); and *Curating Difficult Knowledge: Violent Pasts in Public Places* (Palgrave, 2011), as well as numerous articles. In 2013 she curated the exhibition *Souvenir, Talisman, Toy* and in 2018-2019 co-curated *Terribly Close: Polish Vernacular Artists Face the Holocaust*, both at the Kraków Ethnographic Museum (MEK) in Poland.

Toma Muteba Luntumbue is an art historian, artist, educator and independent curator. He teaches at the Ecole de Recherche Graphique (ERG) and Ecole nationale supérieure des arts visuels de La Cambre in Brussels, Belgium. He was the artistic director of the 4th and 5th Biennale de Lubumbashi, DR Congo in 2015-2017. He also curated the following exhibitions: *Exitcongomuseum* at the Royal Museum for Central Africa in Tervuren (2000-2001), *Transferts* at the BOZAR Centre for Fine Arts, Brussels (2003), and *Ligablo* at the Royal Library of Belgium, Brussels (2010-2011).

Sharon Macdonald is Alexander von Humboldt Professor of Social Anthropology in the Institute of European Ethnology, Humboldt-Universität zu Berlin, where she founded and directs CARMAH – the Centre for Anthropological Research on Museums and Heritage. She also leads a multi-researcher ethnography of museum and heritage developments in Berlin – *Making Differences* – and is PI in the Excellence Cluster *Matters of Activity* and of the recently completed *TRACES: Transmitting Contentious Cultural Heritages with the Arts* (EU). She is a research associate of the Pitt Rivers Museum, Oxford, and a member of the advisory boards of both the Berlin Exhibition in the Humboldt Forum and the House of European History. She has written widely on questions of culture, museums, and heritage. Recent publications include, as co-editor, *Refugees Welcome? Difference and Diversity in a Changing Germany*; *Engaging Anthropological Legacies* (a special section of *Museum Worlds*); and the paperback editions of the *International Handbooks in Museum Studies*. The co-authored *Heritage Futures. Comparative Approaches to Natural and Cultural Heritage Practices* is in press.

Wayne Modest is the head of the Research Center of Material Culture, the research institute of the Tropenmuseum (Amsterdam), Museum Volkenkunde (Leiden), Afrika Museum (Berg en Dal) and Wereldmuseum (Rotterdam). He is also Professor of Material Culture and Critical Heritage Studies (by special appointment) in the faculty of humanities at the Vrije Universiteit, Amsterdam (VU). Modest was previously the head of the curatorial department at the Tropenmuseum, Amsterdam; Keeper of Anthropology at the Horniman Museum, London; and Director of the Museums of History and Ethnography in Kingston, Jamaica. His research interests include issues of belonging and displacement; material mobilities; histories of (ethnographic) collecting and exhibitionary practices; difficult/contested heritage (with a special focus on slavery, colonialism, and post-colonialism); and Caribbean thought. More recently, Modest has been researching and publishing on heritage and citizenship in Europe, and on ethnographic museums and questions of redress/repair. His publications include *Museums and Communities: Curators, Collections, Collaborations* (Bloomsbury Academic Publishers, ed. with Viv Golding, 2013), *Museums, Heritage and International Development* (Routledge, ed. with Paul Basu, 2013), *Victorian Jamaica* (Duke University Press, ed. with Tim Barringer, 2018), and *Matters of Belonging: Ethnographic Museums in a Changing Europe* (together with Nicholas Thomas, Doris Prlic, and Claudia Agusta)

Bonaventure Soh Bejeng Ndikung (born in 1977 in Yaoundé, Cameroon), is an independent curator, author, and biotechnologist. He is Founder and Artistic Director of SAVVY Contemporary Berlin. He was Curator-at-Large for documenta14 in Athens and Kassel; Artistic Director of the 12th Rencontres de Bamako, a biennale for African photography (Mali, 2019); as well as Guest Curator of the Dak'Art Biennale (Senegal, 2018). Together with the Miracle Workers Collective, he curated the Finland Pavilion at the Venice Biennale in 2019, and is Artistic Director of Sonsbeek 2020-2024, a quadrennial contemporary art exhibition in Arnhem, the Netherlands. He was Guest Professor in Curatorial Studies and Sound Art at the Städelschule in Frankfurt, and is also a recipient of the first OCAD University International Curators Residency fellowship in Toronto in 2020.

Margareta von Oswald is an anthropologist trained at the Institut d'Études Politiques (Bordeaux), the École Normale Supérieure (Paris), the École des Hautes Études en Sciences Sociales (Paris), and the Humboldt-Universität zu Berlin. Since 2016, she has been a research fellow in the multi-researcher and multi-location ethnography project *Making Differences: Transforming Museums and Heritage in the Twenty-First Century* at the Centre for Anthropological Research on Museums and Heritage (Berlin), led by Sharon Macdonald as part of Macdonald's Alexander von Humboldt Professorship. Based on a two-year-ethnography in Berlin's Ethnologisches Museum and the Royal Museum for Central Africa (Tervuren), Margareta von Oswald's doctoral research analyses the restructuring processes and accompanying controversies of anthropological museums in Europe. In particular, she has been interested in the ways in which the museums relate to and deal with their colonial legacies and their reverberations in the present. From 2016 to 2019, she co-organised the seminar series *Rewriting the Colonial Past: Contemporary Challenges of Museum Collections* (EHESS, Paris). In 2015, she curated the exhibition *Object Biographies* with Verena Rodatus (Humboldt Lab Dahlem, Berlin).

Roger Sansi was born in Barcelona (Spain) in 1972. After studying at the universities of Barcelona and Paris, he received a PhD in Anthropology from the University of Chicago (2003). He has worked at Kings College and Goldsmiths College, University of London. Currently, he is Professor in Social Anthropology at the University of Barcelona. He has worked on Afro-Brazilian culture and art, the concept of the fetish, and on contemporary art in Barcelona. His publications include the books *Fetishes and Monuments* (Berghahn, 2007), *Sorcery in the Black Atlantic* (edited with L. Nicolau, Chicago University Press, 2011), *Art Anthropology and the Gift* (Bloomsbury,

2015), and *The Anthropologist as Curator* (2020, Bloomsbury). He is a member of the research group GRECS, and was a founding co-convenor of ANTART, the *Anthropology and the Arts Network* of the European Association of Social Anthropologists (EASA), with Jonas Tinius (2018-2020).

Alexander Schellow is a German filmmaker and artist based in Cologne and Brussels, where he is a professor and directs the department of time-based practices and animation at the ERG (School of Graphic Research). Since 1999, he has been developing a continuous practice of memory (re)construction through drawing and animation. Several series of drawings, animations, installations, and performances have been circulated internationally. He has cofounded the production platform index.film (Berlin) as well as the collective AnimationResearchGroup (Brussels), and he regularly collaborates with the label Lowave (Paris, Singapore) and the production company Films de Force Majeure (Marseille).

Arnd Schneider is currently Professor of Social Anthropology at the University of Oslo, and was formerly Reader in Anthropology at the University of East London, and Senior Research Fellow at the University of Hamburg. He writes on contemporary art and anthropology, migration, and film. He was a co-organiser of the international conference "Fieldworks: Dialogues between Art and Anthropology" (Tate Modern, 2003). His main publications include *Futures Lost: Nostalgia and Identity among Italian Immigrants in Argentina* (Peter Lang 2000) and *Appropriation as Practice: Art and Identity in Argentina* (Palgrave, 2006). He edited *Art, Anthropology, and Contested Heritage* (Bloomsbury 2020), and *Alternative Art and Anthropology: Global Encounters* (Bloomsbury 2017); and he co-edited (with Chris Wright) *Contemporary Art and Anthropology* (Berg 2006), *Between Art and Anthropology* (Berg 2010), and *Anthropology and Art Practice* (Bloomsbury 2013). He co-edited with Bernard Müller and Caterina Pasqualino *Le terrain comme mise en scène* (Presses universitaires de Lyon, 2017). *Experimental Film and Anthropology* (co-edited with Caterina Pasqualino) was published by Bloomsbury in 2014. Between 2016 and 2019, he was a partner of TRACES (*Transmitting Contentious Cultural Heritages with the Arts: From Intervention to Co-production*) under the European Union's *Horizon 2020* programme.

Anna Seiderer is Senior Lecturer at the Arts Department of the University Paris 8/Vincennes, Saint-Denis. She is a member of the Laboratory of Anthropology of Contemporary Worlds (LAMC) of the Université Libre de Bruxelles and the Gesellschaft für Ethnographie (GfE) of the Humboldt

Universität zu Berlin. Since 2017, she is a member of the Scientific Committee and is in charge of the "Creations" section of the *Slaveries and Post-Slaveries Review* (CIRESC/CNRS). Her PhD in aesthetics was devoted to the transmission at work in/by/despite post-colonial museums in Benin, and she coordinated the European project *Ethnography Museums and World Cultures* [RIME]. Her continuing research is dedicated to contemporary artistic practices dealing with colonial history.

Nanette Snoep is director of the Rautenstrauch-Joest Museum. Kulturen der Welt in Cologne. Between 2015 and 2018 she was director of the Grassi Museum für Völkerkunde in Leipzig, the Museum für Völkerkunde in Dresden and the Völkerkunde Museum in Herrnhut. In Dresden she curated an experimental growing exhibition in 10 steps, *Prolog #1-10, Stories of People, Things and Places* (2016-2018) which explored the ethnographic museum about his colonial legacies in an ongoing process. This curatorial concept was then taken up at the Grassi Museum in Leipzig under the name *Werkstatt Prolog* in 2018. For Leipzig she initiated a series of exhibitions *Grassi invites #* inviting external curators, artists, theatremakers, refugees, communities and students to bring out new perspectives on the museum's collection and permanent exhibition. *Grassi invites #1 Fremd* (2016), *Grassi invites #2 Dazwischen/in/Between* (2016), *Grassi invites #3 Masks!* (2016), *Grassi invites #4 Tattoo&Piercing* (2017). Her last exhibition she organized in Saxony, *Megalopolis – Voices from Kinshasa* (2018), gave carte blanche to a collective of artists from Kinshasa to curate and produce their own exhibition at the Grassi Museum. Prior to her appointment in Germany in 2015, she spent 16 years at the Paris Quai Branly Museum as Head of the "Historical and Contemporary Globalization collection". She curated in France 1931. *Les étrangers au temps de l'Exposition coloniale* (Cité Nationale de l'Histoire de l'Immigration, Paris 2008), *Vodou. L'Art de Voir l'Invisible* (Musée du Vodou, Strasbourg 2013), for the Quai Branly Museum, *Recettes des Dieux. L'Invention du Fétiche* (2009), *Exhibitions. L'Invention du Sauvage* (2011) et *Les Maîtres du Désordre* (2012) with venues at the Kunsthalle Bonn in 2012 (*Narren. Künstler. Heilige. Lob der Torheit*) and at the Fundacio La Caixa 2013 in Madrid (*Los Maestros del Caos*). Between 2004 and 2014 she also taught African art history at the École du Louvre in Paris and at the Université Nanterre.

Nora Sternfeld is an educator and curator. She is documenta Professor at the Kunsthochschule Kassel. From 2012 to 2018 she was Professor of Curating and Mediating Art at the Aalto University in Helsinki. In addition, she is Co-director of /ecm – MA Programme in Exhibition Theory and Practice at the University of Applied Arts Vienna, part of trafo.K, Office for Art, Education and Critical Knowledge Production based in Vienna (w/Renate Höllwart, Elke Smodics); and of *freethought*, a platform for research, education, and production based in London (w/Irit Rogoff, Stefano Harney, Adrian Heathfield, Mao Mollona, Louis Moreno). In this context she was one of the artistic directors of the Bergen Assembly 2016. She publishes on contemporary art, exhibitions, politics of history, educational theory, and anti-racism. Monographs include *Das radikaldemokratische Museum* (de Gruyter, 2018), *Kontaktzonen der Geschichtsvermittlung. Transnationales Lernen über den Holocaust in der postnazistischen Migrationsgesellschaft* (Zaglossus, 2013), and *Das pädagogische Unverhältnis. Lehren und Lernen bei Rancière, Gramsci und Foucault* (Turia+Kant, 2009).

Anne-Christine Taylor is a social anthropologist trained at the University of Oxford, and at the École des Hautes en Sciences Sociales, under the academic supervision of Claude Lévi-Strauss. She has conducted extensive fieldwork among the Achuar, a Jivaroan group of the upper Amazon, and has published widely on various subjects relating to Jivaroan culture, to theoretical and historical issues in anthropology, and more recently on the role of anthropological museums. Her main fields of interest have been kinship studies, forms of indigenous historiography and non-Western regimes of historicity, and, since around 1995, the study of indigenous conceptualizations of consciousness. From 2005 to 2014, Anne-Christine Taylor was in charge of the Musée du Quai Branly's department of research and university-level teaching. From 1995 to 2005, she was head of the Equipe de recherche en ethnologie amérindienne at the CNRS. Besides being editor in chief of the journal *Gradhiva – revue d'anthropologie et d'histoire des arts*, published by the Musée du Quai Branly, Taylor is a member of the editorial board of the *Journal de la Societe des Américanistes*, of *Terrain*, of the Ecuadorian journal *Memoria – Revista de historia y antropologia andina*, and of the journal *Systèmes de pensée en Afrique noire*.

Jonas Tinius is an anthropologist of art and a post-doctoral research fellow on the *Making Differences* project at the Centre for Anthropological Research on Museums and Heritage (CARMAH), based at the Department of European Ethnology, Humboldt-Universität zu Berlin, Germany. He is funded by the Alexander von Humboldt Foundation as part of the research award for Sharon Macdonald's Alexander von Humboldt Professorship. After studying British and American Studies as well as social and cultural anthropology at the universities of Münster (Germany) and Cambridge (UK), he completed his doctoral thesis on theatre and migration at the Department of Social Anthropology and King's College, University of Cambridge (UK). His post-doctoral research explored how Berlin-based curators, contemporary artists, and art institutions engage with notions of alterity, otherness, and diversity through their curatorial practices. Together with Professor Roger Sansi (Barcelona), he was a founding co-convenor of the *Anthropology and the Arts Network* of the European Association of Social Anthropologists (2018-2020). He is editor of *Anthropology, Theatre, and Development: The Transformative Potential of Performance* (2015, Palgrave, with Alex Flynn); *Otherwise. Rethinking Museums and Heritage* (with colleagues from CARMAH, Berlin, 2018); *Der Fremde Blick. Roberto Ciulli und das Theater an der Ruhr* (with Alexander Wewerka, Alexander Verlag, 2020).

Visual constellations across the fields

1 The entrance door to the archive. Photograph by Marion Benoit, © Ethnologisches Museum der Staatlichen Museen zu Berlin – Preußischer Kulturbesitz
2 Archival files stored in the museum's archive. Photograph by Marion Benoit, © Ethnologisches Museum der Staatlichen Museen zu Berlin – Preußischer Kulturbesitz
3 Boris Gliesmann working in the archive. Photograph by Marion Benoit, © Ethnologisches Museum der Staatlichen Museen zu Berlin – Preußischer Kulturbesitz
4 View into the Weltkulturen Labor, Frankfurt, with furniture designed by Mathis Esterhazy and various fish traps from the Weltkulturen Museum's collection. Photograph by Wolfgang Günzel, 2011
5 Weltkulturen Museum Storage Building, Frankfurt am Main. Photograph by Armin Linke, 2013
6 Protest inside the museum. Photograph by Lyse Ishimwe, © Lyse Ishimwe
7 ExitCongoMuseum, Johan Muyle, *L'impossibilité de régner*, 2001, © J.M.Van Dyck
8 ExitCongoMuseum, Philip Aguirre y Otegui, *l'Homme de Tarifa*, 2001, © Koen de Waal
9 Corridor of the Museo Prestorico Etnografio "Lugi Pigorini" (part of Museo delle Civiltà), Rome, with model of Sabratha amphitheatre, and painting from colonial period. Photograph by Wolfgang Thaler
10 *Bel Suol d'Amore: The Scattered Colonial Body*, Preliminary exhibition design, section view, Museo Prestorico Etnografio "Lugi Pigorini" (part of Museo delle Civiltà), Rome, June 2017. Photograph by Cinzia Delnevo

11   Installation view, 'Arrival, Incision: Indian Modernism as Peripatetic Itinerary', part of *Hello World. Revising a Collection*, Hamburger Bahnhof – Museum für Gegenwart, Berlin 2018, © Mathias Völzke
12   Installation view, 'The Museum of Rhythm' at Muzeum Sztuki, Łódź 2017. © Piotr Tomczyk
13   One part of the video projection, with visitors sitting on the radiators in front of the gallery membrane facing Müllerstraße, during the exhibition *Circling Around Oneness* (2016) by Mwangi Hutter, Galerie Wedding © Fernando Gutiérrez Juárez
14   Exhibition view of Viron Erol Vert's dreamatory, *The Name of Shades of Paranoia, Called Different Forms of Silence* (2017) in Galerie Wedding © Johannes Berger
15   Visitors during the opening of Viron Erol Vert's dreamatory, *The Name of Shades of Paranoia, Called Different Forms of Silence* (2017) in Galerie Wedding © Johannes Berger
16   *Canine Wisdom For the Barking Dog – The Dog Done Gone Deaf* at the Dak'Art Biennale 2018; Ibrahim Mahama *No Time for Curation* (1966-2014-2018) © SAVVY Contemporary
17   *Canine Wisdom For the Barking Dog – The Dog Done Gone Deaf* at the Dak'Art Biennale 2018; Pungwe *Tsi I Ge Ge Ha He* (Tree Shrine), sound installation © SAVVY Contemporary
18   'Monday' by iQhiya, installation view of *That, Around Which the Universe Revolves: On Rhythmanalysis of Memory, Times, Bodies in Space* at SAVVY Contemporary (2017), © Raisa Galofre
19   One of two panels (the lefthand) from Zygmunt Skrętowicz's *The Gassing*, from his Auschwitz series (1963). Warsaw State Ethnographic Museum. Photograph by Wojciech Wilczyk.
20   *Die Baustelle*, Rautenstrauch Joest Museum, Cologne, 2019. Credit Vera Marusic
21   Nora Sternfeld, Isa Rosenberger, and the Retired Firemen of Bergen, THE MUSEUM OF BURNING QUESTIONS. The Partisan Café (at Bergen´s historic fire station) with Jenny Moore, Freja Bäckman, Kabir Carter, Tora Endestad Bjørkheim, Johnny Herbert, and Arne Skaug Olsen. Educational and Performative Cafe designed by Isa Rosenberger, in collaboration with Heidi Pretterhofer, Bergen Assembly, 2016. Photograph by Thor

22 Nalini Malani, *Hamletmachine*, 2000. Video installation with four lcd projectors, four dvd players, amplifiers, speakers, salt, mylar, mirror. Installed as projections on three walls and salt-bed (variable). Closed room 1100 x 800 x 400 cm (variable). Video loop 20 minutes, © Nalini Malani, Mumbai
23 Book cover *Black Atlantic* (HKW, 2004), © HKW
24 Wohnungsfrage, 2015, Haus der Kulturen der Welt, Berlin, urban model, housing model, Kooperatives Labor Studierender (Kolabs) und das Architekturbu ro Atelier Bow-Wow, Tokio/ and the Tokyo architecture office Atelier Bow-Wow, Photograph by Jens Liebchen/HKW, 2015

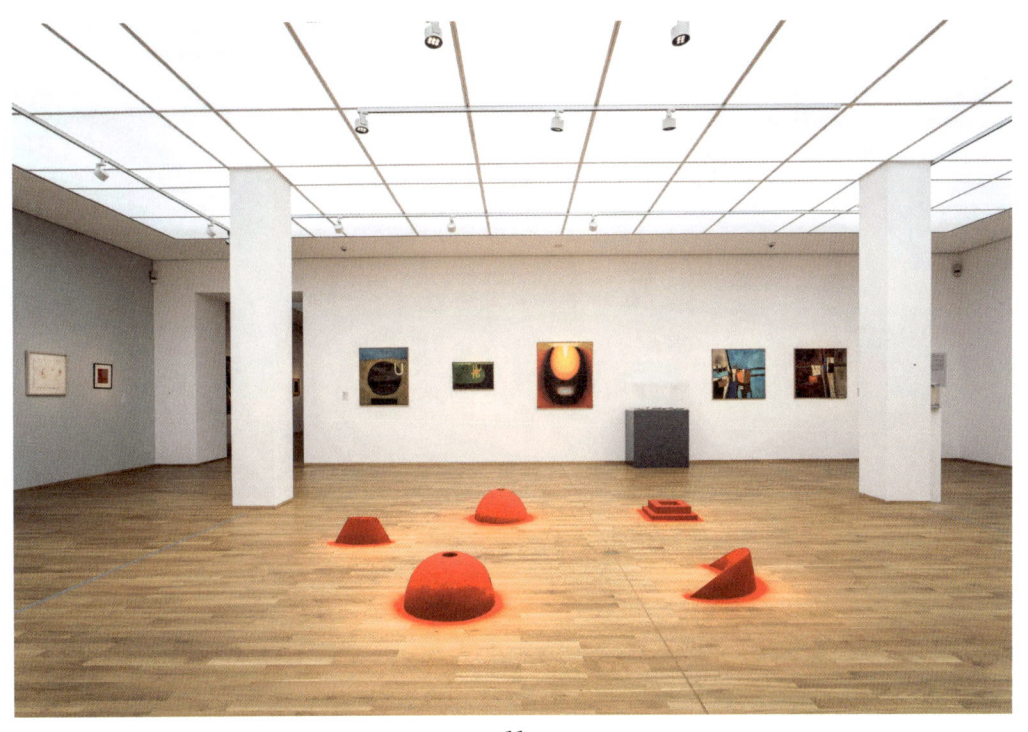

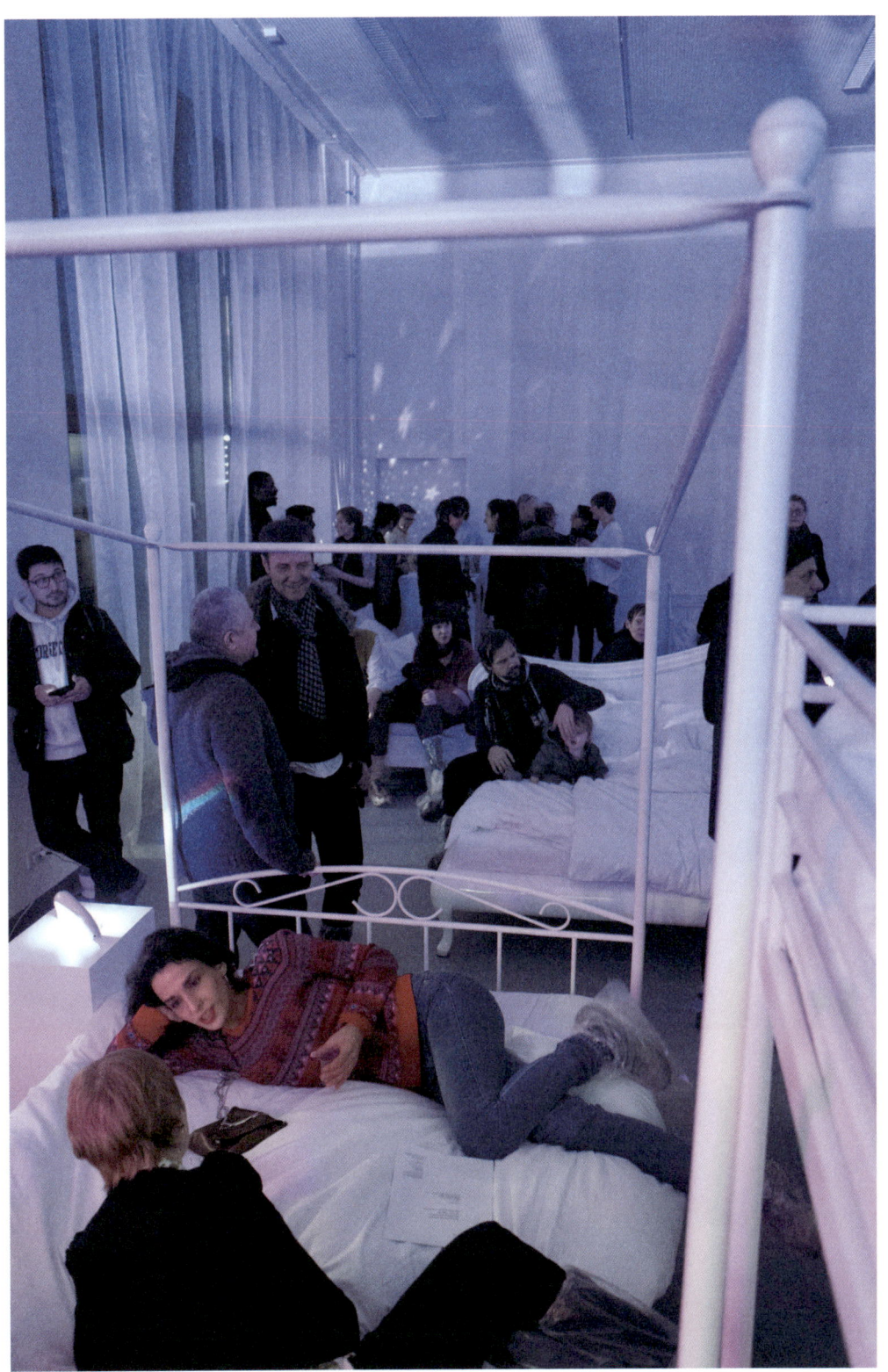

Some lists to inspire the reader

Instead of a generated index, we, as editors, chose to peruse each text with view to keywords, concepts, exhibitions, organisations, adjectives, surprises that may inspire a search. These lists are meant to generate unexpected inquiries, like a book you find by accident on a shelf while looking for an other.

A list of words and concepts

accumulation 145, 309

actant 243, 326

activism 28, 31, 69, 146–148, 181, 243, 302, 364

Afro-descendant 32, 143, 148–151, 160, 164

Afro-feminism 144

alienation 252

alterity 17, 20, 33, 181, 214, 255–258, 327

anachronism 35, 376–380

animism / animacy / animate 78, 84–93, 215, 231

anthropologo-centrism 285

anthropomorphism 85–91, 101

appropriation 295, 304, 305, 313, 371

artefact 19, 77, 81, 82, 84, 102, 115, 135, 139, 154, 161, 175, 189, 193, 224, 231, 306 asymmetrical history 250

authenticity 122, 158, 303, 352

authority 22, 33, 102, 133, 141, 214, 303, 335

awkward 22, 34, 190, 195, 290, 295, 296, 302, 305, 307, 310, 311

Berlin 17, 24–28, 55, 107, 116, 118, 247, 251, 255, 259, 269, 285, 337, 340, 343, 349, 377

Black Radical tradition 66

blind spot 352

canonisation / decanonisation 20, 23, 371

catalyst 24, 257, 306

coeval / coevalness 377, 379

estrangement 32, 53, 78, 81, 93, 103

ethnography 18, 30, 52, 53, 101, 109, 123, 146, 181, 183, 206, 328

ethnological 26, 28, 46, 49, 98, 111, 112, 138, 189

exoticisation 31, 53, 99, 103

expropriation / expropriable 122, 145, 146, 151–155, 164, 165, 232, 300

extraction politics 32, 143–145

fictional diplomacy 216

fieldwork 17, 18, 24, 27, 55, 132, 139, 258, 261, 379

Holocaust 34, 289, 292, 294, 300, 302, 308, 309, 315

hyphen / hyphenated 22, 249

ideology of conservation 134, 136

imperial rationalities / imperial formation / imperial economy 45, 146, 151, 226, 248, 250, 251, 264

indigeneity / indigenous 21, 30–33, 69, 97, 100, 181, 184, 211, 216, 233, 250–252, 279, 302, 308–310, 314, 315, 343 infrastructure 18, 31, 32, 92, 109, 112, 115, 123, 124, 131, 233, 262, 333, 343, 345, 365, 366, 377

institutions / institutional resistance 17–32, 34, 45, 53, 65–69, 73, 100, 103, 119, 122, 131, 132, 136–139, 144–155, 164–166, 189–191, 194–196, 243–249, 250, 258–260, 274, 305, 326, 329, 331–334, 337

intense proximity 20

irony 378

knowledge / knowledge production 17, 18, 22, 30, 45, 51, 52, 80, 81, 97, 99, 100, 104, 107, 109, 111, 115, 119, 123, 131–134, 140, 145–147, 150–153, 160, 164, 183, 188, 190, 193, 202, 211, 214, 215, 248–251, 282, 283, 301, 305, 310, 326, 331, 334, 338–340, 354, 355, 359, 363, 364, 371, 372, 377–380

legacies 17, 19, 22, 27, 50, 67, 107, 258, 289, 294, 326, 377

logos of ethnos 19, 134, 136

mechano-pneumatic 92

membrane 33, 255–261, 265, 270–273

migration 20, 24, 71, 189, 234, 245, 263–266, 270, 303, 306, 328, 333, 354, 376

modernism / modernity 19–23, 35, 45–47, 82, 89, 122, 151, 159, 211, 217, 233, 244–249, 289, 305, 340, 343, 345, 348, 352, 378

morphing 358, 359

naïve 314, 342, 344

nativism / native / nativist 20–21, 100–101, 138, 146, 184, 251–252, 370–371, 377

neo-ethnicity 352

Non-Aligned Movement 214

non-human 31, 46, 53, 72, 73, 77–80, 83–85, 88–90, 101–102, 216

nostalgia / nostalgic 25, 223, 233, 235–236

ontologies / ontological / ontological confusion / ontological expansion / racialised ontologies / ontological exteriority 17, 32, 80–85, 153, 155, 160, 164, 189, 196–197, 211, 215, 356

parliament 24, 155–157, 163, 215–216

plaster cast 33, 229, 230

plunder 291–293, 375

polyphony 132, 155, 214, 242, 252

polyversal 141

porosity 195, 259, 265, 271–273

post-anthromorphism 88

post-colonial 18, 21–22, 25–26, 28–34, 55, 82, 103, 145–148, 157–158, 165, 175, 182, 184, 189, 213, 215, 223, 231–233, 236–237, 289–294, 302–303, 308, 328, 331, 334, 337, 343, 346, 352, 354, 375

post-ethnographic / post-ethnological 19, 134, 136, 182

post-modernism 136, 182, 214, 215, 377, 378

post-relational 20

post-structuralist 131, 215

primitivism / primitive 46, 77, 82–83, 88–89, 98, 178, 183, 282

precarity 29

productive refusal 33, 243

promiscuity 20, 73, 74

provenance 25, 28, 55, 107–112, 114–124, 139, 155, 189, 229, 258, 291, 297

queer 73, 161, 215, 243, 353

racism / racialisation / racial domination / racialised economy of knowledge 17, 21, 24–25, 56, 68, 70, 121, 137, 144–154, 157, 164, 178, 184, 218, 229, 245, 259–260, 264, 268–269, 284–285, 298, 308–309, 353, 365, 369–372, 384

redress 34, 103, 163, 290, 305, 307, 349

refusal 33, 153, 243, 244, 266, 355

remediation 32, 139

repair 34, 47, 73, 122, 203, 290, 307, 378, 387

restitution / repatriation 25, 27, 30-34, 55, 99, 103, 108-109, 123, 134, 138, 140-141, 146, 148-150, 153-164, 188, 249-250, 290-294, 303, 306, 309, 311, 334, 375-377

robotics 35, 77-80, 82, 84, 91

Savage Sublime 30, 45-47

scattered body 224-225

shared heritage 189, 192, 309

sheltering structure 132, 137, 140

speculative scenography 82

spybot 84

sovereignty / souverainism 20, 33, 45, 107, 217, 280, 334, 354, 359, 377

stewardship 97, 295, 302

surrealism 19, 82

temporary inclusion 144, 145, 149, 153, 165, 166

trans-anthropological 17, 21, 22-24, 29, 31, 33, 57, 69, 134, 148, 190, 196, 201, 243, 258, 261, 273, 285, 286, 310, 327-329, 375, 378, 379

trans-cultural 22, 98, 359

trans-gender 22

translation / translatability 17, 19, 28, 29, 31, 33, 71, 97-101, 113, 119, 121, 122, 182, 184, 211, 213, 214, 216, 219, 243, 248, 252, 267, 271, 309, 344, 351, 354, 355, 359

transversal / transversality / transversally agentive / transversal agent 23, 27, 29, 31, 32, 97, 132, 136, 175, 211, 212, 378, 379

troubling / troubles / troubled zone 18, 26, 27, 34, 45, 52, 78, 79, 83, 91, 107, 113, 116, 123, 189. 190, 353, 380

uncanny valley 78-89, 91

uncertainty 22, 23, 80, 81, 84

undercommons 74, 365

universal / universality 22, 51, 72, 98, 99, 103, 159, 176, 181, 248, 290–292, 309, 347

urgency 18, 32, 69, 70, 73, 180, 243, 257

violence / non-violence 33, 53, 74, 123, 140, 146, 154, 155, 158, 182, 183, 189, 191, 192, 199, 202, 203, 205, 224, 229–231, 243, 245, 250, 252, 282, 290, 294, 298, 302, 304–308, 313–315, 327, 367

vulnerability 243

Chronological list of cited exhibitions

Objets prétextes, objets manipulés (1984, Musée d'Ethnographie Neuchâtel) 328

"Primitivism" in 20th Century Art: Affinity of the Tribal and the Modern (1984/1985, MoMA, New York) 46, 282

Le Salon de l'Ethnographie (1989, Musée d'Ethnographie Neuchâtel) 328

Magiciens de la Terre (1989, Centre Georges Pompidou, grande halle de la Villette, Paris) 214, 216, 340

The Other Story (1989, Hayward Gallery, London) 340

China Avantgarde (1993, Haus der Kulturen der Welt, Berlin) 342, 344

Tanzania. Masterpieces of African Sculpture (1994, Haus der Kulturen der Welt, Berlin; Städtische Galerie im Lenbachhaus, Munich) 342

Other Modernities (1995, Haus der Kulturen der Welt, Berlin) 344, 345

Colours: Art from South Africa (1996, Haus der Kulturen der Welt, Berlin) 344

La Différence (1996, Musée d'Ethnographie Neuchâtel) 328

Derrière les images (1998, Musée d'Ethnographie Neuchâtel) 328

Portrait Africa: Photographic Positions of a Century (2000, Haus der Kulturen der Welt, Berlin) 346

Heimat Kunst (2000, Haus der Kulturen der Welt, Berlin) 346

Century City: Bombay-Mumbai 1992-2001 (2001, Tate Modern, London) 349

ExitCongoMuseum! (2001, Royal Museum for Central Africa, Tervuren) 32, 176, 386

Off the Silk Road: Art and Culture from Central Asia (2002, Haus der Kulturen der Welt, Berlin) 351

Musée cannibale (2002-2003, Musée d'Ethnographie Neuchâtel) 328

DisORIENTation: Contemporary Arab Artists from the Middle East (2003, Haus der Kulturen der Welt, Berlin) 351

subTerrain. Artists in the cityfold (2003, Haus der Kulturen der Welt, Berlin) 347, 349

Distant Proximity: New Positions of Iranian Artists (2004, Haus der Kulturen der Welt, Berlin) 351

Black Atlantic: Travelling Cultures, Counter-Histories, Networked Identities (2004, Haus der Kulturen der Welt, Berlin) 352, 353, 356

Spaces and Shadows. Contemporary Art from South East Asia (2005, Haus der Kulturen der Welt, Berlin) 351, 352

What is a body? (2006, Musée du Quai Branly-Jacques Chirac, Paris) 77, 81

Anders zur Welt kommen (2009, Altes Museum, Berlin) 138

Recettes des Dieux. Esthétique du Fétiche (2009, Musée du Quai Branly- Jacques Chirac, Paris) 329

The Making of Images (2010, Musée du Quai Branly-Jacques Chirac, Paris) 77, 81

Ligablo (2010-2011, Royal Library of Belgium) 179, 180

Exhibitions. L'Invention du Sauvage (2011, Musée du Quai Branly-Jacques Chirac, Paris) 329

Animism (2012, HKW, Berlin) 87, 93

Maîtres du Désordre (2012, Musée du Quai Branly-Jacques Chirac, Paris) 329, 330

8th Berlin Biennale (2014, KW, Berlin) 246, 247, 248

Wohnungsfrage (2014, Haus der Kulturen der Welt, Berlin) 357, 359

4th Lubumbashi Biennale 'Réalités Filantes' (2015, Lubumbashi) 177, 178, 203

Wir sind alle Berliner. 1884 – 2014 (2015, SAVVY Contemporary, Berlin) 27

Post-Otherness Wedding (2015-2017, Galerie Wedding, Berlin) 33, 259, 260, 262

Persona (2016, Musée du Quai Branly-Jacques Chirac, Paris) 31, 53, 77, 78, 80, 81, 82, 85, 88, 90, 91, 92, 101, 102

German Colonialism: Fragments Past and Present (2016-2017, German Historical Museum Berlin) 28

5th Lubumbashi Biennale 'Eblouissements' (2017, Lubumbashi) 177, 178, 203

Bel Suol d'Amore – The Scattered Colonial Body (2017, Pigorini Museum, Rome) 224, 237

documenta14 (2017, Kassel/Athens) 27, 268

My Museum, a museum about me! (2017, Curating and Public Scholarship Lab, Concordia) 300, 315

Beyond Compare: Art from Africa in the Bode-Museum (2017-2019, Berlin) 55

Unsustainable Privileges (2017-2019, Galerie Wedding, Berlin) 33, 259, 260, 262, 267

Untie to tie: On Colonial Legacies and Contemporary Societies and Movement. Bewegung (2017-2020, ifa gallery, Berlin) 27

10th Berlin Biennale (2018, KW, Berlin) 27

13th Dak'Art Biennale (2018, Dakar) 27, 280, 283

Canine Wisdom For the Barking Dog – The Dog Done Gone Deaf (2018, Dakar) 283

Hello World. Revising a collection (2018, Hamburger Bahnhof, Berlin) 247, 249, 250

Most Wanted. The Popular Culture of Illegality (2019, Volkenkunde Museum, Leiden) 72

Terrible Close. Polish Vernacular Artists face the Holocaust (2018/2019, Ethnographic Museum, Krakow) 315

Berlin and the World (forthcoming, Humboldt Forum Berlin) 55

List of cited institutions / organisations

AfricAvenir (Berlin) 25

AFROTAK TV CyberNomads (Berlin) 25

Artefakte // anti-humboldt (Berlin) 25

BAMKO-CRAN (Brussels) 146, 147, 149, 150, 153, 154, 155, 157, 158, 159, 160, 161, 163

Bergen Assembly (Norway) 34, 137, 365–369

Berlin postkolonial (Berlin) 25

Bode-Museum (Berlin) 55

BOZAR (Brussels) 143, 162, 177, 178, 187, 192, 194, 195, 202

CAFE CONGO (Brussels) 157, 161

Centre for Anthropological Research on Museums and Heritage (CARMAH, Berlin) 28, 35, 50, 56, 59, 256, 273

City Palace / Stadtschloss (Berlin) 24, 25, 54, 377

COMRAF (Comité de Concertation MRAC-Associations Africaines, Brussels) 158, 159, 163

daadgalerie (Berlin) 26

documenta institute (Kassel) 372

École de Recherche Graphique (ERG, Brussels) 187, 194, 206

Ethnologisches Museum (Berlin) 26, 31, 107, 109, 111, 112, 119, 249

freethought (London) 34, 365

Freie Universität Berlin 249

French Ministry of Research and Higher Education (Paris) 98

Galerie Wedding (GW, Berlin) 33, 256–259, 262

German Federal Cultural Foundation (Halle an der Saale) 26

German Historical Museum (Berlin) 28

German Lost Art Foundation (Berlin, Magdeburg) 109

Goethe-Institute 340, 342, 343, 347, 348, 355

Grassi Museum (Leipzig) 328–330, 332

GREYZONE ZEBRA (Brussels/Paris) 190, 194–196, 199, 202, 204

Haus der Kulturen der Welt (HKW, Berlin) 19, 34, 54, 93, 326, 340, 342, 343, 345, 346, 355–359

Hayward Gallery (London) 73, 340

Holocaust Memorial (Berlin) 56, 315

Horniman Museum (London) 66

Humboldt Forum (Berlin) 24–28, 31, 46, 54–56, 107, 111, 112, 138, 140, 251, 258, 328, 377, 387

Humboldt Lab Dahlem (Berlin) 26, 124

Humboldt-Universität zu Berlin 28, 50, 56, 260

ifa-Gallery (Berlin) 27, 258

Initiative Schwarze Menschen in Deutschland (Berlin) 25

Iziko Museum (Cape Town) 203

Jewish Museum (Prague) 315

Khiasma (Paris) 165, 194, 201, 202, 206

l'Ecole nationale du patrimoine (Paris) 97

Laboratoire Agit'Art (Dakar) 137

Le Louvre (Paris) 329

Musée du Quai Branly-Jacques Chirac (Paris) 20, 31, 53, 77, 97

Museo delle Civiltà (Rome) 224, 229, 237

Museum für Naturkunde (Berlin) 57

Museum of Asian Art (Berlin) 24, 249

Museum of European Cultures (Berlin) 56, 57

Museum of Islamic Art (Berlin) 56

Museum of Mankind (London) 133

Museum of Modern Art (MoMA, New York) 46

Museum Rietberg (Zurich) 34, 258

Museum Volkenkunde (Leiden) 53, 71

National Gallery of Canada (Ottawa) 312

National Museum of the American Indian (Washington, D.C.) 314

No Humboldt 21! (Berlin) 25-27

No Name Collective (Brussels) 161

NYC Museum of Natural History (New York) 46

Palace of the Republic (Berlin) 24

Pigorini National Ethnographic Museum (Rome) 224-230

Police Museum (Bahia, Brazil) 376

Prussian Cultural Heritage Foundation (Berlin) 58, 111

Rautenstrauch-Joest-Museum (Cologne) 326, 334

Research Center of Material Culture (Leiden) 31

Royal Library of Belgium (Brussels) 179

Royal Museum for Central Africa (Tervuren) 32, 143, 147, 175, 181, 187, 188, 190, 204, 380

SAVVY Contemporary (Berlin) 27, 33, 258, 280-284, 286

School of Oriental and African Studies (London) 132, 343

Smithsonian Institution (Washington, D.C.) 133

Tanzania-Network (Berlin) 25

The British Museum (London) 25, 46, 133, 309

The Museums of History and Ethnography (Kingston) 65

Weltkulturen Museum (Frankfurt am Main) 134, 140

Yad Vashem Institute (Jerusalem) 296, 308